DEVELOPMENT

OF

CONTAINERIZATION

Success through Vision, Drive and Technology

Cover: Photograph by Frans A.J. Waals

Cover: Design by Corien Smit

DEVELOPMENT

OF

CONTAINERIZATION

Success through Vision, Drive and Technology

Hans van Ham   Joan Rijsenbrij

IOS Press

Published by IOS Press under the imprint Delft University Press

Publisher
IOS Press BV
Nieuwe Hemweg 6b
1013 BG Amsterdam
The Netherlands
tel: +31-20-6883355
fax: +31-20-6870019
email: info@iospress.nl
www.iospress.nl

ISBN 978-1-61499-146-5 (print)
ISBN 978-1-61499-147-2 (online)

PRINTED IN THE NETHERLANDS

This book is printed on G-Print (Forest Stewardship Council Accreditation: FSC MIX).

PREFACE

This book describes the development of containerization, which due to the tremendous cost and time savings in maritime cargo transportation proved instrumental for a globalized economy. The help of rapid developing technologies, available from many disciplines, and the innovative approach from engineers and logistic managers accelerated a worldwide expansion of containerization into a globalized, fast and cost-effective transport system. This facilitated the development of global just-in-time logistics and simplified the large-scale (intercontinental) transport of consumer goods and semi-finished products. Obviously, the evolution of IT systems helped to control the massive cargo flows with tens of thousands box handlings per day at major ports. At present, containerized transport has matured and contributes substantially to a higher wealth in the world.

From the start of our professional careers, in the early 1970s/mid-1980s respectively, we were impressed by the rapid technological changes in marine cargo transportation, shown by ever larger container vessels and new port infrastructure and terminal handling facilities, with all types of new equipment and information control systems. The various types of co-operation between shipping lines (including takeovers) and ways to control the total transport chain were also intriguing.

Many of the impressive developments in containerization were achieved by enthusiastic and driven pioneers such as Malcom McLean (Sea-Land), Stanley Powell (Matson), Lord Sterling (P&O), Maersk Mc-Kinney Møller (Maersk), Dr. Chang Yung-fa (Evergreen), Frank H. Brown (WP&YR), W. Bruce Seaton (APL), Li Ka-Shing (Hutchison Whampoa) and Gerrit Wormmeester (ECT). They had a vision and together with their entrepreneurial talents and managerial skills they motivated engineers and managers to realize their ideas through the use of technology. These professionals have considerably influenced the development of vessels, transshipment equipment and container handling concepts. Some of them deserve special mentioning: Keith Tantlinger, Bill Casper, Charles Cushing, George G. Sharp, Rudiger Franke, Les and Don Harlander, Charles Hilzheimer, Mike Jordan, Ron Katims, Murray Montgomery, Jules Nagy, Gene Pentimonti, Hans Tax, Ernst Vossnack, Jelis Verschoof, Larry Wright and Chuck Zweifel. Author Joan Rijsenbrij had the privilege to meet most of these key executives from the pioneering stage; it was a great pleasure to exchange views on conceptual designs and to discuss future developments. It showed that innovative transport systems can only be realized when based on vision, drive and the application of technology.

During the most recent decades, several books and publications have touched upon the various topics within containerization. Especially the shipping aspects and transport economics have been covered in great detail. A comprehensive history of containerization with a technological emphasis was still missing. With this book we have tried to present a worldwide overview of all major system components and the drivers that have contributed to the great success of containerization. Since today's dynamic life style does not allow going deep into history, the book is structured in developments per decade, whereas some key technological topics are examined in greater detail. It is illustrated by many pictures (seeing is believing), some of them of moderate quality from a photographer's point of view but relevant for the interested reader. We assume that the developments and lessons learnt will be valuable for students in transportation, designers of terminals and transport systems and all those who are fascinated by the impressive transport systems, supporting the prosperity of our society.

ACKNOWLEDGMENT

A long-distance call in July 2005 from Hans van Ham to Joan Rijsenbrij in Langkawi started a co-makership in writing a book about the impressive developments of containerized cargo transportation. The combination of research skills (both authors active for the Delft University of Technology), general knowledge on trade and transport policies and decades of operational experience in container operations appeared to be a good starting point to present history, motives and background of a transport technology that really boosted globalization. Publications and lots of (private) information collected over years from experts both from shipping lines, terminals and equipment manufacturers have been used as a start. From there, facts and figures were checked with literature and research documents. Surprisingly, many students and young employees of transport-related companies and authorities showed their interest and sometimes even contributed with new information and pictures.

Over the years, students have supported the structuring of photographs and the search for information. We are grateful to Henk-Jan Schilperoort, Bob Ham and Michiel van Haersma Buma. Mr. Itsuro Watanabe was very helpful with information on vessel characteristics and the developments of containerization in the Far East. Mr. Oudendal shared the knowledge about his long-time ISO-TC104 standardization activities just like many other colleagues and business friends out of Joan Rijsenbrij's ECT period who exchanged valuable information.

Much help and support was given by Jozephina Spoek-Schouten who processed large parts of the (hand-written) concept. We are grateful to Dick Mensch, who helped with layout and management of documents and pictures. His patience and dedication helped to maintain our motivation to complete this book. The authors have appreciated the precise editorial work of Frans Waals, his critical reading and knowledge of containerization generated many changes in text and layout, which improved the manuscript considerably.

The authors want to thank the holders of copyright who have granted permission to use their material. Every effort has been made to determine and acknowledge holders of copyright. We regret any oversight that may have occurred and will gladly make proper acknowledgment in future printings after written notice has been received.

For the overall presentation of information, illustrations and views about the development of containerization the responsibility remains with the authors.

TABLE OF CONTENTS

Development of Containerization

CHAPTER 1

CONTAINERIZATION

A Boost for Globalization

In general, the line is taken that containerization started in the United States of America in 1956, followed by the first intercontinental container shipping services between the US, Europe and the Far East in 1966. Within 50 years, containerization developed into a global transportation system, with over 5,000 vessels, shipping around 2 billion tons of general cargo annually through more than 500 ports. In these ports the containers are consolidated and distributed to and from thousands of inland destinations and origins using trucks, barges or rail. Containerization enables a fast and reliable carriage of base materials, components and semi-finished products to regions with attractive production facilities (often in low labor cost areas) and in reverse, the distribution of consumer goods all over the world.

Figure 1: Early shipping by the Egyptians

The maritime container really boosted globalization within a few decades. However, it should be realized that the process of globalization already started 500 years ago, in 1492, when Columbus (Cristobal Colon) discovered some Caribbean isles and connected the Americas with Eurasia.

Colon's early intercontinental sea voyage was a result of some thousands of years of navigation along coastal waters and inland rivers. Curiosity was the start of shipping, but it were also the drive of mankind for area expansion, the exchange of cultures, the trading of products and the transport of treasury goods and building materials that created shipping as we know it from the Egyptians, Phoenicians, Greek, Romans and Asian cultures such as China, Philippines and Indonesia (see Figure 1).

Figure 2: The Cog

During the Middle Ages, shipping was used for regional trading (Mediterranean, North West Europe and Asia) and the transportation of (mostly luxury) goods between Europe, the Middle East, Asia and West Africa (see Figure 2). The drive to find a faster (and more secure) route to the Indies and the availability of simple navigation instruments allowed Columbus to sail the Atlantic westbound and discover some Caribbean isles, followed by the Spanish colonization of major parts of the Americas.

During the 17th and 18th century, seafaring people, such as the Arabs, Chinese, Dutch, English, Portuguese and Spanish, started global trade: the Spanish between the Americas, the Philippines and Europe; the Chinese between Mainland China and Asian trade bases set up by the Portuguese; and the English and Dutch for trade with Europe, Africa and the Middle East. The first two large shipping and trading companies were the East

Figure 3: VOC cargo vessels sailing the Indies in the 17th (left) and 18th century

Indian Company (London) and the "Verenigde Oost-Indische Compagnie" (VOC, The Netherlands). The latter became the first multi-national, with regular services by up to 350 vessels per year sailing from The Netherlands to India, Japan, Malaysia, Java and Philippines, already using cargo lists, letters of credit, bills of lading, etc. In Asian waters, feeder operations were organized (often by the Chinese) to major trading hubs like Manila, Macau, Deshima, Batavia and Suratte.

The slowly-growing world population (due to a shortage of food in some regions and many diseases) and the limited transportation capacity of sailing vessels (50-1,500 tons) caused a steady but moderate increase in the transportation of goods. During the 19th century, technology helped improving service reliability, travel speed and cargo capacity of oceangoing vessels. Good examples are the Clipper, capable of sailing at more than 15 knots with around 1,000 tons of pay load (see Figure 4).

Figure 4: American Tea Clipper (painting A. Jacobsen)

The invention of steam engines (expansion machines, first in paddle wheelers and later for propeller propulsion) boosted vessel sizes further. The independence of wind improved schedule integrity, resulting in more trade and reduced transportation cost. The very labor-intensive loading and discharging activities (with own gear or dock-mounted, steam-driven cranes), kept the vessels in ports for several weeks. This, together with a moderate travel speed, resulted in intercontinental voyage times of several months.

The introduction of steam turbines and diesel engines matured shipping and supported a continuously-growing trade with cargo shipments all over the world. The building of the Suez Canal and later the Panama Canal shortened sailing distances considerably, enabling a steady of intercontinental trade during the 20th century.

After the worldwide economic depression of the 1930s and the Second World War (1939-1945), the world had to recover from the massive destructions. The US helped with a major financial support program (the Marshall program for European and some Asian countries), facilitating trade between the US, Europe and Asia.

Shipping developed and during the 1950s general cargo vessels of up to 14,000 dwt were used, with speeds of up to 21 knots and, in general ,with their own handling gear on deck. Despite increased sailing speeds, all-in voyage times remained rather long, as most vessels called at many ports and in each port had to stay several days up to weeks because of slow, labor intensive load and discharge operations. The ship's handling gear offered rather low productivity. Some ports (mostly European) installed faster general cargo cranes (lifting capacities of 5-15 tons, outreach 20-35 m.), but bundling cargo in the holds remained time consuming. Moreover, cargo damages and pilferage were major issues in many ports, making some shipping lines decide to invest in vessels with side ramps, inboard elevators, etc. However, these technological improvements with mechanized devices did not take off at a large scale, due to a lack of standardization, the reluctance of established shipping lines and the fact that still a lot of stevedoring was required to bundle or palletize the general cargo before lifting it mechanically from the quay into the vessel's holds.

The development of containerization, described in detail in this book, changed the world of cargo transportation dramatically. As from the 1960s, purpose-designed container vessels were introduced and within 20 years vessel capacity increased from 15,000 tons in the 1950s to over 60,000 tons in the 1970s. Economies of scale, the invention of fuel-efficient diesel engines and the considerable reduction of port-handling costs resulted in a remarkable decrease in cargo transportation cost and a substantial reduction of damage and pilferage. Technology supported the development of vessels (see Figure 5), handling equipment and container terminals (see Figure 6) but equally important was the technological development in information control and communications.

Figure 5: Containership (SL-18, Sea-Land)

The advantages of standardized load units were proven during the Korean and Vietnam wars and also the manufacturing and logistics industries discovered the potential of shipments in standardized containers. The availability of reliable, low-cost and fast transportation changed the manufacturing of consumer goods: spreading manufacturing towards low labor cost areas. The introduction of the maritime container resulted in savings for all parties in the supply chain, while during the much short-

Figure 6: Container Terminal (ECT Delta Terminal, Rotterdam)

er voyages the cargo was protected against weather and pilferage. Standardization resulted in simple transportation and handling equipment and proper tracking and tracing during the whole trip.

Unquestionably, containerization today is a worldwide transportation system with many coastal, domestic and intercontinental shipping services. Economies of scale, fierce competition and pressure from shippers have resulted in low transportation costs and frequent (often daily), reliable services. This has enabled multi-national companies to realize global logistics, with a reduction of the number of production facilities to only a few in the world and allowing economies of scale in their production processes as well. In many cases, the worldwide demand for a certain product (varying from tea bags to cars) is supplied out of fewer than 5 production locations. Despite the distances of thousands of kilometers (regularly several 10,000 km) travelled by materials and components before their final assembly, transportation cost represents only a few percent of the end product's selling price. For instance, a shipment of TV sets from the Far East to Europe will take less than 4 weeks at a cost of about 10 US$ per TV set. A return load of waste paper (low revenue cargo) will be shipped for less than 30 US$ per ton. The container has resulted in cheap and efficient cargo transportation, which in turn has accelerated worldwide trade and just-in-time logistics; certainly a combined result of vision, technology and a drive for improvements from many parties involved, triggered by some visionary entrepreneurs.

A detailed description of all the developments and the many success stories (and failures!) behind this remarkable change in cargo transportation is not possible within the context of only one book. For that reason the authors have chosen to present the chronological order of the shipping aspects, in decades (1956-1966-1976, etc.) per chapter. In between, key issues in the technological developments are presented. This combination provides the reader with the most important facts and issues that determined a revolution in general cargo handling and which supported a globalization of production and consumption. Nowadays containerized transport is a real utility, indispensable for a global economy.

CHAPTER 2

PROLOGUE

Until World War II, the maritime breakbulk and general cargo sector had virtually remained unchanged for decades. The cargo packed in bags, bales, crates or casks was stowed and transported in (and on) general cargo ships. In 1950, an average vessel was smaller than 10,000 Gross Register Tons (GRT) and had a service speed of approximately 15 knots. They were fitted with loading and discharging equipment, the most common rig being the married fall system. The marine terminal acted as a point of interchange between water and land. Two basic types of construction can be identified: the pier and the wharf. The pier is a long and relatively narrow structure that juts out into the harbor waters. A transit shed is used for temporary storage. This type of terminal was common in the US, for example in New York and San Francisco. Basically, it is an extension of the city's road network. In contrast, the wharf or quay is constructed along the shoreline, a concept often applied in river ports. Both in Europe and North America warehouses were often located close, 10 to 20 m., to the quay wall.

At that time, dock-side cranes were common in Europe and many other parts of the world, but rarely seen in the United States. The advantage of such cranes is the large outreach. A crane picked up loads out of the hold of the vessel and dropped it on the dockside anywhere within reach of the crane's jib. This feature has more advantages for wharf type terminals with a wide apron with railway tracks than for (narrow) pier type terminals.

The shift from manpower to mechanically and/or electrically-driven equipment was an important development in cargo handling, allowing loads much larger than man loads (up to 60 kg.). In the United States this move took place during the 1930s, while in Europe mechanization started during the 1950s and early 1960s. During these years, many firms bought their first dock tractor and/or lift truck. On a marine terminal, dock tractor-trailer combinations were pieces of equipment used for hauling cargo, i.e. the horizontal movement of cargo for distances of over 100 m. Handling is the vertical movement and/or short horizontal movement of cargo. The fork-lift truck is the

Figure 7: Handling of Liberty ships in New York during WW2

most widely-used piece of handling equipment. A hydraulic lifting device is capable of raising loads on either skid or pallet. No longer hampered by the lifting capabilities of man, it became possible to strap many small packages on pallet boards. This started the process of unitization that will be scrutinized in this chapter. Due to the advance of mechanization, the development of unitized maritime loads started in North America, but other parts of the world followed suit. First, palletized loads and wooden "boxes" will be considered. Subsequently, the use of small steel containers will be described and finally detachable truck bodies or "van" type containers will be introduced.

2.1. SMALL UNIT LOADS

Palletized loads and wooden boxes

The stevedoring pallet is used to handle cargo on the marine terminal. Because of their heavy duty, they are made of heavier material than other types. Several sizes exist, as this pallet must be capable of accommodating a large number of commodity types and sizes. For large packages, such as furniture, the 4 by 7 ft (1.22 x 2.13 m.) proved convenient, for smaller packages the 4 by 5 ft (1.22 x 1.52 m.) size was often used. Another type of pallet found on marine terminals was the shipping pallet used for sending pallet loads from shipper to consignee. The size of this pallet is 4 by 4 ft (1.22 x 1.22 m.) or 4 by 3' 4" (1.22 x 1.02 m.). The first is suitable for road or rail transport when an open platform bed is used; the latter is fitted for closed-body trucks and box cars. In Europe, 1.20 x 0.80 and 1.20 x 1.00 m. pallets were introduced. Moreover, a large (stevedore-owned) pallet, 1.80 x 1.20 m., was often deployed as load unit between vessel and warehouse.

Figure 8: General cargo ship for palletized cargo (Great Lakes)

Because palletized loads are more economical to handle than loose cargo, palletized operations were quickly introduced. Some shipping lines utilized ships with side ports, elevators and/or decks with limited clearance in order to achieve (substantial) efficiency gains. In some trades, pallets evolved to small unit containers such as wooden cribs (consisting of a pallet and secured by removable sides and top and bounded by metal banding) and larger guards, boxes, with a lining of corrugated metal.

Amongst the firms pursuing alternative handling techniques, Matson Navigation Company was the most prominent one. This long-time West Coast-Hawaii shipping line estimated that cargo handling amounted to 48% of the total cost of seaborne commerce. Moreover, cargo handling costs were increasing rapidly. Running its own shore facilities led the company into developing new long-shoring methods and cargo transshipment and distribution techniques, particularly in the field of unitization. In the early 1940s, specially-designed plywood boxes of 6 by 6 by 4 ft (1.83 x 1.83 x 1.22 m.) were fitted with hinged doors and locking devices including numbered aluminum seals. Named after the president of Matson Terminals, J. Harding Jensen, these "Jensen Boxes" were stuffed with commodities that were sensitive for pilferage such as liquor, candy, drugs and small appliances. At the same time, it protected against breakage. Its successor, the also wooden cargo guard container, was slightly smaller: 4 ft by 5 ft by 6 ft (1.22 x 1.52 x 1.83 m.). It could hold 135 cu ft (3.83 cubic meters) or three tons of cargo. The moment the cargo arrived at the dock, the commodities were placed in the box. When loaded, it was sealed and the seal was not to be broken until it reached its destination. In the early 1950s, each vessel in the West Coast-Hawaii trade carried, on average, 25 of these boxes.

In other parts of the world, shipping lines developed similar transport concepts, like in Denmark, where in the early 1950s DFDS shipping line introduced small wooden containers. Two ships, *Axelhus* and *Riberhus*, were purposely designed for domestic service (incl. passenger transport). They were small, i.e. 471 grt, and equipped with a 1,200-bhp diesel engine enabling a cruising speed of 14 knots.

The blue containers were transshipped using a so-called "pallet loader". The successful service, which was extended in the late 1950s, lasted for 17 years (see Figure 9).

Steel containers

In the early 1940s, Leathem D. Smith, an innovative shipyard owner from Sturgeon Bay (WI), toyed with an idea that would greatly facilitate the ship and shore handling and transportation of cargoes. He envisioned the construction of ships specially designed to carry cargo in uniformly-sized, stackable steel containers. These boxes had high doors at one end and bore collapsible legs to lock them onto the deck of the ship. The containers could be attached to each other, when stacked, via sockets located in the upper four corners of each container (UK pat. 623.550).

Because there was sufficient clearance between the surface and container, this allowed the insertion of a fork lift truck or a lift tractor. Moreover, they were equipped with lifting eyelets, which enabled placement of the containers upon or removal from a ship, railway car or truck. The blue prints were drawn in 1943, and in 1944, Agwilines, a New York ship operator, showed great interest. Certain refined features, particularly in dimensions and folding legs, were the result of discussions between Smith and shipping line officials. In 1945, production started and in the fall of that year twelve containers were used by Agwilines in an experimental run. Relative success was experienced and more shipping lines were to use these boxes. By the spring of 1946, about a hundred units were manufactured. Up until this time the devices were of a "knock-down" variety, i.e. they

Figure 9: Wooden containers used by DFDS

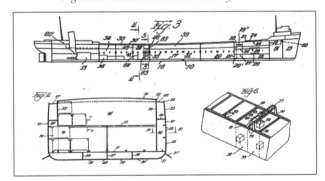

Figure 10: Laethem D. Smith's patented containership (1946)

could be taken apart. The first of the rigid type was placed in use in early 1947 and by March 1948 some 500 containers had been sold. After the sudden death of Smith in a sailing accident in June 1948, talks started with the Dravo Corporation. Based on Smith's concept the Dravo Corporation started to manufacture its own steel unit container, the Transportainer. The outside dimensions were 7' 9" x 6' 8" x 6' 5.5" (2.36 x 2.03 x 1.97 m.). The inside capacity is 275 cubic ft (7.79 cubic m.) and the weight capacity amounted to approximately 6 tons. These containers were of welded steel construction and provided considerable protection for the cargo shipped in them. They could be lifted by fork-lift truck or hoisted by ship's gear. One of the largest users of the Transportainer was Bull Line. In the early 1950s, they applied between 500 and 600 units on their New York-San Juan (Puerto Rico) route.

During World War II, the US army started to combine items of uniform size and lashed them onto a pallet. Convinced by the advantages of unitization, they started experimenting with small containers for the shipment of supplies. In 1947, a first series was developed and tested by the Transportation Corps. These so-called Transporters were rigid steel reusable containers capable of carrying approximately 9,000 pounds (4 tons). Its dimensions were: 8' 6" long, 6' 3" wide, and 6' 10" high (2.59 x 1.91 x 2.08 m.). It had a double door on one end, was mounted on elevated skids and had lifting rings on the top four corners. Its distinctive shape included rectangular corners. Because of the Korean War, an additional 500 containers were purchased for use between the army's General Depot in Columbus and the Far East. They were used to ship items via Japan to Korea and subsequently forwarded by rail to army supply bases.

Figure 11: Transporters in the Korean War theatre

These experiences, along with the study of household goods shipments, showed the effectiveness of the container against damage and pilferage. It also proved the efficiency in the moving of troop materials from continental US to overseas commands as well as the signifi-

Figure 12: CONEX boxes in multi-modal operations in the 1950s

cantly-reduced handling costs and transportation time. Based on the Transporter, the Container Express (CONEX) was developed. The basic dimensions were, more or less, the same, but a smaller modular unit (4' 3" x 6' 3" x 6' 10.5"/1.30 x 1.91 x 2.10 m.) was also introduced. By 1965, there were approximately 100,000 CONEXES in use by the US military forces. From an economic point of view the employment of these containers has been lucrative.

The dimensions of the small steel containers, including railway containers, enabled haulage with different transport modes without major adjustments. The White Pass and Yukon Route (WP&YR) railway opted for a more comprehensive approach. This Canadian transport company had been involved in many ventures over the years including a series of lake and river steamers, a trucking line, an airline, as well as the well-known railway that connects Skagway (Alaska) with Whitehorse (Yukon). However, the company relied upon other carriers for the overseas haul of goods. In 1953, the company decided to look into containerization as WP&YR president Frank H. Brown saw the need for integrating ship, train, and truck operations. The panacea was the development of a "box" that could be moved quickly and cheaply from one transportation mode to another. After evaluating the financial feasibility of such an integrated ship-train-truck "container" transportation system, a test container was built.

The first cargo load to be shipped north in the company's test container consisted of large rolls of paper. This commodity was selected because it had always caused trouble. On the test run the rolls were stacked vertically, the container was locked and customs sealed and swung aboard the ship. However, the test container had "bugs". The doors became wedged against each other but were eventually opened with a cutting torch. Nevertheless, the rolls of building paper were in perfect condition and the container concept was perceived a success. The company decided to proceed with the idea and contracted the Canadian Vickers Shipbuilding Company of Montreal to build a ship specifically designed to handle containerized freight. The ship, the 4,000 ton *Clifford J. Rogers*, was commissioned in October 1955. The ship had 2 holds and 4 hatches. There were no "tweendecks". It could carry 165 containers, stacked 3 high, one on each side of the center line of the vessel. The other space was used for general cargo such as lumber and plywood.

By November 1955, containers and the ship were brought together. Vancouver (British Columbia) became the testing ground for the first integrated container operation. On November 26, the *Clifford J. Rogers* set sail for Skagway with her first load of containerized freight. At Skagway the containers were transferred onto special flat railcars with tie-down equipment to secure the boxes for the 110 mile (177 km.) journey to Whitehorse. Drayage was ensured by WP&YR's Highway Division with a truck fleet of flat bed chassis compatible with the new containers. The new ship and containers, coupled with the upgraded (narrow gauge) railway and truck fleet, made the first integrated container system operational in the world.

Figure 13: Clifford R. Rogers (un)loading at Skagway, Alaska

At the heart of the system was the 8' x 8' x 7' (2.44 x 2.44 x 2.13 m.) container, capable of carrying up to 5 tons of freight. Firstly, 550 containers were acquired, while later another 90 boxes were added. Four types of containers were in use: dry, vented, heated and refrigerated. Dry containers were used for "hard" goods. Vented containers permitted a constant flow of fresh air and (in summer) they contained hardy perishables, such as apples and potatoes. Freight that had to be kept warm during freezing weather was transported in heated containers. Finally, refrigerated containers were equipped with a controlled air cooling system.

The container concept has been at the Yukon service ever since, albeit in 1965 the system switched to -off standard- 25' 3" x 8' x 8' (7.70 x 2.44 x 2.44 m.) containers and new equipment including a bigger vessel, the *Frank H. Brown*. It also showed that in order to justify the high initial investment, two-way traffic for containers was essential. This rule still holds true today since an empty container occupies a lot of valuable shipping space without earning any revenue.

Figure 14: 1st and 2nd generation WP&YR container

2.2. LARGE UNITS

Vehicles

Materials handling becomes more efficient when the size of the unit increases. Already during the 1920s, Graham Brush, a civil engineer and former naval aviator, has carried this idea to its extreme. He bought a cargo ship and had it adapted to carry railway freight cars. Four sets of railway tracks were laid side by side from one end of the ship to the other on the three lower decks, and a fourth set on the main deck. A midship hatch was modified so that freight cars could be loaded directly onto the tracks on each deck. Once the cars had been placed on the tracks, they were pushed toward the bow and stern and were fastened in place with wheel chocks, jacks and turnbuckles. Not surprisingly, the company was called Seatrain.

Brush had his eye on the offshore trade with Cuba. Albeit independent after being liberated from Spanish rule in the Spanish American War, Cuba was in fact an economic colony of the United States. Its rail lines were built to the standard gauge used in the states and it sent many tropical products, most notably sugar, rum and cigars, to the mainland in exchange for a variety of industrial goods. From 1912 until the mid-1930s, the Florida East Coast Railway used roll-on/roll-off railway ferries to move loaded railcars between Havana and the railway terminal at Key West. Since most of the freight trade to Cuba was carried in oceangoing ships operating between Havana and New Orleans, Brush chose this port as its US port of call. Large gantry cranes were constructed at the docks in New Orleans and Havana to handle any type of freight car on and off the ship without using stevedores. An additional advantage of the Seatrain transport system was that it did not require covered piers or warehouses.

In January 1929, the "trainship" *Seatrain New Orleans* with four sets of tracks on the main and three lower decks, departed from New Orleans carrying its first set of loaded freight cars to Havana, The innovative transshipment process allowed quick turnaround times, so the "trainship" spent more time at sea than any traditional general cargo ship.

The New Orleans-Havana run turned out to be a huge success. In the first three years, Seatrain Lines Inc. carried twice as much tonnage between New Orleans and Havana as the three competing shipping lines, who operated four times as many (general cargo) vessels. Carriers who watched helplessly as shippers abandoned them for the new service immediately implored the government to protect them from this disruptive innovation. The Chicago Association of Commerce and the Mallory and Morgan Steamship Lines, which operated in the protected coastwise service, filed a request with the Interstate Commerce Commission (ICC), a federal agency with jurisdiction over coastwise, inter coastal, inland and Great Lakes water carriers. But the question was: is Seatrain engaged in coastwise carriage? The answer was clearly no, as Cuba was an independent nation. The ICC therefore rejected the request on the grounds that Seatrain was engaged in international maritime commerce, over which the ICC had no jurisdiction.

Brush's next step was to offer services out of New York. Because Seatrain needed rail access to the waterfront in New York, Seatrain bought the Hoboken Shore Railway, which had originally been built to bring coal to the docks. He also ordered two new ships, *Seatrain New York* and *Seatrain Havana*. They were built at the Sun Shipyard in Chester, Pennsylvania, and were delivered in September, 1932. Although laid out like the original *Seatrain New Orleans* they were larger and faster than the older ship. Each of the new ships could carry 100 loaded freight cars (the equivalent of a train of a mile long!). They could steam 16.5 knots, making them the fastest freighters on the ocean and providing fourth-morning delivery to Havana and sixth-morning delivery to New Orleans, as arrangements could be made to transfer freight cars from one ship to another in Havana. By using an offshore port as switching point for an in essence domestic service, it turned into an international trade. Furthermore, the notion that railcars bound for New Orleans would be moved from one ship to another was largely a ruse because many railcars went from New York to New Orleans without being offloaded in Havana.

Seatrain offered the service against tariffs half the rail fare. Atlantic shipping lines, seaboard railways and unfriendly shippers protested bitterly to the Shipping Board and the Interstate Commerce Commission that the Seatrain service was damagingly unfair competition. According to the Merchant Marine Act of 1920, better known as the Jones Act, transport between US ports was provided on all essential trade routes by ships built in the US and owned and manned by US citizens. The first sailing of the *Seatrain New York* was almost postponed by a Shipping Board ruling. In a last-minute decision, while the *Seatrain New York* was already fidgeting in New York Harbor, Seatrain Lines Inc. was allowed to proceed for a six-month trial period. The service continued until 1959 (Cuban Revolution).

Figure 15: Seatrain's transshipment facility in New York

Not only rail cars but highway semi-trailers too could be transported by ship. A specially designed roll-on/roll-off ship used in conjunction with a dedicated terminal would allow quick and easy (un)loading. The first ideas were based on amphibious operations in World War II by so-called tank landing ships (*LST*: landing ship, tank). These naval vessels could carry large quantities (up to 1,900 tons) of vehicles, cargo, and landing troops and disembark directly onto a shore. A 50-ton, on-board A-frame hoist derrick could also be used for discharging the load. Michael Bustard of the Atlantic Steam Navigation Company saw the commercial use of the LST and approached the British Admiralty. Three vessels were hired by the Atlantic Steam Navigation Company and deployed in North West Europe sailings with government/army goods between ports, such as Antwerp, Rotterdam, Hamburg and Tilbury. The adapted LSTs were successful and stayed in service from the maiden voyage of the *Empire Baltic* on 11th September 1946 until December 1966 when the *Empire Nordic* was withdrawn.

In the United States, Trailerships Inc. bought in April 1947 two LSTs to haul trailers between New York and Albany. Their stern was considerably altered to speed up the roll-on/roll-off process. The two "trailer ships" *New York* (ex *USS LST-969*) and *Albany* (ex *USS LST-970*) were deployed on the Hudson River until September 1955.

Figure 16: USS LST-970 in military (left) and commercial service (right) as Albany

Roll-on/roll-off traffic gained momentum and shipping lines developed plans for new services and vessels. For example, the Pacific Coast Steamship Company intended to build two fast, large trailer ships, with a length of 563 ft (171.6 m.) and a speed in excess of 20 knots, connecting San Francisco and Long Beach. Although these plans did not materialize, the idea was not lost. Most notable were the plans, in 1953, for the development of a similar service between the Southeastern and Northeastern coast of the US. Initiator was the McLean Trucking Company. By the early 1950s this North Carolina-based firm with 1,776 trucks and thirty-seven transport terminals along the eastern seaboard possessed the largest trucking fleet in the South and the fifth-largest in the country. As the trucking business matured, many states adopted a new series of weight restrictions and started levying charges.

So it became a balancing act for truckers to haul as much weight as possible without triggering any fees. McLean realized that there had to be a more efficient way to transport cargo and he thought of a sea-land, trailer-ship service. The ships were a design of the Bethlehem shipyard and each had to cost over US$ 5.5 million. They would have a length overall of 638 ft (194.5 m.), a maximum beam of 87 ft (26.5 m.) and a draft of 20 ft (6.1 m.). Equipped with four cargo decks these ships could carry 286 35-ft (10.67 m.) semi-trailers. The total capacity of the two principal trailer decks amounted to 208 semi-trailers; an additional 78 units could be accommodated in the hold and on the boat deck. Ramps or elevators would be used to move trailers from the main deck to the hold and from the first deck to the boat deck. Stern ports at the level of both the main deck and the first deck facilitated direct loading and unloading to and from each deck. Double-ended, four-wheel drive tractors would be used to pull the trailers to the end of the ramp, turn around and push them up the ramp to their assigned positions aboard ship. The anticipated time spent in port by trailer-ships was 26%, slightly less than the Seatrain vessels (31%) and significantly below conventional port operations (47%).

The proposed operation was geared to the requirements of merchandise traffic movements and would be a common carrier service available to all on a first come first serve basis. Four ships would offer three weekly sailings between Wilmington (NC) and New York (NY) and between Wilmington and Providence (RI). In addition, weekly services would be provided at Charleston and Savannah or Jacksonville. The effective (compared to road transport) area of operation included the five South Eastern States (North and South Carolina, Georgia, Alabama and Florida) on the one hand and, on the other, ten Eastern and New England states ranging north from Delaware. However, McLean's plans for trailer-ships were not carried out and Bethlehem Steel shipyard at Sparrows Point, MD cancelled hull numbers 4,529 through 4,532. But, McLean did not abandon the idea of transporting trailers by ship.

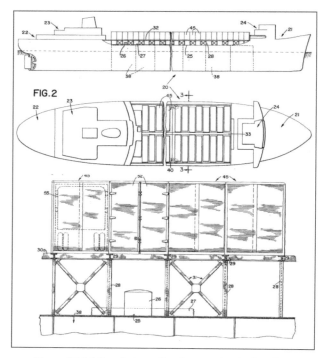

Figure 17: McLean's invention for containerized trailers

One of McLean's ideas was to place a complete semi-trailer (incl. wheels) inside a metal box and then bring this box onboard a bulk ship, modified with a spar deck (see Figure 17). This would be attractive as extra revenue, when shipping liquid bulk. The container was perceived as a sheet metal box (aluminum was mentioned), with outside stiffeners and D-rings as lifting lugs. Inside there should be means to secure the semi-trailer using inflatable members at the side-walls and a fixed support under the king pin.

His patent US 2,853,968 (filed 26 August 1954 and awarded 30 September 1958) mentions a capacity of 84 semi-trailers, in two rows of 42. The semi-trailers were placed perpendicular on the ship's length direction. Obviously, he later decided that this approach was less feasible then using the actual trailer to be secured on the spar deck or using trailer-bodies (containers), detachable from road chassis.

When he acquired Pan-Atlantic in early 1955, his plans were to convert the shipping line into a trailer-carrying steamship company. Shortly after, he purchased two T2 tankers, *Whittier Hills* (renamed *Alameda*) and *Potrero Hills* (renamed *Ideal X*), they were fitted with spar decks in order to carry trailers. In this case transshipment was based on the "lift on/lift off" principle. At the Bethlehem Steel shipyard trials were carried out to improve this technique (see Figure 18).

Figure 18: Trials at the Yard

Another company, Alaska Steamship Lines, also carried trailers, complete with chassis and running gear. The trailers were lashed to the main deck of general cargo vessels. This sometimes called "fishy back" service was primarily used to haul perishable foodstuffs from Seattle to defense bases. The volume of this service, however, remained small.

Figure 19: Alaska Steamship's "fishy back" service

"Van" type containers

From about 1900 onwards, railway companies started with containers that could be moved from trucks onto standard railway wagons. In the United Kingdom railway container designs were standardized during the late 1920s when the Railway Clearing House approved standards based on the existing designs. Closed or "van" type containers emerged as the most common ones. Those were built from wooden planks. They were all between 6' 6" to 7' 6" (1.98 to 2.29 m.) high, 7' 7.5" (2.32 m.) wide and came in two floor sizes: the short closed container (6' 11"/2.11 m. long) was called Type A, the long version (16' 5"/5.0 m. long) Type B. There was a

Figure 20: BD container on Conflat wagon

second letter added to the container prefix to indicate the specific type, for example the BK is a furniture container. The most common type was the BD which had side doors as well as an end door. The containers were secured to the (mostly) "Conflat" wagon.

Many thousands of containers were built, mainly to the standard pre-war "van" type designs. Although production ended in 1958, they were in use until the early 1970s. These containers were also used in overseas trades, especially to/from the Netherlands, Belgium, France and (Northern) Ireland. They were transported in cargo vessels often owned by British Rail (BR) and its predecessors (before 1948). In order to accelerate the transshipment process, British Rail commissioned in 1958 two ships specially designed for carrying these containers, the *Container Enterprise* and *Container Venturer*. The dimensions of these 982-grt vessels were 80 m.

Figure 21: Container Venturer for BR containers

(length) by 12.5 m. (beam). They were deployed in a new container service between Heysham (England) and Belfast (Northern Ireland). These ships were nearly 20 years engaged in BR container transport and sold in 1979.

In road transport, the concept of trailer bodies that could be detached from their chassis was in 1906 adopted by the Bowling Green Storage and Van Company for overseas removals. They used 18 x 8 x 8 ft (5.49 x 2.44 x 2.44 m.) detachable wooden trailer bodies, i.e. lift vans that could be hoisted aboard steamships in one piece (see Figure 22).

Matson also experimented with larger units. At their Honolulu marine terminal a truck could be loaded or discharged in one single operation of less than 30 seconds. A so-called straddle truck or Ross carrier (because the Ross Company was the first to build the machine) was used for handling as well as hauling "truck size" cargo. In the forest industry this type of equipment was already in use for rapid handling of lumber, later it was applied for lengths of all kinds such as pipe and steel rails. The abovementioned carrier was based on this principle, however with increased vertical clearance and width to pass over the bed of a semi-truck. A "box" filled with pineapples was picked up from bolsters on the ground by the hoisting arms of the unit carrier. After moving the load to the truck, the box was released by reversing the process. In order to prevent the load from being displaced when travelling, the load could be gripped to the undercarriage.

Figure 22: Early advertisement for lift vans

However, the "real" predecessor of the modern container was initiated by Alaska-based Ocean Van Lines. A contract for hauling US Army military supplies from the Seattle area via the port of Valdez to Camp Richardson, Alaska, was the incentive for the first regular service with "van" containers. As in 1949 no such container existed, they approached the Thoburn C. Brown company in Spokane (Washington). This company built all aluminum, semi-monocoque trailers. They were also the first to install a nose-mounted mechanical refrigeration unit called "Thermo King". Ocean Van Lines requested two hundred 30' x 8' x 8' 6" (9.14 x 2.44 x 2.59 m.) containers that could be stacked two high. Since a 30-ft flat front, stressed aluminum skin trailer was already in production, engineer Keith Tantlinger of Brown Trailers only had to devise a means of withstanding the stacking loads and provide lifting and securing points. By feeding a 2½-inch pipe down the existing extrusion and putting a steel casting on top, basically the container was ready for use. Stacking of loaded containers was no problem. Over time it became clear that the vertical component of the lashing chains was the greatest force (see Figure 23 and Figure 24).

In addition, sixty-nine skeleton trailers were needed for transporting containers to and from the ports. Since this type of trailer did not exist before 1949, it had to be designed and built according to specific requirements. For example, chassis strength was determined when the semi-trailer was used without container. Once the container was secured on the chassis rigidity was unimportant.

For their Alaska service Ocean Van Lines joined forces with both barge operators and the Alaska Steamship Company. The containers were transported between Seattle and Valdez, where they were transferred to trailers. Service began in early 1951, but operations were shut down in less than two years. Difficulties in (un)loading the containers from the vessel were, in part, the culprit. However, OVL containers did not disappear, because other carriers placed them into service for years afterward. Some of them were stretched to 40 ft, others became semi-trailers.

Figure 23: Ocean Van Lines containers are loaded and transported to Seattle

Figure 24: OVL containers carried in general cargo ships or on ocean going barges

IN RETROSPECT

Mechanization started a revolution in the maritime breakbulk and general cargo sector, because manpower did not limit handling anymore. The introduction of the forklift truck made palletization possible and, in due course, these pallets were placed in small wooden or steel containers. Shipping lines interested in efficiency gains fitted these containers rather seamless in their conventional operations. Among the frontrunners of the unitization concept were Matson, DFDS (Denmark), Bull Line and the US Military with its large-scale CONtainer EXpress (CONEX). The transport company that fully exploited the concept of containerization was the White Pass & Yukon Railroad. Based on their 8' x 8' x 7' (2.44 x 2.44 x 2.13 m.) container the company reorganized their complete transport system including the first purpose built containership, the *Clifford J. Rogers*.

Also, with regard to large units the innovation came from outside the maritime sector. Railway and trucking companies were heavily involved in searching for new methods of transportation. Complete vehicles such as boxcars, wagons and trailers were (dis)embarked by roll-on/roll-off or lift-on/lift-off techniques. Pioneers were Seatrain (rail), Atlantic Steam Navigation Company and Trailerships (road). However, carrying the frame and running gear is in fact not necessary. In this respect, a container is essentially a trailer body or van without chassis or a boxcar without wheels and underframe. British Rail (and its predecessors) were using this concept for overseas trade and even acquired two specially designed containerships. However, in the advent of modern containerization Ocean Van Lines earns the credits. They ordered 30-ft (9.14 m.) aluminum containers, built by the Brown Corporation, which also designed the skeleton trailer. Although their Alaskan service lasted less than two years, it was the first case of modern containerization.

CHAPTER 3

TAKE OFF OF A CONCEPT
(1956-1966)

April 26, 1956 is generally considered the start of containerization. That day the *Ideal X* of the Pan-Atlantic Steamship Corporation sailed from Port Newark, New Jersey to Houston, Texas, with fifty-eight 33-ft containers on deck.

The venture was the brainchild of trucking magnate Malcom McLean. According to popular belief, he had been watching longshoremen in the port of New York in 1937 taking bales of cotton out of his truck and load them into ships. It came to his mind that this cumbersome way of transshipment could be easier. However, it took until the 1950s before action was taken. At first he wanted to roll-on/roll-off and, later on, lift-on/lift-off trailers aboard ships. After these ideas were abandoned, he em-

Figure 25: Ideal X sailing between Newark and Houston

braced the idea of only transporting the bodies of trailers. On the West Coast Matson Navigation was soon to follow. Slowly but surely, other steamship lines and railroad companies adopted the concept as well. New initiatives in this field emerged not only in North America but all over the world.

3.1. PAN-ATLANTIC'S SEA-LAND SERVICE

McLean's intention to diversify into shipping needed approval of the Interstate Commerce Committee (ICC), as it was unlawful for anyone to take control or management in a common interest of two or more carriers. Anticipating problems, he created a new company, McLean Industries Inc., in January 1955 with Malcom as president, his brother James as Vice-President and his sister Clara as secretary and assistant treasurer. Then they put control of the trucking company in a trust and the McLeans resigned as directors of McLean Trucking. Soon after, on 21 January 1955, McLean Industries bought the capital stock of Pan-Atlantic (and Gulf Florida Terminal Company, Inc.) for US$ 7 million. This shipping line was established in 1933 by the Waterman Steamship Corporation, Mobile, Alabama to conduct coastwise operations. Later that year, after negotiating a US$ 40 million loan, the stock of Waterman including 30 vessels was also acquired.

Albeit the company possessed shipping and docking rights, plans could not proceed because seven railroad companies accused McLean of (still) violating the Interstate Commerce Act. Although McLean had resigned from the presidency of McLean Trucking and placed his ownership in a trust, it was not enough to secure the ICC's endorsement. Ultimately, he was forced to choose between his well-established trucking company and a speculative shipping endeavor. Showing his entrepreneurial spirit, he sold his remaining interest in McLean Trucking and focused on Pan-Atlantic.

3.1.1. Trailer-ships

The first vessel to carry containers was a World War II emergency tanker, officially classified as T2-SE-A1. These tankers were of a commercial design that the Sun Shipbuilding & Drydock Company had been building for Standard Oil of New Jersey (ESSO). During the war 481 of these ships had been launched. Due to a shortage of gear boxes, they were equipped with steam turbines and electric machinery producing a shaft horsepower of 6,000 (maximum 7,240), which enabled a speed of 14.5-15 knots. The dimensions of the tanker were approximately 160 m. length over all, 20.7 m. (molded) beam and a loaded draught of 9.2 m. The displacement tonnage was 21,880 and the deadweight tonnage 16,613 whereas the designed tonnage was 10,448 gross, 6,150 net.

Two of these vessels were acquired by Pan-Atlantic soon after the takeover. The *Ideal X* was built as *Potrero Hills* by the Marinship Corporation in Sausalito, California and commissioned in January 1945. After the vessel was conveyed to Pan-Atlantic in August 1955 the vessel was sent to Bethlehem Steel Co's yard at Sparrows Point (Baltimore), Maryland, for alteration. Spar decks for the carriage of trailers were added. Already during wartime, cargo (including airplanes) was transported on portable cargo decks without affecting the oil-carrying capacity. Before the *Ideal X* was equipped with a spar deck Pan-Atlantic's T2 tanker *Almena* (formerly known as *Whittier Hills*) was already converted and subjected to tests. Two other T2 tankers, *Coalinga Hills* and *Black River*, were acquired in 1956 and altered for container service at the company's shipyard in Mobile, Alabama. The latter was renamed *Maxton* (after Malcom McLean's place of birth).

In the early spring of 1955, two test containers were ordered from Brown's manufacturing facility in Toledo, Ohio. Because 33-ft (10.06 m.) containers were a catalogue item in the Brown sales manual they could be delivered on short notice. Within two weeks, the all-aluminum stress skin containers were transported to the Baltimore shipyard.

Keith Tantlinger, a Brown employee, was the linking pin between the Pan-Atlantic venture and the Ocean Van Lines project. He guaranteed McLean the robustness of their container. When he arrived at the shipyard Malcom McLean and others were actually testing the strength of the container by jumping on the structurally riveted roof. The experiment was convincing. Two hundred 33-ft containers were ordered at Brown's. Later, Fruehauf took over the manufacturing of containers (according to the Brown design).

For loading containers on and off the tankers, revolving cranes were preferred, but they could not be delivered on short term. Two secondhand cranes were bought, dismantled and adapted by cutting over 6 m. out of the gantry structures to lower the boom hinge. One crane was transported to Port Newark, New Jersey, where the port authority had already reinforced the dock apron and installed the crane rails and electric power supply. The other crane was installed on reinforced dock number 16 in Houston. Tantlinger, who had joined Pan-Atlantic as Vice-President of Engineering and Research

Figure 26: Loading of containers with an automatic spreader on 26th of April 1956

in 1955, designed an automatic spreader for the 33-ft containers. Thus the need for labor to manually engage the four pendant hooks from the spreader was eliminated. However, because of the swinging of the containers, longshoremen were still needed (see Figure 26).

Moreover, the US Coast Guard and the American Bureau of Shipping needed the assurance that freight stowed in containers did neither endanger the crew, the vessel nor other cargo. According to the demands of the Coast Guard the containers were lashed on the spar deck and contained vulnerable cargo during the roundtrips between Port Newark and Houston. The test continued until bad weather was encountered and the Coast Guard was convinced that the containers could retain their cargo in rough weather at high seas.

Terminal operations were based on the use of trailer chassis. For loading the cargo aboard the ship a container on a trailer was driven alongside the vessel. Then the outbound container was discharged by the quayside crane and transferred to the spar deck. Within the same cycle the unloading of an inbound container took place in reverse order. The short in-out cycle required a streamlined organization. McLean concluded an agreement with both the International Brotherhood of Teamsters and the International Longshoremen's Association (ILA) about their respective jurisdiction. Pickup and delivery away from the pier was outsourced to independent trucking companies whereas teamsters moved containers in Sea-Land tractors in the immediate terminal area. The trailer with container was driven into position at the pier side by a trucker who would also undo the clamps that tightened the container to the chassis. In addition, longshoremen secured the hooks to the top of the container. In 1959 a levy of US$ 1 was placed on each container and went to the ILA. Three years later the ILA gained the right to consolidate container loads of up to 80.5 kilometers from the port. This is known as the 50-miles rule.

When the cargo was not immediately transported to its final destination, the trailers with container were stacked at the terminal. This means that huge open areas were needed for the stacking yard. New York's finger piers were not suited for container operations. Port Newark boasted a modern wharf type terminal that had a wider apron, a 15.2 m. gauge crane rail track, a shed with a tail gate high freight platform and two railroad tracks. The ship berth length amounted to 168 m. Moreover, it was situated near the New Jersey Turnpike, which is part of the Interstate network. Construction of this highway was completed in 1952. Close by locations such as New York City and New

Figure 27: Promotion for the new service

Jersey's industrial centers as well as destinations further away e.g. the US industrial heartland were well accessible. An advertisement claimed that a truck could travel from Port Newark to Chicago without having to stop for a single traffic light!

3.1.2. Cellular containerships

Although millions of dollars had been spent on modifying ships, purchasing containers, chassis and tractors and, last but not least, reinforcing dock aprons and installing huge cranes, the project was short-lived. Already in 1956 the conversion of C2 freighters into cellular containerships with shipboard gantry cranes started at the Waterman owned Gulf Shipbuilding yard in Chickasaw, Alabama.

C2 vessels were designed by the United States Maritime Commission in 1937-38. They were all-purpose cargo ships with 5 holds. In all, 173 were built between 1940 and 1945. The first C2s were nearly 140 m. long, 19.2 m. wide, had a draught of 7.6 m and a speed of 15.5 knots. Later ships varied in size and tonnage (see Figure 28).

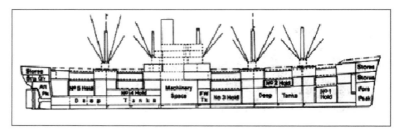

Figure 28: Longitudinal cross section of a C2 all-purpose cargo ship

The selected Pan-Atlantic vessels belonged to the (smaller) C2-S-E1 type with a capacity of 6,190 gross tons. A total of 30 ships of this configuration were exclusively built by Gulf Shipbuilding Corporation, Chickasaw (AL). Six vessels were to be converted: *Gateway City, Azalea City, Bienville, Fairland, Raphael Semmes* and *Beauregard*. In order to meet the strict conversion schedule the Mobile-based engineering firm of Ewin, Campbell and Gottlieb was contracted for 90 days and George Sharp, a well-known naval architect from New York City, was hired. Keith Tantlinger acted as the supervisor of the work that moved ahead in unexplored territory.

The hull conversion encompassed the removal of all the "tweendecks", hatches and conventional cargo gear. By adding sponsons on both sides of the ship the longitudinal strength (and stability during loading) was improved (see Figure 29). This was necessary because the hatches were made larger. Moreover, deck capacity could be extended. Finally, vertical batten guides were installed forming six cells into which the containers could be loaded. Below deck the boxes were stacked on top of each other and secured by their own weight, the guides forward and aft, and the hatch covers on top. In addition two layers of containers were stored on deck. The capacity of the ships increased to 9,014 gross tons.

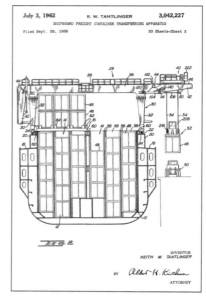

Figure 29: C2 cross section

Figure 30: Pan-Atlantic trailer for 35-ft gooseneck container

The early 33-ft containers were not used for the C2 ship operations, instead the renowned 35' x 8' x 8' 6" (10.67 x 2.44 x 2.59 m.) Sea-Land container was introduced. The length of the new containers was determined by the maximum length of trailers then allowed on Pennsylvanian highways. Each container had a frame with eight corner castings that could resist stacking loads. In this way the hinge vulnerability problem could also be solved. Also, the process of engaging a container by the spreader needed to be redesigned because the vertical cells restricted movement outsides its profile. Inspired by a bolt-action rifle that worked on the principal of a rotating locking mechanism, Tantlinger designed the twist lock and the box corner fitting.

Since working with the land-based rotating cranes was slow, it was considered more efficient to use shipboard cranes. Moreover, it made transshipment independent from port facilities. Since these cranes could be positioned over a row of containers, the crane operator only had to work in two dimensions. Searching for a manufacturer of suitable cranes, a small producer of logging equipment was found. The Skagit Steel and Iron Works of Sedro-Woolley, Skagit County, Washington, had the know-how and flexibility to construct a container handling hoist to be mounted on a ship gantry. One gantry crane was located forward of the deckhouse, the other one aft. Each crane was equipped with a diesel engine on top providing the power needed. The only thing that did not work out was the position of the crane operator. The idea was that, in order to handle the loads more carefully, "the operator would ride the spreader". Later, the operator stood on a platform on top of the trolley from where he could control the operation of the spreader. The cycle, from the moment the trailer body was lifted until lowered into position in the hold was approximately 2 minutes and 20 seconds.

There had been much debate among naval architects about the type of vessel to be converted into containerships: freighters or tankers? In general, existing tankers were more suitable for conversion. Calculations indicated that the cost per container slot for a T2 tanker amounted to US$ 7,800 and for a C2 freighter US$ 13,650. Albeit exact figures are not available, the estimated costs of Pan-Atlantic's C2 conversions amounted to over US$ 3.5 million per vessel. This complies with the above-mentioned numbers. Interestingly, a request by McLean Industries to purchase a number of T2 tankers from the Government was rejected in the congressional year of 1956.

Notwithstanding these clear figures, shipping lines simply used ships already in their possession. They were happy that an existing ship could quickly and successfully be converted to a useable containership for approximately one-third of the price of a new containership. Moreover, freighters were more suited for partial conversions.

Late 1957, the first vessels with a capacity of 226 35-ft containers (approximately 396 TEU, Twenty feet Equivalent Units) became operational. On October 4, the *Gateway City* sailed from Port Newark to Miami, Tampa and Houston. In 1958, Puerto Rico became the first offshore destination. Ports served on a regular basis included San Juan, Jacksonville and Miami, in addition to Newark and Houston. In due course, the four T2 tankers were removed from the service.

Figure 31: Ship mounted gantry crane

Figure 32: Gateway City on its maiden voyage near Miami

Increased operations made the company decide to relocate its headquarters from Mobile (Alabama) to Port Newark (New Jersey). Soon after, Pan-Atlantic Steamship Corporation changed its name to Sea-Land Service, Inc, "to better describe the services offered".

Adjacent to the terminal, but within the boundaries of the city of Elizabeth, the Port of New York Authority (since 1972: The Port Authority of New York and New Jersey) began developing Sea-Land's new US\$ 19 million terminal. In 1962, New Jersey Governor Richard Hughes dedicated the 82 hectares (203 acres) port area to Sea-Land that gradually developed the area over the next two decades.

3.1.3. Expansion

In 1962, Sea-Land introduced its first intercoastal container service between the East and West Coasts. The first containership, *Elizabethport*, capable of carrying 476 35-ft containers, arrived on September 27 in Oakland, after a stop at the new Sea-Land terminal in Long Beach. The Port of Oakland had managed to negotiate a lease with Sea-Land to become the Northern California headquarters for its intercoastal service. The agreement contained a 650-ft section of an Outer Harbor berth and the exclusive use of six acres for the staging of up to 340 trailers. In addition, the Port Authority

Figure 33: Intercoastal box shipping by Sea-Land's Elizabethport

had also constructed a new truck terminal. Eastbound, the ships made an additional stop in Puerto Rico before returning to the East Coast. Initially, the service ran on an 18-day schedule, using two ships. Later, four containerships on this service provided a 9-day schedule. Again, WWII tankers were used. Because of their size (152.4 x 20.7 m.) they are classified as T3 tankers. The steam turbines enabled a speed of 15 knots for this 16,387-dwt tanker. They were jumboized by adding a new midbody and their new dimensions became 620-630 x 78 ft (190-193 x 23.8 m.). At that time, these vessels were the largest dry cargo freighters in the world. The *Elizabethport* and her sister ships *San Juan, San Francisco* and *Los Angeles* were equipped with huge onboard gantry cranes for the self (un)loading of containers.

Alaska was added as a destination in 1964. The service ran between Seattle and Anchorage and Kodiak and was linked with other West Coast ports by a feeder service. In this way Sea-Land could offer container services as far as the Eastern seaboard. Operations commenced just weeks after the Good Friday Earthquake. Starting with shipments of badly-needed relief supplies it soon expanded to general cargo.

The service was provided by two containerships: *Anchorage* and *Seattle*. These vessels were former C4 ships acquired during conversion into partial containerships by Bull Line. Later, Sea-Land converted these vessels into full containerships able to accommodate 272 35-ft con-

Figure 34: Sea-Land vessel in port of Anchorage

tainers. The *Anchorage* made history in December 1964 by becoming the first large vessel to batter its way unaided through the heavy winter ice of Cook Inlet. Not so much the steel hull, but the propeller blades were at risk. Ultimately, the vessel reached the port after which she was named. For the first time, Alaskan ports were served on a year-round basis.

In 1969/70, the bows of the *Anchorage, Seattle* and *Baltimore* were joined with the after bodies of three T2 tankers respectively named *Bull Run, Petrolite* and *Esso Roanoke*. This required skilled ship surgery, because of the dissimilar hulls of the T2 and C4 ships. At the point where the 143-ft (43.6 m.) after body joined the 328-ft (100 m.) fore body a mismatch of 3' 6" (1.07 m.) and 4' 3" (1.30 m.) in resp. beam and depth occurred. During the hull conversion the machinery received a complete overhaul. Since the "identity" of a vessel is determined by its stern, it is atypical that they were (re)named *Anchorage, Seattle* and *Baltimore*. The operation led to an increased container capacity of 354 35-ft containers (359 for the *Baltimore*).

The stern and machinery of the *Anchorage, Seattle* and *Baltimore* were joined with a newly-built bow and mid-section and rechristened *Rose City, Pittsburgh* and *San Pedro*. When the job was completed a ship emerged capable of carrying 602 35-ft container.

In 1964, the company moved from the provisional to the permanent headquarters, a three-storey high general office building. A truck operations building, a truck maintenance garage and a 335 m. long general cargo warehouse were constructed on the same location. A 24.7-hectare (61 acres) marshalling yard could hold 2,600 containers with their chassis. For perishable cargoes, a special terminal with outlets to maintain refrigeration in parked containers was built. Clara McLean directed the administration and took care of furniture, equipment, etc.

In order to locate the movement of containers in the system, the company employed an IBM 1440 Data Processing System. In October, a long-time financing agreement with Litton Industries was concluded. This proved to be a firm base for further growth.

In the fall of 1965, Sea-Land began installing dockside cranes with a lift capacity of 30 long tons at its major locations. The first of these US$ 800,000 Paceco-built cranes was installed at Port Elizabeth. Twenty-two more at twelve other ports followed suit. Sometimes, cranes were owned by the port authority e.g. Houston.

On the West Coast the relationship between Sea-Land and the Port of Oakland strengthened in March 1965, when Sea-Land signed a 20-year lease for 10 ha (24 acres) and two deepwater berths in the Outer Harbor. The site was designed to accommodate more than 1,000 truck trailers and comprised two new shoreside gantry cranes, signaling the industry's move away from shipboard cranes. Sea-Land was allowed priority, but other operators could use the facilities as well. The bill for these improvements was US$ 2.5 million. With the completion of this facility, larger ships could be deployed and traffic intensified.

Figure 35: McLean at Port Elizabeth

3.1.4. Vietnam War

Containerization got a real boost when the Vietnam War escalated and the quantity of war supplies that had to be shipped increased substantially. On July 11, 1966, Sea-Land began a containership service between US West Coast ports and Okinawa, the United States major back-up base in the region. Three jumboized T3 containerships formerly active in the intercoastal service carrying 476 containers each were deployed. The use of containers was supposed to be very efficient. Quoting a high-ranking military official (the Deputy Director of Transportation, United States Army Material Command): "Twenty-five men are all that are required to move 20,000 tons of cargo from the ship onto the trailers and into the marshalling yard. They also re-stow the ship with retrograde cargo of empty containers, all within 30 hours. This means it takes 750 man hours to

Figure 36: Oakland's 7th Street Terminal next to US army base

discharge 20,000 tons of cargo. In contrast, it would take almost 12,000 man hours to unload the two 10,000-ton Victory ships. The impact of that kind of manpower saving is obvious."

The Navy contracts were westbound only and guaranteed a minimum number of containers on each trip from the US West Coast (i.e. Oakland and Seattle) to Okinawa and the Philippines. Sea-Land collected additional revenue every time a container was re-stuffed with material to be returned to the US. The payments for eastbound freight were pure profit since the negotiated rates already covered the empty backhaul.

At first, McLean did not meet much enthusiasm in relation to his projected containerized maritime service to Vietnam. Before the buildup of US combat forces, Saigon was the only important deep-draft port in Vietnam. In 1964, a small so-called Delong pier, which could berth two vessels, had been constructed at Cam Ranh Bay 180 miles north of Saigon. In order to handle the tremendous influx of men, equipment and supplies the plan was to develop major logistical bases at Saigon, Cam Ranh Bay and Da Nang and to establish six minor support bases in smaller ports. Although the effectiveness of containerization was proven by a demonstration by Sea-Land, McLean took a considerable risk. The cost of reinforcing the pier at Cam Ranh Bay, assembling the cranes,

Figure 37: Sea-Land container in Vietnam

floating equipment and vehicles across from the Philippines, and building the truck terminals were entirely Sea-Land's.

In November 1966, the Military Sea Transportation Service (MSTS) provided a 2-year contract for containership service from the US West Coast ports to Vietnam. The terms of the contract included:

a) Three self-sustaining C2 containerships, each carrying 274 35-ft containers, providing service from Oakland to Da Nang, and three non-self-sustaining C4 ships of a 609-container capacity each, make the run from Oakland and Seattle to Cam Ranh Bay, arriving at destination every 15 days. A shuttle service consisting of a 247-container C2-type ship running between Cam Ranh Bay, Saigon and Qui Nhon was also established. The schedule of the shuttle self-sustaining ship meets the schedules of the larger non-self-sustaining ships.

b) In addition to the ships, Sea-Land Services provides the necessary containers, chassis, tractors and other gear to furnish complete door-to-door service from CONtinental US (CONUS) west coast ports to inland military depots in Vietnam.

c) Sea-Land Service delivers empty containers to be filled with military cargo at any point designated by the Government within the commercial zone of Seattle or within an expanded commercial zone in the San Francisco-Oakland Bay area.

d) Subsequently, Sea-Land Service drays the filled containers to its own terminal for loading aboard its containerships.

e) Upon arrival of a containership in Vietnam, Sea-Land Service unloads the containers and delivers them with its own tractors to any point designated by the Government within 30 miles of the discharge pier.

f) The Government has 30 days' free time to empty the containers in Vietnam. When empty, the containers are returned to CONUS at no additional cost to the Government.

In the contract a new type of ship is mentioned: C4 ships with a capacity of 609 containers. These were stretched former C4 troopships that after the addition of a 50 m. long mid-body section measured 209 m. and had a speed of 15.5 knots. The names of these ships are *Oakland*, *Long Beach*, *Trenton* and *Panama*. Mid-1966, they were operational.

It took a lot of effort to supply the troops. From 1965 to 1969 Military Sea Transportation Service (MSTS) moved almost 54 million tons of combat equipment and supplies and almost 8 million long tons of fuel to Vietnam. The seven Sea-Land vessels delivered approximately 1,200 containers a month to Vietnam, i.e. 10% of the supplies destined for Vietnam. The remaining 90% required the service of more than 250 other ships. The effectiveness of container shipping for military support in a war zone was undeniable.

However, a few problems occured. One of the challenges was how to get the freight out of the container at inland locations. The military did not have material-handling equipment that could take the container off the chassis and set it on the ground for ease of access. If the doors were opened, a forklift could get the first few pallets out but then the forks couldn't reach all the way back. At first, chains, cables and rope were used to get the freight out of the container. Later, the military developed an extended-boom forklift and low-mast forklifts that could go inside of the container. Another problem was tracking a container and knowing its contents.

Figure 38: Fork lift unloading pallets

Venturing into Vietnam entailed considerable risks for Sea-Land. For example, the US government was liable only for damage to the company's trucks and equipment caused by enemy fire. However, efforts paid off. A fixed rate per container was negotiated. Moreover, the contract required the government to offer "all of its containerizable cargo". This led westbound to utilization ratios of close to 100%. Each roundtrip from the US West Coast to Cam Ranh Bay brought Sea-Land more than US$ 20,000 per day, and each smaller vessel sailing to Da Nang took in about US$ 8,000 a day, at a time when time chartering a large general cargo ship cost US$ 5,000 a day. From almost nothing in 1965, Sea-Land's Defense Department's revenues rose to a total of US$ 450 million in 1973.

Figure 39: Cam Ranh Bay

3.2. MATSON NAVIGATION

The second shipping line heavily involved in early containerization was Matson Navigation, a major player in the California-Hawaii trade. In early 1956, a research department was established that studied Hawaii's special freight problems thoroughly. Operations research was used to find the optimal containerized transport system. The findings were published in mid-1957 and the main recommendation consisted of the adoption of the container concept in two phases.

At first instance, six freighters were converted to carry up to 75 containers on deck, with conventional breakbulk in the holds. The size of Matson's containers, 24' long, 8' 6" high and 8' wide, was determined by road regulations; in California the rule on doubling up trailers was limited to 24 ft for each trailer. On August 31, 1958 the *Hawaiian Merchant*, a C3-class freighter sailed from San Francisco to Honolulu, Hawaii with 20 boxes aboard.

Matson paid a lot of attention to the transshipment process. Extensive research was carried out to determine whether ship-mounted or dockside cranes should be preferred. The latter were chosen because they seemed to be more cost effective for Matson's operations, i.e. a number of ships serving only a few ports. To keep the turnaround time of a containership to a minimum, the loading of containers between ship and shore should be as fast as possible. However, existing cranes did not meet this requirement. For example, the cranes used for (un)loading Pan-Atlantic's T2 tankers lost 2 to 3 minutes per cycle due to poor control of the container at points of pick up and discharge.

Figure 40: The Hawaiian Merchant on its inaugural voyage

For a full containership this would result in a 4 to 8 hours delay, which was considered unacceptable.

Since the study concluded that no crane on the market satisfactorily met all of Matson's requirements, performance specifications were put together and put out for bid. The Pacific Coast Engineering Co. (Paceco), one of eleven bidders, was awarded the contract to do the detailed engineering and final design work. Following its philosophy that the best design has the fewest number of pieces, Paceco began developing conceptual drawings paying particular attention to aesthetics. This resulted in a unique and extremely clean-looking A-frame configuration. The operator's cab was mounted to the main portal in full view of the operation with all controls at hand. In order to latch the container Matson used a modified Cleco clamp system where a hook was inserted into each corner housing and then moved laterally by a mechanically inserted wedge.

The Matson terminal located at San Francisco's old finger piers was not suited for this type of operation. Piers are long and relatively narrow structures with a shed. The slip between two adjacent piers was based on the number of berths. Matson had already modernized its terminal. The 222-ft (67.7 m.) inside area between the two piers had been joined by a pile-supported platform. The center part of the platform was constructed as a depressed well for truck maneuvering and for crane rail track accommodations. The remainder of the slip was utilized for pier and shed widening. However, it did not offer sufficient space for container storage. Moreover, the weight of the cranes could not be supported by the pilings of the pier. Hence, the company moved across the San Francisco Bay to Alameda. On January 7, 1959, the crane was put into service at Encinal Terminals. The new container crane operated a three-minute cycle.

Figure 41: First Paceco A-frame container crane

With an average container weight of twenty tons, this resulted in a productivity of 400 tons per hour.

In 1960, cranes were also installed at Los Angeles and Honolulu where the Diamond Head terminal was improved. At Los Angeles, Matson advanced the port US$ 1 million to get new facilities constructed. Repayment was made from wharfage tolls. The crane was also sold to many other companies. In 1983, the Paceco A-frame container crane was awarded an International Historic Mechanical Engineering Landmark.

Figure 42: Matson's Diamond Head terminal in Honolulu

The introduction of all-container vessels depended on the success of phase 1. The "only deck" phase lasted nearly two years. November 1959 saw the start of the US$ 3.8 million conversion of the *Hawaiian Citizen*. This vessel became the first full container carrier of Matson. She could carry 296 containers in her hull, stacked six high in honeycombs of steel frame, and up to 140 on deck. The total of 436 24-ft containers (523 TEU) included up to 72 refrigerated units. May 19, 1960, the *Hawaiian Citizen* made its maiden trip to Hawaii. Her entry into Matson's service doubled the company's container capacity.

A few months later, two converted C4 bulk carriers, the *Hawaiian* and *Californian*, entered the trade. Westbound, a maximum of 286 containers were loaded, eastbound the load consisted of 3,000 short tons of molasses and 16,000 short tons of sugar stowed loose in the hold and a full complement of nearly all empty containers all above deck. Sugar provided in this case the stability for the lighter load of high stacked empty containers. Even the *Hawaiian Motorist,* an automobile transporter, had deck space for 226 containers.

Distribution of containers from Honolulu to the outports (and vice versa) was done by the *Islander*. This 1963-built, 91.5 m. long barge with the hull of a deepsea vessel had a giant on-board crane and capacity for 155 containers, reefers included. The *Islander* was towed, since unions refused to man such a large barge with only a six-man crew. Hence, a propulsion system was never installed. A weekly-scheduled service between Oahu, Hawaii, Maui and Kauai was established. As a barge with its own gantry crane with automatic spreader on board, the *Islander* carried out a good but somewhat awkward inter-island service.

Although new methods of cargo handling were always re-jected by the International Longshoremen's and Ware-housemen's Union (ILWU), the recognition that the contain-er revolution was inevitable, made the ILWU negotiate a labor agreement that was meant to compensate longshore-men for lost jobs and wages resulting from mechanized car-go-handling techniques. In 1959 the ILWU and the steam-ship lines represented by the Pacific Maritime Organization (PMA) settled upon a pilot agreement which became known as Mechanization and Modernization fund (the M&M fund). The employers donated US$ 1.5 million to the fund whereas the union agreed to lift certain work rules and ac-cepted new labor saving methods. In 1961, the agreement

Figure 43: ILWU leader Harry Bridges

was put into final form and lasted for a period of 5½ years. Employers contributed US$ 5 million an-nually to the fund, basically to allow early and mandatory retirement. In this way the economic bene-fits were split among the shipper, the steamship lines and longshoremen (albeit not evenly). In 1966, a second M&M agreement was concluded.

3.3. OTHER INITIATIVES

3.3.1. Alaska Steamship Company

One of the first shipping lines that encountered containers was the Alaska Steamship Company (Alaska Steam). Transport of 30-ft containers between Seattle and Valdez began in early 1951 but op-erations were shut down within two years. After the demise of Ocean Van Lines Alaska Steam com-menced carrying trailers, complete with chassis and running gear. The trailers were lashed to the main deck. The volume of this trailer service remained small.

Figure 44: Alaska Steamship Company transporting containers in regular service

In 1956, Alaska Steam inaugurated the use of 24-ft containers between Seattle and Seward. The cooperation with Alaska Rail Road (ARR) was instrumental to the success. Both were interested in eliminating the unnecessary labor costs for transshipment. The railroad teamed up with the steamship company and ordered its own containers. By the end of 1957, various types of containers were in use, some owned by the shipping line or railroad, some by road transport companies such as Puget Sound Alaska Van Lines.

Considering containers as the future, Alaska Steam converted two of its Liberty ships into cellular containerships in 1964. The converted *Tonsina* and *Nadina* were capable of carrying 176 24-ft containers athwartships. A third Liberty ship was adapted as partial containership. At the same time a subsidiary of the Alaska Steamship Company, the Alaska Trainship Corporation, started a rail-ferry service with the *Alaska III* (previously Seatrain's *City of New Orleans*) carrying a maximum of 56 loaded railcars between the Canadian port of New Westminster (British Colombia) and Whittier (Alaska).

Competition in transportation between Alaska and the lower 48 States was fierce. Even before Sea-Land started their Alaskan container line, other steamship and barge operators offered state-of-the-art services including roll-on/roll-off and container traffic. Ferry service for rail cars was offered from Seattle every three days by Puget Sound Alaska Van Lines' barges called Hydro Trains carrying up to 42 loaded rail cars. Trucking company Alaska Freight Lines that took over Ocean Van Lines, operated barges that hauled trailers and containers from Seattle to Valdez and transported them by road to Fairbanks. In 1956 Anchorage was added as port of call and by 1961 Seward was served as well. The company was taken over by McLean in 1964 to facilitate their new Alaskan service. Alaska Steamship Company's obsolete Liberty ships could in fact not compete with these services and went out of business in 1971.

Figure 45: Alaska Steam's converted (Liberty) containership with athwartship container cells

3.3.2. Grace Line Inc.

One of the companies that adopted the container concept full swing was Grace Line. This steamship company offered scheduled services from the United States to Latin American ports. Late 1950s. the trade to Venezuela was declining and Grace Line decided that deploying two new general cargo ships and two converted C2 freighters, *Santa Eliana* and *Santa Leonor*, would meet the requirements for the Caribbean. They called their containerized activities "seatainer" service.

The modification of the ships took place in 1959 at the Baltimore-based Maryland Shipbuilding & Drydock Co. The vessels were fitted for the carriage of 17' x 8' x 8' (5.18 x 2.44 x 2.44 m.) containers. Although the conversion was very similar to Pan-Atlantic's, the already bigger S-AJ1-type C2 vessel was lengthened by 13.7 m. Each vessel could accommodate a total of 476 containers (382 below deck, 94 on deck). The gross tonnage increased to 10,485 tons and the deadweight to 8,651 tons. The sponsons contained tanks to facilitate carrying petroleum on the return leg from Venezuela. The expenditure of Grace Line on these two conversions amounted to US$ 6.9 million.

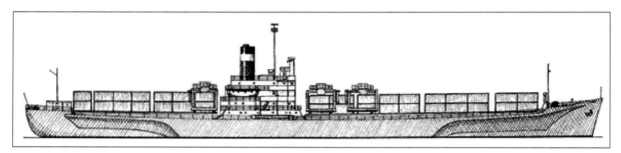

Figure 46: Drawing of Grace Line's C2 conversions Santa Eliana and Santa Leonor

The converted *Santa Eliana* started international container shipping when she sailed for Venezuela in January 1960 with 176 containers containing powdered milk and other general cargoes. However, the longshoremen in Venezuela refused to unload the containers even though some sort of a previous agreement had been concluded by the agency. After 18 days an agreement was reached and the *Santa Eliana* was unloaded with the provision that no more vessels of this type would be used. The sailing of the *Santa Leonor* was cancelled and both vessels were laid up.

When the Saint Lawrence Seaway System opened, Grace Line obtained approval for an operational subsidy for the Great Lakes route albeit the vessels were completely unsuited for the system, in particular, the locks in the Welland Canal. The full-container service connected Great Lakes ports directly with destinations in the Caribbean The venture proved to be a financial disaster and the run was given up after just one season. In 1964 the *Santa Eliana* was sold and deployed by Sea-Land under the name of *Mayaguez*. The same happened to *Santa Leonor* which was renamed *Ponce*. In their new configuration they could carry 274 35-ft containers.

In 1963, Grace Line introduced four new 20-knot, 14,442-ton vessels (the Santa Magdalena-class) carrying passengers as well as freight to/from the West Coast of South America. Each was fitted to carry bananas in three holds. On the southbound voyage these areas were used for carrying cars or palletized cargoes. The other two holds were container holds. Container capacity was 175 20-ft containers. They were equipped with sophisticated cargo carrying devices; five cargo elevators in three holds and

Figure 47: Santa Mariana, a general cargo and passenger ship

four gantry cranes on deck, which, when married in pairs, could handle 40-ft containers. The passengers on board were granted priority by the port authorities, a big advantage in congested ports.

3.3.3. White Pass & Yukon Route

One of the container pioneers, the White Pass & Yukon Route, decided to invest 8 million Canadian dollars in a completely new system. In 1965, the old "Container Route" transportation system with small containers was replaced by -off standard- 25' 3" x 8' x 8' (7.70 x 2.44 x 2.44 m.) aluminum containers with steel frame. The containers came in four types: dry, vented, heated and refrigerated. A new 6,000-ton containership, *Frank H. Brown*, was equipped with a heavy shipboard gantry crane with retractable arms (Munck). Its lifting capacity was 36.3 metric tons at an overall reach of 18.3 m. from the center line of the ship. The gantry crane engaged the container latching devices when it was loaded or discharged from the ship. New dock and freight handling facilities were constructed. Straddle carriers handled containers on the terminals. The containers were moved by rail between Skagway and Whitehorse on flatcars and were held in place by a special, cone-shaped holding device.

Figure 48: Frank H. Brown discharging its load at Skagway

3.3.4.   Other shipping lines

The commitment of most shipping lines was limited to include containers in conventional liner services. In this way only minor modifications and investments were needed. Seatrain included containers in their operation by deploying devices that could move containers over the railroad tracks in the hold of the ship. In relation to a US$ 150 million US Navy contract nine tankers were converted to carry containers as well as railway wagons and vehicles.

Figure 49: APL's President Lincoln, a Searacer-class vessel

Sometimes new vessels were designed to carry both general cargo and containers. A good example is provided by American President Lines' two C4-S-1q vessels *President Lincoln* (second) and *President Tyler* (third) were built in 1961. These 172 m. (LOA), 23 m. (beam), 13.6 m. (depth) ships with a draft of 9.75 m, had a general cargo capacity of 13,223 gross tons. The containers were carried just forward of the superstructure, in hold No. 4, which was outfitted with its own gantry crane. They could also accommodate 12 passengers in 8 staterooms. With a speed of 20.5 knots these so-called Searacers, a modified (by George C. Sharp) ver-

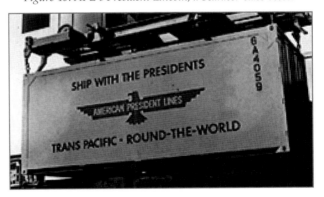

Figure 50: Early American President Lines' container

sion of the common US Mariner design, were deployed in a round-the-world service. Container services provided by these vessels were not very successful. Despite several adaptations the Searacers were never converted into full containerships. Their deployment ended within 20 years.

3.3.5. US railroads

Especially on the West Coast, railroad companies such as Southern Pacific, Union Pacific and Alaska Rail Road became involved in container transport. These companies often owned a fleet of 24-ft containers themselves. They were transported as Container On Flat Car (COFC) or on a chassis called Trailer On Flat Car (TOFC).

The practice of carrying trailers in a train atop a flatcar is known as piggyback. Railroad companies developed piggyback services in order to compete with long-distance road transport. The first Piggy back service was inaugurated in 1926 by the Chicago North Shore and Milwaukee Railroad. However, it was not until the 1950s that an inflexible government regulation was lifted and Piggyback services gained momentum. In the beginning, trailers were moved via a ramp onto flatcars, a technique known as circus loading. Later, cranes with grapple arms were used. This method became common practice for many railroad companies. Containers transshipped in this way also need lifting lugs.

Figure 51: Transshipment On Flat Car (TOFC/COFC)

An innovative way of transferring truck trailers between highway and rail carriers was patented by Flexi-Van. Flexi-Van equipment consisted of specially designed flatcars with two hydraulically liftable and rotating tables, lightweight monocoque trailers and special highway wheel and axle assemblies ("bogies"). At the terminal the trailer van could be (un)loaded in five minutes without additional equipment. Afterwards, the brake line and electrical circuit needed to be (dis)connected.

Figure 52: Flexi-Van service offered by the Milwaukee Road

The New York Central Railroad started the first Flexi-Van service in April 1958, soon to be followed by the Milwaukee Road. De facto, it meant that the North part of the East and West coast were connected. Although initially not intended for maritime use, shipping lines, such as States Marine Lines, joined later. Flexi-Vans were transshipped into seagoing vessels and travelled all over the world. People outside North America who spotted their first (long) container in the early 1960s may well have seen a Flexi-Van.

Figure 53: Flexi-Van loaded aboard a deepsea vessel

3.3.6. Australia

Down Under the Associated Steamships Ltd. of Australia took a bold step when they decided in 1963 upon systematic containerization. They ordered a specially-designed vessel, the world's first brand-new cellular containership, from the New South Wales State Dockyard. The *Kooringa* had a length overall of 126.2 m., 16.8 m. beam and a mean loaded draft in service of 6.9 m. with a corresponding deadweight of 4,353 tons. It had two holds with six hatch covers each. Both holds were divided into six bays by transverse bulkheads, and guide bars on the bulkheads provided further subdivision into individual compartments. For handling the containers it was equipped with two travelling gantry cranes on deck, capable of lifting up to 17 tons. This single-propeller motor vessel had a service speed of 16 knots and was launched 29 February 1964.

The costs of the *Kooringa* reached to one and a half million pounds and another million was spent on the construction of special terminals at her ports of call Melbourne and Fremantle, and on the provision of 16' 8" x 8' 0" x 8' 6" (5.08 x 2.44 x 2.59 m.) containers and other auxiliary equipment. The company pioneered an all-inclusive rate (including drayage at both ends of the journey, port charges, sea freight and a "free" all risks insurance). The odd container size was based on 4-ft D boxes called "Seatainer" already in use in coastal trades. For joint use in the *Kooringa*, the new container was four times larger. Although vessels such as the *William Holyman* transported "Seatainers", they lacked cell guides and cannot be considered as genuine forerunners of the *Kooringa*. Around 1970, a conversion took place for the carriage of 20-ft containers. At the same time the cranes were removed and the sponsons deepened. In 1975 the service was discontinued.

Figure 54: Kooringa at Victoria Dock, Melbourne

Figure 55: Four D-boxes handled as one container

3.3.7. Ireland

Due to its location, Ireland's international trade needed maritime transport. In addition to British Rail, which already offered container services, Irish shipping lines such as the British and Irish Steam Packet Company (B & I Line) and, in particular, Bell Lines embraced containerization wholeheartedly.

Bell Lines Ltd., established in 1963, was a shortsea carrier that operated between Ireland and the United Kingdom. At the end of the 1960s, container services were extended to continental Europe. The company anticipated an integrated transport chain with containers and chartered the first ship specially designed to carry ISO units. It

Figure 56: Non-ISO 20-ft container of B & I Line

was built in Germany by the Sietas shipyard in Neuenfelde near Hamburg and launched in 1966 as the *Hans Hinrich*. Bell Lines arranged a 5-year charter and the vessel was renamed *Bell Vanguard*. The dimensions of the vessel included a length of 70.8 m. and a beam of 12.5 m.

Her capacity was, due to regulations for coastal trades, 499 gross tons or 67 TEU. The 1,320-bhp engine allowed a speed of approximately 13 knots. It had large hatches that covered 80% of the ship's width. Cell guides were not installed. In 1967, the *Bell Vanguard* was joined by two sister ships (*Bell Valiant* and *Bell Venture*) and the *Bell Victor*, a slightly bigger vessel (80 TEU). To facilitate the total transport chain, Bell Lines possessed about 1,000 containers and was heavily involved in terminal operations. The container terminals owned by Bell Lines were

Figure 57: Bell Lines' terminal in Teesport

very efficient. With one gantry crane covering the whole dock area, the operator could not only handle the vessel but also rail wagons and truck trailers. Also, stacking and repositioning of containers was carried out in this way.

3.3.8. United Kingdom

British Railways were familiar with the use of containers in overseas transport. In 1961, they started a new container service between London and Manchester called Speedfreight. The containers were very similar to the pre-war designs but they had recesses on the underside of the floor that engaged with cone shaped mountings on the wagon. Later, a number of light metal "boxes" including 27' long, 8' wide and 7' 4½" high (8.23 x 2.44 x 2.25 m.) CA-type containers were developed. They all had special lifting points on the base, at 9-ft separation. The new containers took less time to (un)load, but required a specially-built crane that had a frame with four rigid arms or large forklifts with grapples. Hence, the container service was limited to yards equipped with suitable cranes. Moreover, Speedfreight service was operated as wagonload traffic.

In many respects, Speedfreight was the forerunner of Freightliner. The idea of moving containers filled with goods within the UK by rail, with final delivery by road, is the basic premise of the Freightliner system. The first Freightliner

Figure 58: Freightliner containers on bogie flat wagon

containers were built in 10', 20' and 27' lengths with an 8-ft square-end profile. Because expected changes in road regulations would permit the operation of bigger road vehicles, 30-ft Freightliner containers were introduced later on. They had grapple lifting points, albeit with 12-ft separation. Later, with the arrival of ISO standard containers, the original Freightliner boxes were steadily replaced by ribbed sided types fitted with top-lift points on their corners.

Due to limited clearance, new designed Freightliner bogie flat wagons had wheels that were only 0.61 m. (instead of 0.94 m.) in diameter. Being of less than normal height, these wagons had no conventional buffers and couplings. Therefore, the last wagon (in a fixed rate of 5) had a raised buffer beam and conventional coupling at one end. Air-operated disc brakes were fitted as standard. The maximum 1,000 ton trains had a maximum speed of 75 mph, but operated, on average, at 50 mph.

The first Freightliner wagons were ordered in 1964. On 15 November 1965, the first Freightliner container train travelled from London Kings Cross to Glasgow loaded with, amongst other items, 15 tons of confectionery, 5 tons of foodstuffs and lots of metal. On its return journey, it carried beer, firebricks and paper. Other terminals followed suit. By 1969, every workday Freightliner offered 140 train services between 30 terminals. Part of the success was based on a flat rate per container, regardless of the value of the contents. This boosted the use of containers for low-value goods such as steel sections and standard house bricks.

Although the service was intended for domestic use, the Freightliner system facilitated seagoing containerized freight. Terminals emerged in seaports initially for coastwise trades, but they handled deepsea containers too. Early 1968, British Rail launched its daily Sea Freightliner service between Harwich and Zeebrugge, Belgium. Two 4,000-dwt containerships with cellular holds, *Sea Freightliner I* and *II*, were built by John Readhead & Sons LTD., South Shields, England.

Figure 59: Sea Freightliner II in the port of Zeebrugge

These vessels were the first new cellular containerships designed according to ISO standards i.e. 30-ft containers. With an overall length of 118.3 m. and beam of 16.4 m. they could carry 222 TEU each. From 1970 on, slightly smaller containerships were deployed on the Irish Sea. Each vessel could accommodate 180 TEU at a speed of 14.5 knots.

The containerships were operated by the British Railways Shipping Division. The Freightliner sea terminals were equipped with two 30-ton cranes for ship to shore movements. Ship discharge/loading productivity rates of over 30 containers per hour were the standard. For rail to road transfer two cranes were on hand.

IN RETROSPECT

Until 1966, containerization was introduced and matured predominantly in domestic North American maritime trades. In the beginning only a few shipping lines i.e. Sea-Land, Matson and Grace Line embraced the idea of containerization full swing. They, like some overseas companies, successfully operated specific routes. Each company had its own system with dissimilar container dimensions, hoisting methods and onboard or on shore cranes. Other shipping lines included containers in their regular operations. These new entrants as well as railroad companies provoked even more variation which hampered the exchange of containers between companies. For example, container lengths differed widely: 8, 10, 17, 20, 24, 25, 27, 30, 35 and 40 ft. This emphasized the need for standardization. Intercontinental trades were still served by traditional general cargo vessels. In general, shipping lines took a conservative approach and were reluctant to start massive change programs for (expensive) container vessels and handling facilities. On top of that it required huge investments in containers since one box cost approximately US$ 5,000 in those days. The South America experiences of Grace Line did not encourage them either.

Still, the first period of containerization clearly showed the anticipated advantages: less damage and pilferage and lower handling costs. Transshipment of traditional general cargo required a lot of effort and the productivity of longshoremen had dropped after World War II. Containers sped up the trans-shipment process and, therefore, the time ships spent in ports could be reduced considerably. Moreover, the cargo moved to the hinterland without reloading. These benefits of containerization were uniquely demonstrated in case of supplying the US troops in Vietnam. (Standardized) containers were about to conquer the world!

CHAPTER 4

STANDARDIZATION
A must for global spreading

The loading and discharging of goods was centuries long a process performed by men carrying loads up to 60 kg (in sacks, bundled, etc.). Only heavy loads (marble blocks, wooden trunks, etc.) required innovative tools, in the Middle Ages resulting in fixed or revolving cranes (see Figure 60). Those cranes were driven by people or animals (hand winches and treadmill). The invention of steam engines and the subsequent industrial revolution induced all kinds of mechanized tools. They allowed a faster handling of goods and caused a relief for the extraordinary "struggle" related with the handling of goods at production or consumption places and/or interchange areas, such as railway stations and ports. Stowage of goods in vessels, carriages, railway cars and trucks, was often focused on the maximum utilization of space and thus a very labor intensive activity.

Nowadays, most of the handling activities in transportation are performed with the help of mechanical devices. Mechanization provides a faster and more reliable handling and also results in much better working conditions for labor. Obviously, it requires a structuring in handling and transportation processes as demanded

Figure 60: Equipment in the Middle Ages

by the handling/transportation functions in the overall production and distribution chain. In many cases, packaging of goods, standardized loads and shipment volumes were determined by the available handling methods and transportation means (such as carriages, tow boats, railcars and ocean going vessels). Standardization is probably the most important pre-requisite for a fast, safe and efficient handling and transportation. Standardization is important for the shape, size and weight of unit loads, but also for all the interfaces where loads meet transportation vehicles (like vessels, railway wagons and road trucks). Standardization helps to design mechanized equipment and to introduce standard work procedures which are important to guarantee safe working conditions. Standardization does not require that every piece of equipment or handling process is designed identically. To the contrary, standardization can be limited to functional requirements in combination with a limited number of essential components and measurements.

Standardization must concentrate on the essential characteristics and eliminate little-used types and sizes, so society can benefit from reduced costs for handling, transportation and information control. In general:

"Standardization is nobody's best, but better for all".

This statement is illustrated in particular in the transportation of goods. When mechanization evolved in the 19th and the beginning of the 20th century, many parties within the transportation chain developed their own standards. Such as cars and platform bases for the railways: boxes, bags and crates for the shipping industry and special handling tools for the handling in ports (slings, dock-tool pallets, etc.). Some shipping lines developed their own boxes, like KNSM, which operated a number of collapsible containers (see Figure 61) to avoid the spacious, costly shipping of empty boxes on a return trip.

Figure 61: Foldable container (Dutch patent: 81889)

Railways and trucking

As from the 19th century, there have been some attempts to standardize railcars and even container-like boxes to be used on railcars. However, in the 1920s and 1930s and even more after the Second World War the railroad companies standardized containers, based on the maximum suitable width (rail clearance cross section) and an efficient length to be accommodated on the most commonly-used rail cars. In the 1930s many US railroads adopted the 9' width and the size group of 7' x 9' x 8' (L x W x H) was predominant (load capacity approximately 5 tons). By 1933, thousands of steel containers were in use on the American railroads (see Figure 62).

Already in the 1930s, some policies for US Interstate and Foreign Commerce for trucking were developed, including regulations for the maximum width (8') and maximum height (12' 6") for trucks and trailer bodies. The maximum width resulted in some conflicts with the already-standardized pallet dimensions. Although the American Standards Association

Figure 62: Small containers used by US railroads

announced standards for 16 standard pallet sizes, the most common sizes were: 64" x 48" (1,626 x 1,219 mm.), 48" x 32" (1,219 x 813 mm), 48" x 40" (1,219 x 1,016 mm) and 40" x 32" (1,016 x 813 mm). From these measurements it can be learned that already in those days the maximum width of 96" (8') resulted in a conflict for some pallet sizes when striving for a maximum truck or railcar utilization.

In Europe, various national railroads introduced small to medium-size containers for the transportation of goods such as in France, Germany, the Netherlands, United Kingdom and Sweden. In the United Kingdom the first boxes were introduced around 1900 (only one example of a private British coalmine railroad has been earlier) and by 1926 the first regular container services were introduced. In 1933, containers were an integral part of the railway transportation system. Their outside dimensions were widths of about 7'-7'¼" and lengths from 7' 11" to 16' 5" and designed for loads up to 4 tons.

The British Railways used quite a variety of box types, such as covered types (including special ones for furniture and bicycles), open types (half height), ventilated and insulated types and boxes for bulk cargo. In the 1950s, there were more than 50,000 of such containers in use.

In Germany, the first rollable containers were introduced in 1924 and already in 1935 approximately 12,000 small containers (up to 3.5 m³) were utilized, see Figure 63.

Figure 63: Small containers used by the German railroads in the 1930s

In the same year, nearly 250 large containers (up to 20 m³) were in operation as well. The German Railways adopted the Dutch Box system already before the World War II. After 1950, a large number of such (mid-sized) boxes were used both by the railways and private companies (in the 1960s about 25,000 of such containers and approximately 5,700 dedicated railcars). The container length remained with 3,100 m. (the maximum allowed railcar width), the width was in general below 2,300 mm and the total mass was 5-6 tons. Remarkably, some special types had a length of 5,990 mm, a width of 2,500 mm and a maximum load of 11.1 tons. The mid-size containers (MC-types) were promoted for door-to-door services and special trailers were able to pick up and deliver the boxes (provided with bottom side wheels) from the ground.

The Netherlands showed similar developments. The first intermodal (rail-road) activity was introduced by the Dutch Railways (NS) and a large consolidator Van Gend & Loos (see Figure 64).

Figure 64: Dutch intermodal box system, Van Gend & Loos (1936)

In France, a subsidiary of the SNCF the Compagnie Nouvelle des Cadres (C.N.C.) and a consortium of trucking companies, GTTM (Groupement Technique des Transporteurs Mixdes), organized containerized cargo transportation using open (height 2,550 mm.) and closed types (height 2,000 mm.), with a width of 2,300 mm. and a length of between 1,490 and 5,000 mm. For some decades the U.I.C. (Union Internationale des Chemins de Ferre) studied Standardization of these middle type containers and their recommendations were presented in their code 590: conditions for conveyance in international traffic.

In the US, the call for Standardization became louder after World War II not only for vans (trucks with an enclosed load area) but also for semi-trailers, including the specifications for all kinds of piggyback (trailer-on-train) operations involving the American Standards Association (Van Container subcommittee) and the Truck Trailer Manufacturers Association.

Shipping

In the described perspectives in the US and Europe a new maritime container type (both for shipping, trucking and railways) was launched by early starters such as Ocean Van Lines, Pan-Atlantic Steamship, Matson and Grace Line. Their main objectives were speeding up port-handling operations, the reduction of damages to goods and the avoidance of pilferage. In this respect, the following statement of Mr. Francis G. Ebel is illustrative. During a panel discussion in July 1960, he said: "The whole thing comes down to economics. The handling of cargo on the waterfront between the land and the ship is about the most horrible example of materials handling that the world has ever seen and the use of containers appear to be about the best prospect for improving this problem!!"

The container improved the handling efficiency and speed dramatically (5 to 10 times better). According to Mr. Ebel: "There are other secondary advantages which are extremely important. For instance the outturn of cargo, i.e. the prevention of damage by the use of containers is really remarkable. Also the pilferage of anything they can get their hands on seems to be accepted practice on the waterfront, and when you have the cargo locked in a box it makes it pretty hard. There are also savings in export packing. While, basically, the saving in handling costs is the primary reason for containerization, these other benefits are very important and are now playing a part in the steamship companies going into this form of handling."

The launching shipping lines in containerization introduced a variety of containers lengths: Grace Line 17'; Pan-Atlantic (later Sea-Land) 33' and later 35'; Matson 24', Ocean Van Lines 30', Seatrain lines 27', etc. (see Figure 65).

Figure 65: Early type containers: Sea-Land 33' and Ocean Van Lines 30'

On this multitude of unitized loads the American Standardization Organization started their work in the 1950s in order to come to a limited number of container sizes. In those years the European and Japanese transportation companies were (not yet) involved. They were engaged in standardizing railroad, trucking, unit loads and handling equipment.

Remarkably, already before containerization started, the Federal Coordinator of Transportation called for the standardization of equipment in 1953. However, not earlier than in 1958 an initiative from the Maritime Administration resulted in two committees (composed of MarAd and Industry representatives) for the development of maritime container standards; one committee should focus on container dimensions (sizes and weights), the other one was asked to come up with recommendations for construction and fittings. The activities were guided within the Sectional Committee MH-5: Standardization of freight containers of the American Standards Association (later shortly named USASI and now ANSI: American National Standards Institute). In the same period the Van Container Subcommittee of the MH-5 Sectional Committee was also studying standard specifications for containers.

The Marad/Industry Committee recommended a container height and width of 8' and lengths of 12, 17, 20, 24, 35 and 40 ft with the following gross weights:

	Length	Gross weight
•	12 ft	28,000 lbs (12.70 tons)
•	17 + 20 ft	44,800 lbs (20.32 tons)
•	24 ft	56,000 lbs (25.40 tons)
•	35 + 40 ft	67,200 lbs (30.48 tons)

These combinations were derived for maritime and intermodal applications as a compromise out of many influencing factors such as highway restrictions, maximum axle loads, tandem axle arrangements, payload optimization and cargo densities.

The Van Container Subcommittee came up with the same series of lengths however, supplemented with lengths of 13, 25 ft and 26.5 ft (regional use). This proposal was not received positively in some US states (opposition against the 12, 17, 24 and 35-ft length). This made MH-5 decide to come up with 10, 20, 30 and 40 ft only, with an 8-ft height and width. This standard was ASA approved at April 14th, 1961.

In the early 1960s, US shipping companies already operated a large variety of lengths (10, 12, 17, 20, 24, 24.5, 27, 30, 35, 36 and 40 ft) wherein 17, 20, 24 and 35-ft length containers by far dominated (Sea-

Land, Matson, US Lines and Grace Line). The 24 ft was economical for Matson's Hawaii operation and 35 ft was the maximum length allowed in all States. Therefore, the 10, 20, 30 and 40-ft length standardization resulted in opposition from those shipping lines operating a non-standard container fleet (especially Sea-Land and Matson). Joint forces from Matson and Sea-Land eventually resulted in getting their 24-ft and 35-ft length sizes introduced in the ANSI standards in 1971 (this was important to avoid discrimination in legislation).

After an initiative by the US, the ISO installed a technical committee on Freight Container Dimensions (ISO TC 104) in 1961. In September 1961, the first meeting took place. The committee determined that a standard should focus on operational exchangeability and should avoid any directives for design details and materials used.

In 1963, the Dutch delegation, supported by other West European countries, proposed to increase the width to 2,500 mm. but the US, UK and Japan blocked this proposal. The first draft standard on dimensions concluded 4 types:

Type	L mm, (ft)	W mm, (ft)	H mm (ft)	Gross Mass Kg/(Lb)
1 A (40')	12,192 (40')	2,438 (8')	2,438 (8')	30,480 (67,200)
1B (30')	9,125 (29' 11¼)	2,438 (8')	2,438 (8')	25,480 (56,000)
1C (20')	6,058 (19' 10½)	2,438 (8')	2,438 (8')	20,320 (44,800)
1D (10')	2,991 (9' 9¾)	2,438 (8')	2,438 (8')	10,160 (22,400)

These dimensions and weights were finally presented in ISO 668 and later amended with heights of 8½ ft and 9½ ft and an increased gross mass of 24,000 kg for the type 1C (20 ft). In the 1970s, this was the accepted standard for dimensions and ratings, lasting a few decades, before further modifications were discussed and partly accepted.

Corner fittings and lifting provisions

For centuries, the handling of bags, crates, heavy loads, etc, was done by slings, chains or cords, requiring a lot of improvisation and muscle strength from port labor. Upon the arrival of boxes for intermodal operations (as of the 1900s), many operators of larger boxes were looking for more efficiency and safety and they often designed their own methods, handling equipment and tools. Some used the widely-spread hooks, fitting in lugs connected to the box; others developed special provisions to enable a fast and safe pick up and handling. When containerization started in the 1950s, there were many types of fittings provided at the various boxes and lifting was performed by provisions mounted at special frames or directly connected to the handling equipment (see Figure 66).

Figure 66: Various types of handling fittings (CONEX, Dravo and Brown)

Some early box operators even patented their solution as they believed that their special design would bring commercial success.

Sea-Land's first 33' boxes (at the *Maxton, Ideal X, Almena* and *Coalinga Hills*) were handled with hooks. Later, Keith Tantlinger designed a spreader bar with a drive mechanism to bring the hooks into 4 corner lugs, thus avoiding the (expensive) support from 2 to 4 dock workers required for attaching the so far used universal hooks onto the container (see Figure 67).

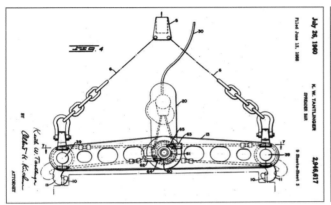 

Figure 67: Automatic spreader by Tantlinger (US patent 2,946,617)

However, this first "automatic" spreader bar design proved to be difficult when connecting such a hook-type spreader bar to containers stowed in vessels with vertical cell guides under deck (to avoid under-deck lashing) as provided in the larger Sea-Land vessels (e.g. the *Gateway City*, which as of October 1957 carried 8' x 8' 6" x 35' boxes). The new cellular type of vessels triggered Keith Tantlinger to invent a new method of handling containers, stowed in vertical cells under deck. He came up with 8 corner castings at the box corners and the use of twist lock bolts enabling the handling from the top and fixing boxes onto railcars or trucks and on top of each other (e.g. on deck).

For the idea of the twist lock bolt, Tantlinger was inspired by his knowledge of bolt-action rifles, in which a strong locking device prevents disengagement under load. The corner fittings were also provided with a side drain (to prevent the built up of water, which could freeze) and so came the first designs for twist lock and corner casting; the original patent is shown in Figure 68.

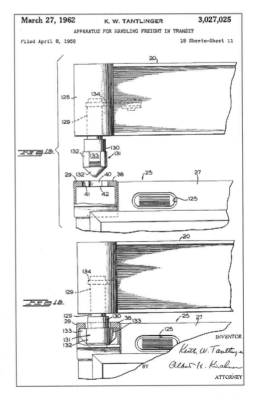

Figure 68: Patent corner casting and twist lock

The introduction of the twist lock proved to be a great success, however, in the beginning, there were some minor teething problems. One almost destroyed the Gateway City Inauguration Event at Mobile, Alabama. For the first corner castings delivered obviously the manufacturer had misunderstood the functionality and had provided an inner web for strengthening reasons. Although Tantlinger had ordered to remove all of that inner webbing (to allow the twist locks to rotate in the corner casting). During the ceremony, with demonstration of the container handling, one corner casting could not be engaged by the spreader. Tantlinger suspected the problem and removed a forgotten web. After that, the demonstration could continue and showed the simple and reliable design of corner casting and twist lock for the handling of Sea-Land containers.

The Matson engineering staff conquered the same problem, however, in a different way. Matson developed their corner posts with attached corner castings to provide sufficient effective bearing, maximum diameter openings for maximum self-alignment on positioning cones (e.g. on deck), side openings for locking pins and/or lashing hooks and requiring a minimum of usable inside space. The corner casting could accommodate a simple self-aligning hook. The alloy steel hooks (test load 74,000 Lb= 329 kN) were hydraulically forced to fit in the wedge-type corner edges. Figure 69 illustrates the Matson design and just like Sea-Land, Matson as well had their own spreader design fitted with tiltable guides for easy positioning and a mechanical interlocking to prevent disengagement during the handling process.

In the same year, Sea-Land and Matson filed their patent documents. National Castings as well filed their so-called Speedloader system, also for use in intermodal load units such as maritime and railroad containers. This concept was adopted by Grace Line and some other smaller shipping lines and later, for a short period, as the national standard in the United Kingdom.

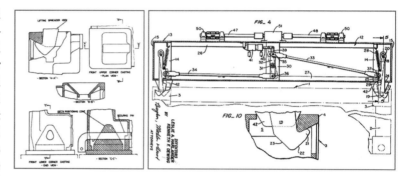

Figure 69: Matson corner fitting and spreader (US pat. L. Harlander 3,078,115)

Setting the Standards: A time-consuming "dog fight"

For more than a decade, many companies and institutions, active in the fields of trucking, railroads, shipping, railcar and trailer manufacturing, standardization, etc., have been disputing the minimum set of standards required to establish an effective interchangeability for maritime and intermodal containers.

Keith Tantlinger (the innovative engineer involved in numerous patents related to containerized transport) worked for Malcom McLean (Sea-Land) and later as VP of engineering for Fruehauf. In both positions he was a representative to many meetings on standards and he describes the process of standardizing container dimensions and corner fittings as a real "dog fight". Similar revelations were recorded from Leslie Harlander (Matson), Ron Katims (Sea-Land), Charles Cushing (Sea-Land, later independent naval architect) and Frans Oudendal (Werkspoor and later Dutch Railways). Obviously, there were tremendous economic interests at stake for those companies who already had invested so much money in containers, ships, trailers, handling equipment, etc.

One of the first thoughts on the need for standardized load units and transport equipment was expressed in December 1935 in a report by Joseph B. Eastman, the US Federal Coordinator of Transportation. This report covered the railroad industry, reviewing railway equipment and related methods, practices and standards. Recommendations were made for further research in improvements for operations and equipment.

As earlier mentioned, it was in 1953 that again the Federal Coordinator of Transportation called for more "uniformity of operations in the everyday handling of containers". Under the umbrella of the American Standards Association (ASA), a section committee MH-5 "Freight Containers" started in July 30 1958 (chairman Herbert Hall and secretary Fred Muller) and appointed 4 subcommittees (Pallet Container, Cargo Container, Van Container and International Coordination). During a number of meetings it became clear that an all-supported standardization of dimensions and corner fittings was still far way. Many committee members suggested modifications and new concepts. For instance, in one meeting it was even proposed to mount retractable kingpins in the container bottoms. As mentioned, in 1961, ASA already approved the basic dimensions (length 10', 20', 30' and 40' x 8' wide and high), but there was no consensus on the fittings (see Figure 70).

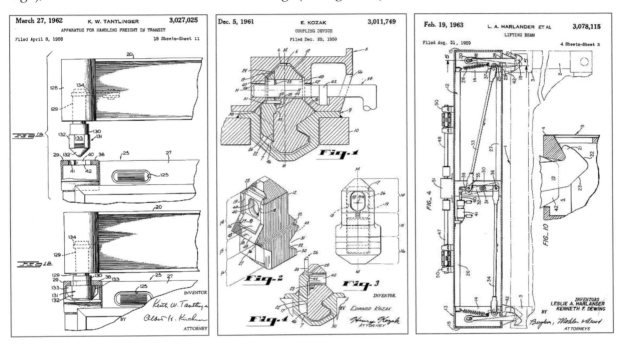

Figure 70: Corner fitting solutions by Sea-Land (left), National Castings and Matson (right)

In order to come to a worldwide transportation system the ISO/TC 104 "Freight Containers" was established in 1961 and three working groups became active (dimensions, strength requirements and lifting standards). The subcommittee on lifting standards made little progress. Many companies were involved; some of them had patents on their lifting provisions. The US ASA MH-5 Handling and Securing Task Force finally came to a breakthrough. Regardless heavy opposition from National Castings, Strick and some other self-interested members, forming a majority of the task force, were in favor of the technically superior Sea-Land concept. During a 1962 meeting, Fred Muller and Keith Tantlinger discussed the Sea-Land corner fitting and twist lock design to become the standard on the condition that Malcom McLean would agree to release the patent, free of charge and no strings attached.

Malcom McLean agreed to release its patent nr. 3,027,025 and after some dimensional modifications the design of a box-type fitting with rotatable engaging lug was accepted as an US American Standard with support from both the ASA and TTMA (Truck Trailer Manufacturers Association). During the ISO/TC104 Hamburg meeting (October 1964) there was still no consensus amongst the US delegates, but Tantlinger described the major characteristics and presented half-size ceramic models to delegates from other countries. A major dispute between National Castings and four leading shipping lines (Sea-Land, Matson, Alaska Steamship and APL) remained, but at a meeting of ASA September 16, 1965 a modified Sea-Land fitting was accepted as a US standard and was to be presented at the ISO/TC 104 The Hague meeting (late September 1965). The US delegation had not managed to send the required documents in advance (such as drawings and descriptions) and during the The Hague meeting it was decided that the proposal could be accepted when the proper documents were received.

A Dutch delegate, Mr. Frans Oudendal, working with Werkspoor Utrecht (a company active in the field of railroad equipment and containers) offered his facility and some draftsmen. Keith Tantlinger (Fruehauf Trailer), Gene Hinden (Strick Trailers), Leslie Harlander (Matson) and the draftsmen worked day and night and produced a set of drawings both in metric and imperial measurements during the meeting (see Figure 71). The British delegation, who had proposed the National Castings design as its national standard, stopped its opposition and the modified Sea-Land design

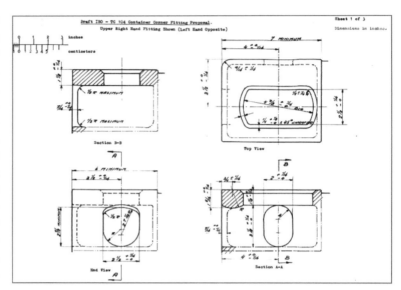

Figure 71: Original design proposal of corner castings (1965)

was accepted with considerable support. However some disputes on design details continued, followed with a number of field tests under a variety of load combinations. This again resulted in some minor modifications (somewhat thicker wall) at some spots and then at the ISO/TC 104 Moscow meeting June 1967, the twist lock and corner fittings were approved as an ISO draft standard.

Towards one International Standard

The ISO-accepted standard (dimensions and lifting concept) included a major modification program (many millions of dollars) for almost all the container shipping lines. Sea-Land and Matson were probably the most affected lines as both their container dimensions and corner fittings did not conform to the ISO draft standards. Their major concern was the requirement of MarAd to allow subsidies only to US companies adhering to the MH-5 standards. During 1965 and 1966, disputes continued involving executives like Leslie Harlander (Matson) and Ron Katims (Sea-Land) trying to convince the MH-5 committee of their optimum dimensions. This resulted in the acceptance of an 8' 6" height but no allowance for their 24' and 35' container. Finally, the issue was brought to the US Congress, which accepted the economic arguments from Sea-Land and Matson. MarAd was ordered to give equal treatment to US shipping lines using non-standard containers, which assured Sea-Land and Matson with vessel construction subsidies and other US supports for the maritime industry.

It took until 1970 before the ISO published the first draft (ISO 668) and nowadays the use of maritime containers is standardized by the following most important standards:

- ISO 668   Series 1 Freight Containers - Classification, Dimensions and Ratings;
- ISO 830   Freight Containers-Terminology;
- ISO 1161   Series 1 Freight Containers - Corner fittings, Specifications;
- ISO 1496   Series 1 Freight Containers - Specification and Testing;
- ISO 3874   Series 1 Freight Containers - Handling and Securing;
- ISO 6346   Freight Containers - Coding Identification and Marking;
- ISO 9711   Freight Containers - Information related to containers on board vessels;
- ISO 9897   Freight Containers - Container Equipment Data Interchange;
- ISO 10374   Freight Containers - Automatic Identification.

The above standards have been developed and accepted over a period of more than 20 years, showing the slow but important standardization process, including international proposals, meetings, disputes, arguments, economics, politics, compromises, etc.

In the 1960s, shipping lines introduced their own method for container identification of their owned containers, often combined with unit type or with serial numbers referring to the type of container (e.g. C for clip-on unit; G for general cargo, aluminum; H for general cargo, plywood; I for general cargo, steel; O for open top; R for refrigerated, aluminum, etc.). In October 1969, the TC104 committee presented a draft standard for the coding of containers taking almost 15 years before ISO standard 6346 was accepted as standard for coding, identification and marking of freight containers presenting the following major elements:

- Identification:
    - Owner code: four capitals, the fourth to be U (unit);
    - Serial number: six numerals;
    - Check digit: one numeral, a means of validating transmission accuracy, based on a standardized algorithm, using owner code, serial number and a weighting factor.

- Coding:
    - Country code, consisting of 2 capitals (ISO 3166);
    - Size and type code, consisting of 4 numerals. The first 2 relate to the size, the second 2 numerals relate to type characteristics (e.g. 20 for 20-ft containers; 40 for 40-ft container), e.g.:
        - 00 = general purpose with opening(s) at one or both ends;
        - 32 = refrigerated and heated container;
        - 50 = open top container with opening(s) at one or both ends;
        - 75 = tank container for dangerous liquids; test pressure 4 bar.

- Marking:
    - Mandatory operational marks such as gross and tare mass and cube;
    - CSC safety approval plate;
    - Optional operational marks e.g. excessive height (9' 6") or width (2.5 m., pallet-wide);
    - Size, location and layout of marks.

Almost every shipping line appreciated the existence of a worldwide standard and by the end of the sixties and beginning 1970s large numbers of 20' and 40' containers were purchased; the majority still 8' high, but already some smaller numbers at 8' 6" high. Some early container types are presented in Figure 72.

Figure 72: Early container types

For some specific trades, specially-designed containers were introduced, more or less fitting into the newly-accepted International Standard, e.g. half-height 20' open top containers designed for 23 metric tons (gross mass) used for high density cargo (see Figure 73).

Figure 73: 20' half-height open top with off standard maximum gross mass

Matson slowly converted from 24' towards 20' and 40' and Sea-Land predominantly switched to 40' (and leased 20') containers. Parallel to this, Sea-Land started a major conversion program by stretching the 35' boxes (with Sea-Land corner fittings) into 40' boxes (with ISO corner fittings). These containers could be handled by either 35' or 40' spreaders. This forced a number of terminals where Sea-Land vessels were calling, to operate telescopic spreaders with so-called multi-use twist locks (asymmetric) supported in floating bearings (see Figure 74). This spe-

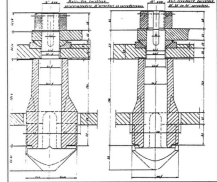

Figure 74: Asymmetric multi-use twist lock versus normal ISO twist lock

cial asymmetric design twist lock was required to adjust to the two different center-to-center distances related to the Sea-Land corner fittings (c-t-c 2,286 mm.) and the ISO corner fittings (c-t-c 2,260 mm.), see Figure 135 in Chapter 6.

For many years, Matson and Sea-Land operated their off-standard containers in rather captive markets (Matson to Hawaii; Sea-Land to the Caribbean and South America). But, when Brazil refused to allow 35' containers on their infrastructure, Sea-Land decided to convert its entire fleet to ISO standard containers.

Nowadays, the worldwide containerized maritime transport system operates a container fleet larger than 30 million TEU (20', 40' and 45' containers, in many different designs and for many various commodities). About half of that fleet is owned by shipping lines, the rest is in the hands of leasing companies, NVOCCs and shippers. The order book for container vessels will certainly cause a further growth of the container fleet (a vessel requires a container fleet of 2-3 times its TEU-slot capacity).

Figure 75 presents only a few of a large family of containers types, wherein general purpose, refrigerated, open top and tank containers represent the mainstream, however with hundreds of other designs, dedicated to special commodities and/or customers.

Figure 75: Present container types

Threats to the strength of standardization

An American saying goes: "There is always room for more" and this saying is surely valid for the development in container sizes. The container heights have been standardized towards 8' 6" and 9' 6" (2.59 m. and 2.89 m.) and in some trades even higher (non-standard) heights are applied (e.g. car-containers, containers for Boeing airplane parts, etc., see Figure 76). There is somewhat more reluctance to increase container width. Already in the start-up phase (1963), the Dutch delegation in the ISO/TC 104 proposed the 2,500 mm width, which would much better accommodate the standard European pallet sizes (1,000 x 1,200 and 800 x 1,200 mm.). However this was rejected by Japan, the UK and the US

Figure 76: Off-standard over-height boeing containers

(although the US allowed passenger buses up to 2,590 mm width). Much later the US proposed 2,600 mm but then the Europeans could only accept a maximum of 2,550 mm, and thus, the 8' width remained the standard.

In 1984, US shipping lines (APL and Sea-Land) introduced the 45' container. Some years later, APL ordered a few thousand 48' containers (to compete with the US and Canadian domestic road transport companies). Nowadays, the 53' long, 8' 6" wide, 9' 6" high container is regularly used in the US and Canada. Shipping line OCEANEX already operates a vessel with 53' cell guides below deck. But worldwide only the 45' container is regularly used by a number of shipping lines; mainly as deck cargo but some vessels have a number of 45' cells under deck.

In the most recent decades, a large variety of non-standard containers have been introduced (see Figure 77), always with limited applications and dedicated to special niches in the market. Examples are the Stora Enso container (SECU = Stora Enso Cargo Unit dimensions: length: 13.7 m. x width: 3.1 m. x height: 3.0 m.). The fruit carrier United Brands operates 43' long containers, providing a better utilization and volume/payload ratio. In Europe (especially for European domestic cargo), the pallet-wide container (with standard ISO corner fittings) is becoming more and more popular. Even a 45' long pallet-wide container was introduced by Geest Line (see Figure 78). Although trucking legislation did not allow semi-

Figure 77: Non-standard, over-wide bulk container

trailers longer than 13.60 m. (45'=13.72 m.), the pioneering work of Geest Line finally resulted in a legal status of these containers but with modified (rounded) corner castings. The question arises whether these developments really support a global interchangeability and further cost control. In many cases terminals and transportation companies accept these non-standards including all the extra attention and additional planning efforts and yard space; the extra costs are covered by the large quantities of standard containers that really support the economies of scale. How long will the system partners accept the extra cost for these exceptions, only beneficial for a limited number of operators?

Figure 78: Over-sized containers, Geest (left) and StoraEnso (center and right)

Maybe, after some 50 years there is again the need for some powerful visionists who set standards for the next 50 years.

IN RETROSPECT

It is remarkable that at the start of the standardization process, many meetings were attended by driven, executive people from companies and institutions; people who were responsible for operations, engineering or commercial activities. In the most recent decade, many companies active in containerized transport have reduced their staffs and top managers focus on their core business and their shareholders value. As a result, meetings for Standardization Committees are nowadays attended by some experts and lower staff members with only limited power of attorney and possibly less keen on maintaining a limited number of standard dimensions and ratings.

The pioneering stage in container standardization has learned that the efforts of the early time decision makers have paid off. The results of their standardization efforts enabled a worldwide interchangeability with a tremendous transport service at rather low cost. It should be remembered:

"Standardization is nobody's best, but better for all"

CHAPTER 5

COVERING THE GLOBE
(1966 - 1976)

The roll out of containerization was supported by standardization. A summary of the most important facts is presented here. Already in 1958, the Materials Handling 5 Sectional Committee (MH-5) of the American Standards Association (ASA) started developing standard dimensions for a US domestic container. In 1961, the MH-5 committee settled on a width and height of 8 ft and on lengths of 10, 20, 30 and 40 ft. However, these dimensions were not acknowledged by Sea-Land and Matson. On the contrary, they convinced the US Department of Commerce to accept the 35-ft and 24-ft container, too.

In 1961, an ISO committee on container dimensions was installed: the ISO Technical Committee 104 (TC104) on freight containers. It consisted of three working groups: on terms and definitions, on dimensions and on specification, testing and marking. TC104's sole aim was to achieve operational exchangeability and the container was perceived as a performance standard. This put an end to discussions on whether containers should be made of aluminum (US) or steel (Europe).

The international standard, Series 1 containers, was based on the MH-5 proposal. In addition, European representatives proposed a smaller container that was in use by Europe's national railways. Therefore, container dimensions were supplemented with the lengths of 6' 8" and 5' in 1963. These sizes could be coupled together to form a standard unit. The Series 1 standard was published in February 1968. In 1969, the US delegation proposed a height of 8' 6", which was used by North Atlantic Services. Although initially accepted exclusively for the 40-ft container, in 1972 this height was also accepted for 20 and 30-ft containers.

Another hot issue was corner fittings. The subject was raised in the ISO TC104 meeting in 1962. Three options, all of US origin, were available. One was the Sea-Land twist lock; the others were developed by the National Castings Company and Matson. The National Castings' solution was turned down because it could not be verified in general use and, moreover, was not cost effective. The success of the Sea-Land corner fitting and its twist lock proved itself in every day service. However, all options were patented and therefore not suited as national standard. Although Sea-Land was earlier affronted by the rejection of their 35-ft container as a standard, McLean released the patent in January 1963 with no strings attached. Even dimensional changes in its box corner fitting and rotatable engaging lug were permitted. The American Standard Association and the Truck Trailer Manufacturers Association agreed but other parties, mainly shipping lines, did not accept the proposed standard. Therefore it could not be presented as the American standard at the ISO meeting in Hamburg in 1964. One year later, in the The Hague meeting, the design was evaluated and accepted unanimously.

It should be emphasized again that the generosity of Malcom McLean (after the pursuing activity of Keith Tantlinger) was in fact the start of a worldwide standardization. It was a prerequisite for the global spread of containerization.

5.1. TRADES

5.1.1. US East Coast - Europe

Although the first containers from the United States of America arrived in Europe in the early 1960s, the first scheduled (weekly) container services across the Atlantic Ocean started in spring 1966. Three companies inaugurated a Transatlantic container service at roughly the same time: Moore-McCormack, United States Lines and Sea-Land. Other shipping lines followed suit.

Moore-McCormack

Moore-McCormack was probably the first to provide container services across the North Atlantic. The company launched the first regular container route to Europe in February 1966. Modern C4, Constellation-class general cargo vessels were deployed. The first of a series of six US$ 10.4 million cargo ships, the *Mormacargo* had a gross tonnage of 10,599 and a container capacity of 292 TEU. These vessels sailed at average speeds of nearly 25 knots. They were the first US-built, fully-automated merchant ships that could be controlled from the bridge. They ran with a crew of only 32.

At the end of the 1960s, these vessels were replaced by four combination freighter/container/Ro-Ro vessels of a unique design. In order to increase its capacity of either container or roll-on/roll-off vehicles, they were fitted with false decks and special hatches. The 11,750-grt *Mormacsky* was the first Sea Bridge-class vessel to join the Transatlantic service in 1968, followed by three sister ships (*Mormacstar*, *Mormacsea* and *Mormacsun*). Although these vessels were well suited for Moore McCormack's important African and South American trades, the limited container capacity of 800 TEU proved to be unfavorable for the European trade. In November 1969 the vessels were sold to American Export-Isbrandtsen Lines (Mediterranean Marine Lines) and shifted to the US East Coast-Mediterranean trade. Here, they had to compete with the *Prudential* and Grace Line's 1,500-TEU LASH ships.

Figure 79: Moore-McCormack's general cargo ship Mormacaltair and Ro-Ro/container vessel Mormacsky

United States Lines

United States Lines' (US Lines) first vessel to bring containers to Antwerp and Rotterdam was the *American Racer*, an 11,250-grt Challenger II-class freighter. The ship was part of an extensive vessel-replacement program started in the early 1960s. The *American Racer* was built in 1964 at Sun Shipbuilding and Dry Dock Company in Chester, Pennsylvania. In 1966, two holds were equipped with cell guides. This class of five 21-knot vessels could carry 112 TEU below deck and 48 TEU on deck. When the *American Racer* set sail for Europe on March 18, it must have looked like any other general cargo ship with kingposts and booms since the first fifty 20-ft containers were stowed below deck.

May 1968, United States Lines launched an all-container newbuilding, the *American Lancer*, the first of (ultimately) 8 vessels. The original plans called for a general cargo vessel, but a fast redesign converted it into a fully-cellular containership, the first to breach the 1,000-TEU barrier. Although the hull was lengthened and widened, it still held the characteristics of a traditional vessel. It had a container capacity of 1,178 TEU and a service speed of 22 knots. As the on-deck TEU capacity was increased significantly for the last vessels of the series, those could carry up to 1,434 TEU. Remarkably, several of these ships made it into the 21st century. From September 1970 on, the American Lancer-class vessels were deployed on the US East Coast-Far East trade and replaced the converted 1950s general cargo ships. These American Leader-class vessels had a service speed of nearly 20 knots and could carry 929 TEU.

Figure 80: United States Lines' American Racer on the Thames

Figure 81: American Lancer, US Lines' first cellular containership

Sea-Land

The first Transatlantic service with fully-cellular containerships started on April 23, 1966, nearly 10 years after the start of containerization, with Sea-Land's *Fairland* setting sail from Port Elizabeth (NJ) to Europe, calling at Rotterdam (the Netherlands), Bremen (Germany), and Grangemouth (Scotland). Together with three sister ships, each of which could carry 226 35-ft containers, the shipping line operated a weekly service. Although these vessels had their own on-board cranes, Sea-Land arranged its own A-frame-shaped container cranes to be installed in Bremen, Rotterdam and Grangemouth. Already in the first year, Sea-Land transported 6,000 containers to and

Figure 82: Sea-Land's Fairland discharging in Rotterdam

from the port of Rotterdam. After a few years, the C2 containerships were replaced by bigger C4 Portland-class vessels. They had been converted in 1968/69 and could carry 366 35-ft containers. Due to the limited number of ports, Sea-Land used feeder services to link other destinations.

In the early 1970s, Sea-Land introduced four newbuildings in this trade. Two vessels were designed by Matson for its Transpacific route and under construction in Bremen, Germany. Since Matson withdrew from international trade and no longer needed these vessels, Sea-Land added them to its fleet in 1970. At first, they became known as *SL-180* and *SL-181* and later as the *Sea-Land Venture* and *Sea-Land Economy*. In their original configuration they could carry 1,175 24-ft and 148 40-ft containers. The vertical cells were flexible; they could be adjusted to handle more 40-ft containers. This greatly enhanced the conversion to Sea-Land specifications and when put into service they could accommodate 552 35-ft and 181 40-ft containers. Note that Sea-Land's adoption of the ISO container becomes apparent for the first time. Two other SL-18-class vessels were acquired from Pacific Far East Lines (PFEL) when they were still under construction at Bethlehem Steel's shipyard at Sparrows Point (Baltimore). These containerships were also designed by Matson but sold to PFEL, who changed its original configuration to 1,664 TEU. When they joined the Sea-Land fleet, they could accommodate 120 20-ft and 613 40-ft containers. Additionally, 159 spaces on top of the hatches could accommodate either Sea-Land's 35-ft containers or 40-ft ISO containers. These two vessels were named *Sea-Land Producer* (see Figure 83) and *Sea-Land Consumer*. Together with the *Sea-Land Venture* and *Sea-Land Economy* they were deployed between North Europe and the US Gulf Coast.

In 1972, the first of eight SL-7 vessels, the *Sea-Land Galloway* (see Figure 84), was commissioned. These vessels could carry 1,096 containers. They were built in Germany (5) and The Netherlands (3). Its 120,000-bhp power plant and fine(r) hull lines allowed the containership to reach a service speed of 33 knots. The *Sea-Land Exchange* crossed the North Atlantic on August 1973 at 34.92 knots, only 1 knot slower than the famous passenger liner and Blue Ribbon holder *United States*. On average, a Transatlantic voyage took 4.5 days. However, the SL-7 could not keep service speed without excessive ship motions in Beaufort 6 and higher. In the United States only the port of New York/New Jersey was visited whereas Rotterdam and Bremerhaven where the European ports of call. The high fuel consumption became critical when oil prices soared due to the 1973 oil embargo. Although lower service speeds of 22 knots decreased fuel costs significantly, the

Figure 83: Sea-Land Producer about to cross the Atlantic ocean

Figure 84: Sea-Land's first SL-7 vessel, the Sea-Land Galloway

(still) high operational costs made successful commercial exploitation of the SL-7s difficult. This led to the sale of six ships to the US government in fiscal year 1981 and the other two one year later. All eight were converted into Fast Sealift Ships during the period 1984-1986 (For more details about the SL-7 vessels, see chapter 6).

American Export-Isbrandtsen Lines

Another company that joined the East Coast North Atlantic trade was American Export-Isbrandtsen Lines. As Container Marine Lines, they started in November 1966 a fortnightly service with Le Havre, Amsterdam and Bremen as European ports of call. The Mediterranean region was also served. At first, two adapted bulk carriers with a capacity of 732 TEU, the *Container Despatcher* and *Container Forwarder*, were used, but later they were replaced by the first American ships designed and built by Bath Iron Works, Maine, to solely carry ISO containers. The keel of the first vessel, the *Sea Witch*, with prefix CV, was laid on October 18, 1966, and delivered nearly two years later, on September 4, 1968. The 17,900-grt vessel could carry around 1,000 TEU and was equipped with a General Electric-geared turbine power plant, which allowed a cruising speed in excess of 20 knots. In 1969, the sister ships CV *Lightning* and CV *Stag Hound* joined the service whereas in 1972/1973 three similar containerships were delivered. Because containerization meant to American Export more than just state-of-the-art containerships, it also included a trucking company and facilities needed for intermodal services.

During the first part of the 1970s, the steamship company suffered heavy losses and Isbrandtsen withdrew its interest in 1973. The passenger liners as well as tankers were sold and in 1976 the city of New York bought their Staten Island Marine terminal for US\$ 47 million. Nevertheless, American Export-Isbrandtsen Lines filed for bankruptcy in 1977.

Figure 85: CV Stag Hound leaving the port of Le Havre

Seatrain Lines

Rather late, Seatrain Lines started its European service in December 1969. During 1971 and 1972, the first four converted C4 freighters were replaced by German-built 1,920-TEU gas turbine-powered containerships, called *Euroliner, Eurofreighter, Asialiner* and *Asiafreighter,* respectively. The advantages of this type of power plant, basically a marine version of the well-known Pratt&Whitney FT 4A-12 aircraft engine, included limited dimensions, light weight and easy replacement. These vessels had a cruising speed of approximately 27 knots. Noticeably, a speed of 36 knots was reported by a pilot on duty. They could transit the Atlantic in four or five days. Despite, the advantages of these engines were outweighed by their excessive consumption of relatively high-grade, hence expensive, fuel. When bunker prices soared after 1973, no new gas turbines have been installed in merchant marine vessels.

Figure 86: Seatrain Lines' Eurofreighter at sea and in port (Clydeport, Greenock)

Seatrain Lines was one of the pioneers of the "landbridge" system. Since the all-water route from Tokyo to New York took 30 days, transshipping containers onto trains in West Coast ports could cut 10 days from the transit time. In addition, containers could be transported to Europe. Moreover, the company assumed full responsibility for the container cargoes. The system became a success and was copied by other steamship companies.

Atlantic Container Line

In contrast with US shipping lines, European steamship companies adopted cooperation in containerization. Already in 1965, four major European steamship companies from Sweden (Swedish America Line, Wallenius and Transatlantic) and The Netherlands (Holland-America Line) agreed on establishing a joint venture named Atlantic Container Line (ACL) to serve the trade between Europe and the East Coast of North America. Before Bermuda-based ACL was officially established, the French

Compagnie Générale Transatlantique (CGT) joined and soon after British Cunard Line completed the membership. With this cooperation the individual shipping lines gave up their own identity and became shareholders of Atlantic Container Line, which acted as the operating and marketing company for the North Atlantic. Since the Swedish shipping lines were hesitant to order fully-cellular containerships, the consortium ordered vessels in which only part of the ship's capacity was specifically designed for containers. Wallenius had ordered two roll-on/roll-off containerships and sold one to Holland-America Line. Both vessels were deployed by ACL. In addition, two other vessels were contributed by the other participating Swedish shipping lines.

The *Atlantic Span*, the first ship of this series of four, sailed from Gothenburg, Sweden, on September 4, 1967 and called at Bremerhaven (Germany), Antwerp (Belgium) and Rotterdam (The Netherlands) en route to New York. On board there were more than 500 20-ft containers as well as over 1,100 automobiles and large rolling units, such as cranes, tractors and machinery stowed on her trailer decks.

Additional ports in the United Kingdom, France and Canada were added to the itinerary once the second generation Ro-Ro container vessels entered service. Six, 900-TEU container/Ro-Ro ships were added to ACL's fleet in 1969/70. Now multiple sailings per week could

Figure 87: Atlantic Song (after lengthening in 1976) in Liverpool

be offered to and from major ports. After Moore-McCormack stopped its Transatlantic service, ACL became the only shipping line handling both containerized and roll-on/roll-off freight.

Hapag-Lloyd

In Germany, two shipping lines, Hamburg-America Line (of Hamburg) and North German Lloyd (of Bremen), put aside their century-long rivalry and joined hands in order to establish a full container service in the North Atlantic. The so-called "Hapag-Lloyd Container Line" operated four fully-cellular containerships in the 700-TEU range. The first vessel, delivered in October 1968, was the 13,382-grt *Weser Express*, owned by North German Lloyd. Its sister ship, *Mosel Express*, was launched within three months. Capacity was 624 TEU and service speed amounted to 20 knots. Hamburg-America Line's *Elbe Express* and *Alster Express*

Figure 88: Hapag-Lloyd's Alster Express

were slightly bigger (736 TEU) and faster (22 knots). When in January 1969 the last ship was delivered, a weekly container service was started with Hamburg, Bremerhaven, Antwerp and Rotterdam as European and New York, Baltimore and Norfolk as US ports of call. In 1973, each vessel was stretched to nearly 1,100 TEU by adding a mid-body section.

Dart

Another consortium entering the Atlantic trade consisted of Compagnie Maritime Belge, Bristol City Lines and Montreal-based Clarke Traffic Services. This joint venture named Dart Container Line had its headquarters in Bermuda. The service commenced in 1969 from the port of Halifax with three chartered ships with a container carrying capacity of 210 TEU, at a speed of just over 16 knots. From Halifax the containers were forwarded by rail to Montreal, Toronto and Hamilton. A second service was operated between Antwerp, Southampton, New York and Norfolk.

Figure 89: The Dart Europe in its striking livery

When three new containerships were introduced in 1970/71, they combined these services. The *Dart Europe* (CMB, built by Cockerill), *Dart America* (Clarke Traffic Services, built by Swan Hunter) and *Dart Atlantic* (Bristol City Line, built by Swan Hunter) were capable of carrying 1,556 20-ft containers. The majority of containers were stowed in the cellular holds, as on deck a stacking of maximum three tiers was possible. These vessels were the first large containerships powered by a single low-speed, 29,000-bhp diesel engine providing a service speed of 23 knots.

5.1.2. US West Coast - Europe

In September 1968, Swedish Johnson Line started container traffic from Europe to the US West Coast with a general cargo ship that was lengthened and rebuilt for containers. However, already 1966, five container vessels were ordered from the Wärtsilä shipyard in Finland and in June 1969 the first of these special-built 744-TEU containerships with 2 holds for refrigerated cargo, the *Axel Johnson*, was delivered. In the next two years the other four vessels followed. Initially, these vessels had two shipboard cranes (1 x 20 tons and 1 x 30 tons). These were removed a few years later to increased deck capacity. When in 1972 the Danish East Asiatic Company and the English Blue Star Line joined, each with two new containerships, the consortium was named Johnson Scan Star.

Conferences have always existed on the North Atlantic, but the introduction of containers in the Transatlantic trade put pressure on traditional agreements. Due to the US anti-trust legislation, conferences found in trades serving the United States are "open conferences". Any common carrier can be a member and can join at short notice. So, these agreements are, in practice, little more than arrangements for fixing freight rates. Early 1970, a rate war erupted on the North Atlantic. Having hardly any financial reserve, Moore-McCormack abandoned its container service within a few months.

Figure 90: Johnson Lines' Margaret Johnson in the Panama Canal

The increase of tonnage that had sparked the rate war, lead to a pool agreement in June 1971:

- Atlantic Container Line   20.25%
- United States Lines   18.00%
- Sea-Land   17.00%
- Hapag-Lloyd   14.17%
- Seatrain Lines   11.25%
- Dart Container Line   10.58%
- American Export-Isbrandtsen Lines 8.75%

Interesting to see is that US-based shipping lines, which started the container revolution on the North Atlantic, negotiated only a small majority of the trade.

5.1.3. Canada - Europe

Conferences operating between the United Kingdom and Canada were so-called "closed conferences". Entry of such conference is restricted and new members are only admitted by unanimous vote of the current members. Membership is not transferable and withdrawal is on a three-month notice. Changes in the agreements require a unanimous vote, but other matters only a two-thirds majority. Conferences found in the trade between the North European ports (between Bordeaux and Hamburg) have arrangements broadly similar to the United Kingdom/Canada conferences.

Sailings to and from Canada were carried out mainly by specialized shipping lines such as Manchester Liners (ML) and Canadian Pacific (CP). Already in November 1968, the first company started, with fully-cellular containerships, a weekly container service between Manchester and Montreal. Total capital investment, including 10,000 20-ft containers, was about £ 16 million, whereas the cost equipment, such as gantry cranes and straddle carriers, was in the order of £ 2 million.

In 1967, ML ordered four 527-TEU containerships from a British shipyard. The first vessel was the *Manchester Challenge,* which needed seven days berth to berth under normal weather conditions. Soon, three sister ships, *Manchester Courage, Manchester Concorde* and *Manchester Crusade,* joined. In order to reach the port of Manchester the ML containerships had to navigate the 60-kilometer-long Manchester Shipping Canal. Therefore, ship size was restricted by the dimensions of the locks. When the *Manchester Courage* entered service, one of the locks was hit and the Ship Canal was closed for many weeks.

Figure 91: Manchester Crusade at Manchester

In Canada, during the eight months "open water season", ML operated a feeder service between Montreal and the Great Lakes ports such as Detroit, Cleveland, Milwaukee and Chicago. However, during the winter months, when the Great Lakes are frozen, freight had to be carried by rail.

As of September 1965, Canadian Pacific transported containers Transatlantic from Antwerp and London to Montreal, Toronto and Hamilton (and back). The 6,000-ton heavy, 408-ft (124.4 m.) long *Beaveroak* could carry 100 20-ft containers. Later, by adding a 57-ft mid-body section (increasing her capacity to 322 containers), the *Beaveroak* was converted into a containership. She returned into service on October 2, 1970 as the *CP Ambassador*. The following year, the *Beaverpine* was converted and became the *CP Explorer*, entering service December 13, 1971.

Full container service between London (i.e. Tilbury), Rotterdam (and later Le Havre) and Quebec City started early 1969 with chartered tonnage. Later the 779-TEU *CP Voyageur*, *CP Discoverer* and *CP Trader* were deployed on this route. These 15,680-grt vessels had a service speed of 18 knots. A new container terminal in Quebec City was opened on December 5, 1970 with the *CP Ambassador* on its dockside. The

Figure 92: CP Trader

terminal was equipped with one 35-tons crane for loading and offloading ships and a smaller one for handling containers between trucks and trains. Interestingly, CP was one of the first shipping lines that offered half-height 20-ft containers with a gross mass up to 23 tons, for heavy weight cargo such as sheet metal.

Changes due to competition and a surplus of capacity saw an agreement at the end of 1973 with Manchester Liners to co-ordinate routes. This resulted in selling off the two older and smaller ships, *CP Ambassador* and *CP Explorer*, as CP struggled for profitability.

5.1.4. US West Coast - Far East

Containers i.e. Flexi-Vans already appeared in the Pacific Rim in the early 1960s. However, the first full container service was introduced several years later. Things got started when in February 1966 the US Maritime Administration approved Matson's proposal to operate a non-subsidized container service between the US West Coast, Hawaii and the Far East. Because Japan, Taiwan and Hong Kong generated cargo well suited to containers, Matson planned to

Figure 93: Matson's converted C3 freighter Pacific Banker

take advantage of its experiences. The company had two of its C3 freighters converted at Japanese shipyards. The *Hawaiian Planter* was rebuilt to a 14,246 ton full containership at Mitsubishi Kobe shipyards and renamed *Pacific Trader*. The *Hawaiian Craftsman* was similarly adjusted in Shimonoseki Shipyard and renamed *Pacific Banker*. Both vessels had a capacity of 464 containers and 49 cars. The *Pacific Trader* inaugurated the Far East service by calling at Kobe and Tokyo and returning to the US West Coast on September 20, 1967.

From the beginning Matson co-operated with the Japanese steamship company Nippon Yusen Kaisha (NYK) Line. This long-standing shipping line reacted enthusiastically when Matson's president visited Japan in October 1965. Matson and NYK Line set up a co-operation based on slot chartering. Later, Showa Line was also assigned to this container service by the Japanese government.

NYK Line was the first Japanese shipping line to deploy a fully-cellular containership, the *Hakone Maru*. The ship's length amounted to 187 m. and its beam was 26 m. This 16,240-grt vessel could carry 752 20-ft containers at a speed of 23 knots. On September 23, 1968 the *Hakone Maru* (see Figure 94) arrived at the newly-dedicated 7th Street terminal in the port of Oakland. About 200 containers loaded with radios, TV sets, electrical appliances, textiles and china were discharged. The next day the ship sailed for Tokyo carrying containers with cargo such as chemicals, raisins and meat. Soon afterwards, the very similar *Haruna Maru* of NYK-Showa Line joined this transpacific service.

By midsummer 1970 Matson had withdrawn from the service due to disappointing financial results. At first, the service was successful and, early 1969, Matson moved towards extensions of the container service to Manila, Taiwan, Hong Kong and Korea. Shore facilities and representation were established. The company envisioned the "landbridge" concept for moving containerized freight between the Far East to Europe via the US by train. The rationale behind this was a time saving of at least one week. In order to implement this concept, Acme Fast Freight Inc., with terminals in 116 cities throughout the US and organizations in

Figure 94: Japan's first fully-cellular ship NYK's Hakone Maru

amongst others Canada and Mexico, was purchased. But business went sour due to various reasons. Moreover, Acme was losing money. Alexander & Baldwin, who had acquired Matson, realized that the financial prospects deteriorated and did not plan to invest the money needed for full-scale container services. On the contrary, Matson's Far East service was suspended and disinvesting began by selling the *Pacific Trader* and *Pacific Banker*. Two more vessels, *H.P. Baldwin* and *S.T. Alexander*, still under construction in Germany, were sold to Sea-Land (SL-180 and SL-181). Two similar vessels designed and ordered from Bethlehem Steel's Sparrows Point shipyard were conveyed to Pacific Far East Line. However, this company filed for bankruptcy before these 1,664-TEU containerships were delivered and Sea-Land also acquired these vessels and deployed all four in the Transatlantic trade. NYK line took over Matson's Japanese container facilities and a few years later Acme was sold.

Meanwhile, Matson focused on its core business, the US West Coast-Hawaii route. In December 1969 the 23,800 ton *Hawaiian Enterprise* was delivered (see Figure 95). Its sister ship, *Hawaiian Progress*, followed suit. Both vessels could carry 988 24-ft and 94 40-ft containers at a speed of 23 knots. They were sailing between US West Coast ports and Honolulu. In addition a feeder service was offered by the *Hawaiian Princess* with a capacity of 156, and after raising the height of the on board gantry crane, 212 24-ft containers. This 6,807-dwt vessel had two diesel engines and two propellers. When this containership was delivered in January 1967, it was the first fully-cellular newbuilding from a US shipyard (Bethlehem Steel, Beaumont, Texas).

Figure 95: Hawaiian Enterprise

Competition in this trade came from US Lines which used fast vessels on the Los Angeles-San Francisco-Honolulu run, and from Seatrain operating old vessels between San Francisco and Honolulu. Cargo from Los Angeles was transported by truck to the Seatrain terminal in San Francisco. In 1974 Matson took over this service including Seatrain's chartered vessels and 27-ft containers.

Government involvement played an important role in Japanese containerization. In September 1966 the Japanese Council for Rationalization of the Shipping and Shipbuilding Industries released a report with recommendations for the containerization of the transpacific trade. In order to derive maximum national benefit from this new technology, excessive competition should be avoided. The integrated use of containers and terminals was promoted and shipping lines were urged to establish some sort of cooperation. Japanese lines were offered attractive loans for their containership investment programs. In addition, new port legislation was approved in August 1967. Standardized container terminals were established in Japan's key ports.

All parties involved acted right away. For example, in October 1966 a Japanese delegation including employees of the Ministry of Transport and port authorities, and representatives from the transport sector and companies involved in the production of containerships and container-handling equipment visited the port of Oakland. The second group of Japanese shipping lines consisted of Mitsui OSK, Yamashita-Shinnihon Kisen (YS Line), Kawasaki Kisen Kaisha (K Line) and Japan Line, chose the port of Oakland as their base for container operations. Their 8-acre (3.2 ha) terminal encompassed a container handling and marshalling yard, a 724-ft (221 m.) long berthing area (of a 1,589-ft (484 m.) long wharf) and a container crane. The first vessel, the 705-TEU *American Maru* of Mitsui OSK Line, arrived on November 9, 1968. The other shipping lines followed within a month and weekly sailings between California and Japan were provided. Dedicated terminals were used in Japan (Tokyo and Kobe) and California (7th Street Terminal in Oakland and ITS Long in Beach).

In the summer of 1970 a combined service to the US Pacific North West Coast and Canada was offered by the six Japanese shipping lines. Three new ships came into service, each one jointly built and owned by two of the steamship companies. By 1973 all but one company (Showa) were involved in a weekly service with larger vessels (around 1.800 TEU) to the US East Coast. It gave Japan a head start in the Pacific.

At the same time Sea-Land began transpacific container services from Yokohama to the US West Coast. This company could easily enter

Figure 96: K Line's 792-TEU Golden Gate Bridge

the trade because nearly all containers destined for military bases in South East Asia returned empty to the US. Sea-Land contacted Mitsui, Japan's oldest and largest trading house, and hired the company to build a terminal, to act as its agent and to handle all domestic trucking within Japan. Even with little business, they still made money. The company soon expanded its container network by introducing an interport service connecting Hong Kong, Taiwan, Korea and Japan. When the SL-7s became available, they operated between Long Beach, Oakland, Seattle and Yokohama, Kobe, Hong Kong and Kaohsiung.

American President Lines had been offering transpacific services for a long time but was reluctant to wholeheartedly embrace containerization. Until 1972, vessels were only partially fitted for carrying containers. From 1973 on conversions started and four new Pacesetter-class 1,508-TEU containerships were commissioned. Quite remarkable since APL transported more containerized than traditional general cargo since 1970.

More US shipping lines considered the future of containerization indecisive. American Mail Line commissioned in 1968/69 five Alaskan Mail-class general cargo ships, conventional freighters that could carry 332 TEU. Around 1972 the company converted four of its early 1960s freighters into full containerships but soon lost autonomy when it merged with American President Lines. Another American shipping line involved in this trade was the Pacific Far Eastern Line (PFEL). This steamship company owned five Mariner-class vessels capable of carrying a limited number of containers and also operated two converted C4 ships with a container capacity of 500 TEU. In the early 1970s PFEL spent US$ 127.8 million on six LASH (Lighter Aboard Ship) vessels that were introduced in the service between the US West Coast and Japan/Far East, South Pacific and Australia. In addition to 43 barges (of 500 tons each), these ships could transport 334 TEU. Los Angeles and San Francisco were the US ports for these LASH vessels.

The principle of the various barge carrier systems is that the sea-going vessel picks up barges by shipboard crane or lift. Therefore, the mother ship's berth need only be a buoy and the barges can be (un)loaded at shallow

Figure 97: President Grant (left) is ex- PFEL's LASH vessel Golden Bear (right)

berths. Moreover, they could avoid berthing in Asian ports plagued by congestion. For a number of reasons these ships did not meet the high expectations and two LASH vessels were sold to Farrell Lines in 1975. Because of the combination of containers and barges, shipping lines became caught up in the additional complexity of trading the vessels as containerships (calling at container terminals) and as barge carriers. In order to resolve this problem PFEL was in the process of converting the remaining LASH vessels into full containerships before the company went bankrupt in 1978. However, the conversion was completed and American President Lines added three 1,856-TEU containerships to its fleet. The last vessel renamed *American Trader* went to United States Lines.

The first Asian shipping line to offer an independent full container service in the Pacific South West was Orient Overseas Container Line (OOCL) in 1969. Soon after, the Pacific Northwest became also served. The company had ten old Victory-type ships adjusted, one of the last large-scale conversions of WW II tonnage. The shape of the vessels remained the same with the exception of the wheelhouse, which was raised to get good visibility. All cargo-handling gear was removed and cell guides were fitted into hatch openings. Finally, the deck was reinforced and equipped to carry con-

Figure 98: OOCL's converted WWII Victory ship Tsui Yung

tainers in three tiers and seven rows. These Oriental Ace-class containerships were the first cellular deepsea vessels carrying substantially more containers on deck (211 TEU) than in hold (89 TEU). They were deployed for only a short period of time; within a decade they were removed from the fleet.

In 1971, OOCL acquired, for the first time, two new 1,394-TEU containerships in its Far East-East Coast service. Four new vessels with a capacity of nearly 1,000 TEU followed suit. In 1975, Evergreen launched its containership project including four new Ever Spring-class vessels with a capacity of 646 TEU. By April 1976, when the fourth vessel had been delivered, a fortnightly service linked Pusan, Keelung, Kaohsiung and Hong Kong with the US East Coast ports New York, Baltimore and Charleston. In October 1976 a direct container service was established between the Far East and the US West

Coast. Initially this trade was served by semi-containerships but when in 1977 the Ever Spring-class vessels were lengthened and capacity increased to 860 TEU, they were used. Larger (i.e. 1,214 TEU) Ever Valor-class newbuildings were deployed on the US East Coast route.

Maersk Line, a well-established shipping line with a large number of cargo liners and semi-containerships in service all around the globe, introduced in 1975 and 1976 nine German built 1,200-TEU containerships. Maersk's Mc-Kinney Møller demanded single-propeller vessels because with two propellers too many things could break down. At that time it was not possible to build diesel engines that could provide enough power for the high service speed of such vessels with only one propeller. Therefore steam turbine propulsion was installed. The *Adrian Maersk* and other A-class vessels were operated in a liner service linking the US with the Far East. Due to their high service speed these containerships sustained a tight schedule with a high degree of reliability. Within three years after delivery an extra hold of 150 TEU was added. In 1984/85 these ships were equipped with diesel engines at Japanese yards. Simultaneously, the capacity of six of them was increased by adding a new section and three were given new sterns including loading ramps and Ro-Ro storage (i.e. garage).

Figure 99: 1,200-TEU Adrian Maersk in the Panama Canal

Figure 100: Svendborg, the one of a kind

Before the A-class vessels were ordered, the diesel-powered *Svendborg Maersk* had been delivered (see Figure 100). This standalone fully-cellular container vessel had a cargo capacity of about 1,800 TEU and a speed of up to 26 knots. Although initially meant for the Europe-Far East trade, it had no clear deployment. It was often used as a substitute for ships that were in dock.

In contrast with Maersk, the Danish East Asiatic Company ordered seven so-called Liner Replacement Vessels for its new Transpacific Line. They could transport traditional as well as containerized general cargo; three of the five holds were equipped to carry containers. 542 TEU could be carried in the modified holds and on deck. A round trip resembled a traditional liner service: thirteen ports of call and a cruising speed of 14.5 knots. This was no match for competing full container services.

5.1.5. Europe to Australia

Even before the consortium of Atlantic Container Line (ACL) was established, four major British shipping lines joined forces to form Overseas Containers Limited (OCL) in September 1965. Ocean Steamship Company, Peninsular and Oriental Steam Navigation Company (P&O) Furness Withy and British and Commonwealth Shipping contributed 49%,

Figure 101: OCL's Encounter Bay ready for departure

30%, 13.4% and 7.6% respectively of the initial £ 50 million. Including the containers needed, the costs amounted to £ 77 million and an additional £ 4.5 million was invested in UK port facilities. In January 1967 orders were placed for six fully-cellular containerships, five in Germany, one in the UK (*Jervis Bay*). Design of the containerships was carried out by Ocean Fleets, the ship design division of Ocean Steamship Co. The first of these Bay-class ships, named after renowned Australian bays, was the *Encounter Bay*. The vessel was delivered in February 1969 and could carry 1,300 TEU (1,540 TEU after modification), a new standard in containerships.

The container service commenced the next month calling at Fremantle, Sidney and Melbourne. On the return trip to the UK perishables were carried in insulated containers that were connected to a central cooling system. Most of the hatches were fitted for under-deck refrigerated containers, cooled from a central plant. Additionally, self-contained clip-on units were attached to the container when the demand for refrigerated capacity exceeded that available under deck. These "clip-on" cooling devices were also used during transport to/from the port. In the ports large, centrally cooled reefer plants were installed.

Figure 102: Slots for porthole containers

Since other British liner operators were rebuffed by OCL, five of them (Ben Line, Blue Star Line, Ellerman Lines, T. and J. Harrison and Port lines (a Cunard subsidiary)) established Associated Container Transportation Ltd (ACT). All containerships were ACT pre-fixed. The first two vessels had a carrying capacity of 1,223 TEU. The approximately 26,500-dwt *ACT 1* and *ACT 2* were delivered in the first part of 1969 and started ACT's container service to Australia, often called ACT(A). The next series of ships *ACT 3* thru *ACT 6* joined in 1971/72. They could carry nearly 1,200 TEU. The ACT vessels were somewhat smaller than their OCL counterparts.

The service was scheduled in close co-operation with OCL to provide regular sailings for shippers. In September 1970 the Australia Europe Container Service (AECS) was formally established to co-ordinate the services. The initial participants included OCL, ACT, the Australian National Line (ANL) which until then only operated in domestic waters, Hapag-Lloyd, Nedlloyd, Compagnie des Messageries Maritimes and Lloyd Triestino.

A full round trip lasted 68 days. The journey from Europe's last port of call to Australia's first's port of call took 23 days whereas traditional general cargo ships needed 35 days. The container service was an instant success; vessels sailed near capacity.

Figure 103: ACT containerships were just numbered

A clear distinction between OCL and ACT(A) was the ownership of the containerships. OCL owned the majority of its container vessels and operated all of them. If required, OCL arranged the inland transport of containers. In contrast, ACT(A)'s containerships were owned by its shareholders and chartered to ACT(A). Management of the vessels was carried out by the shareholding companies. A separate company, ACT Services Limited, provided marketing and documentation services, which were available to the ACT consortium, and also made arrangements for internal haulage where this was required.

In August 1972, ACT withdrew its containerships and the two vessels it managed for ANL (*Australian Endeavour* and *Australian Exporter*) from AECS. However, they continued as a member of the AECS conference and rates were not undercut. After the split up, AECS represented eleven pooled containerships on behalf of its five remaining members. Apart from the six OCL "Bay" vessels, Hapag-Lloyd provided the *Melbourne Express* and *Sydney Express*, Nedlloyd the *Abel Tasman*, Compagnie des Messageries Maritimes the *Kangourou* and Lloyd Trestino the *Lloydiana*, all with a container carrying capacity between 1,500 and 1,700 TEU. In 1977, New Zealand was also included in the sailing schedules of AECS which name was transformed into ANZECS. The newly founded New Zealand Shipping Corporation became a participant and contributed a vessel called *New Zealand Pacific*.

Additional container capacity was offered by ScanAustral A/S, a joint operating company established by three Scandinavian shipping lines, East Asiatic Company (Denmark), A/B Transatlantic (Sweden) and Wilh. Wilhelmsen (Norway). The service started in July 1970, when the first of ten multi-purpose vessels with container capacity was deployed in a direct North Europe-Australia service. During 1972/73, five new 1,320-TEU Ro-Ros were introduced, gradually replacing the multi-purpose vessels. With a service speed of 22 knots they provided a fortnightly service.

Figure 104: Messageries Maritimes' Kangourou

5.1.6. Australia - Japan/Far East

As early as 1969, containers could be transported between Australia and Japan. K Line had started a joint operation, the Eastern Searoad Service (ESS), with Australian National Line and the Flinders Shipping Company with three identical Ro-Ro vessels that could carry 600 20-ft containers. When the last ship was delivered sailings every ten days could be offered.

In August 1970 a full container service was inaugurated. The Australia Japan Container Line (AJCL) was established by Australian West Pacific Line, the China Navigation Company Ltd. and the Eastern and Australian Steamship Company Ltd., all shipping lines that had been operating conventional cargo services for many years. AJCL started, in conjunction with OCL and ACT, a fortnightly sailing from Brisbane, Sydney and Melbourne to Yokkaichi, Nagoya, Yokohama and Osaka with the 976-TEU *Arafura* and 1,122-TEU *Ariake*. When NYK, Mitsui OSK and YS Lines with their approximately

Figure 105: Yamashita-Sinnihon Line's Tohgo Maru

1,000-TEU containerships began to operate a combined service with AJCL, a weekly service could be offered. Although the service was introduced on an integrated basis under slot charter arrangements, marketing and booking of the cargo was each partners' own responsibility. Australian ports of call included Melbourne, Sydney, Brisbane and occasionally Fremantle. Whereas New Zealand ports called at were Wellington, Lyttelton, Port Chalmers and Auckland.

5.1.7.   Australia - North America

One of the reasons of ACT(A)'s withdrawal from AECS was the cancellation of an antici-pated service also calling at New Zealand ports. By September 1972, ACT operated an independent container service between Europe and Australia/New Zealand. The basic route was from UK (Liverpool/Tilbury) and the con-tinent (Zeebrugge/Le Havre) to Austral-ia/New Zealand via Cape of Good Hope and back via Panama Canal or Cape Horn. Other

Figure 106: Farrel Lines' Austral Envoy

vessels serving in the Pacific America Container Express (PACE) service between Australia and the US East Coast. This route was from St. John (New Brunswick), Newark (New Jersey), Norfolk and Philadelphia, via Panama to Australia and New Zealand. PACE was not the only container service between Australia and the US East Coast. In 1965 Farrell lines had bought the profitable Australian service for US$ 7 million from US Lines and in the summer of 1969 they bought several of their (Rac-er-class) partial containerships to put on the US East Coast and Gulf to Australia and New Zealand route. In 1972 the first of four (new) fully-cellular containerships, the *Austral Envoy*, was commis-sioned and soon all partial containerships were replaced. In 1970 Columbus Line, a division of Ham-burg Süd, also began its container service between New York, Australia and New Zealand with gen-eral cargo vessels. However in 1971 a full container service with the *Columbus America*, *Columbus Aus-tralia* and *Columbus New Zealand* (22,000 dwt, 1,187 TEU) started.

From March 1971, a direct service between Australia and US and Canadian West Coast ports called PAD (Pacific Australia Direct) was also operated by ACT and ANL in combination with A/B Transat-lantic from Sweden. Although not a full container service, the three 20,000-dwt Paralla-class roll-on/roll-off ships had a capacity of approximately 1,200 TEU in an all-container configuration. Later, Columbus Line containerized its traditional liner service in this trade by deploying 750-TEU vessels.

5.1.8.   Europe - Far East

After Europe-Australia, the Europe-Far East/Japan trade was the next route to be con-tainerized. In order to offer attractive sailing schedules shipping lines worked together. Trio (Ben Line, OCL, Hapag-Lloyd, NYK and MOL) was the first. Their service started early in 1972 and by autumn 1973 renowned ships such as the record breaking 3,010-TEU *Hamburg Express* (Hapag-Lloyd), *Liverpool Bay* (OCL), *Benalder* (Ben Line), *Kamakura Maru* (NYK) and *Elbe Maru* (MOL) had been delivered.

Figure 107: Hapag-Lloyd's 3,000-TEU Hamburg Express

The total investment exceeded £ 300 million. The 3,000-TEU containerships of the European shipping lines, with a service speed of 26 knots, were substantially larger and faster than before. Their beam of 32.3 m. (13 containers wide) was determined by the dimensions of the locks in the Panama Canal. This was the only available route since the Suez Canal was closed at that time. Trio was able to schedule a weekly service between Tokyo, Kobe, Kaohsiung, Hong Kong, Singapore, Hamburg Bremerhaven, Rotterdam and Southampton.

Figure 108: Two containerships of Ben Line in Southampton

A competitive spur in the Europe-Far East trade was added by a Scandinavian consortium (Scanservice) that consisted of Swedish East Asia Company, Danish East Asiatic Company and Wilh. Wilhelmsen, from Norway. With four fully-cellular containerships of about 35,000-dwt and a container carrying capacity of approximately 2,400 TEU they offered a sailing every 15 days. The first vessel, Swedish flagged *Nihon,* started the Far East service from Götenborg in June 1972. The East Asiatic Company's *Selandia* and *Jutlandia* and Wilh. Wilhelmsen's *Toyama* followed suit. High ser-

Figure 109: Triple-propeller Jutlandia in dock in Hamburg

vice speeds were characteristic for these containerships. For example, the triple-propeller sisterships *Selandia* and *Jutlandia* were equipped with three diesel engines (total of 75,000 bhp), giving them a service speed of 28 knots. (One 12 cyl. center engine was coupled to a controlable pitch propeller and two 9 cyl. outboard engines were each connected to a declutchable fixed propeller).

When TRIO membership was denied to Nedlloyd (Netherlands) they joined the Scanservice consortium that was in return renamed ScanDutch. Nedlloyds contribution consisted of two 2,950-TEU vessels *Nedlloyd Delft* and *Nedlloyd Dejima.* The last to join was the French shipping line Messageries Maritimes. Their 2,800-TEU *Korrigan* resembled the *Benalder* and its sisterships. These developments enabled ScanDutch 4 sailings each month. In contrast with TRIO, ScanDutch had no Asian participant. This changed when in April 1977 the Malaysia International Shipping Corporation (MISC) joined and contributed two 2,450-TEU newbuildings (*Bunga Surai, Bunga Permai*). At the same time a third Nedlloyd containership, *Nedlloyd Houtman,* entered the trade. By the end of the 1970s ScanDutch operated 10 vessels in their Europe-Far East service.

Figure 110: The Nedlloyd Delft in ScanDutch service

A third consortium, the ACE group, emerged mid-1975. Its members were basically Asian shipping lines such as Orient Overseas Container Line (OOCL), Neptune Orient Line (NOL) and Kawasaki Kisen Kaisha (K Line). One European company Franco Belgian Services (FBS) formed by French Compagnie Maritime des Chargeurs Réunis and Compagnie Maritime Belge and Ahlers Line, joined the consortium. Most vessels had a capacity of around 1,500 TEU with the exception of K Line's *Seven Seas Bridge* and *Verrazano Bridge* (1,908 TEU each) and OOCL's *Hong Kong Container* (2,068 TEU).

Figure 111: FBS' 1,450-TEU Chevalier Paul, in ACE service

5.1.9. Europe - Caribbean

The Caribbean Overseas Line (CAROL) started a container service between Europe and the Carribean in 1976. The initiating partners were Hapag-Lloyd, Harrison Line and Koninklijke Nederlandsche Stoomboot Maatschappij (KNSM). They ordered in Poland six 1,160-TEU containerships with an onboard crane; two vessels per company. When the Compagnie Génerale Transatlantique joined, it took over one of the KNSM vessels. A fifth partner, Horn Line, chartered space only. In the same year a service between Bordeaux and the French Antilles was started with two 680-TEU vessels.

Figure 112: KNSM's Hollandia operated in CAROL service

The CAROL service included in Europe seven ports of call whereas in the Caribbean ten ports could be visited if sufficient cargo was available. Later, sailings in the Caribbean were restricted to fewer ports. It took some time to containerize perishables and, very important, coffee. After many trials they succeeded in transporting these commodities without loss of quality.

5.1.10. Europe - South Africa

It took some time before State owned shipping line South African Marine Corporation (Safmarine) was allowed to take up containerization. The Southern Africa-Europe Container-Service (SAECS) consisted of two routes: South Africa to Northwest Europe and the Mediterranean. Safmarine operated the latter trade in cooperation with Lloyd Triestino whereas Deutsche Afrika-Linien (DAL), Messageries Maritimes, Chargeurs Réunis, Compagnie Maritime Belge, Nedlloyd, Union Castle and

Figure 113: SA Waterberg, one of Safmarine's Big Whites

Ellerman/Harrison were the European partners. Nine containerships of approximately 2,450 TEU and a service speed of 23 knots were deployed. Lloyd Triestino's *Africa* inaugurated the new service in July 1977. When all vessels were deployed four to five sailings each month were offered.

5.2. THE EFFECT OF CONTAINERIZATION ON THE PORTS

Not only ships and shipping companies were affected by containerization, ports and terminals also needed modifications. European ports with a focus on general cargo shipping were often located upstream and their facilities for transshipment and storage were unfitted for handling the new containerships. So, existing terminals should be adapted or new container terminals had to be established, In either case, port authorities and stevedore companies were faced with huge investments. The developments in British and Commonwealth ports may serve as an example.

The London Docks are typical for many UK ports. These docks with enclosed non-tidal basins accessible through locks had limited quayside space and many warehouses in the backyard. The London Docks were located near the city center, some distance up the Thames River. A rail system was available for the distribution of goods from the docks. Later, road transport became important as well.

With the advent of containerization, the use of these docks was already in decline. The docks at Tilbury were the last ones to be constructed and closest to the sea. In 1965 the Port of London Authority further extended the Tilbury dock facilities and started the development of a new container terminal which was ready for the first containerships in 1968 with full service due to be opened in 1969. However, it started with a 13-month strike of longshoremen at Tilbury. In May 1970, operations started at the new £ 20 million terminal. This state-of- the-art facility possessed nearly 3.2 km of deepwater quay (up to 44 ft (13.4 m.) at some berths) forming 13 berths, six of which were for container traffic. However, the Tilbury dispute resulted in vessels having to load and discharge in other ports; the proposed Far East container line link was captured by Southampton. Tilbury did eventually come to succeed as a container port for London, being chosen as the European terminal for OCL. Plans to expand this success to the other London docks failed. They fell into disuse as docks (e.g. the Royal Docks and Millwall Docks) and were redeveloped into residential areas, commercial, exhibition or recreation centers or, even, into an airport.

Figure 114: Tilbury Docks with OCL containerships, in 1970

Figure 115: Felixstowe's box terminal before its latest expansion

Another port benefitting from its location close to sea (and the high London port rates) was Felixstowe (see Figure 116). Being a small East Coast port it was no part of the British Transport Docks and could operate independently. Felixstowe opened its first purpose-built container terminal (see Figure 115) in 1967 and transformed within a few years into the largest container port in the United Kingdom.

One of the success stories of adaptation is Southampton where the existing facilities, designed for passenger shipping and general cargo, came available and were suitable for container transshipment. Southampton had long been the terminus for the North Atlantic passenger shipping. Due to the sheltered deepwater approaches and the long quays required for passenger liners, it was in 1965 decided to turn Southampton into a container port. British Transport Docks constructed a £ 3.5 million container terminal with a 1,000-ft (305 m.) deepwater quay backed by 20 acres of

Figure 116: Container terminals in port of Southampton

paved working area, which was commissioned in October 1968. As more container companies chose Southampton as their main UK port, a £ 14 million further development was started. Rail infrastructure including a Freightliner terminal was extended and improved. Southampton is now the second largest container port in the UK.

On the European continent port authorities had less influence on (private) stevedore companies which operated their terminals. A fragmented approach would involve considerable risks for the individual company without achieving economies of scale. Hence concentration of facilities was profitable and, moreover, made better use of the available dockland with sufficient depth. In Rotterdam the municipal port authority succeeded in getting the divided stevedores in a negotiating room. As a result Europe Container Terminus (ECT) was created, with five stevedore companies and the Dutch National Railways as its shareholders. In August 1967, ACL's *Atlantic Span* was the first ship to arrive at the new terminal in the Margriethaven.

Singapore, directly on the Europe-East Asia trade route, was established in 1812 as an entrepot center, for which it was eminently situated. Its dock complex was built in the late 1860s and consisted of an enclosed basin and waterfront quays. It also had a good harbor and anchorage. The dock complex was similar to many to be found in Britain, be it the small dock at the original Felixstowe port or the Royal Docks at London, but with the addition of extensive waterfront quays. It was built for, and was of course suitable for, conventional general cargo shipping.

Figure 117: The original port at Singapore in the 1960s

With the advent of containerization in the late 1960s, Singapore port had to be adapted if it was to retain its position as a prestigious port and trading/transshipment center. It started the development of a container terminal by rebuilding the Tanjong Pagar wharves (see Figure 118) into a container terminal. The first containership to use this facility was the *Nihon* in June 1972.

The older dock basin and waterfront quays were retained and continued to be used until the Brani Terminal opened in 1992. After redevelopment -the basin was filled in and new quays were built- it became the Keppel Terminal.

It became clear that containerization also meant concentration; shipping lines called at less ports with large(r) hinterlands. Sea-Land is a representative of this trend, especially after the SL-7s had been introduced. Feeders transported containers to and from these hub ports.

In 1975, Sea-Land opened a terminal in Algeciras, Spain, strategically located inside the Straits of Gibraltar (see Figure 119). However, this terminal was not a regular terminal but a transfer facility where containers could be exchanged between different trades. Containerships serving Transatlantic trades could drop off containers meant for ports in the Mediterranean region and Middle East.

The abovementioned illustrates only a few developments of ports and terminals; more details are presented in chapter 12.

Figure 118: Singapore Tanjong Pagar Docks

Figure 119: Sea-Land Terminal, Algeciras

IN RETROSPECT

The pace of containerization in the period 1966-1976 was astonishing. Within a few years, fully-cellular containerships were deployed in every important trade and other routes followed suit. This required a lot of investment for both new vessels and port facilities. The way shipping lines and (port) authorities dealt with these developments varied per continent.

Since containerization started in North America, US shipping lines had more experience than their overseas counterparts. Due to strict anti-trust regulations, these companies operated "stand alone". Investment decisions on new ships were problematic and subject to financial limitations. In hindsight state of the art general cargo ships (States Marine Lines), LASH vessels (Delta and Pacific Far East Line) and fast but fuel consuming containerships proved wrong: some well established US shipping lines did not survive.

European shipping lines collaborated within a conference or, usually smaller companies, cooperated more closely in a consortium as a regular shipping line. This latter form was especially successful in long distance trades where a lot of vessels had to be deployed, to get a weekly service. As newcomers their containerships were state of the art (up to 3,000 TEU) and often equipped with diesel engines. Hence they were less vulnerable for high oil prices.

Japanese shipping lines were forced by the authorities to work together. In return the Japanese shipping and port sector could benefit from financial contributions. In the Pacific their collaboration took shape as liner agreements; in the Europe-Far East they were reliable partners in the various consortia. Compared with their European counterparts their containerships were slightly smaller.

During this period containerization has spread and matured. A huge fleet of modern containerships had emerged and shipping lines seemed to enter a period of steady expansion.

CHAPTER 6

THE SEA-LAND SL-7 PROGRAM
A systems approach in door-to-door Logistics

Already in August 1960, at a panel discussion on the "The Outlook for Containerization", during the Truck Trailer Manufacturers Associations Summer Meeting, some speakers emphasized that a systems approach should be taken in order to fully benefit from the potential of a standardized container. Malcom McLean and his team of young enthusiastic employees developed their transportation concepts in line with this philosophy. Moving the trailers (a word still used by McLean for Sea-Land containers) from door to door in a fast, efficient and cost-effective way was the final goal.

Within Sea-Land there was no history of long-standing liner services with cargo-based rate structures and no extensive calling patterns from sailing schedules built up around a port-to-port philosophy. In the second half of the 1960s, Sea-Land developed an impressive new concept: door-to-door delivery of containers on road chassis from continent to continent (US-Europe and US-Far East). This was supported by a hub-and-spoke concept with very fast mainline vessels, connecting only a limited number of major terminals (the hubs) and regular high-frequency feeder ships carrying boxes from there to their final destination port, from where they were distributed inland using Sea-Land-owned road chassis.

In those days the competition was using general cargo liner ships designed to carry containers on deck. The majority of those vessels were running at speeds of between 19 and 21 knots, although APL deployed a series of 14,000 dwt "Seamaster" general cargo vessels with an average speed of 25 knots (Figure 120). This probably convinced Malcom McLean to introduce a very fast ship type, the so-called SL-7. The original order for five SL-7 vessels was eventually extended to an 8-unit program.

In 1968, Sea-Land analyzed worldwide services and concluded that a speed of approximately 32 knots would allow a fast and attractive alternative on any major trade route. Fast ships would connect new, upgraded terminals able to handle a vessel within 24 hours, at a productivity of 75-100 containers per berth per hour. This required more, larger and faster on shore quay cranes and provisions for such new features as stacking frame and hatch cover storage (instead of on-dock). Speed was certainly a selling point and McLean selected a 33-knot vessel design, with a capacity of 1100 containers (896

Figure 120: APL Seamaster-class vessel President van Buren

35-ft and 200 40-ft boxes) distributed over 15 bays, with 700 containers in the holds and 400 deck. In retrospect, this SL-7 program encompassed one of the largest investment programs any shipping line, or better transport company, had ever made: eight main line vessels, 20-30 feeder ships, more than thirty new or expanded terminals (quay walls and storage area), more than 70 quay cranes, some ten thousand new containers (dry cargo, reefer and tank containers), more than ten thousand road chassis (also used to store boxes on the terminals) and, on top, information and planning systems to monitor and control logistics between the Far East, Europe and the United States. The total value for this massive program must have been more than 4 billion US Dollars (in those days!), spent in less than 5 years! Obviously, the Reynolds Tobacco financial power must have been instrumental in this operation.

The breakthrough was the logistic concept that allowed door-to-door transport between the US and Europe within 7 days! Three components from this concept attracted attention: the SL-7 vessels, the enlarged terminals and their quay cranes.

6.1. VESSELS

In October 1968, the naval architects of J.J. Henry Co. started the design of the SL-7 and delivered the plans for a worldwide tender by April next year. Surprisingly, already in August 1969, a contract was signed with a European consortium of the Rotterdamse Droogdok Maatschappij, Netherlands (three vessels), A.G. Weser, Germany (three vessels) and Rheinstahl Nordseewerke, Germany (two vessels).

Figure 121: SL-7 model at Netherlands Ship Model Basin

Figure 122: SL-7 under construction at RDM and Wilton Feijenoord, Rotterdam

In those days, the European shipyards, supported by renowned shipbuilding experts from the Universities of Berlin, Delft and Hamburg were the only ones able to carry out such a large project. US shipyard facilities were too small and the Japanese ones were not experienced enough. Only yards in Sweden, Germany, the Netherlands and the UK had the expertise to build large container vessels and passenger liners. After an extensive model test program at the Netherlands Ship Model Basin, speed/power and stability/trim relationships were optimized, leading to the following main dimensions (see Figure 121):

- Length overall   288.4 m.
- Length between perpendiculars   268.4 m.
- Beam, molded   32.2 m.
- Design Draft   9.1 m.
- Scantling Draft   10.6 m.
- Displacement at scantling draft   51,815 LT
- Cargo capacity   1096 containers
- Estimated average container mass   15 MT
- Gross Tonnage   41,127
- Shaft horsepower   120,000 HP
- Max speed at design draft   33 knots
- Two propellers (5-blade) diam. 7 m.   135 rpm
- Propulsion:
  - 2 Foster wheeler boilers (58 kg./sec.)
  - 2 sets of Gen. Electric cross compound turbines each with a:
    - HP-turbine (60 bar) at 5,038 RPM
    - LP-turbine (7 bar) at 3,574 RPM

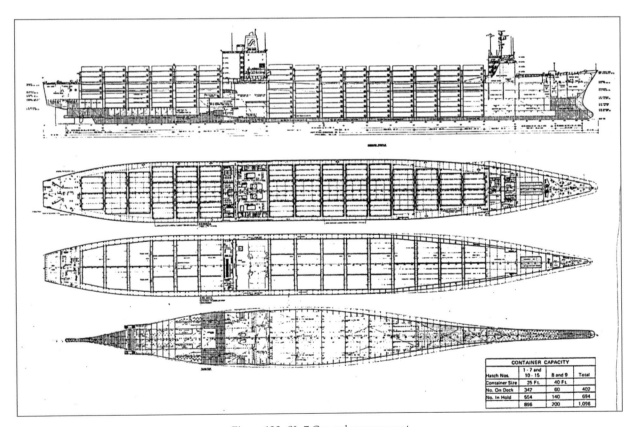

CONTAINER CAPACITY			
Hatch Nos.	1 - 7 and 10 - 15	8 and 9	Total
Container Size	35 Ft.	40 Ft.	
No. On Deck	342	60	402
No. In Hold	554	140	694
	896	200	1,096

Figure 123: SL-7 General arrangement

Figure 124: SL-7 in front of the CNJ Railroad Bridge

A minor, but interesting design feature was the vessel height (air draught) allowing it to cross the CNJ Railroad Bridge in New York (see Figure 124).

During trials it became obvious that the world's fastest cargo vessel was a real breakthrough in vessel design. Even in reverse the ships reached speeds of 14 knots, an amazing experience for the crew of a tanker that was overtaken by an SL-7 vessel during one of its trials while sailing backwards!

The first vessels were delivered in 1972, while the last three ones were commissioned in September and December 1973. The project manager, Mr. Sjoerd Hengst, opined that the success of the project was partly due to the central engineering and purchasing office (the Containership Construction Center), staffed by employees of the three shipyards, the design agent and the American Bureau of Shipping. The United States Coast Guard (USCG) could not provide assistance, a problem Malcom McLean solved by attracting retired USCG staff to ensure complying with USCG codes.

Coincidentally, a large number of Dutch shipbuilding engineers were involved in the SL-7 project: Mr. D.J. de Koff (project manager at J.J. Henry Co), Mr. J.J. Muntjewerff (Vice-President of NSMB and responsible for many major design details), Mr. Dassen (chief designer of RDM) and Mr. S. Hengst (contract manager, responsible for the activities of the three shipyards).

During the first years after commissioning, some minor teething problems were solved (fairwater and propeller cone, and strut bearings), however, in general, the vessels performed as specified and expected, sailing from Seattle to Kobe in almost 6 days and from Rotterdam to New York (Port of Newark) in 4.5 days. Seakeeping in heavy weather at the Atlantic was sometimes problematic (not in the Pacific). The average speed reached between 31.1 and 33.3 knots. Those achievements were impressive, but at the expensive of a massive fuel consumption:

- 614 tons/day at 33 knots;
- 439 tons/day at 30 knots;
- 240 tons/day at 25 knots.

This is a lot of fuel for just 1,100 containers (about 2,000 TEU), in particular when compared to an 8,000-TEU, 2005-built vessel at 25 knots burning 225-250 tons/day only.

The handling performance in ports increased considerably due to faster terminal cranes and efficient lashing of on-deck containers (in three layers, see Figure 125). Strict standardization of length, width and height of the boxes allowed the designers to use lashing frames (horizontal space frames) connecting containers to deck-mounted buttresses. This turned out to be very effective, fast and safe for both the crew as well as the stevedores.

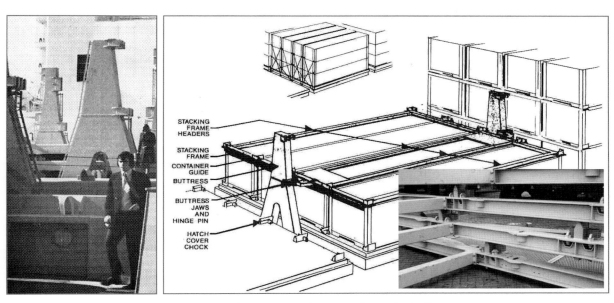

Figure 125: SL-7 lashing system with stacking frames fixed at buttresses

Unfortunately, the vessel's main feature, speed, became its Achilles' heel. The two oil crises, in 1973 and 1978 caused fuel prices to explode to around US$ 150/ton by the end of the 1970s (Figure 126). On average, during this decade, fuel cost as percentage of overall vessel cost rose from around 20% to 50%. For the SL-7 this percentage was probably even higher, what made Sea-Land decide to reduce service speed to 27/28 knots.

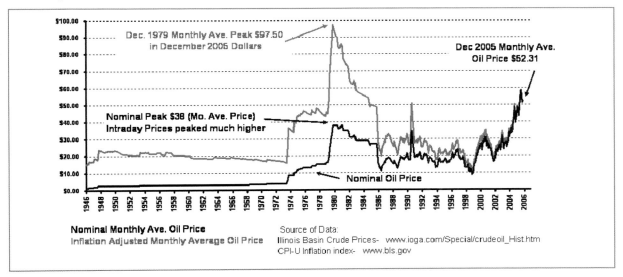

Figure 126: Oil price development

As the SL-7 vessels were rather small and had very high operating cost but were only at one third of their expected lifetime, the question was what to do with them? Charlie Hiltzheimer, president of Sea-Land, C.R. Cushing, naval architect working for Sea-Land, and some others came with the following dilemma: Who needs speed and does not care too much about fuel cost?

Exactly, the US Navy, used to steam turbine-powered vessels. At first, the Pentagon was reluctant and Sea-Land threatened with re-engining to about 25,000 bhp. Later, Charlie Cushing's company converted an SL-7 test model into a military equipment carrier. His team produced a thousand scale models of jeeps, tanks, artillery, etc. and within a few weeks Sea-Land presented its idea to the US Navy admirals in the Pentagon. The converted model was convincing (seeing is believing!) and by the end of 1981 all eight SL-7 vessels were taken over by the Navy for its Rapid Deployment Service of

Figure 127: SL-7 converted into a navy equipment carrier

the Military Sealift Command. During 1982-1983, a major conversion took place at Pennsylvanian Shipbuilding, Avondale Shipyard and NASSCO, resulting in a ship with space for more than 700 army vehicles and several helicopters. The vessels were equipped with on-deck cranes (twin 35 tons and twin 50 tons) and side ramps. They had become self-sustained vessels to support military operations with sailing speeds equal to that of cruisers and destroyers (see Figure 127).

Since 1984, the converted SL-7 vessels have been involved in several operations such as Dessert Shield/Dessert Storm (1990-1991) and Enduring Freedom (started in 2001). While after 40 years they are still the world's fastest cargo ships, the SL-7 vessels have been renamed as follows:

Sea-Land McLean	→	Capella	Sea-Land Trade	→	Bellatrix
Sea-Land Galloway	→	Antares	Sea-Land Finance	→	Altair
Sea-Land Market	→	Pollux	Sea-Land Commerce	→	Regulus
Sea-Land Exchange	→	Algol	Sea-Land Resource	→	Denebola

Some other fast ships from the early 1970s, the Jutlandia and Selandia (EAC), were also converted and are still working for the Military Sealift Command (Figure 128).

Figure 128: The converted Jutlandia and Selandia (EAC), left, and converted SL-7 (right)

6.2. TERMINALS

The philosophy behind the SL-7 program was speed and predictability for the shipper. The vessels operated in mainline services, both on the Atlantic and the Pacific trade, in a weekly schedule and with only a few hub ports per continent (Europe: Rotterdam, Bremerhaven and later Algeciras; US East Coast: New York, Jacksonville, Miami and Norfolk; US West Coast: Seattle, Oakland and Long Beach; Far East: Yokohama, Kobe, Hong Kong and Kaohsiung), see Figure 129.

Figure 129: Sea-Land terminals in Rotterdam (left) and Oakland

The early seventies showed a tremendous growth in container shipping and Sea-Land prospered due to its logistic concept. The terminals in the hub ports handled the mainline calls and served the large amounts of relay cargo (containers from mainline vessels to feeder vessels and reverse). Moreover, they also connected the hinterland by road or in some ports also by rail (e.g. Bremerhaven and Long Beach). The turnaround time of the SL-7 vessels required 1,000-1,500 container lifts in 24 hours, while simultaneously, and before and after the mainline call, feeder vessels had to be discharged and loaded. In some ports the relay share was 60-70% and so one SL-7 could easily generate 2,000-2,500 lifts, to be carried out within 48-60 hours.

Sea-Land's background as trucking company and its belief in simplicity and service made it a great supporter of the on-wheeled storage systems (every container on a road chassis with an easy pick-up and delivery by the trucker). However, storing chassis-mounted containers is area consuming (parking places and drive lanes), resulting in an area utilization of 100-110 containers per ha. Thus, the terminals in the SL-7 program required large amounts of land for storage. Moreover, Sea-Land believed in control over all its major activities, so a Sea-Land terminal always comprised the following facilities:

- Sufficient quay length for handling the mainline vessels and feeders, including some lay-by berth length for feeders;
- 2-4 quay cranes for Sea-Land use only;
- Storage area for on-wheeled boxes;
- Reefer plug-in connections;
- A marine building for stevedoring and operations planning;
- Maintenance facilities for cranes, spreaders, etc.;
- Maintenance and repair facilities for containers and road chassis (sometimes also terminal chassis);

- Maintenance area for reefer containers including connections for the pre-tripping of refrigerated containers and cleaning facilities;
- Storage area for empty containers (MT depot);
- Container freight station to consolidate and distribute LCL cargo and to store special commodities (e.g. cigarettes from Reynolds Tobacco in special lockers);
- Last but not least, a gate with sufficient incoming and outgoing lanes for equipment inspection (status of containers and SL-owned chassis), customs inspection and information exchange for their logistics.

Already in the early 1970s, Sea-Land used a type of Automatic Equipment Identification system (AEI) using plates with bars and color codes, attached to the containers and readable from quite a distance (approximately 10 m.) both from fixed stations or with the help of mobile equipment mounted on a truck, driving through the parking lanes (Figure 130).

Figure 130: AEI plate on Sea-Land container (left) and terminal vehicle with AEI reader

The annual throughput of Sea-Land's main hubs reached several hundred thousand container moves and the terminal's area grew substantially (e.g. Port Elizabeth terminal to 93 hectares, Rotterdam to 33 hectares). But, at many terminals space was at a premium or not available at all, which made Sea-Land accept and introduce more dense stacking systems such as Rubber Tired Gantries (Algeciras, Yokohama, see Figure 131), straddle carriers (Bremerhaven, Rotterdam), Rail Mounted Cranes (Norfolk) and even overhead bridge cranes, stacking 4-high underneath of the large CFS in for example Hong Kong.

In particular, in Europe it was difficult to manage the pool of road chassis as various countries had different national design requirements (axle loads, brake systems, lighting). This caused many difficulties, e.g. when bringing a load to Germany and returning via Switzerland for a new pick-up.

The large driving distances on the expanded (deeper) terminals also caused some problems in maintaining high crane productivity at reasonable cost. But to some extent Sea-Land could compensate this by applying the dual cycle concept. This concept worked well for under-deck containers. After clearing the first cell in a hold, while the next cell was being discharged the first cell could be reloaded. This allowed tractor drivers to bring a loaded chassis under the crane and then, after lifting, wait for the next container to be discharged and carried to the stacking yard.

In general, Sea-Land managed its yard operations quite well, supported by its ability to realize short dwell times for the containers in the yard. In the 1970s, dwell times at their major hubs regularly stayed under 3 days, which was much better than usual during the first decade of the 21st century. Eventually, the arrival of more container types and the formation of alliances (bringing other line-owned boxes and lease boxes) together with area shortages and the arrival of trucker owned chassis in Europe and the Far East, changed the typical on-wheeled container storage yards at Sea-Land terminals into RTG, RMG and straddle carrier-based terminals.

Figure 131: Early 4-high stacking with RTGs at Algeciras

6.3. CRANES

The introduction of the SL-7 vessels required Sea-Land to install a substantial number of new cranes on their terminals, not only because they needed more handling capacity to achieve the required performance, but also because the new vessels had a Panamax beam (32.2 m.) and the crane's outreach and lifting range had to be increased.

Sea-Land specified higher speeds for main hoist and trolley travel, provisions for load control (to limit sway) and provisions for the storage of hatch covers and stacking frames. The objectives were clear: much faster cranes, for heavy duty use during 3,500-5,000 operating hours per year and designed for reliability and low maintenance demands.

Figure 132 shows a general arrangement of the SL-7 crane. This so-called "modified A-frame" had to be adapted for various crane track gauges, e.g. 50' in Rotterdam and Bremerhaven; 80' in Hong Kong and 100' in Long Beach. Almost every newly installed crane had landside box girders, a lattice type boom and a rope driven trolley. Most of the cranes were built by Paceco (Pacific Coast Engineering Company) or its licensees. The SL-7 cranes in general had the following characteristics:

- Outreach 115' (35 m.), backreach 50-75' (15.2-22.9 m.), rail span 50-100' (15.2-30.5 m.);
- Crane width 79' 6" (24.23 m.) buffers compressed (for reduced operational interference);
- Lifting height above quay wall approximately 85' (26 m.);
- Main hoist speed full load 160 FPM (49 m./min.) empty load 385 FPM (120 m./min.);
- Trolley travel speed 500 FPM (152 m./min.) and 0.6 m./sec^2 acceleration rate;
- Heavy duty, mill type, separately excited DC motors for the main drives.

The crane specifications asked for a sway control system limiting the sway amplitude to maximum 12 inches (± 30 cm.) to be reduced to 1/4 within 5 seconds. Paceco installed cranes with a split trolley (allowing increasing the reeving angle to the head block when coming out of the cells) and 6 ropes to the sheaves at the head block. The crane duty cycle was based on the handling operations on the SL-7 vessels including dual cycling onto 3-5 truck lanes within the rail gauge (and this explains the rather moderate trolley travel speeds).

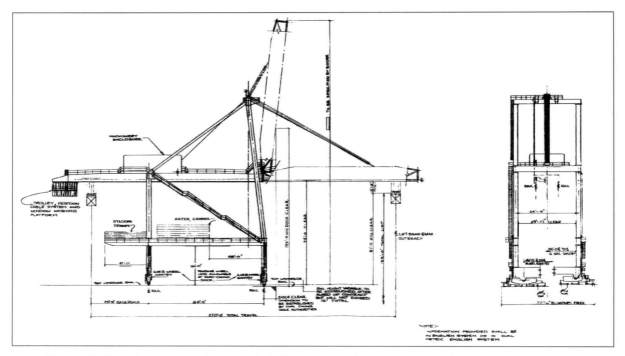

Figure 132: General arrangement SL-7 crane including provisions for the storage of hatch covers and stacking frames

The cranes were colored black (very dominant on the horizon) and had white machinery houses to limit sun heating (see Figure 133, the original SL-7 cranes before and after the takeover by Maersk). It is remarkable that Sea-Land specified these high-capacity cranes already in 1970-1971, only 12 years after the first Paceco A-frame was installed in Alameda, California.

Figure 133: SL-7 cranes (Rotterdam 50' gauge, left; Long Beach 100' gauge, right)

But, the Sea-Land engineering department envisaged even further developments. The crane specs asked options for provisions to automate hoist and trolley motions and to register hoist and trolley position; even load weighing at 0.5% accuracy was demanded. Manufacturers were required to prove their wind load calculations with wind tunnel model tests at an Aeronautical Laboratory. Also, the requirements for fatigue, stability, buckling and surface preparation were amongst the highest in those days. Understandably, after some years of operations, some engineering features showed disadvantages. Crane drivers did not appreciate the split trolley as they were exposed to additional cabin movements, outside their control (the trolley splitting drive was actuated automatically at a certain spreader lifting height). The two main hoist ropes that controlled the sway (in the middle of the headblock) wore out rather quickly. Especially in the 100' cranes, the high hoisting speeds caused jamming of the hoist cables (the empty load hoist rope sagging could be 4-5 m.). Also the stowage of hatch covers and stacking frames in the cranes often caused operational hiccups (see Figure 134) and these provisions in the crane never got general application. The Port Elizabeth terminal introduced special wheeled frames to support/move stacking frames outside the crane.

Figure 134: SL-7 cranes (stacking frame in the crane, left; wheeled stacking frame, right)

Sea-Land usually purchased its cranes without spreader. They had their own specifications and spreaders were attached to the head block with four twist lock-type bolts for reasons of fast exchange. Spreaders were fitted with multi-use twist locks, capable of connecting to both 35' SL-type containers (corner casting center-to-center distance 2,286 mm.) and to 20' and 40' ISO type containers (corner casting center-to-center distance 2,260 mm). Details are shown in Figure 135.

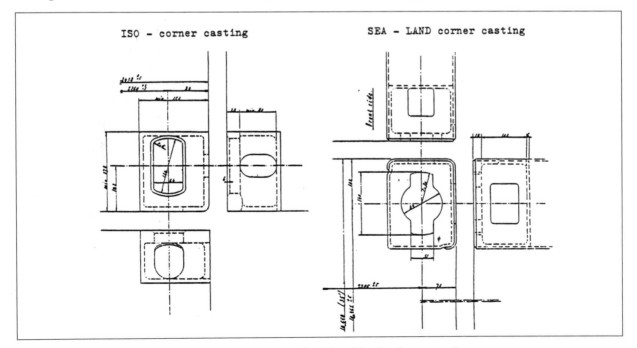

Figure 135: Different shapes for ISO and Sea-Land corner castings

Some special crane concepts were installed in terminals where a nearby airport restricted the maximum height (e.g. Port Elizabeth, New York, Miami, see Figure 134 and Figure 136). The shape of this sliding boom cranes is still remarkable. Figure 136 also shows the crane turntable at the Port Elizabeth Sea-Land terminal in New York, a rare and expensive terminal feature.

IN RETROSPECT

In retrospect it can be concluded that the SL-7 program started with 8 very fast vessels (Figure 137) surrounded with a new logistic concept. This concept resulted in a new generation of container quay cranes and many of these cranes have been operating for almost forty years thanks to the rigid specification with high-level functional demands and many detailed engineering requirements for quality and reliability.

Figure 136: The Sea-Land terminal in Port Elizabeth N.Y.

Due to the oil crises in 1973 and 1978 and the tremendous growth in container shipments the SL-7 vessels became unattractive after 7 years (too expensive in operation, too small to follow the growth). However, the investments in large terminals and about 70 next-generation cranes paid off well, during various decades after the start of the SL-7 program. It definitely allowed Sea-Land to realize short connection times based on proper planning tools, control over their operations (including inland transportation) in true carrier haulage. Obviously, in times where terminal volumes ranged up to 500,000 lifts per annum.

However, the present day tendency of large shippers/consignees to organize their own inland transport (to save money at the landside leg) has resulted in less efficient door-to-door operations due to more parties being involved, less potential for scale advantages in inland transportation and more waiting times at the connecting nodes.

Figure 137: The SL-7 vessel crossing the channel

NOTE FROM THE AUTHORS

Sea-Land realized that it had to provide systems and facilities for the overall transport, including a cost effective balancing of all their investments in that door-to-door logistic chain. Nowadays the shipping lines push ports and terminals to invest in (over)capacity, to satisfy their hunger for economies of scale. If one considers the massive investments in hinterland terminals and transportation infrastructure, it is questionable whether today's imbalance between vessel size and call size and the demands posed on facilities in ports and the hinterland is effective from a cost point of view for the whole industry.

CHAPTER 7

EXTENDING THE SYSTEM
(1977-1986)

When the era of conquering the globe came to a close, a robust transport market had materialized. Since containerization was profitable, shipping lines continued to invest in more container capacity. However, due to the second oil crisis in 1979/80, the growth of the world economy and international trade slowed down. In these circumstances the many newbuildings created overcapacity and put transport rates under pressure. Moreover, soaring fuel prices caused substantial cost increases for shipping lines. Most companies tried to protect their market share whereas new firms emerged and challenged their competitors. At first, these developments are examined for various trades. Subsequently, the efficiency measures, both technical and organizational, will be described. Again, a vibrant period in containerization had started.

7.1. DEVELOPMENTS PER TRADE ROUTE

North Atlantic

By the end of the 1970s and beginning of the 1980s the North Atlantic was still the busiest trade route. This can be exemplified by the busiest container ports at that time: New York (until the end of 1980) and Rotterdam (1981-1986). After the rate war of 1970/71 the market had stabilized and the shipping lines remained the same with the exception of Farrell Lines that took over the entire fleet of American Export Lines after it had filed for bankruptcy in 1977. But difficult financial times also hit this company, and Farrell Lines dropped all of its North European routes and sold 38 of its 44 ships.

Due to the large market share of US shipping lines no comprehensive conference agreement had been established in the US East Coast-North Europe trade. Still, European steamship companies were reluctant to start rate wars. In 1980 debt burdened Seatrain fired the opening shot of a new rate war by bolting from the conference. In order to attract more traffic the company substantially lowered its rates. The other shipping lines reacted immediately. The already weakened company could not sustain the cutthroat competition and Transatlantic services were soon suspended. In August 1980 Seatrain sold its Atlantic ships to Trans Freight Lines (TFL), a subsidiary of Australian Thomas Nationwide Transport (TNT). TFL had recently

Figure 138: Transshipment in the port of Rotterdam in the 1980s

taken delivery of six 956-TEU containerships and these vessels were deployed in the Transatlantic service. However, their presence on the Atlantic was short lived and in 1986 their service was taken over by OCL.

Figure 139: Trans Freight Lines' Democracy in Hamburg

Another interesting development took place in relation to Dart Containerline in mid-1981. The company was equally owned by Canadian Pacific (i.e. CP Ships), Compagnie Maritime Belge (CMB) and, since 1973, the C.Y. Tung Group (OOCL). At that time four former 1,050-TEU Seatrain containerships, acquired by the Tung Group after the demise of Seatrain, were used on the North Europe-US East Coast run.

With regard to Canada, the above mentioned companies formed the Saint Lawrence Coordinated Service (SLCS), basically a slot-charter operation. The participation of CP Ships amounted to 40% and CMB (thru Dart Canada BV) 30%. The remaining 30% was the responsibility of the Tung Group that had acquired Furness Withy in the early 1980s and now owned Manchester Liners. A weekly service between Montreal and North West Europe was offered by deploying the former Dart vessels. By jumboizing these containerships in 1981 the capacity increased to approximately 1,850 TEU. By replacing the previous service that was operated with 12 small ships, the efficiency gains are clear. Other competitors in this trade included ACL, which operated four approximately 500-TEU Ro-Ro vessels from 1976 thru 1982, and CAST, which used several adapted bulk carriers which combined the transport of (eastbound) bulk commodities with (mainly westbound) container cargo, thus benefiting from the reverse imbalance. Moreover, CAST was the first carrier to give a fixed rate per container.

In October 1983, Tung arranged a decisive buy-out deal that gave Dart full control of the US service. For the Canadian service CMB and CP Ships teamed up in Canada Maritime and Tung's participation was renamed Dart-ML Container Line. However, the SLCS slot charter agreement stayed intact.

Pacific

In the Pacific the downturn in the shipping business began later. During the second half of the 1970s, competition had considerably increased. Besides Maersk that had been containerizing its cross trades in the Pacific, several (new) shipping lines from South East Asia entered the trade. These companies included Evergreen and Yang Ming (Taiwan), Orient Overseas Container Line (OOCL) (Hong Kong), Neptune Orient Line (NOL) (Singapore), Korean Shipping Corporation (KSC) and Malaysia International Shipping Corporation (MISC). Another newcomer was the Far Eastern Shipping Company (FESCo) from Russia. Most companies were individually able to offer fre-

Figure 140: CAST Caribou on the Saint Lawrence river

quent pendulum services from the Far East to the US West Coast, sometimes extended to the East Coast. This substantial increase in competition put pressure on rates. Albeit all shipping lines suffered, US companies were hit hardest. In 1981 Seatrain went bankrupt. By that time a number of US companies, among others States Steamship Company and Pacific Far East Lines had already ceased operations. Against this background Sea-Land decided to withdraw from the main transpacific conferences in 1980.

In an unprecedented move, the remaining US shipping lines (Sea-Land, American President Lines, US Lines, Lykes Bros. and Waterman Steamship) applied for permission from the Federal Maritime Commission (FMC) to enter into mutual slot-chartering agreements. The way Japanese companies cooperated in the Pacific served as an example. Two years later APL and Sea-Land gained permission for a joint feeder service between the Philippines and Kaohsiung. Eventually, a new comprehensive US Shipping Act that streamlined FMC-procedures especially in the area of rate regulation and agreement processing, was passed in 1984. In this law antitrust immunity for carriers, conferences and ports was redefined. The legislation also allowed through rates for intermodal transport.

Some Asian companies also sought cooperation to rationalize their transpacific services. In May 1981, NOL/KSC/OOCL filed an application for a joint service. As of May 1982, they were allowed by the FMC to deploy up to 18 large containerships in services to both coasts of the US. This slot-sharing agreement meant for NOL that the four vessels used for its 10-day Far East to US West Coast service would be deployed in a weekly Far East to US West Coast loop and a separate weekly Far East to US East Coast loop (as a result of the Tripartite Agreement Consortium Sea-Land, short of capacity, was able to charter vessels from OOCL (2) and NOL (1)).

Not only US shipping lines were affected by these developments, Japanese companies responded as well. The Japanese Ministry of Transport allowed the breakup of the "great six". Mitsui OSK and K Line established direct connections with mainland East Asia and Korea. Although Mitsui OSK operated a joint East Asia-California service with K Line, they teamed up with the Danish East Asiatic Co. for other destinations. Based on experiences in the ACE group, K Line chose NOL and OOCL as new partners. The remnants of the "great six" were the YS-Japan Line group (which became Nippon Liner Services in 1988) and the somewhat imbalanced partnership of NYK and Showa.

Far East-North Europe

The Far East-North Europe trade was characterized by a powerful conference (FEFC) which consisted of three consortia: Trio (Ben Line, OCL, Hapag-Lloyd, NYK and MOL), Scan Dutch (EAC (DK), EAC (S), Wilhelmsen, Nedlloyd, Compagnie Generale Maritime (F) and Malaysia International Shipping Corporation (MISC)) and Ace (OOCL, Franco Belgian Services, K Line and NOL). Due to the long distances, regular sailings demanded the deployment of many vessels. It was difficult to enter the trade as an independent shipping line. Therefore, several emerging Asian shipping lines such as Korean Shipping Corporation (KSC) and Cho Yang joined the Ace group in the late 1970s.

Figure 141: Yang Ming's 1,984-TEU YM Sun

Maersk started a containerized service in this trade at the end of 1976, albeit with converted general cargo vessels that became available after the A-class containerships were introduced in the Pacific. The 21-knot vessels could carry 500 TEU and provided a fortnightly service. The next delivery of newbuildings entered service in 1979 thru 1981. By the end of

1981 four 2,100 L-class containerships had replaced the old vessels. Two similar vessels followed suit pushing services up to a ten-day frequency. Contrary to common practice Maersk aligned itself with the FEFC for some time but pulled out in June 1982. In an Inter-Group Agreement (IGA) FEFC's main three consortia offered 550,000 tons in November 1980 for Maersk. Moreover, Evergreen, which already provided a Middle East/Mediterranean link, extended this service, on a 10 day basis, to North Europe. The company negotiated a three-year "tolerated outsider" agreement with the FEFC in mid-1982. Another shipping line from Taiwan, publicly held Yang Ming Marine Transport Corporation, followed Evergreens "Mediterranean first" approach when it cautiously replaced and extended its existing service by bigger vessels (i.e. 1,984 TEU, see Figure 141). With four vessels, a 17-18 day schedule was maintained. Like other shipping lines such as ZIM, Polish Ocean Lines and Cosco, Yang Ming continued its outsider status.

South America

One of the last important trades to be containerized was South America. Until 1980 only small volumes of containers were transported by traditional general cargo vessels. One of the first shipping lines to deploy two (converted) full container vessels was Hamburg Süd, a well-established German company that had served the South American East Coast for more than a century. These vessels, *Monte Sarmiento* and *Monte Olivia*, could carry 530 TEU including 300 20-ft porthole containers. In 1981/82 two 1,185-TEU newbuildings, *Monte Rosa* und

Figure 142: Hamburg Süd porthole container with clip-on unit

Monte Cervantes, followed. They were fitted with onboard cranes because many South American ports lacked transshipment facilities for containers. Moreover, they were equipped for carrying large numbers of porthole containers. At the same time Hapag-Lloyd had, for its South America West Coast service, freighters converted into semi-containerships that could carry 322 TEU.

US shipping lines continued serving South American with general cargo ships. Moore-McGormack offered links from the US East and West Coast to the East Coast of South America. Delta linked these destinations from several Gulf ports, but was, after the acquisition of Prudential's Latin American services, building a comprehensive South American network. Since 1969, Prudential Lines included Grace Line, which had served the North and West Coast of South America. However, these shipping lines did not have the financial resources to invest in

Figure 143: Delta's Santa Clara, a former Grace Line freighter

containerships. In 1983, United States Lines took over Moore-McGormack and, soon after, Delta.

Round-the-world services

The acquisition of Moore-McGormack and Delta fitted in the innovative concept of Malcom McLean, the owner of United States Lines since 1977. From the moment he took control of US Lines there were signals that he was planning substantial changes. Early 1979 he announced to build twelve (initially fourteen) gigantic, highly automated containerships. These vessels would be deployed in a one way round-the-world service. The idea was not new. For example, American President Lines operated a combined passenger/freight round-the-world service for many years. US Lines expected that in this way the return cargo problem on two way routes could be eliminated. In addition, liner services linked regional markets with the round-the-world service, e.g. Delta to and from South America. This would provide US Lines the competitive edge in deepsea container transport. Rather late, a US$ 570 million contract was signed for 1983-85 delivery of twelve 4,354-TEU containerships. In order to accommodate these containers, the vessels looked like "shoeboxes" or "bathtubs". They had low speed type diesel engines installed that provided a service speed of 16-18 knots (which is relatively low for containerships). These containerships were called Econships.

In July 1984 the *American New York* sailed on its maiden voyage. The vessels were deployed in an 84-day eastbound round-the-world service but encountered difficulties in keeping the schedule. For US Lines it meant entry in new trades in the US/Mediterranean/Middle East/Indian subcontinent/Far East, something Sea-Land tried to achieve with a hub terminal in Algeciras (Spain). Since vessel deployment on the existing routes stayed -more or less- the same, the new service added annually 963,000 slots.

Figure 144: US Lines' American Washington in Khor Fakkan

By mid-1984, Evergreen was also due to inaugurate a round-the-world container service. In contrast with United States Lines, this service was eastbound as well as westbound. Although introduced by Evergreens chairman and owner Chang Yung-fa as just a "rationalization", a new Transatlantic service was added. In this way three East Coast and five North European ports were connected directly. Evergreen started its initially 10-day itinerary with new G-class 2,728-TEU containerships. While the new vessels poured in the frequency increased to a weekly service by the end of 1985.

Although proclaimed previously, the introduction of full-scale round-the-world services in

Figure 145: Evergreen's Ever Grade transshipping containers

1984 shook the container sector to its roots. Two years later the experiences were mixed. As such the round-the-world service was, and has always been, a viable concept. The success depended on how shipping lines filled in their service. There were big differences between the US Lines' and Evergreen's approach. In the beginning US Lines "low fuel consumption" strategy paid off. When fuel prices dropped, the cost advantage evaporated. However, with the diesel engines installed higher service speeds were not attainable. Since competitors had also reduced rates, shippers preferred fast services. Moreover, US Lines' high expectations of Middle East cargo did not materialize. Losses were piling up and on 24 November 1986 the company filed for protection under Chapter 11. Attempts to revive the company failed and US Lines went bankrupt. By late 1986, Evergreen operated 52 ships and 160,000 containers, whereas US Lines was left empty handed.

7.2. TECHNICAL MODIFICATIONS

Propulsion

Before 1974 many vessels were fitted with steam turbines that enabled high service speeds. These power plants had several advantages, amongst others, compactness and low repair and maintenance costs. Moreover, the boiler could burn low-grade fuels. In the United States building vessels with steam turbine plants was common practice. Also, in Japan and Europe most large containerships were fitted with powerful steam turbines. In that era, the most powerful steam-powered Japanese containership was the 1,569-TEU *Japan Ambrose,* with a 50,000-bhp turbine, whereas the propulsion of the larger European vessels in the Europe-Far East trade reached up to 88,000 bhp. The ultimate showcase of the power of steam turbine plants is the SL-7 containership that could achieve unprecedented service speeds of 33 knots with two compound (i.e. two turbines linked together) steam turbines producing 120,000 bhp. Using one boiler and two turbines the SL-7 could still maintain 24 knots.

Gas turbines in containerships were only installed in four Seatrain owned vessels. These German-built 1,920-TEU containerships were fitted with two Pratt&Whitney aircraft engines that produced a total of 60,000 bhp enabling a cruise speed of approximately 27 knots. Their excessive (i.e. 300-380 tons/day) fuel consumption of relatively high-quality fuel was a disadvantage. After bunker prices had soared, no new gas turbines were installed in containerships.

Japanese and European shipyards also applied diesel engines. The use of medium-speed diesels was restricted to smaller vessels such as the 458-TEU containerships used by Manchester Liners. Larger containerships e.g. DART vessels were equipped with slow-speed diesel engines. As service speeds of large, purpose-built containerships rose, the performance of diesel engines increased too. Containerships such as the 2,370-TEU *Selandia* with a service speed of 28 knots showed the capabilities of state-of-the-art Bŭrmeister & Wain diesel engines; one 12 cylinder center engine and two outboard 9 cylinder engines produced together 75,000 bhp. At that time problems such as piston wear were not solved, yet. Reliable high-output X-head diesel engines became available in the mid-1980s.

Figure 146: 12-cylinder engine of the Selandia

Nuclear-powered fully-cellular containerships have never been built albeit a few general cargo vessels were in service for some time (e.g. *Savannah* (US), *Otto Hahn* (Germany) and *Mutsu* (Japan)). Still, American Hawaiian S.S. had in the early 1960s designs made for three nuclear-powered containerships but the plans did not materialize. UK-based Vickers Limited Shipbuilding Group also offered nuclear powered vessels. In the early 1970s research on a 2,000-TEU nuclear containerships was carried out in Japan. For a service speed of 33 knots it needed a 90 MW (around 120, 000 bhp) nuclear reactor. The plan never made it further than a trial design.

Officially classified as a LASH vessel, the nuclear Russian icebreaker *Sevmorput* has probably transported the most containers. After several years of construction the reactor was started on October 26, 1988 and the NS *Sevmorput* was put into operation in January 1989. A 30 MW power plant enabled a service speed of 20 knots. The 260 m. long vessel was intended for transportation in Arctic regions and equipped with an ice-breaking bow. It can carry 74 lighters of 300 tons each or 1,328 20-ft containers. The vessel is still in service.

Figure 147: Nuclear icebreaker Sevmorput with containers

The rise in bunker prices since 1973 had a profound effect on the choice of propulsion machinery for new containerships; diesel engines were preferred over steam turbines. Big steam turbine-engined ships had a fuel consumption of 370 tons a day (up to 600 tons for SL-7s) whereas similar diesel powered vessels with a slightly reduced speed of 23 knots needed only 170 ton/day. When oil prices soared again in 1979 and continued to be high, many shipping lines considered switching to diesel propulsion. Most of the relatively new vessels, especially big ones, were re-engined from steam turbine to diesel. For example, 20 out of 22 steam turbine vessels deployed in the Far East-Europe service were converted to diesel. The nine A-class containerships of Maersk were rather late (1984/85) re-engined at Japanese yards. The most extreme shipping line in relation to propulsion was ACL that replaced its five remaining G2 steam turbine Ro-Ro ships delivered in 1969/70, but kept their four G1 diesel powered vessels from 1967.

One of the few US shipping lines that started re-engining was Sea-Land. It hired Mitsubishi Heavy Industries to convert four of its older vessels (*Elizabethport, Los Angeles, San Juan* and *San Francisco*) into diesel-powered containerships. From the originally T3 tankers, enlarged by new mid bodies, the bow and stern were removed. Newly-built bows and sterns were added and a six-cylinder diesel engine was installed. The slightly-increased length (approximately 35 ft (10 m.)) offered a larger carrying capacity of 673 40-ft against 476 35-ft containers. These first diesel-powered containerships in the Sea-Land fleet were designated the D6-class. They rejoined the fleet as *Sea-Land Leader, Pioneer, Pacer* and *Adventure* in 1977/1978. The US Coast Guard considered them completely new vessels and issued new official numbers when they formally enrolled as US merchant vessels.

In the US, large diesel-powered ships were ordered for the first time in 1982 by APL. Avondale shipyard built three 2,590-TEU containerships, *President Lincoln, Washington* and *Monroe*, the first US-built diesel containerships. However, APL was not the first US shipping line to acquire new diesel powered vessels. In 1980/81, the twelve vessels of Sea-Land's D9-class of 1,678-TEU containerships (later recalculated as 1,780 TEU) had been delivered by Japanese and South Korean shipyards to replace the renowned SL-7s.

Figure 148: APL's President Monroe in Seattle

Ship configuration

By the end of the 1970s, the fully-cellular containership had become the most popular vessel to transport general cargo. The maximum dimensions of containerships were already established in the early 1970s by vessels such as Hapag-Lloyd's *Hamburg Express*, which were deployed in the Europe-Far East service. At that time the Suez Canal was closed and often the route via the Panama Canal was used. Hence Panamax dimensions were applicable for these vessels. The dimensions of containerships reached up to 294.13 m./965 ft (LOA) by 32.23 m./106 ft (beam). Under deck containers

Figure 149: Hapag-Lloyd's record-breaking Frankfurt Express

were stowed 10 wide and 9 high. In contrast with similar vessels in the Europe-Far East trade, which carried containers 12-wide, 3 high on deck, these containerships could carry 13 containers abreast. Their capacity (slightly) exceeded the 3,000-TEU mark. It took until 1981 until Hapag-Lloyd again built a record-breaking containership, the (stand-alone) *Frankfurt Express*, which could carry the equivalent of 3,045 20-ft containers. In 1988 this capacity was increased to 3,430 TEU.

Although this might sound simple, Panamax vessels face serious stability problems. The locks in the Panama Canal require a length to beam (L/B) ratio that is high and causes instability. Vessels such as the *Frankfurt Express* needed vast volumes of ballast water. The ballast tanks at both sides of the vessel acted as counterweight. However, the space needed for these ballast tanks limited the stowage of containers under deck to 10 wide. The 10-row/8-tier in hold and 13-row/4-tier on deck boundaries were fully utilized by US Lines' Econships. Each vessel was suited to solely carry 40-ft containers, its carrying capacity amounting to 2,177 FEU (4,354 TEU).

However, the typical newbuilding was in the 2,000-TEU range. Many companies ordered ships in the 2,000-TEU range such as Sea-Land (D9s: 1,780 (12x)), Maersk (L-class: 2,100 (10x)), Yang Ming (Ming class: 1,846 (11x)), United Arab Shipping Company (A2-class: 2,100 (9x)). In the course of time many of these vessels were jumboized. The emphasis was on cost per slot. The developments can best be demonstrated by Evergreen. In 1975/76 their first fully-cellular containerships, four 600-TEU S-class vessels, were delivered. A crew of 30 members was needed to operate these ships. Soon these vessels were stretched to 878 TEU. Moreover

Figure 150: Evergreen's Ever Vital berthing at ECT Home

the ships were automated and crews reduced to 24 member. Their second series of 7 (V-class, see Figure 150) containerships was larger i.e. 1,214 TEU and needed a crew of 22 whereas their 4 L-class vessels of 1,800 TEU was manned with a crew of only 16. The fuel efficiency of these vessels was high. In order to reduce operating costs further, many of these ships were registered under flags of convenience with home ports such as Panama and Monrovia. It is clear that Evergreen was a competitive newcomer.

Containerships had marginalized other types of vessels that specialized on unitized cargo such as LASH-vessels and pallet ships. Existing types of ships that were also able to carry containers remained on the scene and developed to become more efficient. Ro-Ro vessels can serve as an example. Especially, Scandinavian shipping lines were proponents in this respect. The latest vessels of Atlantic Container Line, G3 Ro-Ro ships, were fitted with container cells on deck. This made lashing of the containers redundant (see Figure 151).

Figure 151: ACL's 3rd generation Ro-Ro Atlantic Companion

In cases of structural trade imbalances sometimes dry bulk carriers were also used for container transport. These so-called conbulkers were often used as container carrier in one direction to fill the empty haul. CAST offered such a service between Canada and Europe. Their ships were not the first of this type. In 1970 Australian National Line started operating the Darwin Trader a nearly 12,000-dwt cellular container/bulk carrier.

Even a round-the-world service was provided by ABC Containerline from Antwerp. The first ships 42,562-dwt *Deloris* and *Helen* with a capacity of 1,100 TEU, were commissioned in 1978. Two similar conbulk ships (*Antwerpen, Brussel*) that could carry 400 TEU more, followed suit whereas the *Ellen Hudig* (42,077 dwt, 1,100 TEU) and sister ship *Cornelius Verolme* joint in 1983. In order to secure the containers in the holds, plates with stacking cones for the cell guides (so-called bridge fittings) were used on the bottom of the hold. However, these plates could not be installed permanently as the bulk operation required a flat bottom. This proved to be a weak point in the first series of conbulkers but was later taken care of in the design phase.

Figure 152: ANL's Darwin Trader on her maiden voyage

Figure 153: 1,100-TEU conbulker Deloris

Based on a long term contract to carry mineral sands from Western Australia to the US Gulf, an (eastbound) round the world service was operated. It was agreed with US shipping lines that no containers would be discharged in US ports, i.e. Houston and Charleston. About half of the container space on the US Gulf to Europe leg was chartered out to Trans Freight Lines that joined the ABC fleet with conbulker *TNT Express*.

7.3. HINTERLAND TRANSPORT

Containerization becomes intermodal freight transportation when two or more transport modes are used for seamless door-to-door transportation. Since vessels only call at a limited number of ports, hinterland transportation needs to be organized in a structured way. In many countries e.g. Japan and Australia, major cities are located adjacent to the sea. In these cases coastal or shortsea shipping is complement to the part of the trip and inland transportation is usually carried out by road transport. In Europe and North America, the location of cities is more scattered over the continent. Due to longer distances freight trains, and sometimes barges, also play an important role in hinterland transportation. The focus in this decade is on establishing adequate transport networks including inland terminals able to provide seamless intermodal services.

Europe

The only country in Europe that had a well developed intermodal rail network available when the container era arrived was the United Kingdom. In continental Europe domestic container transport was carried out in mixed trains by state-owned national railway companies whereas long distance, cross-border container transport was taken up by Intercontainer, an organization established in 1967 by a number of these national companies. Transport capacity was hired from its affiliates. The European rail sector comprised two separate markets for transporting (semi-)trailers and containers. The European piggy-back companies were organized by the road sector, in the Union Internationale des Sociétés de Transport Combiné Rail/Route (UIRR). In 1983, the two organizations struck a bargain, the Montbazon agreement, that concluded that transportation of ISO containers by rail would be Intercontainer's prerogative; the market for transport of trucks, tractor/trailers and semi-trailers by rail would be UIRR's domain. Both organizations were allowed to take swap bodies i.e. domestic/European containers.

From Amsterdam, Rotterdam and Antwerp (the so-called ARA ports) inland navigation became important too. A scheduled liner service between Rotterdam and Mannheim in Germany, along the river Rhine, started in 1974. At the same time barge operator Nieuwe Rijnvaart Maatschappij (NRM), a branch of shipping line Koninklijke Nederlandsche Stoomvaart Maatschappij (KNSM), began operating between Amsterdam and Basel in Switzerland. Conventional (dry bulk) barges could be used without alterations but equipped with adjustable wheelhouses enabled an extra tier of containers. In anticipation of the new service, NRM had three barges built with a box-shaped hold, extendable wheelhouse and perpendicular bow to push unpropelled barges.

Figure 154: NRM barge Stroomwijk

New barge terminals mushroomed along the river and transport volumes to/from The Netherlands increased from 60,000 TEU in 1980 to 200,000 TEU in 1985.

North America

Since the opening of the Panama Canal in 1914 transport between Eastern and Western seaboard locations in the US has been a choice between water and rail. After a period in which the railroads were dominant, containerization revived intercoastal transport when Sea-Land inaugurated its California service in 1962. However, the question remained: fast but expensive land transport or slow and cheap all water services.

This problem gained momentum in the early 1970s when US shipping lines started offering eastbound Far East-Europe services. In order to cut (in relation to westbound services) unfavorable transport times, trains could be used to transit the North American continent. Seatrain was one of the frontrunners. Its "landbridge" system i.e. transport of containers by dedicated trains between East Coast and West Coast US ports shaved 10 days from the all-water transport time. The system was also used to reach ports as final destination; the service is then called "minibridge". Finally, "microbridge" refers to transport between ports and an inland point of origin or destination.

Figure 155: Early Landbridge Seatrain/Atchison, Topeka and Santa Fe Railway

By the end of the 1970s, American President Lines replaced its all-water service to and from the East Coast by a "bridge" service. Under the new president W. Bruce Seaton, acquainted with all types of surface transportation modes, intermodalism implied seamless transfer of containerized shipments between ship, train, and truck. Since single-car delivery was unreliable APL developed the Liner Train concept. By operating dedicated trains on a fixed schedule the unpredictability of single-car delivery was eliminated. Moreover, railroad companies quoted unit train rates which made rail transport more competitive.

Figure 156: APL Liner Train being loaded

At that time the lion's share of container transport by rail was Trailer on Flat Car (TOFC) also called piggyback transport. Only a few rail terminals were equipped to handle containers. APL's first liner trains hauled their containers piggyback style i.e. mounted on trailer chassis. In contrast with other countries, Containers on Flat Cars (COFC) was in the US the exception to the rule.

It were the shipping lines who pushed developments ahead. In order to raise efficiency the idea of putting one container atop of another was initiated by Sea-Land. But the conventional flatcar was not suited for this. However, because a considerable amount of equipment hung underneath the wagon, it should be possible to lower the floor. By lowering the floor of the railcar, two shipping containers could be stacked where only one went before, so the cars could carry double the freight in the same space. The double-stack concept was developed by Southern Pacific and Sea-Land. Southern Pacific No. 513300, the first double-stack container car (or 40' Wells COCF), was delivered in July 1977 by the American Car and Foundry Company. This standalone wagon fitted with bulkheads was followed by a three unit specimen (SP 513301) in March 1979. In the second half of 1981, 42 5-40' well cars (SP513302-513343) were delivered. The last configuration, a set of five wells, became the industry standard. The railcar itself is articulated, meaning there are wheeled trucks in the intermediate positions and at each end. The much smaller number of couplers significantly reduced the slack action. Together with the low point of gravity of well cars, this also resulted in a decrease in cargo damage.

Early double-stack well cars were employed with bulkheads to secure the top row of containers. Besides a high(er) weight, these cars were less flexible with regard to larger off standard containers such as of 45, 48 and 53-ft length. Cars without bulkheads, called IBC-type cars, in which the top container is held into place by stacking cones, were introduced in de mid-1980s. Also, longer double stack well cars were built. At first three 45-ft cars were placed in the middle of a five-well car unit, soon followed by five 45-ft, 48-ft and even 53-ft

Figure 157: Southern Pacific No. 513300 at Sacramento

cars. The "heavy capacity" double-stack trains were composed of five-well, articulated cars, provided with 125-ton wheel trucks (62.5 per axle). Their light-weight design allowed a pay-load of 56.7 metric tons per well (for one double container stack). In addition, single-well and drawbar-connected multiple-well cars were developed to transport heavy containers; they provide more wheels to distribute the extra weight more efficiently.

At first many railroad companies were skeptical, some declaring that they would never own double-stack cars or run them along their lines. There were lots of obstacles. Two containers stacked one on the other meant an increased clearance profile, even after the car's platform was lowered. This meant raising bridge and tunnel clearances, and, in the east also adapting the high voltage overhead catenary wires. Because cars had a wider clearance profile, equipment along the sides of rail tracks had to be moved.

But to overcome these difficulties, shipping lines teamed up with dedicated railroad companies and railcar builders to force the innovation along. Among the first to order new rolling stock were Burlington Northern, Sea-Land and American President Lines. In the mid-1980s the first two companies purchased Twin-Stack cars at Gunderson whereas American President Lines acquired Lo-Pac cars from Thrall. Together APL and Thrall re-engineered existing TOFC cars to carry ten 40-ft containers. The two

Figure 158: Double-stack Sea-Land containers in regular service

bulkheads at either end of the wells were removed because containers could be secured with the same inter-box connectors as used on vessels. Taking off the bulkheads saved IBC-type double-stack cars weight and allowed containers to be loaded and unloaded more efficiently.

As a promoter of Liner Train, minibridge and microbridge connections, American President Lines moved over 80 thousand containers by rail in 1983, paying more than US$ 90 million to the railroads. APL -then perceived as a high-cost carrier offering a premium type of service- was eager to introduce cost-efficient dedicated double-stack container train services. In April 1984 a service once a week between the port of Los Angeles and Chicago was started. Based on earlier experiences American President Lines understood that the success of double stack depended on making the whole system work. This meant not only managing the double stack trains itself but also operating terminals and providing trucking services to assure customer delivery in time. In this concept the activities of railroad companies were limited to "hook-and-haul".

Marketing of double stack was also carried out in-house. An essential problem consisted of the lack of export traffic. APL acquired National Piggyback Services Inc., the largest US piggyback shipping agent, and attracted other third party intermodal companies to fill the empty backhauls with domestic cargo. Amazingly, the increase of domestic cargo soon outpaced the already double digit growth of Asian imports. After APL had introduced the first 45-ft maritime container in 1980, a 48-ft and 53-ft container followed, especially for this domestic trade. For the trucking industry these large containers signified increased competition with the railroad sector.

Figure 159: 45-ft APL container on top of two 20-ft containers

The above mentioned developments were enhanced by deregulation in the transport sector. The Motor Carrier Act and, especially, the Staggers Rail Act of 1980 had a profound impact on intermodal transport. No longer did ICC regulations apply for the rail portion of piggyback carriages. Moreover, rail-owned truck companies were allowed because the requirements for entering the trucking business were loosened. In this way railroads could offer more competitive TOFC/COFC services. In addition, the Shipping Act of 1984 permitted intermodal through rates to be established.

Figure 160: APL-stacktrain on its way to Chicago

IN RETROSPECT

In 1977, the future looked bright for shipping lines involved in containerization but outlooks worsened when economic growth slowed down and oil prices stayed high. Cutthroat competition on established markets such as the Atlantic and Pacific drove various US shipping lines out of business. European and Japanese companies were better suited to sustain difficult economic times. Being conference members, they sticked to the agreements and kept, more or less, their market shares. Traditional non-conference members such as Maersk and emerging Asian shipping lines benefitted most from this situation. Evergreen established its position by successfully operating an innovative round-the-world service.

Many shipping lines put a lot of effort in cost reduction. Since fuel prices were still high, most, relatively new, steam turbine containerships were re-engined with diesel propulsion. Labor costs could be decreased by deploying smaller crews on new vessels. Reflagging was also a popular measure to decrease costs. Although (re)organizing hinterland transportation could be interpreted from a cost point of view, for many shipping lines it meant taking control of the transport chain. The most spectacular developments took place in North America where double stack container trains were introduced by American President Lines and Sea-Land. This company understood that container transport by rail was not only a technical issue but also required an adequate organizational structure. In addition, new US legislation enhanced the cooperation between various transport modes. Containerization had turned into intermodalism.

CHAPTER 8

THE STRADDLE CARRIER
Workhorse for almost a century

The first straddle truck was developed by Mr. H.B. Ross in 1913 to replace horse-driven carts used at lumber mills for the transportation of timber. The machine was built in Seattle, Washington, by the Stetson-Ross Machine Works for Woodworks Machinery. It had front wheel steering, could carry a load of six tons and was electric driven (see Figure 161) to avoid the risk of fire near saw mills. Later on, combustion engines were applied to cover longer stretches without the need for frequent battery recharging.

Figure 161: First straddle carrier built by Ross, 1913

After the First World War, these straddle trucks (or straddle buggies) became very popular in the lumber industry on the US West Coast. From there, these straddle trucks spread to other transportation areas, such as steel mills, fruit handling and port operations. The machines had chain drives on two wheels or sometimes even four (see Figure 162). For more comfort and less impact loads, Ross introduced a kind of hydraulic spring system and a drivers cab at the top.

Figure 162: Ross straddle carriers with 2 and 4 wheel chain drive

Independently, in 1920, Carl F. Gerlinger, an inventive engineer from Germany, built a Gerlinger straddle carrier at his Dallas (Oregon) Machine & Locomotive Works (see Figure 163). This machine was powered by a four-cylinder Cadillac engine driving two wheels with hard rubber tires with gear drives and a drive shaft or chain drive.

Figure 163: Gerlinger first straddle carriers

Double coil springs provided some drive comfort. Later, six wheel machines with a coupled leaf spring system and inner chain drives at the center wheels came onto the market (see Figure 164).

Figure 164: Gerlinger carrier with six wheels

The Gerlinger straddle carriers were applied in the lumber and steel industry (lift capacities up to 27 tons), the automotive industry, in port operations and even for the loading/unloading of rail cars. Gerlinger also introduced an all-hydraulic carrier with hydrodynamic wheel supports, see Figure 165.

Gerlinger further developed its straddle carrier for other applications and already in the beginning of the 1960s they delivered a straddle carrier to the Alaska Railroad company for the handling of containers on railcars (see Figure 166), but in general Gerlinger stayed in business for the steel and lumber industry until today.

In 1922, another West Coast company, Willamette Iron and Steel, in Portland, Oregon, built a lumber carrier and known as the Bulldog. In the 1920s, Willamette changed her name into Hyster, which is taken from the term Hyster-it-up or heist-it-up (hoist it). Later, Hyster became well known for its fork lift trucks and other transportation equipment. It introduced a declutchable hoisting mechanism from the engine power take off to the hoisting (lifting) shoes (see Figure 167).

Not surprisingly, the construction of straddle carriers for the lumber and steel industry started in Europe, in 1946, in Valmet, Finland. It was also active in the lumber and paper industry. Valmet machines were 4 or 6-wheel machines (see Figure 168) with lifting capacities of up to 60 tons. After the Second World War, growth at Valmet was very much supported by Finland's War Compensation Program, coming from the former Soviet Union.

In 1953, the Clark Equipment Company (Battle Creek, Michigan, US) acquired the Ross Company and integrated the straddle carrier into its product range of lifting equipment.

And then...., in 1958, Clark (former Ross) was approached by the Matson research team looking for equipment to handle (transport and store) their in-house developed 24' containers. Clark had already experimented with a prototype for the handling of containers, but Matson felt the need to stack containers on top of each other (to save space). This triggered Clark to develop a straddle carrier program for container handling based on existing straddle carriers for the lumber and steel industry. In the US the container was considered a van (Webster: van is a covered vehicle, a large truck or trailer) and so, Clark introduced his proprietary name for its straddle carriers: The Clark Van Carrier. The first machine (Clark model 512) came into service in January 1959 at Matson's Encinal Terminal at San Francisco (see Figure 169).

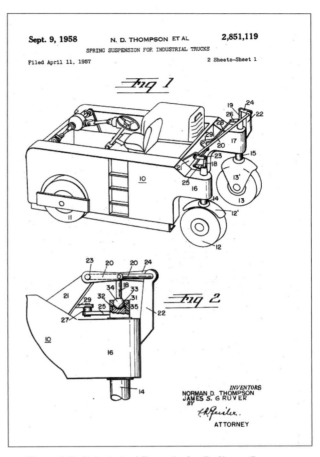

Figure 165: Patent straddle carrier by Gerlinger Company

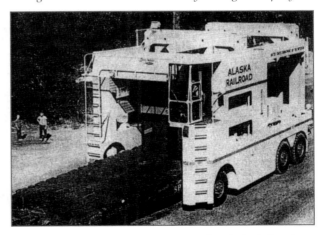

Figure 166: Gerlinger straddle carrier for Alaska Railroad

Figure 167: Hyster straddle carrier (left) and drive line detail (right)

Figure 168: First Valmet straddle carrier (1947) and later model for container handling

Figure 169: Clark straddle carriers at Matson terminals

Different from Matson, Sea-Land based the storage of containers on the chassis system. Therefore, the Clark Van Carrier was not used by Sea-Land during the first two decades of containerization. However, the Clark Van Carrier attracted a lot of attention and when containerization came to Europe, by the end of the 1960s, Clark Equipment Co established manufacturing plants in Belgium (La Brugeoise in Brugge), the UK and Australia, while in Japan a license agreement was established with TCM. The rapid growth of containerization in the 1970s caused a boom in straddle carrier purchases and by the end of the 1970s the Clark Van Carrier reached a market share of almost 70%. The lifting height was 1 over 2 and lifting capacity 30.5 tons under the spreader (see Figure 170).

Figure 170: Clark 20', 3 high at ECT (left) and Model 521 for 40',3 high

The rapid terminal growth in the 1970s and the flexible and multi-purpose functionality of the straddle carrier (applicable both for transportation and storage/stacking) made many manufacturers decide for a "me-too" strategy. During the 1970s, new straddle carrier designs were introduced, such as the Drott (hydrostatic drives) and Raygo Wagner Strad 80 (6-wheel type with two fixed, driven, middle wheels) in the US, Rubery Owen and Karricon (later Rubery Owen Karricon) with 4 and 8-wheel machines in the UK and Peiner and Demag, with their hydrostatic drives, made in Germany mainly for the European market (see Figure 171).

Due to the tremendous growth in terminal operations the straddle carrier's utilization exceeded the 1,000-1,500 operating hours per year and in some terminals annual figures of more than 3,000 operating hours became the standard utilization. Fatigue problems and unreliable, low-cost components (due to the increased competition amongst straddle carrier suppliers) caused many headaches for terminal operators, suffering from high breakdown figures, poor availability and high maintenance cost. In some terminals lifetime figures below 20,000 operating hours were recorded and thus the market started looking for improved designs.

In 1973, ECT purchased 6 Clark Van Carriers fitted with a mechanical hoist system, (diesel engine power take off, clutch, gearbox, hoisting drum and cables) supplied by Nellen Kraanbouw (see Figure 172). The modification was made to overcome the many breakdowns from the Clark hydraulic hoist systems.

In 1977, Mr. Wormmeester and Mr. Rijsenbrij convinced Nellen Kraanbouw to design a faster and more reliable diesel-electric straddle carrier with a minimum lifetime of 50,000 operating hours. This resulted in the first 8-wheel diesel-electric straddle carrier with 2 diesel generator sets, 4 electric motors for travelling and 1 electric motor for hoisting. The first prototype was designed with a box type structural design, while the following machines were designed with a lattice type structure, providing better visibility and improved fatigue resistance. The design was a success and in the beginning of the 1980s, a 4-high machine (1 over 3) supported by 10 wheels (tires 16.00 x 25) was introduced, a novelty in the container terminal business (see Figure 173).

Figure 171: Early straddle carriers from European (top) and US (bottom) manufacturers

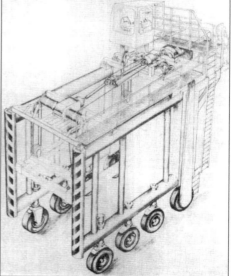

Figure 172: Clark Van Carrier modified with Nellen Kraanbouw mechanical hoist system

Figure 173: Development Nelcon carriers (first prototype; 8-wheel 1-over-2; 10-wheel 1-over-3)

Demag-Junkerrath stopped manufacturing in 1973, but the Peiner straddle carrier (a clever design from Hans Tax) was further improved. The smart, but unreliable hydrostatic travel drive was exchanged for a simpler mechanical drive line. Already in the beginning of the 1970s, the Clark Equipment Co. management in Michigan showed a limited interest to upgrade and further improve the Clark Van Carrier and this, together with the stronger competition, made Clark lose its strong market position. In 1976, Ferranti Engineering (UK) acquired the Clark Van Carrier business and later Ferranti developed a mechanically driven enlarged portal straddle carrier (Figure 174).

Figure 174: Ferranti and Valmet straddle carriers with mechanical travel drives

The experience built up by Valmet with its straddle carriers for the steel and logging industry made Valmet decide to increase the container straddle carrier business in 1976, introducing an 8-wheeled container stacker with diesel mechanical travelling, diesel hydraulic hoisting (horizontal cylinders + chains to the spreader) and hydrodynamic suspension above all wheels. Valmet paid a lot of attention to maintainability, driver's comfort and visibility. Moreover, the Scandinavian and German requirements for robustness under bad weather conditions and for environmental control resulted in a rather reliable heavy-duty machine capable of delivering more than 3,500 operating hours per year.

During the same period, Peiner as well switched to a mechanical drive for travelling, however supplied out of one top-mounted diesel engine.

By the end of the seventies Ferranti (earlier Clark) let its market share to Peiner, Valmet and Nellen (later Nelcon) mainly for Europe and the US, and TCM and Mitsubishi in the Far East (see Figure 175).

In the second half of the seventies, Sea-Land ran out of yard space in many terminals and despite their admiration for the simplicity of on-wheels yard operations; they accepted higher-density stacking (3-high) using straddle carriers. In a study for Piraeus, Sea-Land advised the carrier concept as the most cost-attractive alternative.

The introduction of containerization in South Africa brought another newcomer (after Nellen/Nelcon) at the straddle carrier stage, Briskar, an Australian manufacturer who designed a hydrostatically driven 8-wheel 1-over-2 carrier (see Figure 176, top left). An assembly plant was built in South Africa, but here again the hydrostatic drives were a big problem for the maintenance engineers. Some other manufacturers, such as BM Titan (Boomsche Metaalwerken, top right), Kocks and Belotti (now CVS Ferrari), produced straddle carriers as well, but they never became successful.

Between 1990 and 2004, some mergers changed the names and triggered some further developments. During the 1980s, Peiner was integrated with the Noell Company and, during the 1990s, Valmet and SISU were included in the Kalmar Group. Nellen merged with Conrad Stork into Nelcon and was acquired by Kalmar in 2002. In 2009, Noell was bought by Fantuzzi which company subsequently was acquired by TEREX.

In 2005, the majority of the straddle carrier market was in the hands of Kalmar, Noell, TCM and Mitsubishi, with all manufacturers showing features like PLC controls, Can-Bus technology, 1 over 2 and 1 over 3 stacking, twin lift, telescoping spreaders (20', 40', 45' and even for 2 x 20' containers) and diesel-mechanic or diesel-electric drives with energy saving electronics.

Figure 175: Straddle carriers Mitsubishi and TCM, below left

Figure 176: Straddle carriers with limited market share

In recent years, some new developments emerged due to the trend to save on labor costs, requiring automated stacking. Kalmar introduced a completely automated straddle carrier, in cooperation with Patrick Stevedores, for latter's Brisbane terminal, the AutoStrad (see Figure 177).

Another spin-off from the existing carrier is the shuttle carrier (4-wheel, made by Kalmar) and sprinter carrier (4 or 6-wheel from Noell and later Konecranes). Their main purpose is to feed containers between quay cranes or rail yards and the stacking area (see Figure 178). In the future some manufacturers may enter the field of fully automated sprinter/shuttle carriers (Kalmar, Noell and Konecranes) as an alternative for AGVs, offering some kind of bufferability by grounding the boxes at interchange areas. However, in the end, the cost/performance ratio of this type of automated shuttle carrier will determine whether in the future it will be applied on container terminals.

It is remarkable that one century after the first straddle carrier was built (by Ross in 1913), manually operated and even fully automated straddle carriers are used for the transport and stacking of containers.

Figure 177: Kalmar AutoStrad straddle carrier

Figure 178: Straddle carriers dominantly for transportation (Noell, Kalmar and Konecranes)

IN RETROSPECT

The straddle carrier was adopted from the timber industry and became a real workhorse for container terminals. It is still widely used, but its relative share in container handling equipment has decreased considerably. From the many manufacturers (approximately 20) only a few survived as a result of the small series, moderate demand and price competition. In the early days, the straddle carrier was a universal machine for stacking, internal transport and interchange to trucks and trains. Nowadays the emphasis has shifted towards transportation, wherein the ability of grounding containers is attractive for buffering between subsequent handling processes.

CHAPTER 9

FOCUS ON THE TRANSPORT CHAIN
(1986 - 1996)

Between 1986 and 1996 the volume of world trade increased substantially. On the one hand developed countries were recovering from an economic recession; on the other hand trade restrictions were alleviated. The boundaries within internal markets were lowered, e.g. North American Free Trade Agreement (as of 1994) or, in the case of Europe (1992), removed. Moreover, the Uruguay Round of GATT negotiations that were started in 1986 resulted in the WTO agreements signed by 125 countries in 1994. The core of this agreement was also to reduce trade barriers albeit on a global scale. At the same time manufacturing and trading companies got more interested in logistics.

Shipping lines had to meet growing volumes as well as shippers' logistic demands in terms of geographical coverage and just-in-time delivery. Cooperation became an essential element for survival and companies were looking for new (types of) partnerships. Some of the ships that were ordered in this period were ground-breaking. Therefore the focus is on ship development first. Next, the search for new partners and different types of cooperation is described. Finally, the attempts to take more control of the transport/logistic chain will be discussed. The basis for modern containerization is laid in this period!

9.1. SHIP DEVELOPMENT

Panamax

Since ship size was determined by the locks in the Panama Canal additional capacity had to be found within the given (i.e. 294.13 m. x 32.31 m. x 12.04 m.) dimensions. In the spring of 1988 the Odense Steel shipyard launched Maersk's first M-class containership, the *Marchen Maersk*. By decreasing the transverse spacing between the container stacks and reducing the width of the double hull these vessels were able to carry eleven containers across in the holds. In order to meet the strength requirements a lot of calculations had to be carried out. The twelve M-class vessels were equipped with lashing

Figure 179: Hannover-class Stuttgart Express

bridges so containers could be carried in six tiers on deck. In contrast with United States Lines' Econships which transported 57% of the containers ten across in the holds, the *Marchen Maersk* and its sister ships carried more than 50% of the cargo on deck. Although the official TEU capacity of these vessels amounted to 3,500 TEU, 4,300 TEU is probably a better estimate.

Hapag-Lloyd increased the capacity of its containerships by eliminating the longitudinal stringers that were used to support the inboard sides of the hatch covers. In 1991 the first of eight Hannover-class containerships (see Figure 179) was delivered by Samsung Shipbuilding & Heavy Industries. The 53,783-grt *Hannover Express* had a carrying capacity of nearly 4,400 TEU. Later vessels from this class could carry up to 4,639 TEU and were the biggest containerships at the time.

Post-Panamax

In 1988, the first five Post-Panamax containerships, built by two German shipyards, were delivered to American President Lines. The *President Truman* was commissioned in April, soon to be followed by the *President Kennedy, Polk, Johnson* and *Adams*. With a length over all of 275.3 m, a beam of 39.4 m. and a draft of 11 m. they were classified as C10 vessels (C10-M-F150a). Since wider ships have better stability characteristics, they entail less water ballast and can carry more cargo. The capacity of these 50,205-grt containerships amounted to 4,300 TEU. They carried containers 12 across in the cargo holds and 16 across on deck. The lashing bridges allowed five tiers of deck containers. A 57,000 HP diesel engine enabled a speed of 24.2 knots.

APL's US$ 500 million capital expansion program included also the purchase of new rail equipment and provided enhancements for its shipping terminals and computer systems. The company doubled the size of its Oakland terminal. APL operated a 18.2 hectare terminal with a quay length of nearly 400 m. and a depth of water of 11.3 m. alongside. Two 45-ton Alliance container cranes and one Paceco modified A-frame with working outreaches of 38 m. and 32.9 m. respectively, served the terminal. Adjacent berths with a quay length of nearly 440 m. were rented to bankrupt US Lines and in 1987 assigned to APL. In the new situation a 32 hectare terminal at Berths 60-63 at the Middle Harbor was rented from the Port Authority.

Figure 180: APL's President Kennedy

To keep pace with the new generation of containerships the Port Authority requested US$ 74 million for a dredging project to widen the Outer Harbor Channel and to widen and deepen the Inner Harbor Channel to 12.8 m. In October 1986 the project was authorized by Congress.

At the time experts fiercely debated APL's decision to build such an "inflexible" vessel. It took until 1991 before the next Post-Panamax containership, the *CGM Normandie*, appeared. This stand alone newbuilding by Samsung Heavy Industries was an adapted (i.e. wider) design of an existing vessel. Its dimensions were 275.7 x 37.1 m, which allowed 15 containers across on deck. She could carry a total of 4,419 TEU. In January 2007, severe winds and huge waves in the English Channel caused serious damage to the ship's hull including a crack in one side causing a flooded engine room; the by then *MSC Napoli* was declared a total loss.

Post-Panamax containerships with a length of around 275 m. and a beam of just over 37 m. i.e. 15 containers across on deck became the rule in the early 1990s. In 1992 Hyundai Merchant Marine received three (out of four) 4,469 TEU Post-Panamax containerships. Also in 1992 the Malaysia International

Shipping Corporation (MISC) took delivery of the *Bunga Pelangi*. Three years later a sistership, the *Bunga Pelangi Dua*, was commissioned.

Nedlloyd took delivery of two innovative open-top or hatchcoverless Post-Panamax vessels in 1994/95: the *Nedlloyd Hongkong* and *Nedlloyd Honshu*. These containerships with a length over all of 279.5 m. and a beam of 37.8 m. could carry 4,181 TEU. The designs were based on research of Nedlloyd's Newbuilding Department on cargo handling, port performance and "care for cargo". The basic idea of naval architect Vossnack was to extend the cell guides upwards to embrace all containers and to remove the hatch covers. They were called Ultimate Container Carriers (UCC). A series of

Figure 181: Nedlloyd Honshu at sea

five hatchcoverless Panamax vessels was already in use since 1991/92. Remarkably, most shipping lines that commissioned Post-Panamax containerships in this period were members of the ScanDutch consortium.

Although the Post-Panamax design facilitated bigger vessels, the carrying capacity of containerships was still under 4,500 TEU. In 1995 Asian shipping lines NYK, MOL and OOCL were about to cross that line; NYK and MOL by extending the length and OOCL by widening the beam. The NYK Altair-class consisted of three nearly 300 m. long vessels that could carry 4,741 TEU. For the first time a Post-Panamax vessel had become the biggest containership. The five MOL containerships named after European rivers, had similar characteristics whereas the (ultimately) eight OOCL California-class vessels had a length of 276 m. and

Figure 182: NYK Altair

beam of 40 m. that allowed 16 containers across on deck. Their carrying capacity was 5,344 TEU.

In the same year another six Post-Panamax vessels joined the APL fleet. The length and beam of these C11 vessels differed only marginally from the first series. Nonetheless their draft (14 m.) and Gross Register Tonnage (64,502 tons) increased substantially and their maximum capacity was 4,832 TEU. In order to sustain the same speed, a 66,385 HP diesel engine was installed. For the first time, these new containerships were not named after presidents but received names of oriental countries. *APL Japan*, *APL China* and *APL Thailand* were built by Howaldtswerke Deutsche Werft (Germany) whereas *APL Korea*, *APL Singapore* and *APL Philippines* were delivered by Daewoo Heavy Industries (Korea). At that time, with eleven vessels, APL owned the largest fleet of Post-Panamax containerships.

Hatchcoverless

A few years before Nedlloyd took delivery of the two Post-Panamax hatchcoverless containerships a series of five similar Panamax vessels was ordered at Japanese shipyards Ishikawajima Heavy Industries (3) and Mitsubishi Heavy Industries (2). The first vessel, *Nedlloyd Asia*, was launched in 1991. By deleting the longitudinal beams on which the hatchcovers normally rest, it was possible to stow eleven rows of containers across in the holds. The extended cell guides kept containers up to twelve high. These 266 m. long vessels could carry around 3,600 TEU.

However, the first hatchcoverless containership was the *Bell Pioneer*. The dimensions of this 301-TEU vessel were 118 m. x 17 m. It was specially designed for shortsea traffic between Ireland, the United Kingdom and continental Europe and commenced operations in October 1990. The award winning hull design by Australian-based Advanced Ship Design Pty Ltd included extended side tanks and increased freeboard to protect the containers from "green water". One hold is covered by a folding hatch cover; the other three are open to the weather and

Figure 183: Bell Pioneer, the first hatchcoverless containership

equipped with a series of one-way freeing ports located at a height, equivalent to the freeboard of a traditional ship. In case any seawater, spray or rain gets into the open holds, two 100 ton per hour stripping pumps are available. Computer simulations as well as tank tests proved the viability and safety of the design. When the *Bell Pioneer* encountered a typhoon on its delivery voyage from Japan, the ship took on even less water than predicted!

In the hatchless holds cell guides extent vertically upwards to just above the coaming heights. With the prefabricated (and very robust) cell guides any configuration and container size is possible. Port turnaround times are on average 25% faster than for equivalent TEU-capacity ships. Since a crew of only seven is needed to run the vessel, the *Bell Pioneer* is a very economical containership to operate. In 1992 the Teraoke Shipyard delivered a similar albeit bigger vessel, the *Euro Power*. This hatchcoverless containership could carry 378 TEU and was also deployed by Bell Lines for some time.

Figure 184: Hatchcoverless containerships Atlantic Lady and Norasia Fribourg

Dutch shipyard De Hoop, which had lots of experience with open top vessels, built two 100% hatch coverless containerships. The *Atlantic Lady* (1992, see Figure 184, left) and *European Express* (1993) had a capacity of 1,472 TEU. Their distinctive shape was determined by cell guides on the side tanks and a deckhouse in front. The next year they constructed two smaller hatchcoverless vessels that resembled the *Bell Pioneer* albeit with longer cell guides. The 558-TEU feeders *Reestborg* and *Reggeborg* had two engines and two propellers that provided a speed of 17 knots. Another series of 2,780-TEU hatch coverless containerships were built by German Shipyard Howaldswerke-Deutsche Werft. In 1993 the *Norasia Fribourg,* the first of six vessels, was delivered (see Figure 184, right).

9.2. DEVELOPMENTS IN LINER TRADING

North Atlantic

The North Atlantic trade seemed to represent a rather stable market but shipping lines such as Maersk, P&O Containers Ltd and Nedlloyd entered the trade for the first time. New entries consisted of Asian shipping lines such as MOL, Yang Ming, Cosco and K Line. In 1992 the Trans-Atlantic Agreement united fifteen shipping lines, conference members and outsiders, to rationalize tonnage and impose higher rates.

In relation to the original conference members two groups of shipping lines can be identified. ACL, the oldest consortium had concluded a vessel sharing agreement with Hapag-Lloyd and for Canadian destinations space was hired from OOCL/CanMar. ACL underwent great changes in ownership. The first to leave ACL was Holland America Line that had decided to skip all cargo transportation. In 1975 ACL participant Swedish America Line (Broström) took over all freight operations (including HAL's share in ACL) and called it InterContinental Transport (ICT). However Swedish America Line encountered financial difficulties in the 1980s and sold its shipping interests to Transatlantic. This is reflected in the ownership of the five new (G3) Ro-Ro containerships that were commissioned in 1984/85: *Atlantic Concert* (Wallenius Lines), *Atlantic Conveyor* (Cunard), *Atlantic Cartier* (CGM), *Atlantic Companion* and *Atlantic Compass* (both Transatlantic). The five remaining G2 vessels were scrapped. Within three years after delivery, the G3 vessels were extended by 42 m. and TEU capacity increased from 2,160 to 3,100 TEU. At that moment the cooperation with Hapag-Lloyd was started. To emphasize the collaboration the names of the *Atlantic Companion* and *Atlantic Concert* changed for the time being to *Companion Express* and *Concert Express.* To reduce costs both shipping lines got rid of their oldest, less efficient vessels.

Transatlantic, by now a member of the Bilspedition group, aimed at full ownership of ACL. Wallenius that intended to cease all container operations and CGM were sold out in 1989. Cunard followed suit but it took until 1995 before they sold the *Atlantic Conveyor* to ACL. The next year CGM also decided to sell their *Atlantic Cartier.*

The other high profile Vessel Sharing Agreement was between Sea-Land and newcomers P&O Containers Ltd and Nedlloyd. The latter shipping lines had found each other in a slot-sharing agreement with Trans Freight Lines that was owned for 50% by OCL. In 1986 P&O's Lord Sterling bought the other OCL partners out and P&O was renamed P&O Containers Ltd. One year later, P&O Containers Ltd took over the remaining 50% in Trans Freight Lines. The acquisition of Cunard-Ellerman, mainly consisting of the ACT participation (including the privatized Shipping Corporation of New Zealand), followed in 1991. The *ACT 1/Discovery Bay, ACT 2/Moreton Bay* and *ACT 7/Palliser Bay* became part of the P&O fleet, the other ACT vessels were owned by Blue Star Line.

In 1988, Sea-Land bought the twelve US Lines' Econships at a bargain price of US$ 162 million and renamed them into Atlantic-class. In order to raise their speed to 21 knots, three ships were shortened and enhanced with a streamlined bow. Together with Nedlloyd and P&O Containers Ltd a new joint North Atlantic service was established. In the new service Sea-Land operated seven Econships, P&O Containers Ltd (see Figure 185) three and Nedlloyd two. Because the containerships had been built with US government subsidies Nedlloyd and P&O Containers Ltd operated these vessels through a leasing contract. Maersk got involved in 1991 when the company rationalized its successful Transatlantic service that was started in 1987 by extending the Far East-US East Coast service to Europe. In return for providing space for US West Coast ports, Maersk received slots for East and Gulf Coast ports it did not serve.

The Trans-Atlantic Agreement (TAA) and its successor the Trans-Atlantic Conference Agreement (TACA) initiated member discipline and brought about a profitable trade. The number of members of the TAA/TACA increased from eleven in 1992 to a high of seventeen in 1996.

Figure 185: P&O's Raleigh Bay underway on the North Atlantic

However, the British Shipper's Council began proceedings and the European Commission started an investigation. The European Commission claimed that TACA had mistreated its dominant position and, in a landmark ruling, issued a fine approximately US$ 310 million (ECU 273 million). This fine was apportioned to the TACA members according to their market share in 1994.

Pacific

Partly as a response to the round-the-world services, cooperation between shipping lines on the Pacific had strengthened. Examples are the collaboration between OOCL, NOL and KSC (short time) and between the two groups of Japanese shipping lines. Facilitated by the US Shipping Act of 1984 a TransPacific Westbound Rate Agreement (TWRA) was concluded by nineteen companies in early 1985. In this way a minimum rate for the very competitive market of backhaul containers was established. Later that year an agreement on the eastward leg was reached. Albeit less powerful than the TWRA, the Asia North America Eastbound Rate Agreement (ANERA) reversed to some extent the downward trend of freight rates. Still, overcapacity was huge. In a Transpacific Stabilization Agreement thirteen shipping lines decided to cut capacity by ultimately 13%.

The problem of overcapacity was also addressed by the Japanese government which was involved in the container industry from the beginning. They issued a policy document stating that the Japanese container shipping lines involved in West and East Coast trades should be reorganized in three groups of two companies. K line and MOL were the first to leave the liner agreements. Together they operated a direct service from mainland Asia and Taiwan to the US West Coast. Their space charter arrangement aimed at improving, stabilizing and rationalizing their operations without giving up their separate and individual operating staff, sales and marketing divisions. However, this cooperation was limited to Californian ports. For the Pacific North West MOL teamed up with the Danish East Asiatic Company whereas K Line joined the NOL-OOCL consortium. Of the four remaining shipping lines, NYK was the strongest one. Showa was the smallest and left the liner shipping business in 1988. In the same year Yamashita-Shinnihon Steamship Co. and Japan Line merged into Nippon Liner System which was taken over by NYK in 1991. Within a few years the number of Japanese container shipping lines was cut in half.

A similar program was initiated by the Korean government. Under the directive of the Shipping Industry Rationalization Policy, the Korea Marine Transport Corporation (KMTC) was forced to transfer its assets to Hyundai Merchant Marine. In this way Hyundai got access to the main Korean trades and started an East Asia-US service with five 2,970-TEU vessels. Another merger, later takeover, was between Korea Shipping Corporation (KSC), which had inaugurated the first major Korean container liner service in 1975, and Hanjin. Cho Yang was not affected. The three surviving shipping lines were considered big enough to benefit from the economies of scale in the container shipping industry.

Figure 186: NLS and NYK reefers sharing the same well car

It became clear that TWRA en ANERA had a limit for individual shipping lines. Hence the formation of slot sharing consortia became popular. NYK (incl. Nippon Liner System) and NOL were the first to join. Surprisingly, MOL and K Line combined forces to maintain market share. Another example of a slot sharing agreement was concluded in 1991 between Maersk and Sea-Land.

Europe - Far East

From the beginning of containerization, consortia, such as TRIO, ScanDutch and ACE were of great importance for the Europe-Far East trade. In 1987, ACE split in two when Franco Belgian Services (a combination of French shipping company Chargeurs Réunis and the Belgian Compagnie Maritime Belge) was sold to Maersk. Korean Hanjin (incl. KSC) and Cho Yang also left. The remaining members K Line, OOCL and NOL decided to increase their capacity by more than 50%. In June 1990 the partnership between Hanjin and Cho Yang ended. Hanjin preferred to operate a self-reliant pendulum service between Europe-East Asia-US West Coast. The smaller Cho Yang joined the German partners DSR Senator Lines in their round-the-world service. In this way, so-called Tricon could offer 7-day frequencies. Later, Hanjin joined as well.

In June 1990 EAC took over the interests and containerships of the Scandinavian partners Transatlantic and Wilh. Wilhelmsen in ScanDutch. The company allied itself with crisis-ridden Ben Line Steamers Ltd (from the TRIO consortium) in a 2:1 joint venture. Ben Line's only assets consisted of three older containerships which had be taken over by the bank as security for its debt. Nevertheless, millions were invested in containers, terminals and a new headquarters near London. After only six months Ben Line collapsed. EAC put up her shipping interests for sale and in 1993 Maersk acquired EAC/Ben Line's nine containerships including containers and four services between Australia and South East Asia. The sale included the two 4,000-TEU containerships *Arosia* and *Alsia* which were delivered to EAC in 1990. Later, EAC sold the fast, 1970s containerships *Selandia* and *Jutlandia* to the US Navy (see chapter 6).

The first participant to leave TRIO was the aforementioned Ben Lines. More important were the ventures of OCL, TRIO's the biggest contributor. When the consortium agreement expired in 1991 OCL's new owner P&O teamed up with Maersk on the Europe-Far East route. Together they could offer customers two weekly departures. Precisely these high frequencies were the reason why P&O rejected a similar agreement with Ben Line.

Alliances

The reduced consortia TRIO (Hapag-Lloyd, MOL and NYK), ScanDutch (Nedlloyd, MISC and CGM) and ACE (OOCL, K Line and NOL) were not stable. The cooperation within TRIO was under pressure due to the incompatibility of the Japanese shipping lines. In 1994 Hapag-Lloyd, which had invested heavily in new capacity, chose NYK and its partner in the Pacific, NOL. Through slot chartering Hapag-Lloyd returned to the Pacific and gained access to intermodal systems of NOL and NYK. Alternatively, the Asian shipping lines were offered Transatlantic services. Moreover, NOL had started a successful service from Singapore to New York via the Suez Canal in 1991. This significantly affected the importance of West Coast ports for the Mid-West and the Eastern seaboard. It was estimated that, in terms of transport time, the journey between Singapore and Toronto either via the Pacific Ocean and Vancouver or via the Suez Canal and Halifax took about the same time: 26-30 days (depending on the directness of the sea leg).

The formal dissolution of ScanDutch took place in 1992. CGM, in the process of restructuring its container services, sold its rights on a fifty-fifty basis to the remaining members Nedlloyd and MISC and withdrew from the Europe-East Asian trade. MOL, looking for new partners joined Nedlloyd and MISC. APL that had decided to venture onto the Europe-Far East trade, took also part in the cooperation.

When finally the ACE consortium dissolved, NOL moved its Europe-Far East service to the Hapag-Lloyd/NYK group and OOCL, APL's partner in the Pacific joined Nedlloyd/MISC/MOL/APL. The latter group formed the Global Alliance. In contrast with the old consortia this alliance covered all major East-West trades. Quite surprisingly, P&O ended its cooperation with Maersk in May 1995 and joined the Hapag-Lloyd/NYK/NOL group, which was renamed Grand Alliance. This left K line isolated, until it joined forces with Yang Ming.

The new partner of Maersk in the Europe-Far East trade became Sea-Land. The two shipping lines already cooperated in transpacific and, to a lesser extent, Transatlantic services. The ocean-side cooperation was geared towards providing reliable multi-week sailings, achieving faster transit times and extending the service network by direct calls at outlying (regional) ports. In addition, terminals and equipment were mutually shared. The cooperation between Maersk and Sea-Land formed yet another firm alliance.

The importance of alliances is best illustrated by figures. Mid-1995 the fleet of fully-cellular containerships consisted of 1,800 vessels with a total capacity of approximately 2.6 million TEU. The alliances held a market share of 29% in the global container fleet and of 45% in vessel capacity (in TEU). The Grand Alliance, Maersk Sealand and Global Alliance encompassed 11.5%, 9.4% and 8.1% of the total TEU capacity respectively.

9.3. TRANSPORT CHAIN

Slot and vessel sharing agreements, alliances, joint ventures, mergers and takeovers are all examples of horizontal integration in the liner shipping industry. Vertical integration i.e. taking more control of other parts of the transport chain such as (inland) terminals and hinterland transportation took also place. However, this is a complex process because other parties than shipping lines are involved as well.

Deepsea terminals

From an organizational point of view terminal operators were confronted with higher volumes. Most stevedoring companies reacted by adding more, slightly modified equipment, extending their premises or building new container terminals. Sometimes inland terminals acted as an extended gate or River Trade Terminals, which could handle and consolidate container cargo prior to dispatch to deepsea container terminals. Fundamental changes in terminal operations were rare. An exception was ECT's new Delta Sea-Land terminal in the port of Rotterdam that opened in 1993. At this advanced container terminal Automated Guided Vehicles (AGVs) were introduced for transporting containers between the stack and the quay cranes. At the stack unmanned, rail-mounted cranes, so-called Automated Stacking Cranes (ASCs), handle the containers from the AGVs and bring them to their location. On the land side of the stacking bay ASCs put containers on the ground for further handling by (traditional) internal transport equipment (for more details see chapter 13).

Terminal operators such as ECT in Rotterdam are by nature bound to a specific location. For the first time stevedore companies started to expand to other ports. A renowned example concerned Hutchison Port Holdings (HPH) that started from Hong Kong. Their first international move was the purchase of 90% of the Port of Felixstowe (UK) for £ 80 million. Worldwide, many other terminals followed. In some cases the Port Authority carried out stevedoring activities. According to, amongst others, World Bank recommendations, the public part including maritime affairs and port development was separated from the more commercial terminal operations. In Singapore this was organized as the Maritime and Port Authority of Singapore (MPA) and the Port of Singapore Authority (PSA). A US$ 500 million joint venture for the development of a container terminal in Dalian was their first international move.

Since the beginning of containerization some shipping lines (e.g. Sea-Land and K Line) had their own transshipment facilities because multi-user terminals could not guarantee preferred treatment. In 1986 Maersk inaugurated a new terminal in Algeciras where East-West trade lanes crossed North-South routes. P&O pursued a policy of acquiring stakes in terminals such as the Shekou Container Terminal near Hong Kong. However, in due course, many shipping lines separated their stevedoring from the liner activities; Compagnie Maritime Belge was amongst the first.

Finally, port authorities can offer dedicated terminals to shipping lines or take financial stakes in terminals. In their land use and concession policy areas adjacent to container terminals can be designated for distribution activities of manufacturing/trading companies or third party logistics.

Hinterland transportation

The transshipment of increasing numbers of containers via deepsea terminals and their transportation over long(er) distances to the hinterland made trucking less attractive. Transport by train and, if applicable, by barge became an alternative.

In many North American ports on dock/near dock rail facilities were upgraded by railroad companies and port authorities. To relief congestion the Ports of Long Beach and Los Angeles completed the purchase of the former Southern Pacific rail track in December 1994 and constructed the Alameda Corridor to connect the national rail system near downtown Los Angeles to the ports. The corridor, which includes an underground, triple-tracked rail line of 16 km (10 miles), is shared by the BNSF Railway and Union Pacific Railroad and went into operation in 2002.

The double-stack rail network was expanded and became denser. Moreover, the Canadian railway companies, Canadian Pacific (CP) and Canadian National (CN), also arranged double-stack services on their networks, which, at the time, started to penetrate the US rail system. On the US side, the number of Class I railways declined to five: Burlington Northern Santa Fe (BNSF, merger in 1995) and Union Pacific Southern Pacific (UPSP, merger in 1996) in the west, Kansas City Southern (KCS) in the center, and in the east CSX and Norfolk Southern (NS), which carved up the assets of Conrail in 1998.

Understandably, APL's double-stack container services were copied by many others. Soon, Japanese and other shipping lines were running their own dedicated double-stack trains. The introduction of double-stack container trains had extended the traditional hinterland of US West Coast ports to the Mid-West and, in some cases, to the Eastern seaboard. For example, in 1991, K Line suspended its all-water service to New York in favor of its dedicated double-stack train network.

Although, shipping lines utilized the huge US Class 1 railroad companies, they were not in the position to acquire them. Conversely, CSX purchased Sea-Land for US$ 800 million from the Reynolds Group, in 1986. In addition to their railroad, CSX operated numerous intermodal facilities. Moreover, they owned the largest US barge company, American Commercial Lines. This company was acquired when CSX purchased Texas Gas Resources Corporation in 1983. On July 24, 1984, the Interstate Commerce Commission ruled that CSX was allowed to keep and operate American Commercial Lines, a change of longstanding government policy against letting railroads own steamship or barge lines.

Rail transport in Europe, passenger as well as freight, was carried out by state-owned companies. For international container transport Intercontainer was established. Containers were transported in combined trains or, if sufficient volume was available, in (dedicated) block trains or shuttles. In 1991, the European Commission issued a directive that forced railway companies to secede the infrastructure and allow new, licensed enterprises to operate intermodal services on their network. For example, Nedlloyd, P&O Containers Ltd and Sea-

Figure 187: ERS Railways train en route in The Netherlands

Land Services established in 1994 European Rail Shuttle, which arranged block trains between Northwest European ports and inland terminals. At first, these trains were run by the national railway companies, while later a full subsidiary, ERS Railways, acted as "traction provider" and supplied the rolling stock. In due course, many other private railway companies emerged. Moreover, some freight divisions of the national railway companies merged, this way restructuring intermodal operations on an international scale (e.g. Deutsche Bahn integrated the cargo division of Dutch Railways into Railion).

Important infrastructural decisions to facilitate intermodal transport included Trans European Rail Freight Freeways, which should provide seamless rail connections between countries and included the construction of a dedicated freight rail link between the port of Rotterdam and the German border. In several ports trucking containers to a central rail terminal replaced the inefficient system of hauling container wagons from far flung corners of the port.

Unfortunately, barges still needed to pick up and deliver their containers from various deepsea terminals. Container transport by barge is in Europe especially important for the ports of Antwerp and Rotterdam. After a slow start, inland navigation gained momentum in the mid-1980s. In 1995, around 700,000 TEU were transported via the river Rhine. Belgian and Dutch domestic trades amounted to approximately 250,000 TEU and between Antwerp and Rotterdam about 400,000 TEU were traded, mainly due to relocating of containers (Bill of Lading) and repositioning of empties. These services are provided by independent barge operating companies in coordination with shipping lines, deepsea and inland terminal operators.

In order to carry containers, existing dry bulk barges only needed minor adaptations such as a retractable wheelhouse. Later, specially designed containerships appeared. The 135 m. long and 16.9 m. wide *JOWI* attracted much attention when it was commissioned in 1998 (see Figure 188). This hatchcoverless vessel is equipped with cell guides and in the hold containers can be stowed in six rows next to each other, in total 398 TEU (4 tiers)/470 TEU (5 tiers). Three 675-kw engines, each with a propeller, and two bow thrusters are installed. Since the dimensions do not comply with traditional ECMT-class waterways, the deployment of *JOWI* is restricted to specific routes.

Figure 188: Inland barge JOWI on the river Rhine

Inland navigation is also important for countries in Southeast Asia. In China inland waterway transport moved nearly as much freight and passengers as the railways. The Pearl and Yangtze rivers have considerably impacted economic development. The Pearl River delta was one of the first regions where large-scale foreign investment was allowed, thus becoming a major manufacturing area. Export goods were transported to Hong Kong and neighboring ports and shipped to all corners of the world. Container transshipment in the Yangtze River delta, i.e. Shanghai and Ningbo, started later.

In port development priority was given to true hinterland gateway ports using waterways such as Pearl, Yangtze and Yellow Rivers (Qiantoa and Llanyugang) or main rail/road arteries as the opening to the hinterland. A new coastal north to south (Beijing to Guanzhuo) rail and highway system will have branches to the major coastal ports. New rail lines will also be constructed parallel to the improved Yangtze River. However, fast container "barge trains" linking Wuhan with Nanjing and/or Shanghai with a three to five day delivery service are supposed to be better and cheaper than rail service. The first container block train from Wuhan and other inland locations to Hong Kong, organized by the China and Canton-Kowloon railway in 1996/97, was also not very successful.

The market for inland navigation is characterized by numerous small operators and only a few large barge companies. In the Pearl River Delta a substantial part of container transshipment is not carried out by gantry cranes at a berth, but by self-discharging (un)propelled Derrick barges. In the port of Hong Kong midstream transshipment (to avoid terminal fees) is common practice. The recent opening of new terminals in Shanghai, many miles from the old port and located in deep water, raises questions about the seaworthiness of the existing barge fleet.

Figure 189: Derrick barge in Hong Kong

Inland terminals

Intermodal networks are shaped by establishing inland terminals. They can be owned by railway or barge companies, port authorities, stevedore companies or even regional development agencies. Their primary function is (un)loading and stacking of containers. Later, additional activities such as repair, cleaning and warehousing followed. Inland terminals often act as regional empty depots for shipping lines, and storage for shippers/consignees nearby.

For intermodal rail terminals in the US, it was important that commercial parties got involved. APL had acquired three freight brokerage firms and established subsidiary American President Domestic. They focused on filling the empty containers to the West Coast with domestic freight. This was so successful that 48-ft and 53-ft containers were introduced for domestic use (see Figure 191). In addition, double-stack train services to Canada and Mexico were inaugurated. In 1988 APL also embraced door-to-door truck load transportation called "Red Eagle" service.

Logistics

The point of view of the users of containers i.e. shippers and consignees, is supply chain integration, just-in-time inventory approach and logistics information system management. Manufacturer Philips considers a container with electrical components on a vessel sailing from Singapore to Rotterdam as pipeline inventory and has already planned the time they will be used for appliances.

Some shipping lines tried to offer shippers/forwarders the additional services they need. NYK opened logistic centers and implemented Worldwide Information Network Services for Logistics (WINS) and Nedlloyd introduced Flowmasters® and, in addition, acquired a large road transport company. Bilspedition, by origin a forwarding company, also pos-

Figure 190: Intermodal facility near Chicago

Figure 191: APL 53-ft container

Figure 192: NYK Logistics' warehouse Los Angeles

sessed a comprehensive transport system, including shipping line interests. Manufacturing and trading companies changed over time from ill-informed shippers and forwarders to large organizations that owned adequate market information.

Instead of carrier haulage where the movement of the container from the origin to final destination is under the control of the shipping line, merchant haulage enables a company to take control from the moment the container arrives at the deepsea terminal. Moreover, perceived savings on inland transport costs, which form a significant part of the total costs of container shipping, are within reach. Hence, shipping lines lost more and more control of the transport chain. In the Hamburg-Le Havre port range the percentage of merchant haulage amounted to around 60% in 1996.

IN RETROSPECT

Containership development got a boost when APL decided to widen their vessels so they could carry sixteen containers across on deck. The beam of 39.4 m. was beyond the maximum Panama Canal width and their first series of five Post-Panamax vessels was much debated. On the one hand they were economical to operate, on the other hand they were considered "inflexible". The latter argument was not valid for APL mainly a transpacific shipping line with an extensive network for double stack container services. In general, their experiences with the new C10-class vessels were positive. Nevertheless it took some time before other shipping lines commissioned Post-Panamax containerships generally with a length of 275 m., a beam of just over 37 m. and a container carrying capacity up to 4,500 TEU. From 1995 on, longer and wider Post-Panamax containerships were built. Due to their characteristics terminals had to be adapted and container cranes modified or replaced.

At the same time Panamax vessels were considerably modified. By decreasing the width of the double hull and eliminating the longitudinal hatch girders, the Panamax containerships could carry eleven (instead of ten) containers across in the holds. Nedlloyd went a step further and launched a hatchcoverless vessel. The basic idea was to extend the cell guides upwards to embrace all containers and to remove the hatch covers. The port turnaround time was significantly reduced which particularly paid off in the feeder and shortsea trades. However, this benefit was offset by higher port and canal fees due to their augmented Gross Register Tonnage (compared to equivalent TEU-capacity ships) and by their increased lightship weight (lower payload).

In this period the container liner shipping industry went (again) through a period of reshuffling. A number of companies withdrew either forced or voluntarily. Well established shipping lines (e.g. EAC, Cunard, Ben Line and Yamashita-Shinnihon) as well as newcomers (e.g. Trans Freight Lines, Korea Shipping Corporation) disappeared from the scene. Other shipping lines were looking for partnerships: Slot and Vessel Sharing Agreements, joint ventures, mergers or takeovers. Although the dissolution of the Europe-Far East consortia played a key role in this process of reorientation, the reshuffling actually started in the transpacific trade. The three remaining Japanese shipping lines formed new partnerships in the Pacific Rim and joined the remaining members of the TRIO, ScanDutch and ACE-consortia. In this way worldwide operating alliances were established. Worth mentioning is also Cho Yang that joined the round-the-world service of DSR/Senator line and formed Tricon. Yet bilateral collaboration between shipping lines such as K Line and Yang Ming or Sea-Land and Maersk were fruitful too.

Cooperation between shipping lines is a form of horizontal integration and took place from the moment containerization began to spread. In this period vertical integration i.e. taking more control of the transport chain is apparent in offering intermodal services (e.g. double-stack trains) and operating deepsea and inland terminals. APL was a frontrunner in this respect. The CSX railroad company acquiring Sea-Land and Bilspedition buying out the other members of the ACL-consortium are examples of other transport companies taking control of the whole transport chain. However, these assets were often sold when the companies experienced difficult financial times.

The point of view of the users of transport, i.e. manufacturing and trading companies, is different: transport as part of supply chain integration. Instead of carrier haulage when the shipping line is in control, merchant haulage enables a company to manage the cargo from the moment the container arrives at the deepsea terminal. Only a few shipping lines offered shippers/forwarders the value added logistics services they needed. Hence others took control of part of the transport chain and merchant haulage became increasingly popular.

CHAPTER 10

CONTAINER QUAY CRANES
Big is Beautiful

Decades before 1956, various types of unitized cargo (barrels, bales and small containers), were handled by dockside or floating cranes or ship's gear. On the shore side, all kinds of cranes were used varying from simple revolving cranes (in the US called "Whirley" cranes) to more complex double link level-luffing cranes, providing a horizontal load path. Especially in Europe there were many manufacturers who developed level luffing cranes with interesting mechanisms to provide a horizontal load path (Kampnagel, Figee, Caillard and Stothert & Pitt, etc.). However both the lifting capacities and outreaches were limited with regard to unitized cargo loads and vessel beams (e.g. 5 tons at 25 m.). Loads in excess of 25 tons were usually considered as heavy lifts, requiring special equipment.

Figure 193: Portal crane, handling rail cars at Seatrain's Hoboken Pier

In the US it was common use to dock cargo vessels alongside a pier and handle the cargo with the vessel's on-board gear. Remarkably, already in 1929, Seatrain Lines Inc. (US) introduced a specially developed gearless vessel, capable of carrying about 100 railcars on 4 decks, fitted with railroad tracks. The railcars were lifted on board with dock-mounted portal cranes, handling the railcars with the help of special cradles. Some cranes even had a double outreach enabling the handling of two vessels alongside one pier, as shown for Seatrain's Hoboken Facility in New-York (see Figure 193). These cranes already showed some functionality later to be recognized in container cranes. Three decades after their introduction, Seatrain still used these cranes for container handling at the start of Seatrain's container services in the 1960s.

10.1. EARLY CONTAINER CRANES FOR DECADES OF USE

The first, small containers, used by the White Pass & Yukon Railways, were handled by the ship's gear (such as the married fall system or the Ebel rig system). This type of ship-to-shore container handling continued throughout the 1960s and 1970s when many containers were carried as deck-load on general cargo and breakbulk vessels. For the handling of their first 30' containers, Ocean Van lines installed a special revolving crane on-board their vessel. However, it still used simple slings and was time and labor consuming (see Figure 194).

Figure 194: On-board crane, handling with rope slings

When Sea-Land (Pan-Atlantic) started its first services with the *Ideal X* and its sister vessels, the containers were handled with traditional Whirley cranes, which offered sufficient lifting capacity and were readily available. The first revolving cranes used in Newark and Houston (1956) were lowered in height and modified (an activity of Bob Gottlieb, crane consultant) to accommodate the first automated spreader (see Figure 195), purposely developed by Keith Tantlinger.

Figure 195: Sea-Land automated spreader (design Tantlinger)

Within a year and a half, Malcom McLean introduced the converted C2-class vessels with a 226 35' container capacity. For those vessels Sea-Land selected another way of ship-to-shore container handling: the shipboard crane with foldable hinged outriggers. This concept was applied earlier for general cargo handling on-board the *Sea Hawk* (1946, in a pilot for efficiency improvement); an alternative was called the extendable overhead cargo gear (see Figure 196).

Figure 196: Onboard gear for general cargo (left portal type; right extendable on dock)

The innovative engineering skills from Keith Tantlinger and Bob Gottlieb (from Ewin, Campbell and Gottlieb, Engineering Consultants contracted by Sea-Land) and the driving force from Malcom McLean with his demands for short delivery times (in this case 90 days!), resulted in the first purpose built shipboard cranes, fitted with a machinery trolley and a new "automatic" spreader with tiltable container guides. Sea-Land selected Skaget Steel and Iron Works (Sedro-Wooley, Washington), a manufacturer of logging equipment who could provide the short delivery time and could cope with the demanding Sea-Land staff and engineering consultants. In the first crane, while being positioned, the operator was "riding the spreader" in a small cabin mounted on the spreader. In later designs (Sea-Land eventually had more than 40 of such cranes on board of converted vessels) the cabin was mounted to the trolley (see Figure 197).

Figure 197: Shipboard cranes with operator cabin on spreader (left) or on trolley (right)

Obviously, this type of shipboard cranes allowed Sea-Land to call at any port with a quay wall and a small apron. There was no investment required for crane rail tracks, dockside cranes and power supply (when the ships were in port, they had sufficient power available). The onboard positioning was precise, however when handling a box onto a chassis on dock, heavy boxes caused some listing of the vessel, hampering a fast positioning. On top of that, the extra crane's deadweight negatively affected the ship's stability and load capacity. The advantage of independency from dock facilities was clearly shown when the Houston Shipping Canal was blocked and Sea-Land could offload the cargo at a different location.

By the end of 1957, when Sea-Land commissioned its first shipboard cranes, Matson, the other pioneer in containerization, took a different approach. Matson's research and development staff studied the best container handling methods and selected dockside cranes. However, they concluded that the crane with sufficient productivity did not exist. So the Matson staff made up their own crane specifications, based on the functional requirements for vessels with a maximum beam of 80 ft (25 m.) and a maximum cycle time of 5 minutes for one load-off/load-on cycle (is dual cycle). Leslie Harlander, department manager of Matson's engineering group, contracted Vietsch Engineering (San Leandro, California) where his brother Don Harlander (project engineer) together with Murray Montgomery (later working for Paceco) prepared a study. The team concluded that bulk handling cranes came closer to the crane Matson needed (horizontal boom; through-leg trolley) and they mentioned cranes from Industrial Brownhoist, Pacific Coast Engineering Co (Paceco), Washington Iron works and others (see Figure 198).

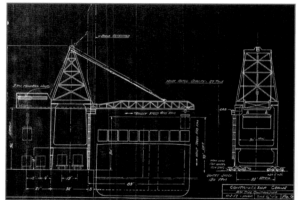 

Figure 198: Matson purchasing specs and example bulk handling crane (Ind. Brownhoist)

In the specifications, the team put emphasis on speed and load control and they selected a rope driven trolley and a reeving system with anti-sway features. The rope-driven (also called rope-towed) trolley resulted in minimal wheel loads on the quay wall, an important characteristic as the crane was planned for a crane track on timber piles. Furthermore, cranes should be fully electrically driven with the latest technology for automatic field weakening in the main hoist motors and semi-automatic position control for hoist and trolley travel. The first crane was contracted to Paceco and was installed at Matson's Encinal Terminal, close to the former Kaiser Shipyard at Alameda, where it was put into service on January 7, 1959 (see Figure 199). Today this crane is a US national historic landmark of mechanical engineering.

The major crane characteristics for this first dockside container crane are presented in Figure 209, later in this chapter where a comparison is provided for container cranes, installed between 1959 and 2011. Later, Matson installed similar types of cranes in Honolulu and Los Angeles.

Already during the first years, a sustained performance of 20-25 containers was realized. This first crane was the base for many more so-called A-frame type cranes installed during the 1960s and 1970s, not only by Paceco and its licensees, but also by European and Japanese crane manufacturers (see Figure 200).

Figure 199: First on-dock container crane specified by Matson, manufactured by Paceco

Figure 200: Various early A-type cranes (Paceco, Boomsche metaalwerken, top, IHI, Mitsubishi)

Development of Containerization

Matson's design team was the trendsetter for the container quay crane and almost everyone, including Sea-Land, followed their approach: a portal type frame with a horizontal main girder and a hinged boom (to be hoisted when the crane was out of operation and avoid vessel collisions).

The introduction of the SL-7 program by Sea-Land resulted in the so-called "modified A-frame" types, suitable for 50', 80' and 100' crane rail gages. Sea-Land developed a crane purchasing program wherein all their cranes were specified in great detail. Crane specifications were generally prepared by knowledgeable engineering consultants, like McKay Engineers and Michael Jordan. They detailed all major functional requirements, some general arrangement drawings, a load-on/load-off scheme for commissioning tests and many engineering details both for the mechanical, electrical and structural design and for the manufacture and erection. In this respect, US companies like Sea-Land, Matson and Seatrain were ahead of starting-up terminals in Europe, Australia and Japan. In those regions it was common use that companies in need of cranes invited a number of renowned crane manufacturers (Caillard, Conrad-Stork, Demag, Kocks, Krupp, MAN, Mitsubishi, Peiner and Stothert & Pitt, etc.), and exchanged thoughts about operational demands and major characteristics, after which the manufacturers returned with their proposals, including all design details, component selections.

Figure 201: From A-frame to modified A-frame (50 ft, left) and with enlarged rail span (100 ft, right)

At the start of containerization in Europe, this approach was continued and many of the first generation cranes (built between 1967 and 1974) were designed and manufactured by well-established European crane manufacturers in a variety of concepts: box girders, lattice girders (triangular and trapezium), double box girders, rope driven trolleys, machinery trolleys, Ward-Leonard drives, thyristor-controlled drives, etc. The manufacturing series were quite small and many crane manufacturers had difficulties in meeting delivery times and world market prices.

Paceco, the successful US West Coast crane builder, contracted a number of licensees (both in Europe: Vickers Ltd UK, Fruehauf Spain and in Asia: Mitsui) and offered very competitive prices for A-frame and modified A-frame types of cranes. Unfortunately, some terminals in Europe were disappointed by the quality of the products from such Paceco-licensees, although it must be acknowledged that some crane contracts were awarded at very competitive prices that could not be met by local or other West-European crane builders maintaining their regular quality standards. Some terminals were disappointed about the quality of such cheap cranes and learned fast. They realized that you get what you specified, which was a problem for many European terminals not acquainted with detailed purchasing specs. Moreover, European crane subcontractors misunderstood engineering specifications from US origin, which resulted in under-designed components. ECT, Rotterdam was one of those terminals who expected to receive a Paceco crane with Sea-Land quality. However the product delivered by Vickers Ltd, (with a Siemens electrical system, erected by Rigging International and provided with many components from unknown subcontractors) was far below Sea-Land's quality demands (which could be noticed in ECT's company, where Sea-Land operated 4 cranes designed and manufactured on Sea-Land's own US-based specs).

ECT went for arbitration and, after many years, won in court. But there was only one real winner: a team of lawyers and engineering experts. In the 1970s and 1980s, a number of terminals learned the hard way that one needs proper crane specifications, not only the functional characteristics but also design details. In those years, a small group of crane consultants recognized the need for expertise on the purchasing side, especially there, where quay loading restrictions and other site characteristics (hurricanes, clearance profile around airports) were imperative. In this respect, Liftech Consultants should be mentioned, a company managed by engineers like Michael Jordan, who introduced all kinds of new designs both conceptual and for crane components. Low profile cranes, articulated booms, snag devices, sway control systems, etc. were designed and specified by Liftech and subsequently further detailed and manufactured by crane builders all over the world.

Figure 202: Low profile cranes for airport areas: articulated boom (top) and sliding boom

During the 1970s, in many ports, hundreds of new larger cranes were installed. The reason was obvious; much larger vessels (Panamax, 13 containers wide on deck, deeper hulls; 3-5 tiers of stacked containers on deck) and demands for higher productivity. Paceco became a leading company, able to offer competitive prices, partly because of its simple design and the large series ordered by Sea-Land. In Europe, this strong competition from Paceco (and later crane builders in Japan and Korea) caused that several well known crane manufacturers did not survive due to strong competition and much lower demand for general purpose level-luffing cranes. For instance, Demag pulled out in the 1970s after the unsuccessful bidding for four cranes for ECT (won by Paceco-Vickers). Other manufacturers, like

Caillard, MAN, and Stothert & Pitt, also withdrew from the very marginal (and often loss generating) container crane business.

The introduction of the 3,000+ TEU container vessels during the 1970s induced a further upgrade of container quay cranes. Sea-Land improved its SL-7 type cranes with features such as split trolley (for better sway control) and increased main hoist and trolley travel speeds. However, the installed higher technical crane handling capacity did not result in a significant increase in operational handling capacity (disturbances from vessel characteristics, waiting for information, load sway, etc.). This recognition made some terminal operators decide to analyze in depth their waterside handling operations, resulting in the awareness that very often the landside organization (stacking system and transportation system between the stacking yard and the quay cranes) could not fulfill the demand to deliver or receive containers in the required timing and sequencing (a failure to feed the hook). It took some years before crane productivity became recognized as a waterside system characteristic.

10.2.   INCREASING CRANE DIMENSIONS: A VESSEL'S DICTATE!

Until the 1970s, many container cranes had truss-type booms with rope driven trolley. However, box girder cranes with machinery trolley attracted increasingly more interest due to their simple design and assumed lower maintenance cost (fewer sheaves, shorter ropes). Obviously, the ever larger vessels (still within Panamax dimensions) required an increased lifting height (rising from 25 m. to approximately 30 m.), although that did not significantly change crane dimensions. Only the hoist and trolley drive speeds increased by sometimes more than 50% and the lift capacity rose towards 50 tons.

The rather controlled developments in container quay crane design ended with the announcement of US Lines' Jumbo-class vessels (Econships). In 1983, the first concerns were raised on the impact of the potential introduction of Post-Panamax vessels, which made some terminal operators decide to specify cranes with an increased outreach. ECT Rotterdam was the first company to order quay cranes suited for handling vessels with boxes 16-wide on deck. Lifting height was increased as well, due to the larger number of container tiers on deck. Despite the larger dimensions for lifting range and outreach, crane width had to be kept below 27 m, because of operational reasons such as maximum flexibility to serve alternate hatches. Obviously, this design requirement had considerable consequences for wheel loads, provisions for crane stability (e.g. stop blocks between sill beam and main equalizers) in gantry travel direction and of course quay wall loads (rail track).

To increase stability in trolley travel direction, without adding ballast, ECT increased the rail span towards 35 m. This wider rail span was followed by other terminal operators (5-10 years later). In the summer of 1984, the first Post-Panamax cranes were commissioned in the port of Rotterdam (ECT). Surprisingly, this was criticized by many experts stating that the investment was a waste of money, as US Lines' Econships remained within the Panamax Canal dimensions. It should be noted that the larger structural dimensions of these cranes increased overall crane cost by less than 5%.

As foreseen and predicted by leading naval architects like Gene Pentimonti (APL) and Ernest Vossnack (Nedlloyd), the first Post-Panamax vessels arrived earlier than most people expected (Post-Panamax ships do not need to carry large amounts of ballast water to maintain proper seakeeping). After the demise of US Lines in 1986, the shipping world was surprised by APL who launched the first Post-Panamax vessels (C10 President Truman-class) with a 39.4 m. beam (16 containers wide on deck) two years later in 1988 (see Figure 203).

In Europe ECT Delta was the only terminal that could serve these 16-wide Post-Panamax vessels, however, to maintain their competitiveness all major ports reacted immediately and within 2 years more than 20 ports installed new cranes with a larger outreach, while many other ports introduced extensive crane raise and boom extension programs.

By the end of the 1980s, it became clear that the increased crane dimensions (outreach, lifting height, higher stacks on deck) resulted in longer crane cycle times and thus lower crane handling productivity (contrary to the favorable scale effects in vessel operating cost). Already in 1988, the innovative Hans Tax proposed new designs to improve the productivity. One design incorporated a height-adjustable main girder, to reduce the pendulum length (better positioning), when at deck-level and below deck and when working smaller (feeder) vessels and barges (see Figure 204).

Figure 203: First Post-Panamax cranes at ECT and APL vessel

This concept could also be provided with a "transfer trolley" to carry containers from the waterside trolley to a landside buffer platform or landside trolley. However, the rather conservative world of port authorities and risk-avoiding terminal operators did not embrace this idea. Innovators like VIT (Virginia) and ECT (Rotterdam) maintained their philosophy for second-trolley systems, and improved yard back-up operations.

But already within 8 years a new stir touched the crane design world. In 1996, Maersk introduced the Regina Maersk-class (17-wide and 6 tiers on deck, 320 m. long), later followed by the larger Sovereign Maersk-class (346 m. long). This required further enlargements in outreach and lifting height. Terminal operators, consult-

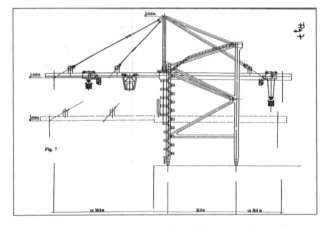

Figure 204: Crane with height adjustable main girder and tower

ants and manufacturers had to manage a boom in structural modifications in quay cranes (crane raise, boom elongations and strengthening) and, again, high investments. The demands for productivity improvements continued and that stimulated crane manufacturers and consultants to come up with new designs (see section 10.4).

During the summer of 1995, Dave Rudolph (VIT's director of engineering) voiced his interest in buying cranes with an elevating main girder. Kone took up the challenge and in the same year presented conceptual drawings for such crane. Although designed with an alternative girder lifting concept, this crane was in principal the same as previously proposed by Hans Tax. Unfortunately for the early innovators (Tax, Kone), VIT postponed the purchase of such crane until 2003 and was then built by ZPMC, the Chinese crane manufacturer who within only a few years captured an impressive market share (see Figure 205).

Figure 205: ZPMC crane at VIT (Virginia) with elevating main girder up (left) and down

Talking about ZPMC, it has been astonishing how fast this Chinese crane manufacturer was able to enlarge its market share. In 1996, it had only 7 cranes on order, while in 1998 it had 20 already. In the summer of 2001, their order book exceeded 100 cranes, while during 2006 ZPMC delivered no less than 244 cranes. In the twenty years up until the end of 2011, ZPMC had built 2000 cranes of which 1000 during the last 4 years. The ZMPC plant in the Shanghai region expanded tremendously by more than 3 km of quay line to erect, test and load cranes onto their own transport vessels (modified tankers). Especially after 2000, ZPMC took a more innovative approach, sometimes triggered by customers presenting their own designs (supported by consultants like Liftech, Casper, Gottlieb and McKay) and in other cases from examples shown by terminals e.g. the Noell Cranes for Burchardkai, Hamburg and the elevating crane at VIT, originally designed by Konecranes.

Obviously the drive of ZPMC to become the world's crane manufacturer had tremendous consequences for the established crane builders all over the world. In the beginning of the 1990s, there were still about 30 quay crane manufacturers (for a combined annual output of about 175 cranes), but in 2006 almost 15 of these crane manufacturers had disappeared or merged. High labor cost, limited economies of scale (overhead cost!) and unfavorable production locations caused manufacturers in Europe, US and Japan to stop their crane building activities. Well-known names such as Boomsche Metaalwerken, Morris, Ansaldo, Caillard, MAN, Conrad-Stork (later Nelcon), Star Cranes, Alliance, Sumitomo and IHI disappeared after decades. The impressive expansion of containerization in China and other Far Eastern regions helped the Chinese crane manufacturers Dalian Heavy Industry, Shanghai Port Machinery Plant and ZPMC to gain more than a combined 80% of the world market; leaving the remainder to about 10 other manufacturers.

In the 1990s, the sky-line of container cranes with their booms stowed in an 80 degree position, changed when APL decided to put the cranes of their new LA facility in a 45 degrees position. This reduced cycle time (boom-up/boom-down) and also avoided boom latches and related limit-switches (a regular cause of breakdowns). Moreover, it improved crane stability, especially for incoming storm loads at the boom side. The APL initiative was followed by many others, particularly in the US (see Figure 206).

Figure 206: Cranes with booms in 45 degrees-stowed position (Port of Long Beach)

In 2000, the idea of significantly larger container vessels further emerged. Experts like McLellan and Wijnolst had already published feasibility studies on 20-26 wide container vessels and Wijnolst and Waals introduced the Malacca-max-class (18,000 TEU). In 2001, there were strong rumors that Maersk was at the brink of ordering a series of four vessels of between 10,000 and 12,500 TEU, to be built by their Odense shipyard. From that year on, terminals, and especially the terminals managed (owned) by APM Terminals (an AP Møller-Maersk subsidiary) started to order cranes with an outreach for 22-wide container vessels and a lifting height above the quay of more than 40 m. (see Figure 207). Between 2003 and 2006 more than 350 cranes with 22-wide outreach capability were installed in major ports over the world. In September 2006, the *Emma Maersk* (the first Maersk mastodon out of a series of 8 vessels) came into service, officially announced for a capacity of 11,000 TEU, but in fact estimated at 14,600 TEU (and later upgraded to 15,600 TEU).

Other shipping lines, like CMA CGM, Cosco, China Shipping and MSC, invested in 9,500-10,500-TEU vessels, but these were still limited to 18-wide containers on deck. Until 2010, almost 10 shipping lines introduced 20-wide ships (ca. 13,000 TEU). This new wave of ultra large containerships (ULCS > 10,000 TEU) has continued up till 2011. As a result of Maersk's investment program in even larger vessels, the Triple-E-class, this will go on for at least another decade. These 18,000-TEU vessels have a beam of 58 m. (23 containers wide), carry 7,000 TEU under deck and 11,000 TEU on deck. By

Figure 207: Crane type suited for 10,000+ TEU-vessels

December 2011, there were already more than 120 ULCS units in service and still more than 170 on order. This forced terminal operators to invest in even larger cranes or modify existing ones to accommodate these large ships, to improve their service (berth performance) and to reduce their cost. The demand for terminal cost reductions was very advantageous for ZPMC, the cost leader in cranes.

Some terminals expect even larger ships e.g. Eurogate tendered for cranes capable of handling vessels with containers 25-wide on deck (69 m. outreach) for their JadeWeserport, Wilhelmshaven. There are even rumors about a 72+ m. outreach. By the end of 2011 the lifting heights reached 50 m. and some ports have installed cranes with a lifting capacity of 120 tons or more (see Figure 208), to allow tandem lift and/or operating double main trolleys.

The deadweight of cranes went up (sometimes close to 2,500 tons) and together with the higher lifting loads, this caused increased corner loads on the quay wall.

Many quay wall designs had to be upgraded in the past and this will continue in the coming years. The larger vessels have initiated these higher loads, forthcoming from wheel loads from the cranes, the increased water depth (vessel draft), the higher bollard loads and the increased fender loads (indeed a considerable cost impact for ports all over the world).

Figure 208: 120-tons crane with two trolleys

Figure 209 shows the developments of major crane characteristics during the period 1959-2010. The load moment went up more than 11-fold (from 576 to more than 6,500 ton-meters) and the crane deadweight increased more than 6-fold (from 325 to more than 2,000 tons).

Characteristics	Type of Crane; Year of Introduction					
	Matson; 1959	Panamax; 1972	Panamax; 1977	Post P.Max; 1990	Super P.Max; 2006	State of the Art; 2011
Outreach from center w.s.rail	24m; 78ft	34m	37,5m	45m	65m	65-72m
Rail Gage	10.4m; 34ft	15.2m./50ft	30,5m./100ft	30-35m	30-35m	30-42m
Backreach from center l.s.rail	8m; 24ft	15m	18m	15-20m	15-20m	15-25m
Lifting Capacity [metric tons]	24	40	50	60	100	100-140
Lifting Height above Apron [m]	15,5	22	25	32	42-48	45-50
Hoist Speed (full/empty) [m./min]	30/160	30/75	50/120	65/125	75/150	90-180
Trolley Travel Speed [m./min]	125	150	180	175/225	225-375	240-375
Gantry Travel Speed [m./min]	45	45	45	45	45	45
Boom Lift (from oper. pos. to stow. pos.) [min]	2,5	5-6	4-5	5	5	5
Crane Dead Weight [tons]	±325	±550	±750	±1000	±1500	±2250
Corner Load [tons]	±100	±275	±425	±525	±700	±850

Figure 209: Developments in crane characteristics (1959-2011)

10.3. BIG IS BEAUTIFUL; SMALL CAN BE SMART

The developments of container vessel size forced about 100 ports to follow with the dimensions of their quayside container cranes (outreach and lifting height above dock). However, only a limited part of the annual throughput is realized through such large vessels. And, besides the top hundred ports, there are a thousand other deepsea ports that do not handle the high end of vessel sizes and thus can do with smaller cranes.

Many regional and feeder ports and certainly terminals with mixed operations (general cargo, breakbulk and containers) have a moderate utilization of their cranes (1,000-2,000 operating hours per year). Then the considerable investments in expensive container cranes, rail tracks, power supply and quay wall infrastructure cause relatively-high operating cost (depreciations, interest and maintenance). This made many terminal operators search for low-cost cranes. Already in the 1970s, some crane manufacturers presented light-weight container quay cranes with limited outreach and lifting range and reduced demands for infrastructure and power supply (Paceco and Kocks).

Another approach came from Europe, where the mobile harbor crane was developed in the 1960s by Gottwald. This type of universal crane was successfully further developed in the 1970s and 1980s and is now common use in many ports, because of its ability to move between berths, the self-sustaining characteristics from the on-board diesel generator set and because it does not require expensive infrastructure (see Figure 210).

Figure 210: Mobile harbor cranes used all over the world (courtesy Gottwald)

This resulted in lower total cost of ownership, often with a reduction of 25-50% compared with a standard portal type container crane (percentage depends on type and utilization rate). The large outreach of up to 45 m. outside the fender face and the ability to handle twin-lift made the mobile harbor crane attractive for the regular handling of Panamax vessels, feeders and barges and as a back-up for the large portal cranes (capable of handling vessels with 18 containers wide on deck). The circular reach proved to be of interest for terminals with a limited quay wall length and a large number of feeders or barges, with a relatively low number of containers per call (0-50). When berthed side by side (up to 5 barges), all barges can be served (see Figure 211). An additional advantage is the heavy-lift capacity up to 200 ton (or 400 when working with two cranes in tandem), which outperforms the maximum lift capacity of a container quay crane with about 100 tons.

Figure 211: Barge operations in Antwerp

It is not surprising that the mobile harbor crane became used in many ports all over the world; both for deepsea operations (see Figure 212) and for inland terminals. The short delivery lead-time (< 6 month), the potential of a simple transfer from one port to another and the possibility of favorable financial arrangements made many terminals decide for this type of crane.

Figure 212: Mobile harbor crane for container (Riviera Beach, Florida, left) and mixed operations (Antwerp)

Already in the 1970s, terminal operators noticed the disadvantages of large portal cranes when handling feeders and barges or when cost savings could be achieved from combining vessel handling and storage close to the quay wall under the crane. Lifting heights of over 25 m. resulted in more complications with sway control, especially when working on shortsea vessels and barges. This resulted in a range of small container quay cranes with lifting heights of 15-20 m. and the ability for stacking within the crane's gauge (see Figure 213).

Figure 213: Feeder and barge cranes (Nelcon, left; Noell and Konecranes, right)

When reviewing the development of ship-to-shore container cranes, the focus always has been on the size and productivity of such cranes. But, from an economics and operations point of view, the small portal crane or mobile harbor crane proved to be an attractive alternative for hundreds of deepsea ports and all inland terminals. Many terminal operators experienced that big might be beautiful but not for them. For their operations small proved to be smart!

10.4. DEVELOPMENTS SUPPORTING CRANE PRODUCTIVITY

Right from the beginning of containerization, crane productivity has been a key issue. Matson's development team studied the first Sea-Land operations and they specified a dock-mounted crane capable of about 25 crane cycles per hour. Already in the first decade it became clear that crane productivity was at the one side determined by hoist and trolley drive characteristics, but at the other side by a number of less controllable topics. Load control (container sway and/or skewing) was important to position a container onto a road (or terminal) chassis or to place a container into a vessel cell or on a stack of containers on deck. Obviously, the crane operator's visibility and his comfort and ergonomics in the cabin also influenced the possibilities to get a good productivity. When the terminals got bigger a major issue came up: transportation of containers from the shore side container crane to the yard and vice versa. The American expression for this was: "You need to feed to hook" stating the importance of guaranteeing a proper connecting transport. However, the partly stochastic crane handling cycle time and the many disturbances in the crane connected handling processes did limit an increase of productivity, regardless the continuing growth in crane hoist and trolley speeds and accelerations/decelerations.

In order to get a more productive crane cycle, Sea-Land and Matson introduced dual-cycling, being a combined load-on and load-off handling cycle. Especially in the first 2 decades that was a considerable contribution to productivity, hence most of the containers were stowed under deck in cells and after emptying one cell, dual-cycling was possible over the entire hatch. Vessels with a large number of equal container bays (like the Sea-Land SL-18-class) and moderate stowage height on deck were very attractive for dual cycling, regularly showing productivities larger than 30 container moves per crane hour.

Growing vessel sizes (requiring higher cranes, causing more load sway) encouraged terminal operators and crane manufacturers to come up with provisions to improve productivity. In the 1970s, Paceco introduced a split-trolley allowing a change in reeving angle (more stable) when the spreader was above the cell guides.

In 1972, ECT installed chassis-loader systems at their quay cranes at the landside sill-beam to speed-up the loading of containers (see Figure 214). These container guiding systems were designed to lower the container onto a chassis and to position the chassis (connected to a tractor, putting its gearbox in neutral position) in length direction, just by embracing the chassis. Although

Figure 214: Chassis-loader at ECT Home Terminal

this was an improvement in productivity, service demands from shipping lines and cost control asked for further productivity increases. The ECT engineering team then introduced a multi trailer train (5 rubber-tired 40'/2 x 20' chassis behind the tractor) and when this train was under the crane up till ten 20' boxes could be delivered to or received from the crane.

In 1977, ECT installed three heavy-duty cranes (still in operation in 2012) with Post-Panamax boom length, a chassis loader system at different positions within the rail gauge (to ensure "every crane its own lane" for undisturbed traffic) and prepared for a fully-automated second trolley system (see Figure 215). This second trolley system was developed by ECT and a first prototype was installed in 1979 on one of these cranes (see Figure 216).

Figure 215: 100' cranes at ECT with chassis-loader and 1st prototype 2nd trolley system (right)

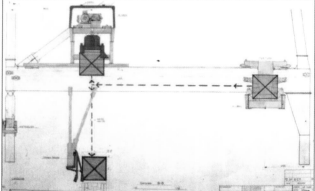

Figure 216: 2nd trolley crane with multi-trailer at ECT (right: schematic)

The crane cycle got divided into two parts; the first waterside part remained a conventional operator controlled cycle between vessel hatch and a platform at about 12 m. height, close to the waterside rail; the second landside part became an automated cycle bringing the container via the moving platform and a fixed hoist near the landside rail onto a chassis at dock-level. The unmanned, fully automated second part of the crane cycle was PLC-controlled and provided with numerous interlockings to become "fool-prove".

The second trolley system raised great interest from many terminal operators, however it took several years before others applied the same or similar systems. APL made full size trials (with chassis loader and multi-trailer trains) at their Oakland facility and the OHI-terminal in Tokyo and the Brani Terminal in Singapore installed a chassis loader system and second-trolley system, built by Sumitomo/IHI, licensed from the ECT design.

In the US the resistance from labor unions blocked a further application at that time and in Tokyo and Singapore maintenance shortcomings and a lack of understanding about the interaction between second-trolley system and waterside transportation caused resistance and doubts about the economics of a second-trolley system. In the early 1980s, VIT (Virginia International Terminal, US) further developed the second-trolley system with the introduction of an elevated, vertically adjustable platform and a sway-controlled second hoist system in the crane's back side (see Figure 217).

Figure 217: 2nd trolley crane with elevating platform (VIT, Virginia)

Both ECT and VIT had the opinion that their second-trolley systems brought a 15-20% improvement on their ship-to-shore container handling. However, one major issue was still at stake: how to feed the hook? Measures like pre-stacking and assigning more tractor/trailers to a crane were applied and ECT introduced the multi-trailer system (MTS) presenting 5 x 40-ft or 10 x 20-ft containers under the crane in one transportation cycle.

It should be noted that indeed the second-trolley systems decreased the stochastic nature of crane cycle times, which was an advantage for the back-up transportation system (less queuing). In practice the increased crane productivity from the second-trolley cranes was sometimes eroded by the increased downtime, forthcoming from the additional second-trolley drives, interlocking and PLC-checker interface, controlling the automatic second trolley cycle.

Some terminal operators tried to increase crane productivity using twin-lift and/or dual-cycling. Twin-lift spreaders were introduced to handle two 20' containers in one crane cycle. Dual cycling (one container discharged and one container loaded during one crane cycle) was applied as well, although such an operation can only serve less than 50% of the vessel call volume.

Figure 218: Early twin-lift cranes with two separate hoist drives (for two 20'-spreaders, or one 40' spreader)

The first twin-lift cranes (to handle two 20-ft containers in one crane cycle) were already introduced between 1969 and 1971 in the UK-Australia trade at the OCL-managed terminals. Two 20-ft spreaders, each connected to their own hoist drive, could be positioned in adjacent 20-ft ship cells (see Figure 218). Later, during the 1980s, twin-lift spreaders became popular through the potential productivity improvement of about 20-50%. But now the twin-lift spreader was connected to one main hoist drive and the lift capacity increased to approximately 65 tons on the cables. To ensure one-by-one transportation using straddle carriers, Stinis introduced the so-called Long-Twin spreader in 1997 (see Figure 219). This spreader allows shifting the 20' containers aside with a gap of 1.5 m. in between.

In 1994, Paceco proposed his Supertainer Crane (see Figure 220) with an intermediate basket ("traverser") running between a shore side trolley and landside trolley (rather equal to the earlier shown Hans Tax concepts), but so far this concept has not been realized.

Reggiane launched its Octopus System (April 1995) with the objective to faster handle the containers between the vessel and a mechanized land based transport system (Figure 221). For 15 years, there were no applications but the Fastnet concept published by Maersk during 2008-2011 shows some similarities.

Figure 219: Long-Twin spreader for twin-lift with adjustable gap

Already in the late 1980s, considerations were made (ECT, amongst others) about a future possibility to berth a container vessel in an indented dock (slip dock), allowing craneage from both sides to work on the vessel (see Figure 222).

The aim was to increase berth productivity by assigning more cranes per vessel (for instance 8-10 cranes, the half from each side) without too much interference from the crane's gantry width. The concept did not receive much enthusiasm from the major terminals. However, almost 10 years later (end of the 1990s) the Port of Amsterdam, together with Ceres Terminals (US) and terminal consultant JWD (Jordan, Woodman and Dobson) convinced the Amsterdam City Council to invest in a new slip dock concept. That concept should attract shipping lines with a demand for increased berth productivity, a service the new Ceres Terminal could offer. The concept was realized (see Figure 223), but never became a big success. The access to the port of Amsterdam via a lock system was not attractive and also the hinterland connections were rather limited and these drawbacks could not be compensated by the potential higher berth productivity. It is still

Figure 220: Paceco's Supertainer Crane

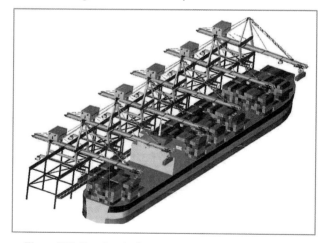

Figure 221: Reggiane's Octopus system with elevated cranes

doubtful whether this concept will ever become attractive when looking to the increased cost of infrastructure, the berthing constraints (tug boats and bunkering), and the limitations in vessel beam width after the selection of the dock width.

In 1999, three large cranes were installed at the new HHLA Burchardkai modified quay wall (in front of the existing outdated one). These cranes were designed by Noell and also provided with a second trolley system (see Figure 224).

Moreover, there was an elevated platform with two container (buffer) positions to connect the main trolley with the second trolley. The platform had provisions to allow the handling of SATLs (Semi-Automated Twist Lock Stackers) or sometimes called IBC's (Inter Box Connectors). It should be remembered that these SATLs were introduced to cater for a much safer lashing on the vessel's deck. However, on the landside the SATLs caused quite some delays in the quay crane-handling cycle. Fixed elevated platforms proved to be helpful to limit the delays (and avoid unsafe situations at dock level), especially when the second part of the crane cycle could be automated. HHLA selected a 35 m. rail span, just like ECT in the mid-1980s, an advantage to limit wheel loads, which were growing due to the increased crane mass (up to 1600 tons). Later, HHLA installed such cranes on the automated Container Terminal Altenwerder, but unfortunately for Noell the contract for the CTA cranes was awarded to ZMPC.

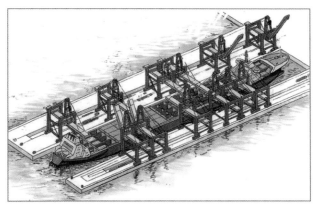

Figure 222: Early concept for 2-sided handling (Rudolf Das, ECT)

Figure 223: Indented dock at Ceres Terminal, Amsterdam

Figure 224: Cranes at Hamburg with machinery trolley and 2nd trolley (Burchardkai, left, and CTA, right)

During the 1990s, the number of 40' and 45' containers further increased and that made some terminal operators and crane manufacturers decide to install tandem-lift cranes that could handle two 40' containers side-by-side, carried below one single hoist trolley. For load stability reasons and to place the container with some spacing on the dock, special spreaders and head-blocks had to be developed. Bromma and Stinis were the first spreader manufacturers who came up with special headblock/spreader arrangements. Stinis patented in 2003 a so-called split head block (see Figure 225), an arrangement later copied by several others (Cargotec, RAM and ZPMC).

Figure 225: Tandem lift with split head block and 2 spreaders (Stinis)

This tandem lifting will further develop into the handling of 2 x 40' containers or even 4 x 20' containers in one cycle however, the connecting transportation and stacking systems must be designed to support the increased productivity (loading is the critical process).

The addition of a second main hoist trolley (as mentioned in section 10.2) also will increase the potential crane productivity as up to 6 x 20' containers can be handled in one crane cycle. The future will learn whether this additional feature has an attractive cost/performance ratio.

So far, history showed that crane productivity improvements must be approached over the whole process: from vessel slot position to the final storage place in the stacking yard.

An isolated increase in crane handling capacity will result in higher crane cost and additional cost increases for quay wall, infrastructure, power supply and energy consumption; the lack of capacity in the connecting handling systems will undo the expected crane productivity increase.

10.5. KEY ISSUES IN QUAY CRANE DESIGN

During the last 50 years, there were a few dominant issues in crane design and as these issues are still relevant it is worthwhile to present them below.

Machinery trolley or rope trolley

At present, the crane dimensions are 3-4 times larger than the first crane Matson installed at Alameda. The trolley travel path has increased from 43 m. towards approximately 120 m., with connected consequences for trolley speed and rope sagging. The lifting height above quay level increased from 15 to more than 50 m. In the first decade, most of the cranes (Paceco, StarIron and Alliance) were designed with a rope towed trolley, resulting in a low moving load, and an enclosed machinery house fixed at the landside main girder. At the arrival of containerization in Europe, manufacturers like Demag, Kocks and Peiner introduced the machinery trolley showing a simple rope reeving and ability for multi-purpose functionality (e.g. Kocks container cranes in Hamburg were prepared for grab handling). In general this machinery trolley concepts show larger moving loads over the main girder, increased corner loads on the quay wall and they produce more noise, both for the operator and the environment.

The present day crane dimensions, the increased attention for environment and maintenance cost and the demand for productivity (and thus load control) have not resulted in one outspoken choice for one of these concepts (see Figure 226 and Figure 227). Some major concept-related topics are presented below:

Figure 226: Early cranes with rope driven trolley (Paceco left; StarIron right)

Rope-Towed Trolley concept:

- Major machinery (main hoist and trolley travel) in an enclosed machinery house; very good accessible components, with integrated electrical control room and provisions for fast exchange of components and rope re-reeving;
- Increased maintenance on much more sheaves and trim-list device;
- Requirements for provisions to prevent excessive rope-sagging (such as catenary trolleys or fixed supports with more complex reeving arrangements);
- Reduced responsiveness for the crane operator when positioning the load (or empty spreader);
- Built-in elasticity to absorb snag-loads as the long cables (>250 m. length) can elongate considerably and thus avoid extreme loads to the crane structure;
- Reasonable corner loads on the quay wall construction;
- Allows high trolley acceleration (although limited to approximately 0.8 m./sec² for operator's comfort);
- Medium-sized festoon cable system to the trolley, as power is only required for spreader and spreader cable drive supply. The low voltage controls do not require much cabling.

Machinery Trolley concept:

- Main hoist and trolley travel machinery on the trolley, with a tendency in the design to limit the weight of components (may affect lifetime!);
- Extensive festoon cable system to the trolley as both power supply and controls are provided out of a fixed electrical room on the main girder(s);
- Simple reeving presenting a good responsiveness to the operator;
- 15-20% higher corner loads to the quay structure as the moving load easily can be 35-50 tons larger than for a rope trolley concept;
- More comfortable movement pattern for the crane operator, due to low trolley acceleration (to avoid high structural inertia loads) however with a somewhat higher sound level.

Figure 227: Monobox girder cranes with machinery trolley (left; early Kocks crane at Eurokai)

In general, the rope driven trolley still is the dominating concept, although both concepts are selected depending on local conditions and demands (preferences). However in the last decade lift capacities have exceeded 120 tons and outreaches up to almost 70 m. have been realized. This topic together with some trends towards dual-hoist tandem lift cranes (= two separately driven head-blocks from one trolley structure, capable of handling 2 40/45' boxes in one cycle) makes the rope towed trolley interesting to limit the cost of quay wall constructions (lower corner loads from reduced crane deadweight and reduced trolley loads).

Sway control

The last decades showed increased crane lifting heights (to more than 50 m.) and 10 containers high stowed under deck. The latter limits the off-lead of hoist cables, a big impact on the stabilizing forces, controlling load sway. Lateral wind loads and trolley acceleration forces become less controllable and especially when the container starts rotating, this yaw is only to stop with the help of guides.

Over the years, a number of companies (like Siemens, ABB) promoted and installed electronic sway control in their main hoist/trolley drives but with moderate success. The average skilled crane driver may benefit from these provisions but the well-skilled crane operator still prefers his manual control, often with more success than the installed sway control devices.

Over the years a few terminal operators did trials with a cabin suspended from a separate track along the boom, to avoid the operator moving with the trolley (and allowing increased trolley acceleration rates, sometimes >1.0 m./sec^2).

Both the split trolley and the separately-moving cabin never became a success. Until today most of the crane operators prefer to move with the load on the trolley. It allows them to control the load sway just by looking downward. Regardless sophisticated electronically-controlled anti-sway drives an experienced crane operator is hardly to beat.

Some research at the TU Delft learned that the enlarged vessel beam (for 10,000+ TEU vessels) and crane lifting height will deteriorate sway control (see Figure 228). The research also showed that a rope trolley has a better potential for sway control, which is shown in Figure 229.

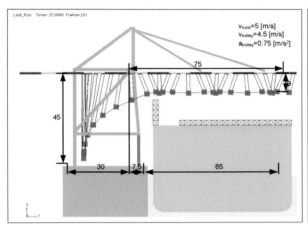
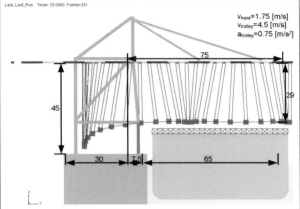

Figure 228: Influence of pendulum length on load sway pattern

Structural Integrity

During the past 50 years the crane sizes increased considerably (e.g. an 11-fold load moment and a tower height of more than 80 m.). However, the crane support base did not change in the same way; the rail gauge increased from 15.24 m. (50 ft) towards 30.48 m. (100 ft) or 35 m. and occasionally to 42 m. but the gantry width is still 27.2 m. for many cranes (even the largest). This has put heavy demands on the structural concept and the crane stability, especially in areas with heavy wind loads, hurricanes or earth quakes. Another issue is the gantry structure motion, induced by trolley and gantry acceleration/deceleration. Structural stiffness is paramount (own frequencies preferably more than 1 Hz) but the drive characteristics as well may influence the excitation of the crane structure (causing discomfort for the operator and additional structural loads).

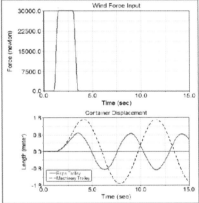

Figure 229: Improved sway control for rope trolley (below right: red line)

The rapid developments in crane sizes during the first decades disclosed all kinds of new structural design topics, so far only known in other fields of crane applications; think of buckling (see Figure 230), alignment of gantry travel truck arrangements, vibration of slender elements (back-stays, diagonals), etc. The continuously increasing crane dimensions during the most recent decades have emphasized the importance of structural integrity.

Figure 230: Low profile crane with reinforcements

Fatigue

Fatigue is one of the most important design issues for container cranes. The expected long lifetime of the crane and the continuing repetitive loads cause (more or less) fluctuating stress patterns on many crane components (both mechanical and structural). In the start-up years of containerization (1956-1970) cranes realized up to about 25,000 handling cycles per year. But in the 1970s, crane utilization increased towards 100,000 cycles per year for some terminals (often Sea-Land and APL used). After the year 2000, 25-40 ports show further increased crane usage often resulting in more than 150,000 crane handling cycles per year and such cranes may easily reach more than 4 million handling cycles during their lifetime.

In the 1970s the first incidents due to fatigue were reported (cracking in structural components, breakdowns in drive lines). Notwithstanding the available know-how of fatigue at many crane builders, new design details and an underestimate of stress fluctuations in various components caused a number of failures. Not surprisingly Sea-Land was one of the first to be faced with fatigue problems (hence they expanded very fast in the 1970s). At their Port Elizabeth terminal, fatigue damaged some of the low-profile cranes in the seventies (see Figure 231) and that was the start of more intensive research to fatigue (e.g. research from Dr. Fischer at the Lehigh University, Pennsylvania).

Figure 231: Sea-Land low profile cranes at Port Elizabeth; boom under repair at dock (right)

It revealed that during one handling cycle, a multitude of stress cycles could occur. In the following years a number of crane manufacturers advised to regularly check critical structural components (e.g. connections between truss and main girder, forestays). In Germany crane manufacturers like DEMAG and Peiner designed truss-type booms with a rather low dead weight which could be obtained by paying much attention to the design details in accordance with the design standards and directives made for fatigue loaded components.

During the last two decades regularly arising breakdowns from fatigue have learned that the intensive use of cranes can result in fatigue damages. Imbalances in rotating equipment, vibration of structural members (e.g. due to Von Karman excitation of slender components) or bad manufacturing details have caused outages of cranes and costly repairs.

The experience with fatigue over the last 30 years and the continuing increase in crane dimensions, productivity, cycles/hour, load pattern and crane utilization learned that fatigue requires a thorough review of structural and mechanical design details.

Loads on the quay wall

The specifications for the first Matson crane addressed the importance of limitations in quay wall loads. This resulted in the truss type, low weight boom and light (rope-towed) trolley, giving crane corner loads of about 100 tons to the quay wall. In 5 decades this figure has increased to 700 tons or more. Many quay walls designed/constructed in the 1960s and 1970s are not suited to support these loads and this has caused major expensive modifications/new buildings in ports. When containerization started wharf designs were a given and the crane designs were adapted to these designs; nowadays it should be an integrated approach from civil engineers, crane designers and the terminal operator.

The impact from additional loads, forthcoming from heavy storms, hurricanes and earth quakes has increased, because of the increased crane sizes. Especially wind loads should be considered in depth. During the 1990s and in the 21st century there has been an exposure from more frequent and heavier storms/hurricanes.

More and more ports are located directly along the coastline or built outside the coastline (Bremerhaven, Rotterdam Maasvlakte and Shanghai Yangshan Islands) and this together with the much higher cranes must be considered in the crane design (larger forces

Figure 232: Crane collapse after hurricane

per m²) and the quay wall design (amply designed provisions for the horizontal forces at crane parking positions and for tie-downs when crane stability is at stake). Figure 232 shows the consequences of such heavy storm loads, in case of insufficient provisions.

10.6. OUTLOOK

The arrival of US Lines' Econships (mid-1980s), triggered terminal operators and crane manufacturers to develop quay cranes with higher hourly handling rates. Main hoist and trolley travel speeds increased and a few terminals installed second trolley systems (ECT, VPA, Seagirt Terminals, Baltimore, and Brani Terminal, Singapore) but the vessels berth productivity remained in the 100 lifts per hour range. The introduction of the Regina Maersk-class and later the Emma Maersk-class clearly showed that an assignment of more than 8 quay cranes on a vessel may look impressive but is not very effective and rather costly for the terminal (see Figure 233). Vessel stowage plan and crane production plan must be well fit and when a disturbance occurs delays are unavoidable.

Figure 233: 11 cranes assigned to Emma Maersk

The number of containers per hatch (on deck and below) grew to over 300, asking for much higher crane productivity. In the period 2001-2006 various new crane concepts have been developed to realize a substantially higher productivity through avoiding time consuming trolley travelling and disturbances from the handling of SATLs (IBCs). Gottwald and Liftech published such concepts, incorporating a 90⁰ rotation of containers and the use of transfer carts between a manned ship trolley and an unmanned automated landside hoist for the connection to waterside horizontal transportation (see Figure 234).

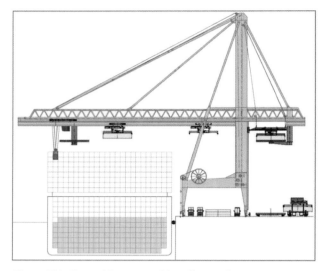

Figure 234: Gottwald concept with trolleys and container rotation

Liftech emphasized the importance of limiting the quay wall loads (as there are many existing quay walls that cannot be amortized) and they suggested spreading the gantry loads over the entire crane portal width (see Figure 235).

In this respect, the TU Delft Carrier Crane goes even further. In this concept the crane portal structure can be moved with normal wheels but when operating the crane is supported by larger pads (see Figure 236). There is no need for the crane to travel (for fine-positioning and changes within a hatch) as trolleys are provided with the possibility to transfer the hoist over a distance of ± 3 m. out of the crane center line.

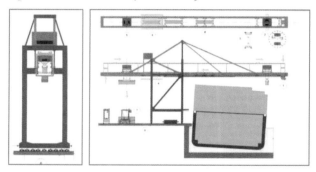

Figure 235: Liftech concept, conveyors and spread quay wall load

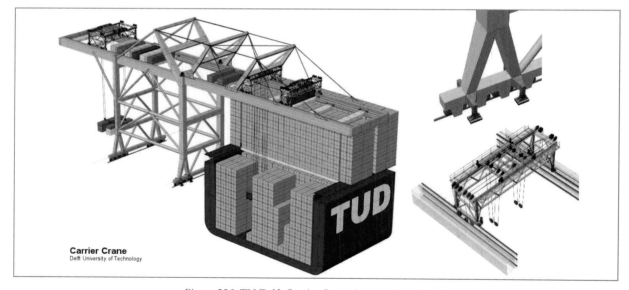

Figure 236: TU Delft Carrier Crane (concept E. Luttekes)

This type of crane will realize about 100 hoist cycles per hour, which will result in an operational productivity of seventy 40' boxes or 140 20' boxes per hour (single lift) or even double when using tandem-lift trolleys.

The announcement of the Maersk Triple-E-class and the likelihood of 20,000+ TEU vessels again pushed the need for faster cranes. In 2008, APMT filed a patent for a waterside container handling system, allowing a much denser assignment of cranes on ULCSs. This so-called Fastnet system was further published in the period 2010-2011, showing a massive infrastructural design, with the ability to apply slender cranes (gantry width probably < 14.5 m.), able to operate at adjacent hatches (see the artist impression in Figure 237). The concept should be capable of a vessel berth performance of 450 boxes per hour, a very ambitious goal compared with the 150-200 boxes/hr. as

Figure 237: Maersk's Fastnet system

state of the art in 2011. The innovation seemed to coincide with the announcement of the Maersk Tripe-E-class vessels, however no indications about realization of this concept were known by the end of 2011. Anyhow, this development shows the pressure from 15,000+ TEU vessel sizes onto the demands for increased terminal handling productivity.

The future will show whether some of these proposed concepts will become materialized. In general, terminal operators and port authorities are risk avoiding organizations and the introduction of the presented innovative concepts requires a systems approach for the entire handling process from vessel to storage yard and reverse.

IN RETROSPECT

After Matson specified the first container quay cranes in 1958, the crane sizes and crane lifting capacities continuously increased as a result of the tremendous vessel size developments. Container quay cranes got a 3-fold outreach, 5-fold lifting capacity, 7-fold crane deadweight and much higher drive speeds. But in spite of impressively high hoisting/lowering and trolley travel speeds and the related large amount of installed horsepower (sometimes > 3 MW) in cranes, the gap between technical handling capacity (about 60 cycles/hr) and realized operational handling capacity has increased.

Real breakthroughs in productivity have not been realized so far. The introduction of Semi Automatic Twist-Lock stackers (SATLs) or IBCs (Inter Box Connectors); the increase in off-standard containers (OH + OW) and the increased pendulum length (crane lifting heights above dock over 50 m.), present negative influences on crane productivity. At many terminals, crane productivities between 25 and 30 containers are still the standard achievement in 2011; not much improvement compared to 1958! But the application of twin-lift/tandem-lift, better (computer) controlled quay transportation and (semi-) automated stacking systems, have resulted in considerable improvements. Some terminals, having properly trained and motivated operators, with smart information control systems and oversized quayside transportation systems show crane productivities larger than 40 boxes per hour and occasionally more than 50. But there is still a huge imbalance between vessel size and crane productivity (in 2011: 15,000-TEU vessels and about 30 containers per hour per crane). Compared to the pioneering stage with vessels up to 1,000 TEU and productivities of 20-25 containers per hour per crane it is obvious that crane productivity developments by far could not follow the vessel size developments. Many small, medium-size and moderately utilized terminals recognized the cost saving potential from mobile harbor cranes. The somewhat decreased productivity is amply compensated by a cost reduction of 30-40%.

Some new crane concepts showed potential for major productivity improvements, however, realization asks for a vision and efforts equal to those shown by Matson and Sea-Land in the early days. Conquering the tripled outreach and lifting height will require engineering skills, project power and teamwork between terminal operator, port authority and crane manufacturer, to really get a breakthrough in crane productivity.

CHAPTER 11

DOUBLED VOLUMES, FLUCTUATING PROFITS
(1996-2006)

After a period of restructuring, new types of collaboration in container liner shipping had emerged. Because many shipping lines were now part of a worldwide operating, multilateral alliance, their focus was now on their core business: accommodating containerized maritime trade. The ample growth of international trade, still significantly affected by business cycles, made shipping lines invest in additional capacity, in particular Post-Panamax tonnage. Additional to ordering newbuildings, merging with or taking over other shipping lines was also a popular strategy. However, economic downturns and overcapacity put pressure on container rates and subsequently on revenues and profits. At the end of this period the list of the largest twenty shipping lines showed considerable changes.

11.1. MERGERS AND ACQUISITIONS

East - West trades

The first major acquisition involved Compagnie Générale Maritime (CGM), which after many loss-making years was privatized in 1996. Privately-owned Compagnie Maritime d'Affrètement (CMA) acquired CGM for US$ 4 million. CMA and CGM legally merged in 1999.

CMA was set up by Jacques Saadé in 1978. Business started with a 200-TEU feeder vessel operating between Marseilles and Eastern Mediterranean ports. Very quickly, the company expanded liner services to North Africa, the Red Sea and later to the Middle East and the Far East. Whereas CGM had withdrawn from the major trade routes, CMA became the number 20 container shipping line (measured in TEU) in 1995. After the takeover, a restructuring of liner services followed. CMA CGM did not participate in an alliance, but worked together with other shipping lines in specific trades. In 1998, the (privatized) remainder of Australian National Line was purchased. In relation to its European feeder activities, various companies from UK-based MacAndrews were acquired in 2002.

Two other shipping lines that merged their activities in 1996 were P&O Containers Ltd and Nedlloyd. P&O Nedlloyd was formed by the amalgamation of the liner shipping interests of both companies in a 50/50 joint venture. In order to balance the shareholding structure, Nedlloyd paid US$ 175 million to P&O's parent company. A complicating factor in the merger was the different alliances both shipping lines had joined earlier. Nedlloyd was one of the founders of the Global Alliance and P&O Containers Ltd had become a member of the Grand Alliance in 1995. Based on their market share in major trades, the Grand Alliance offered the best opportunities for growth.

Soon after this merger the rights of the Australian National Line were acquired. P&O and Nedlloyd had been involved in the Europe-Australia trade from the beginning. Their Mediterranean-Australia trade was strengthened due to the withdrawal of, amongst others, Lloyd Triestino. In this respect, the purchase of Blue Star Line's container business, mainly consisting of the remnants of ACT, can be explained. Further expansion included the buyout of Farrell Lines (US) and the acquisition of the container business of Harrison Line (UK).

The takeover of American President Lines by the smaller Singapore-based Neptune Orient Line (NOL) took place in 1997. APL's expenditure on six new Post-Panamax containerships put a lot of financial pressure on the company. For US$ 825 million, NOL not only doubled its container tonnage but also inherited an extensive North American intermodal network. Moreover, APL was a frontrunner in e-commerce and possessed state-of-the-art electronic data systems. NOL decided to use the prestigious APL brand for its shipping activities. From an economic point of view, the anticipated economies of scale did not materialize. Moreover, the company had paid a high price (nearly 50% over the market price) for APL. When the Asian economic crisis struck in 1997, debts skyrocketed. Among the assets sold was APL's Stacktrain, bought by Pacer International for US$ 315 million.

With respect to alliance membership NOL, which now included APL, faced the same problem as P&O Nedlloyd: should the Grand Alliance (NOL) or Global Alliance (APL) be preferred. In 1998 the Global Alliance was joined. Surprisingly, OOCL and MISC (only Europe-Far East) switched to the Grand Alliance and Hyundai Merchant Marine, which had already concluded a far reaching slot agreement, formally joined the Global Alliance. The latter was then renamed New World Alliance.

In the same year, Senator Lines was taken over for 80% by Hanjin, which already strongly cooperated with these Tricon-members. Senator Lines was a 1994 merger of two shipping lines: DSR-Lines (est. 1956) and Senator Linie (est. 1987) from former Eastern and Western Germany respectively. In 1998 UASC joined Hanjin, Senator Lines and Cho Yang and the alliance was renamed United Alliance. In 2001 Cho Yang went bankrupt and soon after UASC left. Then, Hanjin (incl. Senator Lines) joined the CYK (i.e. Cosco, Yang Ming and K Line) alliance thus forming the Hanjin-CYK group.

Figure 238: DSR Senator California

In 1998, Lloyd Triestino one of the oldest shipping lines in the world (founded as 'Österreichischer Lloyd' in 1835), was privatized and bought by the Evergreen Marine Corporation. Both companies were already partners in a mutual container service between the Mediterranean and the Far East. Over the years the cooperation had intensified. The brand name Lloyd Triestino, since 2006 Italia Marittima, was retained. To make the acquisition a success the services were restructured to (better) fit in the Evergreen liner network. The East-West traffic was strengthened and, for example, the direct Europe-Australia service of Lloyd Triestino was abandoned in favor of transshipment in Singapore. Evergreen proceeded with reorganizing by making its affiliate Uniglory, specialized in Asian feedering, a division in 1999. A few years later Hatsu Marine Ltd was established in the UK. Containerships are easily transferred from Evergreen (prefix *Ever*) to Lloyd Triestino (pre-fix *LT*, now *Ital*) and Hatsu Marine (prefix *Hatsu*) vice versa, and even newbuildings are assigned to different shipping lines (see Figure 239).

Through slot sharing and joint service agreements Evergreen, Lloyd Triestino, Hatsu Marine and other shipping lines could offer liner services to Asia, America and Europe.

In 1999, Maersk acquired the lion's share of Sea-Land. Both shipping lines already shared a decade of collaboration. The first time Maersk seriously engaged with Sea-Land was in 1990 when the company rationalized its newly started Transatlantic service. Maersk aimed at a possible purchase of Sea-Land from CSX but negotiations produced a restructured version of the Vessel Sharing Agreement that had already been concluded between Sea-Land, P&O Containers Ltd and Nedlloyd. In 1991, Maersk started to cooperate with P&O Containers Ltd in the Europe-Far East trade and with Sea-Land in the transpacific trade. When P&O Containers

Figure 239: 8,073-TEU Hatsu Courage

Ltd withdrew from its partnership with Maersk in 1995 this paved the way for a worldwide cooperation between Sea-Land and Maersk. Global strategy, management culture and customer orientation of both companies matched. The ocean-side cooperation was geared towards providing reliable multi-week sailings, achieving faster transit times and extending the service network by direct calls at outlying (regional) ports. Terminals and equipment were shared as well.

Maersk profited more from the alliance than Sea-Land did. Since parent company CSX was under financial pressure, it was decided to split Sea-Land into three divisions: a port division, a domestic and an international shipping line. For US$ 800 million Maersk acquired 70 predominantly leased containerships, 200,000 containers and 15 terminals. Partly due to claims in relation to stevedoring contracts, the price was renegotiated down to US$ 600 million. The remaining Sea-Land terminals were later sold to Dubai Ports and the domestic shipping operations were carried out by Horizon Lines. After the acquisition was approved of by North American and European authorities the company changed its name into Maersk Sealand.

Figure 240: Safmarine Container Lines' container

When Malcom McLean died in 2001, aged 87, his brainchild Sea-Land had ceased to exist. Still recognized as "the father of containerization", containerships around the world blew their whistles on the morning of his funeral.

Another shipping line, Safmarine Container Lines (SCL) was taken over in 1999. Albeit headquartered in Antwerp since the merger of Safmarine and CMB-T(ransport), in 1996, the company was rooted in South Africa. Safmarine purchased the CMB share in 1998 and consequently became the nr. 20 container shipping line in the world. The company's North-South trades complemented Maersk's less developed liner services to the African continent. The acquisition included about 50 vessels and 80,000 containers. Instead of integrating the company into Maersk Sealand, the Safmarine brand was retained.

North-South trades

Maersk was not the only shipping line that was interested in North-South trades. A merger between Hapag-Lloyd and Hamburg Süd was suggested but after some initial activities, rapidly abandoned. Instead Hamburg Süd, financially backed by its parent (i.e. Oetker) company, took over various shipping lines such as Brazilian Aliança in 1998 and Crowley American Transport the year after. Including the acquisitions from the early 1990s, among others several divisions of Furness Withy, Hamburg Süd substantially increased its market share in the Europe-South America trade. By purchasing Kien Hung in 2003, liner services from Asia to South America could be offered as well. In addition, the acquisition of Ellerman Line strengthened Hamburg Süd's position in the NW Europe-Mediterranean/Middle East/East Africa trades. After getting hold of the cross trade activities of the Far Eastern Shipping Company (FESCo) between Australia/New Zealand and North America as well as Asia. Hamburg Süd lastly took over Costa Container Lines (CCL) on December 1, 2007. CCL was specialized in the trades between the Western Mediterranean, South America and Mexico /Caribbean and ran an extensive network of feeder services in the Eastern Mediterranean. Most liner services eventually carry the Hamburg Süd-brand including the renowned Columbus Line that started containerization between the US East Coast and Australia/New Zealand.

Another shipping line that emerged from a niche market i.e. the Montreal-Europe route was CP Ships, the maritime division of the Canadian Pacific conglomerate. The company perceived growth opportunities in the shipping sectors and had generated money for investment by divesting in various other sectors.

In 1993, CP Ships bought the 47% participation of CMB in Canada Maritime (CanMar), established in 1983. At that time the shipping line operated a fleet of thirteen small (800-1,200 TEU) vessels. In 1995 financially troubled CAST, the main competitor in this trade, was acquired. CP Ships now controlled 85% of the container business in the port of Montreal. During the process of integrating CAST into its liner services, US$ 34 million was paid to buy nearly bankrupt Lykes Bros. Steamship Company of New Orleans and CP continued the chartering of eight vessels. Another acquisition

Figure 241: CP Liberator (ex Lykes Liberator)

was the shipping line operations of Contship Containerlines for an estimated US$ 100 million. In 1998, the purchase of two more (small) lines, Norwegian Ivaran and Australian New Zealand Direct Line (ANZDL), followed.

After establishing a joint venture with Transportación Marítima Mexicana (TMM) named Americana Ships, the Mexican partner sold its 50% stake and division of worldwide liner services to CP Ships. Soon after, Christensen Canadian African Lines (CCAL) and Italia Line were taken over. When in 2001CP Ships was spun off, the shipping line was the seventh largest carrier in the world.

Endgame

The main mergers and takeovers in the East-West trades occurred in the second part of the 1990s, rather independent from the developments in the south-west trades. Exception to the rule was Maersk that took over both Sea-Land and Safmarine Container Line in 1999.

This changed when CMA CGM acquired Delmas from the Bolloré group in 2005 for 600 million Euros. Delmas was actually SCAC-Delmas-Vieljeux because Bolloré had merged the Société Commercial d'Affrètements et de Combustibles (SCAC), which was a freight-forwarding firm primarily focused on Africa with shipping line Delmas-Vieljeux. Crucial for the deal was the assurance of CMA CGM that Delmas could stay in Le Havre and operate under its own name. At the same time OT Africa Line, a roll-on/roll-off shipping line, was also purchased from the Bolloré group. These acquisitions significantly strengthened CMA CGM's position in Africa.

The company kept on buying niche carriers in 2006/2007. By acquiring Cheng Lie Navigation Co. all intra-Asia operations could be transferred to this Taipei-based company. The purchase of US Lines allowed CMA CGM, in combination with subsidiary ANL, to become a leading shipping line in de Australia/New Zealand-US West Coast trade. Finally, formerly state-owned Compagnie Marocaine de Navigation strengthened CMA CGM's position in the Mediterranean market and increased its stake in the Tangier Terminal phase 2 to 40%. Unlike most shipping lines CMA CGM still uses the traditional company names.

Another shipping line that expanded its liner services in the North-South trades was Hapag-Lloyd. The company had expressed interest in these trades before and parent company TUI was prepared to pay 1.7 billion euro (US$ 2 billion) to acquire CP Ships. The shipping lines merged in 2006.

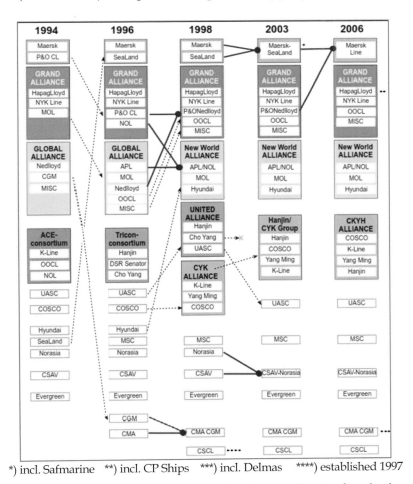

*) incl. Safmarine   **) incl. CP Ships   ***) incl. Delmas   ****) established 1997

Figure 242: Development of alliances and mergers 1994-2006 (Hallvar Gisnås et al., adapted)

However, the most important takeover of 2005 was the purchase of P&O Nedlloyd by Maersk. For US$ 2.9 billion they acquired 150 containerships and 400,000 containers. Although they paid a high price at the peak of the market, ordering vessels would at least be as expensive and would have taken more time. The company was renamed Maersk Line (again). The amalgamation was not without problems. For example, the new computer systems had difficulty communicating. Especially ordering containers went wrong; they arrived too late, not at all or on time but in another port. When in 2006 a sudden downturn ensued, A.P. Møller had to announce an expected profit 40% below that of 2005.

The only company growing organically, i.e. tripled its fleet, was the Mediterranean Shipping Company. MSC was founded in 1970 by Gianluigi Aponte, an Italian with a maritime background. The company started as a freight broker but purchased its first vessel in the same year. The 1,861-grt/2,900-dwt *Patrica* was built in 1955 and later lengthened to 84.3 m. The ship was acquired by the Mediterranean Shipping Co. (Genève) Monrovia for US$ 280,000 and delivered to the new owners on May 24. Management was carried out by the Aponte Shipping Co. S.A., Bruxelles. *Patricia* was sold again in 1973. The second general cargo ship was a former Hapag-vessel that was acquired in January 1971. It was 2,441-grt/4,749-dwt and named *Rafaela* (after Aponte's wife). On 24 December 1977 *Rafaela* went aground during a voyage between Hull and Antwerp. The vessel sustained severe bottom damage and was sold to ship breakers. At that time MSC owned fourteen vessels and had moved its headquarters from Brussels to Geneva.

MSC's first liner service went from the Mediterranean to the Red Sea and Somalia where Aponte had lived the first years of his life. Northern European and East and South African destinations were added in 1977 and the next year liner services were extended into the Indian Ocean. The highly competitive North Atlantic Container trade was entered in 1985 with services from Europe to the US East Coast. In 1989 a service between South Africa and Australia began and was subsequently combined with the South Africa to Europe line in a direct service. South Africa was also connected with the United States and Durban became a port where services could be interlinked. In Freeport, Bahamas, another hub terminal was established in 1988.

In 1984, the Europe-South Africa line was the first service to be fully containerized. Gradually, second-hand fully-cellular containerships were introduced. In 1982 the *Sextum* (ex *Ercole Lauro*) a two year old vessel was bought from financially troubled Lauro Lines. The 27,076-grt containership was built by the Fincantieri shipyard in Genoa and served the company for more than eighteen years. Other second-hand containerships from renowned shipping lines followed, for example, Johnson Lines' *Antonia Johnson* (renamed *Regina D*) and *San Francisco* (renamed *Diego*) joined the fleet in 1985/86. In 1990 the first containerships, owned as well as chartered, appeared with the prefix *MSC*.

Figure 243: MSC Rafaela in the port of Antwerp

Meanwhile MSC had reached the top ten of biggest container shipping lines by a strategy of autonomy. The company was eager to enter the Europe-Far East trade and ordered new containerships for the first time. The *MSC Alexa* (2) and *MSC Rafaela* (2) were delivered in 1996 by the Fincantieri shipyard in Ancona, Italy. With a LOA of 244.2 m. and beam of 32.2 m. these 42,307-grt vessels could carry 3,300 TEU. From 1999 on, numerous newbuildings joined the fleet. Post-Panamax vessels were for the first time delivered in 2002; 75,590-grt containerships with a capacity of 6,750 TEU by Daewoo and slightly smaller ones (i.e. 6,730 TEU) by Hyundai.

11.2. SHIP DEVELOPMENT

Post-Panamax

In the mid-1990s the capacity of Post-Panamax containerships had eventually started to increase. Still, the delivery of the *Regina Maersk* by the Odense shipyard in December 1995 took the world by surprise. It was billed as being capable of loading 4,800 TEU but the hull was subsequently lengthened to enable more than 6,000 TEU to be carried, including 700 reefers. However, this figure is based on 14 ton/TEU, in practice there was space for several hundreds of containers more on the 81,488-grt/84,900-dwt vessel. It was the first of the "mega" containerships with a length of 318.2 m., a beam of 42.80 m. and a draft of 14.5 m. The 54,860-kw engine provided a service speed of 25 knots. The *Regina Maersk* and her five sister ships were categorized by Maersk as K-class containerships. They featured much new and advanced technology and the automation level was high, including a one-man operated bridge. The crew comprised only thirteen people. Accompanying the new vessel was an order of 80,000 new, mainly 40-ft (refrigerated) containers.

Summer 1998 the *Regina Maersk* was sent on a tour of American ports. On July 22 the vessel made an inaugural call at the port of New York and New Jersey. Because the access channels were only 12.2 m. (40 ft) deep the containership arrived at high tide. Moreover, many containers had already been discharged in Halifax and it was carrying approximately 20% of her capacity and as a result, the ship rode high in the water. In order to clear the 46-m. (151-ft) high Bayonne Bridge crossing the Kill van Kull, the communications mast had to be detached. So, having a keel to mast height of 60.4 m. (198 ft),

Figure 244: First call of the Regina Maersk at New York

reaching the container terminals in Port Elizabeth and Port Newark, N.J. would always pose a problem. It was clear that ports needed channels that are deep enough and docks modern enough to accommodate them.

At that time Maersk and Sea-Land were reconsidering the port of New York-New Jersey as the primary East Coast base because the 25-year lease of their Port Elizabeth terminal would expire in 2000. The arrival was staged to send a message to port officials (and politicians) along the Eastern seaboard. Deep water ports, such as Baltimore (MD) and Norfolk (VA), were also seeking the Maersk Sealand business. For New York harbor, which has notoriously narrow and shallow channels, the visit of the *Regina Maersk* intensified the pressure on officials to obtain adequate federal money for deepening the channels. The toughest task would be blasting the shelf of bedrock underlying the Kill van Kull. With a 15.2 m. (50-ft) channel, a ship like the *Regina Maersk* will under certain loading conditions be able to navigate the harbor and to pass the Bayonne Bridge.

The advent of "mega" containerships made upgrading of existing port infrastructure necessary. The adjustments made in the port of New York/New Jersey provide an example of such a comprehensive approach: in a US$ 733 million dredging project the US Army Corps of Engineers deepened the main shipping channel in New York Harbor to a depth of 15.2 m. and the Port Authority launched a US$ 650 million terminal redevelopment program.

The modernization of the thirty-year old wharf structures at the Port Elizabeth Marine Terminal was one of the redevelopment projects. The terminal operator, APM Terminals North America, wanted Berths 82 through 98 modified for handling "mega" containerships. Berths 82 through 88 were originally designed for a depth of 11.6 m. whereas 12.2 m. was applicable for Berths 90 through 98. In 1996 Berth 98 and part of Berth 96 were already deepened to -13.7 m. The existing berths were inspected to determine which structural modifications were needed to accommodate the berth deepening to -15.2 m. and the heavier new container crane corner loads. Six low profile container cranes were built in the early 1970s, two cranes

Figure 245: View of the wharf improvements

were added later. They were replaced by (extra) Post-Panamax cranes capable of servicing vessels up to eighteen containers wide. As a consequence the crane corner loads increased 2.5 times to 730 kN per m. crane track. Furthermore the timber fender system was replaced by a new system capable of resisting the energy of a 152,000 ton displacement vessel. Wharf improvements were carried out in phases which allowed the terminal to be operational during construction (see Figure 245).

The design of the *Regina Maersk* was the basis for the next series of S-, C- and A-class vessels. When the last K-class containership *Kirsten Maersk* was launched in 1997, the first S-class vessel, the *Sovereign Maersk*, was already under construction. These containerships had a LOA of nearly 347 m. and could (officially) carry 6,600 TEU but calculations showed that up to 8,160 TEU was possible. The K- and S-class vessels made Maersk for the first time the number one container shipping line in 1997. After eleven S-class vessels eight C-class containerships were delivered between 2000 and 2002. Both series had the same dimensions, however, the C-class containerships were equipped with more powerful (63,000-kw) engines. Finally, six slightly longer A-class vessels were delivered in 2003/2004. Maersk stated that these 352.1 m. containerships could also carry 6,600 TEU, however 8,272 TEU is a more appropriate number.

Due to the small differences between the S-, C- and A-class vessels and their similar deployment, all 25 containerships are often referred to as S-class vessels. Mid-2011 Maersk embarked on a "capacity boost" program for a

Figure 246: The raising of Carsten Maersk's navigation bridge

number of these containerships, the *Carsten Maersk* being the first. Their capacity was increased by adding two tiers of containers forward of the accommodation block. Therefore the navigation bridge has been raised and the lashing bridges heightened. The number of reefer plugs was also increased. Although the ships' effective capacity (in 14 tons/TEU) has remained almost unchanged, the vessels' maximum capacity has risen to 9,600 TEU. After the first ten ships another six S-class vessels will have their capacity enhanced.

Other shipping lines also ordered 8,000+ TEU Post-Panamax containerships, albeit shorter. The first company that ordered a large series of these vessels was OOCL. In 2003 the *OOCL Shenzen* was delivered to be followed (until 2010) by fifteen sister ships. The first out of five new containerships of China Shipping Container Line, *CSCL Asia*, was record-breaking in July 2004. In December of the same year the new record holder *P&O Nedlloyd Mondriaan*, the first out of a series of eight, was delivered. The first four were christened as *P&O Nedlloyd*-vessels but after the takeover renamed as Maersk-vessels. The latter four containerships were designated Maersk right away. April 2005 Hapag-Lloyd commissioned the *Colombo Express,* the first of eight with a capacity of 8,749 TEU. With the exception of the OOCL Shenzhen-class (323 m.), all other containerships had a length of approximately 335 m.

The last series of record-breaking 42.8 m. wide containerships from the Lindø shipyard consisted of six D-class vessels. Again the design was lengthened so the *Gudrun Maersk* and her sisters had a LOA of 367.3 m. and a draft of 15.5 m. These 115,700-dwt vessels could officially carry 7,500 TEU, but estimates varied between 8,500 and 9,500 TEU. The containers could be stowed in eight tiers on deck. Compared to the A-class vessels the wheelhouse was raised and now contained eleven decks. Once again, more powerful engines were available; the installed 68,640-kw Sulzer enabled a service speed of 26 knots.

In July 2005 the *MSC Pamela* with a capacity of 9,200 TEU officially became the new record holder. However, it was never meant to be that big since the initial (Samsung) design called for a 323 m. long and 42.8 m. wide containership. When in 2003 the deepsea container market started to boom and shipping lines were feverishly looking for capacity, the design was modified. There were two ways to increase the capacity: the ship could either be lengthened or widened. In order to attain the necessary stiffness, a slender hull has to be significantly stronger than that of a wider ship. By increasing the beam to 45.6 m. the vessel could accommodate seven tiers of containers in eighteen rows on deck and ten tiers, sixteen abreast in the holds. With a molded depth of 27.2 m. the *MSC Pamela* was the first containership to exceed the 100,000-grt boundary. Thirteen vessels were equipped with a 69,000-kw engine which enabled a service speed of 25.2 knots.

Figure 247: Record-breaking D-class Georg Maersk and MSC Pamela, both 9000+ TEU

Contrary to the Maersk-vessels the proportion of containers below deck is much higher (over 50%) and these containers can take heavier loads (see Figure 247). However, attention must be paid to the stowing of containers below deck because the maximum load onto a standard container of 3,392 kN (ISO 1496) can easily be exceeded if the ten 40-ft containers are each loaded with maximum 35 tons.

Panamax

Obviously, most attention is drawn to the exciting developments of Post-Panamax containerships but until 2003 Panamax vessels were delivered in (more or less) equal numbers.

In the 1990s, the biggest Panamax containerships were deployed by Hapag-Lloyd. The capacity of the last Samsung-built Hannover-class containership was 4,639 TEU. In 2000, a new series of Panamax vessels was built by Hyundai. The 4,864-TEU *Antwerpen Express* gained an extra bay of containers from a shorter accommodation block. An additional 70 TEU was derived from a change in engine design. Due to the greater power density per cylinder these containerships needed two cylinders less than the nine cylinders used in the preceding vessels.

An innovative Panamax-design by Hanjin Heavy Industries & Construction Co. exceeded the 5,000-TEU boundary for the first time. With a maximum of 5,060 (later 5,089) TEU, these vessels were among the most popular Panamax containerships to be ordered. The six holds could contain 2,282 TEU whereas on deck 20/40/45-ft containers in 6/7 tiers totaled 2,778 TEU. From 2004 on these vessels were deployed by various shipping lines, including Maersk, Italia Marittima/Evergreen and MSC.

Figure 248: 5,089-TEU ITAL Laguna, a Hanjin design

Today, the ultimate Panamax containership can carry over 5,300 TEU. Designed and built by the Chinese Zhejiang Ouhua Shipbuilding, the rather unique design includes a deckhouse that is not fitted on top of the ship's engine room, but in a more forward position (eight bays from the bow). Containers will be stowed on top of the engine room and a single funnel is placed in the middle of a bay for 20-ft containers. With a capacity of 5,301 TEU, the ships are able to carry some 200 TEU more. Similar designs show that it is possible to squeeze 5,600 TEU into/onto a Panamax hull.

Hatchcoverless

One of the few shipping lines that embraced the idea of hatchcoverless containerships unconditionally was Swiss shipping line Norasia Services SA. They asked Nigel Gee Associates to optimize the concept for their anticipated Fast Feeder Containership. The dimensions of these vessels with a draft of 9.0 m. amounted to 217.1 m. (LOA) and 26.7 m. (beam). They could carry 1,185 TEU in the hatchless holds and 126 TEU in two closed holds which hatches could bear an additional 76 TEU. Two 12-MW engines and, to limit resistance, one propeller enabled a speed of 25 knots. Five ships were ordered from HDW in Kiel and another five from

Figure 249: Fast Feeder Containership Norasia Savannah

Jiangnan shipyard in Shanghai. They were delivered at the end of the 1990s, the *Norasia Samantha* being the first of this class (see Figure 249). On its maiden voyage from Zeebrugge to Montreal the vessel achieved an average speed of 26.15 knots. But many of these vessels encountered technical difficulties and consequently schedules could not be met. The financially-troubled shipping line concluded an agreement with Invest AD and all ten containerships went to their joint venture Abu Dhabi Container Lines. In June 2000, Norasia integrated with Chilean shipping line CSAV. The Fast Feeders were successively operated by various shipping lines, MSC often being the last. When the ex-*Norasia Sultana* was sent for scrap in 2012, it was for the youngest containership ever to be demolished (excl. vessels damaged by accidents).

Especially for shortsea and feeder traffic, hatchcoverless containerships boost many benefits. They are economical to operate due to shorter turnaround times and avoided costs for handling hatches and lashing containers. Unfortunately, the cost savings are offset by higher port and canal dues. These charges are usually based on Gross Register Tonnage. The design of hatchcoverless containerships requires a high freeboard which causes high Gross Register Tonnages. Especially in shortsea trades and feedering where equivalent TEU capacity ships have comparatively low freeboards this is a serious drawback. Since the turn of the century some shipyards have designed shortsea vessels that combine the advantages of traditional and

Figure 250: Semi-hatchcoverless feeder Katherine Borchard

open top containerships. Most of the about 120 open-top vessels in service in 2009 are in the 500 through 1,000-TEU range (FeederMax size). In a typical design these vessels have a hatchcoverless section amidships and one or two holds which are equipped with hatch covers to allow the carriage of dangerous goods (see Figure 250).

11.3. ECONOMIC PERFORMANCE

The 1996-2006 period, is characterized by substantial growth of containerized maritime trade. In 1996 container traffic amounted to 150.8 million TEU (loaded and empty) and in 2005 378.0 million TEU, an annual growth of 10.75%. However, business cycles impacted this trend. The first major disturbance was the Asian financial crisis beginning in July 1997. By 1999, countries were beginning to recover though not all Asian countries were hard hit. As a result of the crises many currencies (excl. Chinese Yuan and Japanese yen) showed sharp reductions in value especially in relation to the dollar. This generated additional export good flows until a more global recession struck in 2001-2002. This downturn was followed by a rather sharp upturn. For example, the increase in worldwide container handlings in 2003 and 2004, 16% and 14% respectively, caused severe port congestion.

Increasing maritime trade made shipping lines eager to expand their capacity. Chartering extra containerships was a possibility but time charter rates show the same pattern as business cycles which also applied for second-hand tonnage. Takeovers could provide additional TEU capacity only if trades coincided. So, many newbuildings were ordered but it took some time to deliver these vessels. In order to reduce this lead time, existing designs were used such as Hanjin's 5,060-TEU Panamax containership and Daewoo's 8,400-TEU vessel deployed by various shipping lines. However, additional tonnage often became available when the downturn had already started. In this period of double-digit growth of TEU capacity, the increase in the economic top years 2000/2001 and 2004/2005 was below 10%!

For shipping lines the bottom line of these developments is revenue based on container freight rates. Figure 251 reveals the influence of business cycles causing demand to vary, and the impact of different levels of TEU capacity supply (i.e. overcapacity) on container freight rates. The shape of the business cycles is more profound by the anti-cyclical addition of TEU capacity. Often the downturn had already started when shipping lines needed the money most.

Two remarkable developments can be observed when looking at the graph. First, increasing ship size in these major trades does not seem

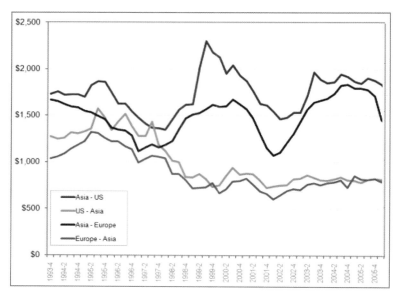

Figure 251: Freight rate by trade area (source: UNCTAD)

to have an effect on (long term) freight rates. Second, the "spread" between eastbound and westbound rates, which amounted to only several hundreds of dollars prior to 1998, increased to about a thousand dollar per TEU. This reflects the fundamental imbalance of good flows in world trade. As a consequence the profits of shipping lines plummeted at the end of the century recovering again as of 2002.

Whereas container traffic in 2005 was 2.5 times higher than in 1996, the TEU capacity of the vessel fleet had expanded by a factor 2.76. Takeovers and major fleet expansions put Maersk in first place, CMA CGM third and Hapag-Lloyd fifth. Asian shipping lines were hardly involved in mergers and takeovers and many lost market share. Evergreen was down to number four and Hanjin slipped to eighth place. The Japanese shipping lines NYK and MOL lost substantial market share whereas K Line maintained its position. The Mediterranean Shipping Company displayed the highest organic growth; with a TEU capacity of the fleet more than eight times higher, they ranked second place. The Chinese shipping lines showed a mixed picture. On the one hand the market position of Cosco, China's traditional shipping line that had been operating container liner services since 1978, deteriorated. On the other hand China Shipping Group's 1997 established container division CSCL ended number six after a modest start in domestic trades using converted vessels (see Figure 252).

Figure 252: China Shipping Lines' Zhen Fen 16 became containership Xiang Bin in 1999

IN RETROSPECT

This period was characterized by ample economic growth and a substantial increase in containerized maritime trade. Shipping lines reacted by ordering many newbuildings to expand their TEU capacity. The ship size of Post-Panamax vessels increased rapidly. In 1996, the 6,000 TEU *Regina Maersk* with a length of 318.2 m., beam of 42.80 m. and draft of 14.5 m., started the era of "mega" containerships. By lengthening the design and increasing deck loads Maersk kept ahead with its vessels. However, in July 2005, the 107,849-grt *MSC Pamela*, the first containership with a beam of to 45.6 m, became the new record holder with a capacity of 9,200 TEU. As a consequence of the development of these "mega" vessels, the existing port infrastructure and superstructure needed considerable upgrading.

Shipping lines also used mergers and takeovers to deal with the need for additional capacity. After the alliances had been established, several shipping lines were taking over companies they already worked with. Evergreen acquiring Lloyd Triestino and Maersk purchasing Sea-Land are examples in this respect. The start of the new millennium showed fewer acquisitions, nevertheless, shipping lines such as Hamburg Süd and CP Ships took over several smaller shipping lines in the North-South trades. Still, the biggest takeovers took place in 2005: Maersk incorporated P&O Nedlloyd, Hapag-Lloyd got CP Ships and CMA CGM acquired Delmas. Due to these acquisitions many brand names of established shipping lines disappeared albeit, in some cases, liquidation would have been the only alternative.

For shipping lines container freight rates are of utmost importance for their profits. Since economic growth was impacted by business cycles, the demand for container transportation varied significantly. During the upturn of business cycles shipping lines took over other companies and/or invested in extra TEU capacity. However, these containerships were often delivered when an economic downturn had already started thus putting container freight rates under even more pressure. When revenues fell at the time shipping lines needed money, companies had to sell off assets (e.g. NOL in 1999) or issue a profit warning (e.g. Maersk in 2006).

The world slot capacity was highly concentrated in the top 20 shipping lines: 7,185,608 TEU i.e. around 59% of total TEU capacity (as of November 2005). The takeovers and fleet expansion earned Maersk a first, CMA CGM a third and Hapag-Lloyd a fifth place. MSC which ended second and, to a lesser extent, number four Evergreen increased their tonnage by organic growth. These top 5 shipping lines controlled more than half of the total top 20 TEU capacity compared to only 42.3% in 1995. Concentration of market power became evident in this period.

CHAPTER 12

CONTAINER TERMINAL DEVELOPMENT

From parking lots to automated high-density stacking logistic centers

During the first decade after World War II, cargo handling in the ports continued in a traditional way, with a limited number of equipment types and an infrastructure built during the 1920s and 1930s. Warehouses (sheds) for short-term terminal storage were located on docks or finger-piers with a complicated arrangement of roads and railroads connecting them or placed at the waterside quay. In some cases the cranes (mostly level-luffing types) were supported by the quay wall and the warehouse building structure (see Figure 253).

During a vessel's dwell time of several weeks, cargo was moved directly under the crane (either on-dock or by the vessel's own gear) mostly by road trucks and railway-wagons. In many occasions even barges were used to connect warehouses to the port area by vessel (predominantly in European ports linked to a waterway network, such as Antwerp, Amsterdam, London, Hamburg or Rotterdam). When cargo was stored in warehouses close to the vessel (before and/or after vessel arrival and vessel operation) the transportation of cargo "to the hook" was increasingly mechanized with equipment developed for the manufacturing industry in

Figure 253: General cargo cranes

the US and Europe. Forklift trucks (electric or with combustion engines), 1-4 ton mobile cranes, simple tractors and carts were the equipment at the apron (see Figure 254).

The vessels themselves had 2 or 3 tweendecks and rather small hatches. So, the cargo had to be stowed in the sides using manpower, often more than 10 dockworkers per hatch. Vessel stowage planning was a manual process focused on maximum vessel utilization (both in volume and weight) taking into account stability and strength of the vessel.

Information control was very much cargo-oriented. Every shipper used his own indications on a large variety of packing types and the stevedore (shipping line related or independent) knew how to recognize destination, location on-board the vessel, type of stowage, etc., from the outside characteristics of the cargo (product type, way of packing, special shapes, smell, colors, etc.). In the whole handling process there was an involvement of many checkers, tally men, foremen, warehouse-bosses, etc.; all using their traditional hierarchic way of control and maintaining their important, indispensable position. It was old-fashioned, costly and not very open to innovations.

Often, there hardly any handling gear (think of the US, the Far East and Africa) and general cargo vessels had to use their on-board deck gear. However, in Europe many ports provided the stevedoring companies with port authority-owned and

Figure 254: Mobile equipment: small crane (left) and early forklift truck

operated cranes with a capacity of 3-5 tons and an outreach of 10-25 m. By the 1950s, these figures had increased to 7.5-15 tons capacity at 30-40 m. outreach. Port authorities in Amsterdam, Antwerp, Hamburg, Marseille, Liverpool, London, Rotterdam and others owned massive fleets of such general cargo cranes; with sometimes a port-owned general power supply network, like pressurized water-power in Antwerp and 600 V DC power in Rotterdam. Until the 1950s, loads of over 25 tons were often considered heavy-lift, which could be handled either at special locations by fixed derrick-type cranes (see Figure 255) or by floating cranes with fixed or revolving structures (see Figure 256).

After World War II, privatization was stimulated and in many ports, quay-side handling equipment was transferred to private (or partly public) stevedoring companies.

Until today, there are still a number of port authorities who own and even operate quayside container cranes (some US-ports, Belgium, France, etc.) to subsequently hire them out to stevedores.

In many ports operations and labor management were organised in a very traditional way, often based

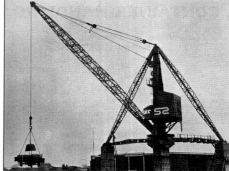

Figure 255: Fixed Derrick cranes

Figure 256: Floating cranes for "heavy" lifts (> 25 tons)

on hundreds of years old "closed shop" organizations. The "Naties" in Belgium, the "Nations" in France and the "Gildes" in the Netherlands and Germany maintained longstanding privileges with strict rules for cargo handling and storage. A lot of activities were not very efficient or even necessary in a modernizing, mechanized world after World War II.

In this traditional port environment with large labor pools (often not very well trained and motivated), causing substantial pilferage and damage to cargoes, the ship owners and shippers got increasingly worried about the cost of stevedoring and cargo transportation. Shipping lines were already satisfied when a vessel spent more than 45% of her time at sea. Therefore, many lines

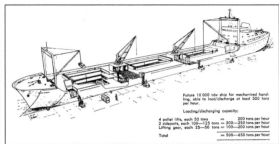

Figure 257: Pallet handling over side doors (Fred Olsen Lines)

were looking for cost reductions and faster turnaround times in port. Some innovative shipping companies introduced unit-load handling using side ramps and on-board elevators (such as KNSM or Fred Olsen Lines, see Figure 257). American companies advocated roll-on/roll-off vessels for complete trailers. Anyhow, during the 1950s a number of (small-scale) improvements showed that there was ground for a breakthrough in worldwide shipping and cargo handling in ports.

12.1. 1956-1966: EARLY TERMINAL DESIGNS; US PIONEERS SHOWED THE WAY

As already mentioned in chapter 3, the introduction of the container changed cargo handling in ports dramatically. It was Sea-Land's and Matson's objective to move the cargo door-to-door in containers, basically only using trailers or railcars at the landside. The packing (stuffing) and unpacking (stripping) of goods in port warehouses, using expensive port labor, could be avoided by doing the same on inland locations or at the shipper or consignee's premises (Full Container Loads, FCL). For smaller parcels consolidated in one container this could also be done outside the port in Container Freight Stations (Less than Container Load, LCL).

The first terminals in the US were developed by Matson, Sea-Land and Alaska Steam. They were basically modifications of existing stevedoring areas where older sheds had been demolished and converted into flat, paved staging areas for containers on trailers (so-called wheeled boxes). Figure 258 (left) shows the limited space for maneuvering trucks alongside the quay. Therefore, parking of wheeled containers was done at any area available close to the quay wall.

When vessel capacity increased, as well as volumes to be stored at the terminal, to assure a high productivity more space was required, preferably as close to the vessel berth as possible. Figure 258 (right) shows a first simple Sea-Land container terminal at Long Beach in the early 1960s. The trucks were identified at the gate and directed to a designated parking slot (either a numbered slot or any free slot in a

Figure 258: Early Sea-Land terminals; Long Beach (right) and Ponce, Puerto Rico

specific row). During vessel operations, the road chassis (semi-trailers) with container were picked up by longshoremen driving the chassis under the on-board crane, with the help of special tractors with a hydraulically liftable fifth wheel. Sea-Land, with its longstanding trucking experience, developed their terminals as a ship-truck interchange area. Their marketing department spoke of LTL (Less than Trailer Load) and TL (Trailer Load) instead of LCL and FCL. Sea-Land owned a large fleet of road chassis allowing them to bring the containers (the semi-trailer) directly under their vessel's on-board cranes. The first series of Sea-Land containers were even fitted with rear lights for road haulage at simple chassis. In the beginning, none of the Sea-Land-operated terminals were fitted with dock-side canes. Road hauliers were used for inland trips to and from the customer and usually they delivered a full container, which was immediately unloaded at the customer's warehouse and back-hauled straight to the terminal or a Sea-Land operated off-dock warehouse (consolidations center or Container Freight Station) shown in Figure 259.

Figure 259: Sea-Land off-dock warehousing (Houston left; Elizabeth)

Sea-Land advocated totally-wheeled operations for maximum speed and flexibility (e.g. late-minute changes in vessel stowage planning). This way, they could subcontract trucking to any company capable of bringing in a truck (bob-tail) with a driver. For many years, Sea-Land maintained this simple and efficient terminal concept, built around their strategy to operate with onboard container cranes. Sea-Land believed in the following advantages of this simple concept:

- No dependency of port handling gear (in many ports not available, or very slow);
- No waiting for berthing or craneage;
- No additional requirements for the dockside and terminal area (no crane rails and power supply and, as wheel loads were equal to public road wheel loads, no special pavement);
- Rather low crane height, resulting in less load sway;
- Simple yard inventory control and terminal logistics.

In contrast, Matson developed their terminal concept in a different way. The carrier did not support the on-board crane concept, as they saw the following disadvantages:

- A loss of cargo carrying capacity of the vessel;
- The ship's stability was negatively influenced;
- A limited vessel berth productivity, as in general only two cranes were available per vessel;
- Underutilized cranes (often less than 30% utilization);
- Low second-hand value of cranes as they were custom-built for a certain vessel type;
- A limited crane productivity negatively influenced by vessel movements when positioning containers onto the on-dock waiting chassis. On top, the crane often had to cope with a significant listing of the vessel, affecting trolley travel motion control.

As indicated in chapter 3, Matson used on-dock cranes and initially moved containers under these cranes on chassis. Already at the start of the 1960s, Matson recognized the shortcomings of on-wheeled container stacking. The all-chassis system requires large parking yards and a huge investment in road trailers. Moreover, it shows limitations in "feeding-the-hook" due to a lack of buffer capacity between yard and dockside crane. And last but not least, the landing of containers onto the (low-weight, simple-design) road chassis caused costly damages to chassis and container bottom rails.

This convinced Matson to introduce the straddle carrier for terminal operations, both for stacking (first 1 over 1, later 1 over 2) and transportation from the yard to the crane (see Figure 260). This resulted in fewer delays under the crane and a considerable saving of land used for container storage. But everything has its price. The straddle carrier terminal concept showed the following characteristics (L. Harlander):

Figure 260: Early Clark Ross straddle carriers for Matson

- More labor involved and the need for skilled straddle carrier operators (training programs!);
- Less operational flexibility and increased carrier cycle times and costs from re-handlings to retrieve boxes stored under other containers;
- More impact from breakdowns as complex straddle carriers showed many technical failures;
- Substantial costs for maintenance and repair, not only from technical failures but also from damages caused by driving in container lanes with very small clearances;
- Higher investment in terminal paving, due to the increased straddle carrier wheel loads;
- Destruction of black top pavement from hydraulic oil leakage.

Nevertheless, Matson's analysis of cycle times and terminal productivity resulted in the straddle carrier concept, which separated the time-consuming container positioning onto chassis from the crane handling cycle, although at an extra cost. Crane handling productivity improved to an average of 25-30 containers per hour. Already in 1961 (Honolulu at the vessel Californian), Matson achieved a record productivity (over the whole vessel operation) of 48 boxes/crane hour. Even in the 21st century, this would still be a very good result!

For the handling of containers onto railcars, Matson inspired Paceco to build the first mobile yard gantry crane (rubber tired), which later was developed into the Rubber Tired Gantry (RTG), also suited for container stacking (see Figure 261). At the more or less dedicated terminals, serving container shipping lines such as Grace Line, American Export-Isbrandtsen Lines, and

Figure 261: Paceco Rubber Tired Gantries for rail handling and stacking

Alaska Steamship Company, productivity regularly reached over 25 containers per hour. This stood in sharp contrast to the handling of containers on and off general cargo vessels using their own gear. For such operations a productivity rate of 5-8 containers per hatch was normal.

The systems approach of Sea-Land, Matson and other shipping companies resulted in an integrated logistic system wherein the shipping company controlled the entire chain including all equipment for providing door-to-door transport. So, the shipping lines owned (leased or controlled) their handling equipment, containers, terminal facilities and road chassis. For that reason the pioneers considered their terminals as a control base not only for the modal interchange but also to store and repair their key equipment: containers and chassis. In the 1960s the terminals had special facilities and space for the cleaning and repair of dry, refrigerated and special containers (such as tanks) and road chassis (brake test equipment, generator set repair, pre-tripping of reefers, container washing plant, etc.), including large areas to park all that (unused) equipment.

Some shipping lines introduced container vessels with roll-on/roll-off possibilities, encouraging general stevedoring companies to convert parts of their terminals into areas for rolling stock and containers on trailers.

In retrospect

Within 10 years, terminals expanded to facilities with a quay line of 300-500 m.; 2-3 container cranes (Sea-Land also introduced the A-frame cranes at their new facilities) and a terminal area of 4 to 8 hectares, with buildings for operations control (the marine building), administration, gate, a container freight station and facilities for Maintenance and Repair (M&R, see Figure 262). Some terminals had on-dock or close by rail tracks to connect containers from the vessel to the railroad, although during the first decade these rail operations were rather limited. In general, terminal operations were dictated by the shipping lines as they introduced a complete carrier (shipping line)-controlled container transport, basically door-to-door.

Figure 262: Early Matson Terminal, Oakland

12.2. 1966-1976: A TURBULENT PERIOD FOR TERMINAL DEVELOPMENTS

In 1966, containerization started spreading from the US to other parts of the world, first to Northwest-Europe (Rotterdam, Amsterdam, Bremen, Grangemouth, London and Liverpool) and, as of 1967, to Japan (Tokyo, Shinagawa and OHI-terminal) and later to Vietnam (supplies to the US army), Hong Kong (1969) and Singapore (mid-1972).

Due to the success of the container in shipping, as shown by Sea-Land, Matson, US Lines and others, all established shipping lines from the old world, developed programs for containerization, including the required port facilities. Between 1967 and 1972, quite a number of US, European and Japanese shipping lines (or consortia) opened container shipping services on important trade routes with vessels ranging from 800-3,000 TEU capacity. This caused a heavy demand for container handling facilities and many shipping lines, joint-ventures and/or consortia (like OCL, TRIO, ACL and ACT) either pushed port authorities to invest in terminals or acquired concessions to operate their own (dedicated) terminals.

In contrast to the US, cargo handling in European ports was in the hands of specialized stevedoring companies, some of them (partly) owned by shipping lines, but others appointed by port authorities and operating more or less independently. Until the 1970s, some US shipping lines managed to obtain their "own" dedicated terminals (e.g. in Bremen, Rotterdam, Grangemouth and Felixstowe), but eventually port authorities and stevedoring companies realized that multi-user facilities could result in higher utilization rates (quay wall and storage area), which was a very important factor to recover the tremendous investments made in the beginning.

In many ports, new companies were formed (sometimes out of existing stevedoring companies and/or shipping lines) to build up facilities and labor organizations capable of handling the large numbers of containers, using all kinds of new equipment so far not known in the ports/terminals. Container handling required large areas both for staging (stacking) and transportation with large, heavy equipment. In most of the existing ports there was insufficient land to accommodate this new handling technology. In the first years (late 1960s), existing terminals were modified, but due to the outlook on considerable growth and the requirement for more space, many ports and stevedoring companies started to develop new port areas dedicated to container handling (and sometimes Ro-Ro operations). Terminal developments in the world showed some regional differences, with the most important areas being the US and Canada, Europe, the Far East and Australia.

12.2.1. US and Canada

In the late 1960s, New York, Oakland and Seattle became important container ports. In New-York, Port Elizabeth was a brand new area accommodating the impressive Sea-Land terminal, one of the many terminals Sea-Land had to expand to support their impressive SL-7 program (see Chapter 6). The Elizabeth Terminal comprised an all-wheeled operation with Paceco sliding boom cranes (a low profile was required as the Newark airport was only a few miles away) and a crane turntable, which allowed the shifting of cranes from one quay to the other (see Figure 263). At the same port area, ITO (International Terminal Operating Co.) and Maher Terminals handled vessels from a number of shipping lines, including ZIM, OOCL and ACL, with combined container and Ro-Ro operations. Both at ITO and Maher, straddle carriers and top lifters were used, besides chassis stacking, as within a few years already the terminals were running out of space.

Figure 263: Sea-Land Port Elizabeth: first phase along the Elizabeth Channel (left) and later expansion with crane turntable (right)

Typical for many US-terminals, the quay cranes were often equipped with bus bar systems, which are piled steel structures accommodating the electric conductors approximately 10 m. above dock level (see Figure 264).

Seatrain had their facilities in Weehawken, along the Hudson River. In front of their new headquarters they modified (1970) a pier type facility with berths on both sides and three low-profile cranes with sliding booms travelling over the pier. The major advantage of these cranes was that they could handle vessels at either side of the pier (copied from their earlier rail car operations). Obviously, there was no stacking capacity at the pier, so containers had to be parked in an area connected to the finger pier (see Figure 265).

Figure 264: Electric supply with bus bars

Figure 265: Seatrain's Weehawken (NJ) facility with sliding boom cranes

The use of finger piers for container operations developed out of the widely-spread use of finger-piers for the handling of general cargo vessels. However, the advantage of being able to use cranes for two opposite berths was much smaller than the disadvantage of traffic crowding under the cranes and the longer travelling distance to the remote stacking areas. Gradually, the finger pier concept almost disappeared for container terminals.

Another large terminal was Howland Hook, serving amongst others American Export-Isbrandtsen Lines and US Lines. There the terminal chassis system was also dominant. However, after several years top lifters were introduced not only for 2-4 high empty stacking but also for stacking full containers (normally up to 3-high, see Figure 266). The large gate building with almost 20 truck lanes in and out and with

Figure 266: Early top lifters (max 3-high)

administrative offices above was a good example of a typical US gate design with a pneumatic tube system to connect the truck driver with the administration clerks working one floor above the trucks.

During the second decade of containerization, in the US and Canada it became clear that many ports could not offer the needed capacity, triggering massive port expansion programs. Some ports could benefit from the radical change from small traditional general cargo facilities towards large area-consuming container terminals.

In New York/New Jersey there were many terminals converted into sites for container facilities. However new terminals at Port Elizabeth and Howland Hook, with much more area and better connections to the railroads and highways, were more attractive for shipping lines.

In Baltimore, the large Dundalk Terminal was converted for container operations and containers were put on the ground (with straddle carriers) to allow for more stacking capacity. Interestingly, the public Port Authority tendered worldwide for container quay cranes and purchased Japanese cranes (IHI; Ishikawajima-Harima Heavy Industries). This is just an example of competition from foreign companies attacking the strong position of Paceco, Alliance and Star Iron, the crane manufacturers that supported containerization in the first decade in the US.

Figure 267: "Tainer-train" with 6-TEU capacity

In Norfolk (Hampton Roads) a large multi-user terminal was realized as a conversion from an older army port and in this terminal both rubber-tired gantries (RTGs) and rail-mounted gantries (RMGs) were installed at tracks, parallel to the quay wall. Probably to serve the close-by railhead in an efficient way, a multi-trailer type of transportation was introduced, the so-called "Tainer-train" capable of transporting about 6 TEU behind one tractor (see Figure 267). At that time this multi-trailer train was not successful (later in the 1980s an enlarged track-keeping 10 TEU trailer-train at ECT became a breakthrough). Many years later more innovations were introduced at this multi-user terminal (e.g. the second trolley crane with a height-adjustable platform).

At Hampton Roads, Sea-Land acquired a 30-year lease for a dedicated facility close to the Portsmouth Terminal. This terminal (see Figure 268) was again of a characteristic Sea-Land design, with an A-frame Paceco Portainer, a yard for chassis stacking, a container freight station and some facilities for maintenance and repair (M&R) of containers, chassis and reefer equipment.

Figure 268: Typical Sea-Land terminals in Portsmouth (left) and Long Beach

A good example of taking advantage of opportunities was shown in Long Beach. Already by the end of the 1960s, it became clear that the established Port of Los Angeles could not expand very rapidly. Long Beach developed a long-term plan with possibilities to reclaim more than 1000 hectares of land during the next 20-30 years. Most of the plan was indeed realized. Due to the variety of tenants, some various terminal concepts were built. Sea-Land remained with their chassis concept, but installed large quay cranes (100' gauge, Paceco MACH, Modular Automated Container Handling). This was necessary to accommodate the increased container flows under the crane when handling the SL-7 vessels in a dual cycle operation. US Lines, next to Sea-Land terminal, followed the same example. The Transocean Gateway Terminal and the K Line terminal (later ITS) installed a combined system:

chassis parking and 4-high stacking (1 over 4) with RTGs. Most of the Long Beach terminals had on-dock rail, used by Southern Pacific, Union Pacific and Atchison Topeka/Santa Fe for connections to the Mid-West and further. Also, the railroad companies developed their own inland (intermodal, mainly train-truck) terminals to serve the fast-growing volumes, often with staging at road chassis and handling with top lifters, such as Raygo-Wagner (see Figure 269).

In a similar way, Oakland developed many new container facilities where San Francisco could not provide the services required from shipping lines (not sufficient stacking space, difficult access for road and rail). The nearby airport forced tenants to install low-profile cranes with sliding boom (Paceco and Alliance). Here as well the chassis system was dominant (Sea-Land, Seatrain, US Lines) but Seventh Street

Figure 269: Container handling with Raygo-Wagner (Piggy Packer, Port Packer)

Terminal (Matson) and the Public Container Terminal used straddle carriers, whereas the multi-user Oakland Container Terminal installed RTGs with a tractor-trailer system.

To conclude the developments in the US, Seattle should be mentioned. Sea-Land started in 1964 and expanded its facility to accommodate military services to Okinawa, the Philippines and Vietnam and by 1973 the SL-7 Transpacific service. And again an all-wheeled operation (chassis parking) asking for short container dwell times (limited space). Other facilities were built for the Japanese lines and Matson with straddle carrier stacking perpendicular to the quay wall (1 over 2). Seattle experienced a massive expansion (already about 500,000 TEU by the mid-1970s) and therefore some later facilities (e.g. Terminal 25) were realized with an RTG stacking system.

During this decade many facilities in the US were modified or newly designed for higher density stacking (Straddle carrier, RTG and RMG) as space was running out. Up till now Sea-Land maintained the chassis system: a simple, low cost operation and attractive for inland trucking if you can organize a short dwell time. No problem, that was a "must" for Sea-Land, as they advertized short door-to-door transportation times (dwell times regularly less than 3 days)!

The first 10 years of containerization, in the US were used by many European and Japanese shipping lines to study the potential of containerization, to overcome their doubts and to review their strategies. When US shipping lines entered their traditional trades a reaction was required. However the European and Japanese shipping industry had a great deal of leeway to make up. The different port structures blocked some developments for a real door-to-door operation. Many non-US shipping lines (and/or consortia) had no possibility to set up their own terminals abroad (some of the shipping lines did not even want it as they argued that such terminal activities did not belong to their core business). The established stevedoring companies and port authorities wanted to maintain their favorable business position. This resulted in a variety of terminal designs outside of the US, when containerization all of a sudden entered Europe and the Far East at a very large scale. Some new terminals were developed by port authorities, others were leased by private operators; some terminals were dedicated to a small number of shipping lines (maintaining their own operating procedures), others were set-up as real public, multi-user facilities.

On top of that there was the influence of an existing handling equipment manufacturing industry (both in Europe and Japan), often supported by their national governments, to participate in the developments for this new port technologies. For those reasons a large diversity of terminal designs came about in the Far East and Europe during the second decade in containerization.

12.2.2. Far East

Japan

Matson was the first shipping line to start a service to Japan, with two self-sustained container vessels (464 containers and 49 cars capacity) enabling them to be handled by any general stevedoring company in Japan. At that time there were still no container facilities. However, this rapidly changed. Japan's fast growing export business (electronics and industrial equipment) required support from Japanese shipping lines and the Japanese Ministry of Transport saw the potential of containerization. A national study group was formed and, together with the Japanese Council for the Rationalization of the Shipping and Ship Building industries (CRSSB), they convinced the

Figure 270: Shinagawa Terminal, Tokyo

Ministry of Transport that massive efforts (investments) were required both for the renewal of the shipping fleet and the construction of new terminals (1966). New port legislation was introduced and Japanese shipping lines were supported by US$ 440 million and favorable investment policies resulting in a large fleet renewal (all vessels were built at Japanese yards!) and a number of new container terminals. This accelerated new container services, all in need of new much larger handling facilities. The first upgrades took place by the end of the year 1967 in Kobe, Osaka and Nagoya, Yokohama and Tokyo (see Figure 270).

Figure 271: Dense stacking at Tokyo, RTGs at K Line (left) and RMGs at OHI 3-5

Much land reclamation was required (e.g. Kobe's Port Island and new wharfs in Nagoya, Osaka and Tokyo). The Japanese approach was based on the lease of (more or less) standard terminal modules comprising a berth length (250-300 m.), sufficient depth, a CFS and an inspection area. In general there were 2 quayside container cranes (to be specified by the tenant and then purchased (and leased back) by the Port Authority. Sea-Land started in 1968 and got access to the Japanese markets by hooking-up with the Mitsui-conglomerate. Quite early, Mitsui got a Paceco-license and so, when Sea-Land started its own terminal at Kobe Island, it was again the A-frame Portainer with a chassis system behind.

Most of the other new terminals used denser stacking. The Japanese started their own production of straddle carriers (Mitsubishi and TCM) and rubber mounted gantries (Mitsui/Paceco). Early attempts on semi-automation were realized at Tokyo's K Line terminal with RTGs (a 2-berth facility at OHI) and at the OHI-terminal (berth 3, 4 and 5), with RMGs (see Figure 271).

After the entering of Japanese shipping lines (NYK, Mitsui OSK and K Line) into consortia serving the Far East-Europe trade (TRIO, ScanDutch and ACE), the expansion of terminal facilities was impressive. Governmental and labor union involvement caused rather rigid regulations (e.g. no operation on Sundays, strict closing hours for deliveries: 48-72 hrs; prices for 40' box handling 50% more than for 20' box handling, etc.). However, productivity in Japanese terminals always has been rather high, not only as a result of the positive labor attitude but also due to the smaller, shipping line oriented terminal sizes (dedicated terminal operations, the use of planning tools and proper housekeeping) and strict regulations.

Hong Kong

Hong Kong Island and Kowloon served as a trade hub for many decades. The British colony was a gateway to China and there was a considerable transshipment activity, although vessel handling was rather primitive. Shore-based facilities were limited, vessels were commonly anchored in the Hong Kong Strait and small boats shuttled the cargo between the shore and the vessels (even today these so-called mid-stream operations do exist for general cargo and containers).

The small, developing country Hong Kong recognized the impact of containerization by the mid-1960s. Their export activities could well be supported with appropriate container handling facilities. A container committee concluded that container operations would spread over the Pacific in a few years and so, Hong Kong had to realize new terminals. It took until October 1967 before the Hong Kong Government initiated a comprehensive expansion program.

Some port operators however took the lead and already started with an upgrading of their existing facilities, in order to accommodate the early container shipping lines (Sea-Land, APL, PFEL and OCL). The Hong Kong and Kowloon Wharf and Godown Company (HKKWGC) improved their Tsim Sha Tsui facility in Kowloon. This common user facility with finger piers got its first A-frame type of container crane in 1971 (see Figure 272, left).

Figure 272: Early Kowloon terminals (pier type, left and a modified ship yard, right)

Another Kowloon company, the Hong Kong and Whampoa Dock Company converted a shipyard at Hung Hom into a container terminal (see Figure 272, right). Their new company Whampoa Terminals installed a sliding boom Paceco crane on a finger pier and two RTGs (Paceco-Mitsui) and a CFS on-shore. Remarkably, this Whampoa Terminals was managed by John Meredith, later to become the president of HIT (Hutchison International Terminals) and later on expanded into the Hutchison Port Holdings Group, a subsidiary of the multinational conglomerate Hutchison Whampoa Ltd.

A third early operator started on Hong Kong Island at North Point, a compact facility with two general cargo cranes (one derrick type) for vessel handling and two Paceco Transtainers (see Figure 273). Interestingly, this facility was backed up by a remote terminal at Kowloon (Kwan Tong) connected through an own-operated fleet of 9 barges (maximum 250 TEU). As such, it was one of the first terminals with a satellite facility.

Figure 273: Hong Kong North Point with general cargo cranes

It took the Hong Kong Government some years to develop a Port Development Plan but finally they decided in 1969 to expand at Kwai Chung (Kowloon). The first three berths (each 1,000-ft long) were tendered and leased to three operators:

- Berth 1 to Modern Terminals Ltd (owners: shipping consortia OCL and ACT and the trading company Butterfield and Swire).
- Berth 2 was acquired by Kowloon Container Warehouse Company Ltd (owners Oyama, NYK, K Line and Japan Line) and after their bankruptcy taken over (1977) by Hong Kong International Terminals (a company formed by Hong Kong and Whampoa Dockyard Co Ltd) that was to exploit Berth 4 as of 1976.
- Berth 3 was leased to Sea-Land, which installed its worldwide terminal concept (Paceco-Mitsui quay cranes, on-wheels stacking and a large CFS (see Figure 274).

Figure 274: Sea-Land terminal Kwai Chung, berth 3

Kwai Chung became the rapidly expanding container port of Hong Kong and all major shipping lines moved to Kwai Chung, many of them with a capital share in one of the Kwai Chung terminals (e.g. Maersk Line, HKKWGC and MTL developed Kwai Chung berth no. 5). After a somewhat slow start, the Hong Kong container terminals were growing very fast, hardly capable of following the massive growth in containerized trade between Hong Kong and Southern China and the rest of the world. Within some decades Hong Kong became the world's container port nr. 1!!

Singapore

After having been a British Crown colony for almost a century and for a few years federated with Malaysia, the Singapore Republic started its independence in 1965. Historically Singapore was a Far Eastern free-trade zone and to support the young republic, the Economic Development Board decided to develop industry and trade. The Port of Singapore Authority (PSA) started already in 1964 and planned four berths for conventional ships. But container shipping developments in the US, Europe and Japan convinced PSA to convert its plans into three berths along the shallow waters around East Lagoon. A US$ 15 million World Bank loan helped to realize an attractive container terminal as well as a decrease in labor gang sizes. After the British announced the withdrawal of their military forces from the island, the Singapore government decided to accelerate their efforts to become a Southeast Asia Trade Center with a modern relay port. This should facilitate feeder services to Thailand, Malaysia, Indonesia, Vietnam and the Philippines.

In 1972, PSA opened its Tanjong Pagar Container Terminal with four Hitachi quay cranes and a straddle carrier-based stacking system. There were three large container freight stations (typically for free-zone trading). Already after 3 years the first rubber-mounted stacking

Figure 275: Singapore Tanjong Pagar Terminal and light-weight Liebherr Tango feeder crane

cranes were introduced and due to the tremendous growth, PSA gradually installed more RTGs (see Figure 275). Within a few years the berth length was further extended to a length of approximately 1,500 m. and an additional feeder berth equipped with two light-weight, 30-tons Liebherr Tango cranes.

Within a decade, the PSA facility ranked in the world top ten container ports and as of the 1990s the port continuously competed with Hong Kong for the position of number one container port in the world. From the beginning, PSA took an innovative approach in container terminal development. Operations were supported by computer systems (IBM 370 model 145 at the start); planning systems for the yard and landside deliveries were developed in-house and a large inland container depot (± 64 hectares) was built close to the terminal. A further reduction in gang sizes (maximum 15 men) and strict procedures for landside receivals/deliveries and for maximum dwell times allowed PSA to offer attractive (low-cost) services for transshipment.

Right from the start PSA took a centralized approach with almost no influence from shipping lines at their facilities development. The policy was (and still is) to plan ahead, realizing the required infrastructure and handling facilities ahead of demands. This, together with large efforts in training and education for a motivated labor staff, made Singapore a top-class container terminal.

12.2.3. Europe

When the major US (semi-)container lines started their operations to Europe as of 1966, the established stevedoring companies, port authorities and shipping lines operating in and from the European ports became very active. Some of them did not believe in the new concept, but felt the competition. Others saw the opportunities and started modification and newbuilding programs. The existing trade lanes between Europe and Australia also triggered terminal developments in Australia simultaneous and almost similar to those in Europe.

In many West-European countries (e.g. Belgium, Germany, France, Italy and The Netherlands) special container terminals were developed either by existing stevedoring companies or by port authorities. In some ports Sea-Land managed to get a dedicated facility (e.g. Grangemouth, Rotterdam, Bremen/Bremerhaven and Felixstowe) and there, Sea-Land introduced their worldwide terminal handling system (on-wheels stacking) and in some ports Sea-Land installed its own quayside cranes (Paceco A-frame Portainers). In the second decade of containerization many ports invested in terminal facilities, not all of them very well utilized. Amazingly, within 5 years (1966-1972) about 50 new terminals were realized in the major European ports (at least 250 m. quay wall; one or more new container quay cranes with 30-53 tons lift capacity and 30-36 m. outreach and sufficient storage), however, with many differences in lay-out and handling concepts. Below, a summary will be given of the major early-built European terminals with issues of interest from a technology and/or operations point of view.

Belgium

In Antwerp (see Figure 276), around the 6th Harbor dock, but especially around the Churchill dock, 5 existing stevedoring companies modified general cargo facilities into pure container or multi-purpose facilities; each with one or two container cranes (lifting capacities from 40-53 tons); most of them with Ro-Ro berthing ramps and ample warehousing. Stacking was predominantly on the ground, with the help of rolling equipment (straddle carriers from Clark, Peiner and Le Tourneau; DEMAG side-loaders; heavy forklifts with a top spreader and capacities up to 30 tons). Right from the beginning the stacking

Figure 276: Antwerp terminal, Churchill Dock

equipment effected the transportation between the quay cranes (some of them with a backreach larger than 20 m.) and the stacking areas. In between the Churchill and 6th dock the Belgium railways installed a 4-track rail terminal directly adjacent to the terminals (this rail terminal was later to be operated by Inter Ferry Boats). In addition the existing railroad infrastructure into the originally general cargo facilities allowed the stevedoring companies to handle containers on railcars at tracks within the gauge of the quay cranes.

Zeebrugge was a port with many ferry boat services including rail ferries and thus, understandably, Zeebrugge designed terminals for sea-rail operations. The first container facility was a shortsea container terminal with two portal type container cranes with a limited outreach of 18 m. and 4 railway tracks inside of the crane tracks (gauge). The objective was to transship directly from vessel to railcar and reverse, but also quite some containers were put on chassis to be picked later by truckers.

In 1971, the Ocean Container Terminal was opened and again there were four rail tracks under the quay cranes. The much bigger Munck quay cranes had a large backreach as well, to connect (via the ground) with a straddle carrier operated storage yard (see Figure 277).

The trains could be moved/positioned by the crane driver using an ASEA, cable-winch driven pull system. Contrary to most other quay cranes in the world, in Zeebrugge the quay cranes had an operator's cabin at the sea-side of the trolley, in order to provide the operator a view on his landside (railcars) operations (induced by the railway origin of this Zeebrugge terminals). After some years of growth in Zeebrugge it became clear, that direct transshipment between deepsea vessels and railcars was difficult to arrange due to delays in vessel/train arrivals, lack of information on connecting transport and waiting for shunting in case of large call sizes.

Figure 277: Zeebrugge terminals: Ferry Boats and OCT (right) with in gauge rail handling

Denmark

In Denmark, Ro-Ro services were widely spread, but container operations were introduced. In 1970, one container crane (30 m. outreach and no backreach) was installed at Copenhagen by Arhus Maskinfabrik, which company later installed a similar crane in Esbjerg. At almost the same time, the Arhus Port Authority installed a quay crane manufactured by Thomas Schmidt from Copenhagen. In Arhus and Esbjerg tractor/trailer transport was combined with forklift stacking and stacking under the quay crane. Copenhagen introduced 2-high straddle carrier stacking (see Figure 278).

Figure 278: Copenhagen (right) and Esbjerg terminal with Arhus Maskinfabrik cranes

France

In France, Dunkirk converted an existing (Ro-Ro) facility into a container terminal with 6 rail tracks under 2 container cranes (Caillard, 53 tons) and a straddle carrier stacking operation.

Le Havre was the largest container port with many Atlantic services (Terminal Quai de L'Atlantique, with 4 Caillard quay cranes) and a mix of a chassis yard system and ground stacking with straddle carriers and side loaders. The "Port Autonome" rapidly developed a second terminal (Quai de L'Europe, 4 Caillard quay cranes), where the established stevedoring companies provided handling systems for stacking (straddle carriers, side loaders and top lifters) and transportation mainly with tractor/trailers or roll-trailers (with gooseneck) between the yard, quay wall and railhead.

In France public interest ("Port Autonomes") owned, maintained and operated the quay cranes; the stevedores only took care of yard operations, inland connections and warehousing. The Port of Marseilles was a typical finger-pier concept, not very suited for large scale container operations. However, at Fos sur Mer (approximately 30 km. west from Marseilles) a new industrial port complex was under construction (e.g. for a steel plant) and there Marseilles realized a large container terminal. This was one of the first European terminals with sufficient land depth for stacking (straddle carriers). At the landside, a 4-track rail terminal was equipped with rail-mounted cranes to handle trains of the French National Railways (S.N.C.F.).

Remarkable was the Paceco quay crane with a 25 m. backreach, enabling backreach block-buffering and connecting to straddle carriers. Also, in Gennevilliers (Port de Paris) en Strasbourg smaller container facilities were realized to service coastal vessels (Gennevilliers) and barges (Strasbourg).

Figure 279: Fos sur Mer (Marseille) showing container cranes with large backreach

Germany

In 1966, Sea-Land started operations in the port of Bremen (with self-sustained vessels) and already after a few years, Sea-Land installed a Paceco A-frame container crane with on-wheel stacking (mainly 35'-containers).

The lengthy access river channel to Bremen was a disadvantage for feeder-operations and already before the 1970s the port of Bremerhaven was built. In both terminals (Bremen and Bremerhaven) stacking was done by straddle carriers (Kocks, Peiner, Jünkerath, Drott and Mannesmann) and only a small number of containers at road chassis (e.g. for Sea-Land, American Export Lines).

At Bremerhaven the new expansion area at Nordhafen West was equipped with Kocks quayside gantry cranes, moreover a number of rail tracks were installed at the middle of the yard, allowing for the handling with straddle carriers. The railcar width (approximately 3 m.) required an increased inside width for the straddle carriers (approximately 3.5 m. instead of the so far usual 3 m.).

Due to the bad experiences with straddle carrier reliability and maintenance cost, already in 1968 the Bremen Terminal introduced the tractor-trailer system for transport of containers between the quay crane and remotely located container stacks.

At the BLG (Bremer Lagerhaus Gesellschaft) terminal in Bremerhaven the straddle carrier was selected again because of its high degree of random access to containers in the yard. However as of 1971 it was decided to use a tractor-trailer system for transportation between vessel and stacking yard. The longer travelling distances in the expanding container yard learned BLG that a transport distance longer than 300 m. made an intermediate transportation system more efficient and gave a better straddle carrier reliability (less driving). From that time on, a typical BLG quay crane back up gang was composed of 4 tractor/trailers and 2 straddle carriers.

In Hamburg there were two container terminals developed around the Waltershof basin: Eurokai, modified out of an existing general cargo pier and Burchardkai (HHLA) with a much larger expansion potential. At the Burchardkai facility stacking and transportation to the quay cranes was realized with straddle carriers. The first straddle carrier stacking blocks had stack rows perpendicular to the quay wall and later parallel; the transportation to the quay crane was done by straddle carriers (both in gauge and in the backreach). Only 2-3 straddle carriers were "feeding the hook", which could be realized by some type of yard planning with stack locations close to the predetermined (expected) berth location. The Burchardkai facility was provided with some large sheds for packing/unpacking and warehousing and some large repair facilities for reefer containers and standard containers (including the popular glass fiber reinforced plywood containers).

Figure 280: Hamburg terminal; Burchardkai (left) and Eurokai

The other Hamburg terminal Eurokai started with straddle carrier stacking and tractors with bathtub-chassis for transportation to the quay cranes and CFS. Limited space at Eurokai resulted at the end of this decade in the use of wide-span, rail-mounted gantry cranes (11 containers wide) for stacking and direct handling of containers onto railcars. These cranes were already connected to a mainframe computer (Siemens 330) for location control and logistics planning. In addition every crane was provided with an on-board mini-computer (Siemens 310) to allow operations even when the mainframe had a breakdown and to allow for minimized hoisting, based on the stack profile when making a crane cycle. Data processing between the central computer and the crane's mini-computers was realized by an inductive loop at a for that time amazing transmitting rate of 1,200 bits/second.

In Hamburg a rather unique facility was built for the consolidation/distribution of general cargo to and from containers. This so-called "Übersee-Zentrum" served as an intermodal hub (connections to rail, road and barges) for general cargo, with more than 1 hectare covered area. But the rapid growth of container traffic directly to shippers and consignees caused a limited use of this facility.

Right from the beginning the German deepsea container terminals were connected by an extensive rail network with more than 40 inland terminals at the beginning of the 1970s. The railways took a considerable share in inland transportation (some years more than 50%) and that was partly forthcoming from the fact that the German railways had already set up a containerized internal network for domestic cargo (the Deutsche Bundesbahn operated about 20,000 DB-owned small containers with a load capacity of 5-6 tons).

The Netherlands

Sea-Land selected Rotterdam as one of their stepping stones to Europe (together with Bremen) starting in 1966, at the general cargo terminal Quick Dispatch, where Sea-Land erected an A-type Paceco crane.

In 1966, the managing director of the Rotterdam Municipal Port Management stimulated a combined effort of existing stevedoring companies (Quick Dispatch, Thomsen's Havenbedrijf, C. Swarttouw, Müller-Progress, Pakhuismeesteren) and the Dutch Railways and they founded Europe Container Terminus (ECT). Already in August 1967 a new terminal at the Margriethaven became operational and in 1970 Sea-Land left their Quick Dispatch location and moved to the North-side of the Alexander dock (operated by ECT, see Figure 281).

Figure 281: ECT (home) terminal, Rotterdam

After a change in ECT's management (in 1970) the focus came on managerial and operational changes (more transparency) and major technological improvements to support a better service and performance. In addition to Sea-Land and ECT some smaller facilities were built in the port of Rotterdam for some shortsea and combined Lo-Lo/Ro-Ro services (Ferry services at the Beneluxhaven and Bell Lines at the Brittaniahaven). Those smaller terminals used wide-span gantries for vessel handling and stacking.

Figure 282: Container Terminal Amsterdam (CTA)

In Amsterdam, CTA started operations in 1968, with some Atlantic (US Lines and Container Marine Lines, a division of AEIL) and shortsea services using 2 MAN quay cranes and a straddle carrier stacking operation (see Figure 282).

The Port of Flushing (Vlissingen) was also rather early with a new container terminal with 2 quay cranes (1 Peiner and 1 Paceco), serving the Australia Europe Container Service for incoming calls (see Figure 283). Their advantage was a large covered area where the sampling and trading of wool could be organized (this was a requirement from the Australian Wooldumpers).

Already after the first 5 years, ECT in Rotterdam realized an annual throughput of approximately 300,000 containers (about 500,000 TEU) and the arrival of consortia in the beginning of the 1970s caused even more concentration of container handling at larger specialized container terminals. Consortia like TRIO (1971) and ScanDutch (1972) made a selection of 5/6 terminals per continent (Europe and South-East

Figure 283: Port of Flushing serving incoming calls of AECS

Asia) and that resulted in quite some rivalry amongst ports and terminals, especially in the Hamburg-Le Havre range. The shipping lines introduced vessels up to 3,000 TEU and required a port stay of maximum 24 hours and of course a good berth performance (50-80 containers/hour) and a guaranteed berth at the planned arrival schedules. The shipping lines used their power to stimulate competition in service and price.

A good example was Rotterdam, where ECT as the largest terminal operator in port expected to attract the newly-formed TRIO group. The TRIO member Ben Line insisted on a second quotation in the Rotterdam port, which resulted in lower prices and a more preferential service offered by Unitcentre (basically a multi-purpose terminal) to TRIO. And so, at the last moment TRIO selected the much smaller Unitcentre.

Nevertheless, ECT experienced a massive growth (already 510,000 boxes annual throughput in 1974); in some years even more than 50%. The growing number of enlarged vessels, the increasing container dwell times and the storage demand for empty containers and shipping lines' owned road-chassis asked for an expansion of storage capacity. This made ECT decide in 1971 to install wide-span, rail-mounted gantry cranes with cantilevers at both sides (see Figure 284).

Once again a partnership between a crane manufacturer and a terminal operator (in this case Conrad-Stork and ECT and earlier shown by Matson/Clark/Paceco) resulted in an innovative stacking crane design. With 14 containers wide between the crane tracks and with rather high gantry travel and trolley speeds, the cranes were partly automated (automatic trolley and gantry positioning on a numerical position). The repeatedly precise positioning could be obtained through a load sway control system at the trolley. New for those days was the

Figure 284: Wide-span, partly automated Conrad-Stork RMG

fact that these cranes were ordered with a functional specification. In a defined type of operation the cranes had to be commissioned with a productivity of 30 container moves/hour randomly in and out of the stack. The crane manufacturer had to select speeds, acceleration rates, etc. by himself.

Unfortunately for ECT, but fine for Conrad-Stork, Unitcentre ordered 6 of the same stacking cranes (although with a rotating trolley) after their successful contracting the TRIO group. Similar types (although from other manufacturers) were later installed at the Tokyo OHI-terminal (Mitsui); at the Modern Terminals facility in Hong Kong (Hitachi) and at the Eurokai Terminal Hamburg (Kocks) (see Figure 285). Although these large stacking cranes gave a good area utilization, some additional space was required for traffic lanes as the stacks had to be connected to the land- and waterside either by means of tractor trailer systems (waterside) or straddle carriers (waterside and landside).

Figure 285: Rail-mounted stacking cranes at MTL, Hong Kong and Eurokai, Hamburg (right)

Ireland and the United Kingdom

Ro-Ro services (railcars and semi-trailers) and coastal services with small container types were in use for many years between many ports in Ireland, the UK and mainland Europe. So, when the large maritime container entered Europe many existing ports modified facilities to accommodate the container. In the UK, the ports of Belfast, Bristol, Clydeport, Felixstowe , Grangemouth, Greenock, Harwich, Liverpool, London-Tilbury, Manchester, Newport, Preston, Southampton and Teesport, they all installed new container quay cranes; similar developments were see in Ireland (Cork, Dublin and Waterford). After some years the major shipping lines determined their major ports of call at the UK: Felixstowe, Grangemouth, Liverpool, London-Tilbury and Southampton.

Shortsea operator Bell Lines took an innovative approach straight away. Operating between only 5 ports, namely 1 in Ireland (Waterford); 2 in the UK (Bellport near Newport, see Figure 286, and Teesport); 1 in the Netherlands (Rotterdam, Brittania harbor) and 1 in France (Radicatel, 30 km. upstream the River Seine). Bell Lines had its own vessels, terminals, containers and some inland trucking activities; a real door-to-door operation. All of their terminals had wide-span gantry cranes (48 m. span), multi-functional for vessel/barge handling, stacking and the inland deliveries to road trucks and trains. In the beginning a standardized manual control system was used at all

Figure 286: Bell Lines with wide-span gantry cranes over the dock

terminals but already after some years the computer was introduced to do much of the manual work including tracking and tracing, statistics, administration and operations analysis. In the UK a much-larger consortium of shipping lines showed a systems approach as well.

After OCL decided to invest in modern container vessels (in 1969 the Encounter Bay-class: around 1,600 TEU and by 1972 the Tokyo Bay-class: 3,000 TEU) for their trade to Australia and the Far East, a series of new terminals was designed and built, most of them under 100% control, in some others with a majority interest. All four shipping lines within the OCL-consortium, (P&O, Ocean Transport,

British & Commonwealth and Furness Withy) decided that the vessel design should be optimized and thus no cranes on board.

The OCL-vessels were provided with large cooling plants (for shipping porthole containers) and as these containers required the circulation of cooled air when stacked on a terminal, all of OCL's terminals had impressive (partly-covered) facilities for these porthole containers (see Figure 287).

Figure 287: OCL Terminals: Sydney (left) and Tilbury (London)

For energy-saving, in some terminals porthole containers were stacked 4 or even 5 high under roof with overhead bridge cranes (see pictures London Tilbury, Melbourne and Sydney). Just like on-board the vessels, containers were stacked in cell-guide frames enabling porthole containers to be connected to a duct-system for cooled, ventilated air. In some terminals straddle carrier stacking was installed including special racks and duct systems to the cooling plants (e.g. Southampton), which is shown in Figure 288.

Figure 288: Stacking of porthole containers: Carrier-based (Southampton, left) and OBC-based (Melbourne, right)

From the start, OCL was focused on efficient, fast door-to-door operations. One of their developments was the twin-lift crane (developed with ASEA), installed in London, and later with Paceco-Vickers for Brisbane, Sydney and Melbourne. Especially in the Europe-Australia trade the 20' container was by far dominant and so crane productivity was very well supported by twin-lift operations. Due to variations in vessel hatch arrangements and cell arrangements the twin-hoist drives were designed to operate separately and the spacing between the 20' spreaders was adjustable as well; a really innovative development (it took two decades, before twin-lift operations envisaged a revival!).

For their UK inland operations OCL cooperated with the existing Freightliner System. This British Rail division started in 1965, originally set up for the rail transportation of domestic cargo. As from 1969, OCL together with the rail operator Freightliner Systems developed a well-organized rail transportation network connecting some major deepsea ports with inland depots (e.g. Container Bases). At such inland terminals, containers could be Customs cleared and consolidated (so-called dry ports). In those days the British motorway network was not very large and often congested resulting in a break-even distance of about 50 miles from where rail transportation became cost-attractive.

It is amazing how well these rail services were operated in the beginning of the 1970s. Mainly block-train shuttles were operated with modern cost-effective sets of railcars (5 cars bolted together). Only the outer wagons of the railcar sets were provided with standard couplings and buffers. The trains were suited for 120 km. per hour and fitted with disc brakes. Most of the more than 30 inland terminals were provided with rail-mounted portal cranes (many with guiding beams between trolley and spreader) to ensure fast handling at the terminals (see Figure 289).

Figure 289: Early rail terminals showing RMGs with guiding beams

Within a few years OCL/Freightliner was running a fast network of rail connections out of Southampton and London-Tilbury with daily connections to their inland terminals (up to Glasgow, Aberdeen), many of them were accepted as clearance depots by H.M. Customs a real contribution to fast door-to-door services. It is regrettable that this service could not keep pace with the impressive growth in container volumes and in later decades the rail service lost some inland market share.

Other interesting issues in Europe

In Scandinavia, Sweden (Gothenburg, Helsingborg, Oxelösund and Stockholm) and Finland (Helsinki) also joined the early European starters with real container cranes at container terminals and inland transportation from their national railways and of course trucking. Italy, Portugal and Spain started at the end of the 1960s.

In the first five years of terminal developments in Europe more than 50 terminals were realized. All of them had rather equal quayside container cranes but with a large variety of equipment for stacking and landside handling: small RTGs, RMGs, various makes of straddle carriers, side loaders (e.g. Lancer Boss), travel lifts and converted fork lift trucks, etc. Material handling equipment manufacturers got aware of the booming containerization and many of them entered the new handling scene with new types of equipment, often diesel-powered with lots of hydraulics ("simple", cheap and suited for large forces). However most of the manufacturers underestimated the tremendous fatigue loads and the intense utilization (sometimes more than 4,000 running hours per year). Hence, operations were rapidly expanding, equipment had delivery times of 6-12 months and so the existing equipment was used up to their limits.

Figure 290 shows a summary of somewhat exotic handling equipment used in the first pioneering period in Europe.

Figure 290: Exotic early equipment at European terminals

During the first decade many changes and new technologies were launched, a number of them are mentioned below.

- In the beginning labor unions were reluctant and not cooperative to accept new rosters, operational methods, etc. (in the UK, France, Italy and Spain), but in some countries a positive approach could be obtained (although sometimes accompanied with strikes), such as in Sweden, Germany and The Netherlands. In ports where the old-fashioned labor organizations (e.g. large labor pools and limited fixed work places per terminal) and non-professional habits of dock-labor continued, an essential change towards an industrial approach, required for the new logistics and technologies, took sometimes 10-20 years.

- The massive investments in reefer plants for porthole containers could not be afforded by terminals with only small numbers of such containers. Therefore small clip-on units were developed and some applications with the injection of liquid nitrogen were introduced at terminals in Belgium, Germany, The Netherlands and the UK.

- Some terminals handled both vessels from Sea-Land and other shipping lines and those terminals were confronted with the varying center-to-center corner casting distances and the different twist lock-designs. This resulted in small changes in spreader design and the use of a-symmetric twist locks (so-called multi-use twist locks). Only many years later (with the disappearance of 35' Sea-Land containers), these modified spreaders could again be replaced with the standardized ISO-dimensions and symmetric twist locks.

- At the start of the 1970s existing railway companies and newly formed rail operating companies (e.g. Intercontainer, CNC France and Transfracht Germany) invested in inland rail terminals to handle containers from rail services connecting deepsea ports. Especially in France, Germany, Italy and the UK extensive inland rail-road terminal networks with more than 20 destinations were developed. Despite this promising start rail operators could not cope with the tremendous growth in the decades to come. Figure 291 shows some of these early inland rail terminals.

Figure 291: Inland rail terminals Germany (left) and Italy

Especially in Europe, but also in Japan and Australia safety became a major issue as the crossing of straddle carrier movements with service traffic caused some severe accidents. For that reason many terminals tried to separate their internal traffic from outside truckers and service vehicles. However, this increased the complicated logistics as various equipment cycles had to be synchronized to get the right box in the right place at the right moment.

In order to improve logistics and to better control the stochastic processes the first scientific engineering attempts were made with the help of operations research and simulation of terminal handling processes (e.g. OCL of London, Tilbury, ECT of Rotterdam and HHLA of Hamburg). At the end of this decade the first computer based simulation models were developed to analyze the stochastic influences from irregular arrival patterns at sea- and landside and to analyze the consequences of unpredictable disturbances in productivities of handling systems. It was the beginning of an ever increasing use of OR-techniques for design and optimization of terminal handling systems.

In the second decade of terminal operations the importance of planning and control of operations became clear. Almost every terminal started with a type of manual control system based upon cards with information such as container ID-number, port of destination, weight, vessel voyage number, seal status, dangerous cargo code, type and size code, etc. Often the control office stored one master card and made copies for vessel stowage, stack location, internal transport movements and gate or quay crane passage.

For berth planning and stack planning a whiteboard or magnetic board was regularly used and in many cases inventory control was just a numerically arranged card collection in a shoe box.

But terminals running over 100,000 TEU throughput per year recognized the shortcomings of the above mentioned "simple" methods and introduced technologies from adjacent industries. Most of them developed their own systems just because there was no container terminal control system available at the market in those early days.

At the start of the 1970s, the first computer applications arrived in container terminals, but in the beginning almost entirely for administrative functions, for tracking and tracing (inventory control) and the time consuming information exchange to shipping lines, customs and port authorities (hazardous cargo) who insisted on daily prints of terminal activities.

In the late 1960s and early 1970s, computer companies like IBM, Univac, Digital Equipment and Siemens installed both hardware and software, with large teams of application engineers for the specific terminal functionality and a large variety of terminal dependent functional demands.

These computer companies assured terminals that their systems would easily solve the rapidly growing logistic bottlenecks in terminals. However, to the contrary: many terminals suffered several years from failures, breakdowns and shortcomings in logistic algorithms.

Some terminals followed a safer way. Firstly, they organized their operations with proven control technologies (guiding cards, optically readable information exchange protocols, etc.) and then, after some years, they applied computer programs for well-defined terminal functionalities.

Illustrative in this respect is ECT, where in 1970 Vice-President Gerrit Wormmeester reversed a planned introduction of IBM computers. At that time he did not believe in computers as long as the logistic control procedures were not properly defined. ECT adopted a well-proven punch card system (from the Dutch National Railways), which was later upgraded and expanded with the help of a (Univac) computer system.

An up-time larger than 99% and proper back-up procedures were vital issues in the early 1970s and many terminals learned the hard way. Some terminals even installed (rather expensive) fail-safe computer systems with built-in shadowing systems and dual operating systems (e.g. STRATUS and Tandem computers).

In retrospect

The second decade in containerization may well be described as the most energetic decade for container terminal developments, with major steps in terminal operations, lay-out designs and operations management. New technologies from adjacent industries were applied with many innovations to accommodate the fast growing container volumes transported around the world. At the end of the second decade (1976) the following could be observed:

- All major trade routes were supported with multi-user and/or dedicated container terminals. They were increasingly confronted with a growing logistic and operational complexity due to the large number of services, a variety of container dimensions (length and height), the many full-container and multi-purpose shipping lines and all kinds of demands from local authorities (customs and safety bodies), shippers/consignees and inland transport companies.

- Containerization caused a tremendous concentration of traffic (mainly trucks and railways) at the terminals as the cargo flows were attracted away from a multitude of small stevedores towards one or a few large container terminals. In Europe, with the exception of typical railroad countries such as the UK, Germany and France, trucking became the dominant mode for inland container transportation (> 80%).

- Limitations of on-wheeled operations introduced all kinds of new handling systems and equipment, however most of them with teething problems and not properly designed for a heavy-duty application, resulting in major fatigue problems and operational breakdowns.

- The tremendous volumes (sometimes over 500,000 TEU/year) and the demand for 24-hour tracking and tracing and yard inventory control became major issues and on top of that the random picking (and deliveries) from truckers and rigid vessel stowage sequences (disregarding the stack lay-out) caused many operational hick-ups.

- The first information control systems, originally set up as simple manually handled card systems (the "shoebox" system) developed into computer controlled administration systems for gate movements, vessel operations, tracking and tracing and invoicing. Only a few terminals managed to install some simple assignment algorithms for logistic control.

- Old-fashioned labor organizations and non-professional practices of dock labor hampered a quick change towards an industrial approach required for the new logistic attitude in containerized transport systems.

- Some pioneering companies (like Sea-Land, Matson, OCL, ECT and Eurokai) introduced new handling technologies resulting from a combined effort from engineers with an industrial background and operations managers with a vision on tomorrow's demands.

12.3. 1976-1986: A GLOBALIZED NETWORK AND SIGNALS TOWARDS AUTOMATION

After two decades in the US and only one decade in Europe and the Far East, containerization further spread over the world. New container services (with either full container vessels or multi-purpose vessels) were introduced to South Africa and later West and East Africa, the Middle East, the Caribbean and Central America and later Brazil and other Latin American countries. In Asia, South Korea and India were connected in the 1970s and before 1985 many countries in the Pacific Region (such as Indonesia, the Philippines and China) had their container services and their container terminals.

During this decade shipbuilding costs were declining partly due to the entrance of industrializing countries (e.g. Taiwan and South-Korea) and this caused a noticeable vessel capacity increase (many shipping lines ordered series of vessels in the Panamax range of 2,500-4,400 TEU, to benefit from economies of scale on their main trade routes). As a consequence shipping lines suffered from lower freight rates in a period with increasing costs (capital cost, fuel and labor). This influenced the pressure on terminal service tariffs and on top of that, a number of non-conference lines entered the scene causing even more tariff pressure.

In some areas port authorities and terminals were operating in a very competitive situation. To a certain extent this was induced by shipping lines, asking for lower prices, and better service, but also because of some concentration on fewer ports in order to better exploit this large (still Panamax) vessels. Such areas with severe competition were the US East Coast between Virginia and New York and North Western Europe (the Le Havre-Hamburg range). Also on the US West Coast, the competition between Seattle and Tacoma, between Oakland and San Francisco and Long Beach and Los Angeles was exemplary.

Some concentration resulted in the development of hub-terminals (e.g. Hong Kong, Singapore, Kaoshiung, New York, Rotterdam and Algeciras); most of them as a multi-user terminal either with shipping lines' operated or commercial feeders. Only a few terminals became real dedicated hubs (Sea-Land, United States Lines).

In this period, the conditions for and requirements to container terminals changed considerably. Despite a second oil crisis by the late 1970s the average throughput growth continued to be 5-10% annually and many terminals even showed double-digit growth rates for several years. As a result, the world's port handling moves more than tripled from 17 million TEU in 1975 to 56 million TEU in 1985. So, almost all terminals had a few common themes: expanding the existing facilities, starting massive newbuilding programs to accommodate future volumes (facilities and equipment) and maintaining or improving their service through changes in operations management and logistic control procedures, for example in Felixstowe, Sidney (Botany Bay), New York, Rotterdam (Delta Terminal) and Kaoshiung. Japan, with its typical modular design approach (300 m. quay wall and about 350 m.

terminal depth) started the design of artificial islands at Kobe and Tokyo. Some highlights from these developments during this decade will be covered below for the various terminal areas.

Waterside activities

Many terminals installed new container cranes, with faster trolley and hoist drives, and larger lifting heights above quay wall to accommodate the growing number of 3,000+ TEU vessels. At the start of the 1980s the first rumors about Post-Panamax wide vessels arrived and ECT, Rotterdam was one of the first terminals to purchase quay cranes capable of handling 16-wide on deck container vessels (40 m. beam). For their new Delta Terminal (opened in 1984) a new quay wall was designed with 16 m. water depth, a crane gauge of 35 m. (later followed by many others), allowable crane corner loads up to 700 metric tons and a power supply through 10 kV flexible cables.

To assure a simultaneous crane gantry travel and driving/parking of service vehicles (lubrication oil for vessels, repair companies) a service road before the waterside crane rail was provided: a real contribution to safety and operational flexibility although at a price. Some terminals followed this idea in a later stage. The use of telescopic spreaders became more common but twin-lift (2 x 20' containers) remained mainly in the UK and Australia (OCL operations). Sea-Land experimented with a spreader type provided with retractable twist locks, in order to avoid holes in the container roofs when positioning a spreader; however this development was not continued (too much maintenance/reliability problems).

Figure 292: Light weight cranes: Paceco in Duluth (left) and Krupp in Longview

As many (smaller) terminals were located at dock sides with limitations in quay wall loadings, some of them purchased light-weight quay cranes (Krupp, Paceco Lightweight, Liebherr-Tango, see Figure 292) at the same time benefitting from an attractive lower investment.

The consequential reduced productivity and lifetime and sometimes increased maintenance cost per move did not bother too much as the number of moves per crane per year was moderate in such terminals.

A few general cargo and multi-purpose terminals in Western Europe installed cost-attractive
mobile harbor cranes (Antwerp and Marseilles), applicable for many commodities and
flexible in their use at various berths without
the need for additional provisions, such as
crane tracks and power supply (see Figure 293).
Waterside productivity became a major issue
and shipping lines insisted on a maximum 24
hour port stay, regardless the call size of their
vessels (often more than 1000 containers/call).
Terminals remembered the typical US ports
saying: "you have to feed the hook". This issue
convinced many terminals to change their
transportation system between the yard and
the quay cranes. Some terminals continued to
drive straddle carriers (in gauge or in the
backreach) directly from the stack to the crane
in combination with a type of stack preplan-
ning close to the expected (planned) vessel
berthing location along the quay wall (Japanese
terminals and Hessenatie in Antwerp). Some
other terminals (BLG in Bremerhaven, Eurokai
in Hamburg and ECT Home in Rotterdam)
used terminal tractor/trailers between the quay

Figure 293: Early Gottwald mobile crane in Antwerp

crane and interchange areas in the stacking yard (stacking crane or straddle carrier operated). A real
up scaling was shown by ECT Rotterdam (the multi-trailer system) and the LUF-system in some
Scandinavian ports (see Figure 294).

Figure 294: LUF-system with 3-high, 2-wide block transportation

The LUF system was basically developed for Ro-Ro operations with passive frames to accommodate
6 x 20' or 6 x 40' containers (3-high on the frame); later they were also used in Lo-Lo-operations with
the objective to reduce labor and equipment cost and to improve buffer ability. The system did not get
much appreciation.

More successful was ECT's multi trailer system, with a patented system for precise tracking (even in curves up to 18 m. radius). After the first trials in 1979 and a few years of pilot operation at ECT's Home Terminal, the efficient trailer-trains (10 TEU) were applied as the only internal transportation equipment at the ECT Delta terminal (see Figure 295).

The buffer at the train supported a crane productivity improvement (in combination with chassis loaders for fast container positioning on the trailer train when unloading) and a cost reduction.

Remarkably a much earlier 6 TEU trailer-train, introduced in the early 1970s at Norfolk International Terminals, Virginia US never became successful. However, the ECT multi-trailer train was introduced later in the 1990s at many other terminals (such as Giao Tauro in Italy, Marsaxlokk in Malta and Felixstowe in the UK).

Figure 295: Multi Trailer System showing the precise track keeping

Safety and operator's comfort got more attention. For lashing activities, special lashing cages to be connected to the spreader, were developed (see Figure 296 right) and sometimes a complete 20' container

Figure 296: Lashing cages

with cut-out corners was used. Some trials with a separate crane operator's cabin on a separate track, independent from the crane trolley, did not get much support as crane operators preferred to have a view on the swinging container below them, in order to have better sway control.

The first developments in waterside automation (ECT's PLC-controlled second trolley system, Matson's quay crane container buffer) arrived at the end of the 1970s. More details are given in Chapter 13.

Stacking operations

In this decade two major aspects influenced a drive towards denser stacking. First, there was the tremendous volume growth and second, many terminals (especially multi-user terminals) were confronted with elongated container dwell times not only for full containers but even more for empty containers (trade imbalances and consortium effects). This resulted in a demand for 5 to 10-fold more stack capacity within a 10-years period.

Matson already showed the way to denser stacking with their straddle carrier operations and this handling system also became very popular in Europe, the Far East, Australia and some US-terminals.

Many US-terminals and dedicated US shipping lines' terminals elsewhere in the world (Sea-Land, US Lines, AEL and Seatrain) were originally in favor of the chassis system, but the low area utilization (ca. 240 TEU/ha) caused a gradual change towards straddle carriers (1 over 2) and Rubber Tired Gantries (up till 1 over 5) with an area utilization of 480 TEU/ha and 700 TEU/ha respectively. Some terminals followed a direction already shown in the early 1970s and installed rail-mounted stacking cranes offering 900-1,100 TEU/ha, depending on stacking height and rail span (e.g. in Hong Kong, Eurokai in Hamburg and OHI terminal in Tokyo).

The chassis system remained popular in the US and in particular for shipping lines offering door-to-door operations (Sea-Land, US Lines, Seatrain and Maersk) with their shipping line owned road chassis (see Figure 297).

During the late 1970s, some terminals (like ECT Rotterdam. Felixstowe, Bremerhaven) could persuade Sea-Land to change from their on-wheeled system to what they called a ground-ing operation. Rising cost of their road chassis (with all the inflexibility forthcoming from

Figure 297: Sea-Land on-wheels stacking at Port Elizabeth

many different National road traffic rules in the various European countries) and the availability of independent truckers with their own chassis, made a change cost effective.

Also the top lifter (very popular in the beginning, due to its relatively simple design and the availability of dock labor) and the side loader lost much ground. Instead of the top lifter a new type of machine came on the scene: the reach stacker, the first ones manufactured by Belotti (late 1960s) and Ormig (both Italy, see Figure 298).

Figure 298: Belotti reach stackers; late 1960s (left) and 1970s

Although somewhat heavier, a higher (front) axle load and more expensive, this type of machine became attractive for small and medium size terminals (operational area utilization 300-425 TEU/ha) due to its better visibility and rather moderate maintenance cost.

Talking on maintenance, this topic was a major concern for terminals during this decade. All terminals established their own maintenance departments (often accommodating 5-10% of their total labor force) with provisions for equipment cleaning, major repairs and spare parts storage. Not only the continuously-growing amount of equipment, but also the gradually enlarged equipment itself (higher stacking straddle carriers, lift-trucks, telescopic spreaders, etc.) caused costly modifications /expansions of maintenance facilities in order to keep pace with the rapidly growing maintenance efforts.

Some terminals recognized the need for an industrial approach, which resulted in structured equipment improvement programs. Especially the heavy fatigue loads and the high utilization rate (often more than 4,000 hrs/year) disclosed many weak components. Some manufacturers failed in adapting their designs, towards the inherent operational demands (functionalities and reliability) and as a result their market share decreased (e.g. Clark Equipment Co.).

The need for reliable, heavy-duty and comfortable equipment made some terminals decide to establish partnerships with manufacturers that were willing to design/build equipment, suitable for the changing demands. Examples are BLG Bremerhaven who challenged Peiner and Valmet to make their straddle carriers more maintenance friendly and with more comfort and less noisy for their operators.

ECT-Rotterdam encouraged Nelcon to build a diesel-electric straddle carrier suited for 50,000 running hours (after experiencing Clark Van Carriers only delivering 15,000-25,000 operating hours with a tremendous maintenance cost). The growing demand for storage capacity resulted in a diesel-electric 10-wheel straddle carrier for 1 over 3-high stacking (see also Chapter 8).

Many terminals discovered the benefits from limiting their number of manufacturers and entered into long term relations with their suppliers, to encourage improvements and new technologies. In this respect a statement from ECT's President Gerrit Wormmeester is very illustrative: "we don't run a zoo, so there is no need to have one piece of every kind".

In later decades this approach was left; economic performance indicators became more dominant, resulting in a multi-vendor approach to encourage competition and reduce purchasing cost. It is doubtful whether this multi-vendor/low investment approach did contribute to minimize total life cycle cost or to improve operational reliability.

One topic in stacking yards required a lot of attention: provisions for refrigerated containers. Many shipping lines operated so-called integrals (the cooling/ventilation plant integrated within the container, only asking for electric supply) but some shipping lines such as OCL, Hamburg Süd, and Hapag-Lloyd used porthole (clip-on) containers, requiring a flow of cold air from an outside source.

The provisions for the plug-in integral refrigerated containers depended on the type of stacking system. On-wheeled and SC-stacking needed a row with rectangular positioned containers (either grounded or on wheels). In the beginning terminals used simple ladders to reach the second layer, but later this was improved to walkways, to enable safe and fast (dis)connecting and monitoring (reading of temperature settings, etc.).

Figure 299: Plug-in connections for integral reefers (straddle carrier, chassis and RTG stacking)

Equal access structures were developed for RTG and RMG stacking systems; however they were positioned inside of the crane track 4 or 5-high with all the difficulties to accommodate 8', 8' 6" and later 9' 6" high containers.

The service of air cooled containers (porthole) was more complicated. One of the first users, OCL, installed either centralized duct-systems in their overhead stacking crane storage yard (Tilbury and Melbourne) or duct-systems especially designed for SC-stacking. However, terminals that only received such containers in small numbers could not effort such expensive installations (requiring a lot

Figure 300: Stand-alone tower units for 2-4 porthole containers

of energy when underutilized due to the bad efficiency for cooling plants when running far below capacity). For such smaller numbers special tower-units were developed (see Figure 300) that could accommodate 2 or 4 containers.

An additional complication arrived when the South Africa Europe Container Service (SAECS) introduced air cooled containers 8' 6" high (instead of 8' for OCL). That caused problems, when stacking air cooled containers more than one high.

In Belgium and The Netherlands, a low-cost method for cooling of these porthole containers was developed using the injection of liquid nitrogen, an acceptable method for deep-frozen cargo but less suited for perishable goods (such as fruit and dairy products) as there was a lack of ventilation.

ECT developed together with Air Products a liquid nitrogen plant including ventilation and a sufficient flow of fresh, cooled air through the containers (see Figure 301). As contrasted with the large-scale duct systems, having 10-12 connections requiring equal temperature setting and compatible cargo (to avoid taint cross-over); this nitrogen plant allowed a per container condition setting. Another advantage was the low (almost none) energy consumption under

Figure 301: Liquid nitrogen cooling plant for individual temperature settings

low utilization rates. The facility as shown in the figure had a remote control station as well, allowing a reduced labor demand for inspection and temperature settings.

In the early 1980s, remote monitoring of integral reefers became a topic of increasing interest due to the high labor cost and damage risk from wrong settings and/or reefer unit failures.

Sea-Land with the largest fleet of reefers (about 9,000 in 1983) developed a system for automatic recording of temperature, unit performance and reefer unit failures without the need for an additional cabling to each reefer container.

The system was based on data transfer between the reefer and a centrally located computer using a communication technology over the power lines (carrier current data transmission). The transmission speed of 300 baud (in a 72 or 83 kHz band) was a good figure for those days and Sea-Land proposed a worldwide standardization of key elements (carrier frequency, signal level, interface RS 232C). The low investment made the system very attractive, however the system was not worldwide accepted. Much later, remote monitoring was standardized however based on additional monitoring plugs.

Landside and intermodal operations

This decade brought a shift in attention towards the landside and inland connectivity, as logistic managers (both from the carriers and shippers) realized that much time was lost at terminals and inland transportation due to insufficient connectivity and failures in information and forward planning.

For landside logistics, carrier haulage (shipping line organized door-to-door transport) was still dominant, but the first shifts to merchant haulage (shipper/consignee arranges the landside leg) were noticed.

In general, the terminal landside had to serve truckers and railroad companies. Starting with trucking, this was the dominant landside mode and during this decade, especially in Europe, the use of shipping line owned chassis gradually diminished. In Europe various countries had differing regulations e.g. the allowed Gross Vehicle Weight varied from 28 tons (Switzerland) to 50 tons (Norway, Netherlands - 5 axles), although the majority of EU-countries was in the range from 38 to 44 tons. On top of that there were all kinds of differences in brake requirements, lighting and registration/taxes. This made shipping lines decide to abandon their road chassis fleets. Even Sea-Land, the most profound believer in the all-chassis concept, gave up also because of the continuously rising maintenance cost (some "creative" truckers changed the good SL tires for their own worn-out ones). Sea-Land was forced in many terminals to set-up swap operations, placing containers from terminal chassis to (trucker-owned) road chassis, a further erosion of the on-wheeled stacking concept.

In the truck interchange area, safety was a major issue and during this decade many terminals decided to fence off these interchange areas from the stacking yard (especially for straddle carrier operations). However for RTG and RMG stacking concepts this was not possible and therefore some terminals decided to introduce an intermediate transport stage between the RMG-yard and trucking using straddle carriers. For RTG-operations the road truckers continued to drive to an indicated RTG-location in the yard with all the related increased chances on damages and elongated service times.

The majority of the landside volume boom was absorbed by trucking causing difficulties for terminals to deliver a reasonable service time. Trucking remained a day-time activity (the consignees maintained their historically developed warehouse opening hours) and during peak-hours, waiting time could mount up to several hours. Some terminals successfully installed a truck appointment system (Hong Kong, Singapore and some shipping line-dedicated terminals) to improve the landside service times.

In Europe, the storage of empty chassis never became a big issue, as the phenomenon of shipping lines-owned chassis was phased out and replaced by trucker-owned chassis. But especially in the US, terminals had to store large numbers of these road chassis, resulting in systems and equipment for a vertical storage (see Figure 302). In many of the US terminals, gates had special lanes only for bobtails (a single truck without semi-trailer).

At the landside a few more facilities could be recognized at many terminals. At first there was the gate with related gate house(s) and overhead inspection areas. For security reasons many terminals developed systems to register the trucker and his truck including the use of camera systems, photographing the truckers license document and container document.

Secondly, many terminals installed large transit sheds for CFS operations (stripping and stuffing LCL cargo). In many Far Eastern countries, the US and so-called freeport terminals (e.g. Hamburg) large warehouses often covered more than 1 hectare in ground area (see Figure

Figure 302: Typical US road chassis stacking (with FLT-rotator)

303). The pinnacle in this respect, were the multi-floor warehouses at terminals in Hong Kong (Sea-Land, HIT and MTL). There, the land area in town was so scarce that the terminals started to realize tremendous warehousing capacity, Sea-Land even on top of a 4-high overhead crane stacking yard (with 1,800 40-ft container capacity!).

Last but not least, terminals were confronted with a growing demand for the storage of empty (MT) containers. When available, terminals designed such MT-depots as block stacks handled with the help of top lifters, converted FLT's with (telescopic) side lift frames and later reach stackers. The regularly appearing off-balances in trade lanes and the arrival of container leasing companies with their related off-hire and maintenance activities resulted in depot-activities outside the marine-terminals (for long-term storage, repair, cleaning, modifications, testing, pre-tripping of reefer containers).

Figure 303: On-terminal warehousing at Burchardkai, Hamburg

The second landside mode, rail transport, had to be connected with the terminals as well. Especially in countries with a long history in rail operations at the port such rail-handling facilities were built at the terminals (on-dock facilities) or close to the terminals (nearby facilities), 1-2 km away and often connected through "internal" roads. Good examples of such on-dock facilities are Norfolk Int. Terminals,

Figure 304: Near-by rail facilities at Long Beach, US

Burchardkai Hamburg, Zeebrugge, Rotterdam ECT, FOS-Marseille and ITS Long Beach. In many ports there was insufficient access or limited space. Some terminals e.g. in the UK (Southampton) and US (Port Elizabeth/Newark and Los Angeles/Long Beach) had to use a rail terminal adjacent or several kilometers away from the terminal (see Figure 304). At most of the on-dock or nearby rail-heads, container handling was realized with rail mounted portal cranes, spanning 2-6 rail tracks and sometimes with one or even two cantilevers. In the UK, Morris cranes and Stothert and Pitt realized the guided-beam trolley concept for rail-mounted cranes, as specified by British Rail engineers and this type of RMGs was later introduced in Italy as well.

In Europe and the US, a few terminals (e.g. Bremerhaven and Tacoma) used straddle carriers (with
extended inside clearance to 3.5 m.),
which required a (costly) split-up of
the train in 150-200 m. parts. In the
US, the existing piggy packer machines (already popular for trailer
and swap body handling) and top
lifters were the favorite types of
handling machines (see Figure 305).

Figure 305: Raygo Wagner Piggypacker (left) and Le Tourneau top lifter

The Freightliner block train concept in the UK, the massive domestic rail movements in the US, block trains in Australia and the historical rail markets in Germany, France and Italy resulted in many inland rail/road terminals hundreds or even thousands km (US, Australia) away from the deepsea terminals. Railroad interests and political support (Europe) realized many inland terminals during this decade but the required growth was often hampered through the lack of track capacity, inflexibility and higher cost in comparison with road trucking.

The larger European rail/road inland terminals were often provided
with rail-mounted portal cranes.
Some rail terminals (UK and Italy)
selected guided beam trolley concepts. This late 1960s crane concept
(Herbert Morris) realized fast and
effective positioning (Figure 289,
right). In the US, the introduction of
double-stack wagon sets in 1981
(Southern Pacific/Sea-Land) and in
1984 the double-stack block train
concept for domestic cargo by APL
(see Figure 306) caused a demand
for huge inland terminals with sufficient space for on-wheeled stacking. For many years simple low-
cost handling equipment (top lifters
and piggy packers and rubber-tired
portal cranes) fulfilled the required
handling capacity. In the drive for
cost control in intermodal inland
rail terminals (to compete with single mode trucking), all kinds of alternative handling techniques for
horizontal transfer were developed
(see Figure 307).

Figure 306: Southern Pacific and APL double stack trains

Figure 307: Railcar-mounted container handling equipment

The objective was a cost reduction, however after many years of development and disappointing performances, none of these techniques became popular. Rail-mounted portal cranes, for terminals handling more than 100,000 TEU, became the standard. For smaller terminals reach stackers, top lifters and RTGs could do the job well enough.

In 1978, ECT introduced one of the first terminal operated block trains to a remotely operated inland terminal (Venlo, at the German border, approximately 150 km from the port of Rotterdam) and in Germany DB/Transfracht introduced fast overnight trains between Hamburg/Bremerhaven and some Southern German cities. Parallel to the marine-bound container movements, the inland (rail/road) terminals were increasingly used for the transportation of domestic cargo (Novatrans in France, Transfracht in Germany, RENFE in Spain, Hupac and CEMAT in Italy, etc.). International container transport was originally introduced by Intercontainer, a European partnership from all major national railway companies, however, in due course more and more other rail operators organized inland container transport.

During this decade inland transport of containers with the help of barging was introduced on the rivers Rhine and Danube. The existence of large US military bases in the Rhine Envelope assured an interesting doorstep for a few large inland terminals. Some of them started as private initiatives, using existing facilities for bulk and general cargo handling. Most of them installed portal cranes with a cantilever outreach and sufficient backreach to store containers within the crane gauge and to handle containers to road trucks or even the railroad. Some examples are given in Figure 308.

Figure 308: Wide span gantries along the Rhine river (KSR Mainz (left), Krupp Basel)

ICT applications

During the 1980s, a large number of ICT applications were developed for the industry in general. Many of them were adapted from the industry for use in container terminals, although with some reluctance from the manufacturers. In many cases they considered the container terminal industry as a small market and that explained why so many terminals took the lead in new technology developments they required. For example: ECT developed together with AEG a "hand-held" radio data terminal to allow fast/reliable container data interchange (ID, type/size, damage status, etc.) between a host computer and mobile equipment or operators in gate or reefer areas. In equipment, additional VDUs could be connected to exchange a number of work orders.

Radio Data Transmission (RDT) was the common technology to communicate between operations centers and centralized computer systems. Motorola and AEG were the first manufacturers to supply RDT terminals in the 450-495 kHz bandwidth with up to 6 lines with 40 characters each. However some disadvantages became clear during this decade. Radio systems were vulnerable to outside disturbances (distortions) and in many countries there was a limited number of frequency bands (even varying per country/continent; e.g. in Europe the 450 kHz-band and in the US 35-80 kHz and 800 kHz band).

Another issue was the fact that until the mid-1980s radio data systems did not accept alpha-numerical input (very inconvenient when processing a container prefix). For that reason some terminals started trials with other techniques. Fiber optics for digital transmissions was used in the equipment itself and some trials were made for quay cranes with glass fiber cores in the high-voltage supply cable.

ECT developed an in-fra-red communication technology for a fast data exchange to its straddle carriers (see Figure 309) that could receive data with a 100,000 baud rate when driving over a ground transmitter (30 degrees active angle).

Figure 309: Infrared data transmission (ground transmitter, right)

Infra red communication required a line of sight and so, over a hundred ground transmitters were installed (with all the requirements for synchronization, etc).

All these developments were necessary to follow the fast growing processing capacities, offered by the computer industry. Here as well, all major terminals developed administrative and operational control programs in a combined effort of their in-house computer experts and outside consultants (often related to computer hardware companies).

So, in the late 1970s, companies like IBM, Univac, Digital Equipment and Siemens installed computer systems at the terminals and obviously most of the operations control software was different for every terminal. Operations control was developed in the areas of ship planning (with a lot of instructions from the shipping lines), yard inventory control, yard work orders and of course a lot of messages to members in the logistic chain (shipping lines, railway operators, truckers, customs, consignees, port authorities, bodies monitoring dangerous cargo, equipment control centers, etc.).

Most of the systems originated from administrative applications, only DEC and Siemens could benefit from their experience in industrial applications, such as the steel and automotive industry. In this ICT world, many terminals had to pioneer as at that moment the ICT industry had no standard solutions available.

Also the first applications for monitoring equipment were developed in cooperation with terminals. In Australia, Glebe Island Terminal installed a "black box" (a type of recorder with built-in memories for 32 functions) in their mobile equipment. And this black-box allowed a monitoring of essential equipment functions, breakdowns/accidents or even operational misuse. Later on, these diagnostic tools further matured, sometimes even into remote-controlled maintenance e.g. shown by STRATUS, the manufacturer of fault-tolerant computer systems.

It should be remembered, that during this decade programmable logic controllers (PLCs) and micro-computers developed at high pace, which helped to connect equipment to host computers for information exchange (work orders, ID checks, etc.). The first developments towards more operator-oriented information systems took place, supported by the availability of data-base systems, query languages and powerful communication software.

US-based companies were the frontrunners in the development of large information systems to support (control) their operations. Shipping lines, like Sea-Land and APL, and terminal operators, such as Maher, developed information systems for tracking and tracing and some operations planning with modules for data exchange with their worldwide subsidiaries and customers.

This also encouraged port communities to install portwide information-exchange systems for fast/reliable data transfer between parties involved in the container transport chain (shipping lines, terminals, shippers/consignees, port authorities, customs, etc.). Such systems were introduced in Antwerp (SEAGHA), Hamburg (DACOSY), Rotterdam (INTIS) and other ports, usually initiated by the port authority.

These early developments in large-scale information exchange systems, taught the importance of standardized data messages and already in this decade international consultation was started, later resulting in the EDIFACT standard messages.

Labor organization and operations management

The rapid growth in terminal throughputs, the application of many new technologies and logistic procedures and the demand for guaranteed service levels triggered major changes in operations and its management. During this decade container terminals developed into a service industry, 24 hours a day, seven days per week and with a 10-25 fold higher productivity (in tons per man-hour) compared to the traditional general cargo handling practices in ports. Obviously, this rapid shift from general cargo towards containerized cargo caused a considerable downsizing in port employment (in some cases more than 50% reduction) and there were major transformations in labor organization, operations management and types of jobs as well. Some of the below highlights will illustrate these changes, experienced in this decade:

- The required new operator's skills and specialized jobs in container terminals reduced the use of general labor pools in ports. The larger terminals attracted their own employees often from outside the port industry, not influenced by labor union practices, motivated and with an industrial or general managerial background. They were offered well-organized work schedules, fixed and fair payments, appropriate training and schooling programs. In some terminals, dock workers from labor pools joined the fixed manning in the terminals and they were schooled as well for the new jobs and associated new techniques and service oriented attitude. Information technology and logistics replaced muscle power and yelling-and-shouting: stack planners were trained in the use of computer-aided stack planning; equipment drivers learned to process container data and work orders with the help of cabin-mounted data communication systems and checkers in the gate became conversant with hand-held radio data terminals;

- The stochastic nature of terminal operations (irregular vessel arrivals, peaks in truck arrivals, etc.) and the variations in service demand did not comply with the fixed rosters that had to be offered to new, motivated employees. However, this could be compensated by the introduction of multi-skill functions where employees were trained to work in 3 to 4 jobs (crane operator, checker, MT-handler driver, etc.) and the abolition of fixed manning schemes, negotiated in the past with labor unions. Flexibility and multi-skilling was the only way to control cost and service in an operational environment with 20-30% idle time. During the times of conventional cargo handling many stevedoring companies conquered this problem with 5-6 days working per week in 2 shifts per day (and sometimes elongated evening shifts) and the majority of manning from labor pools, casual labor and volunteers. But this did not work for container terminals; especially in Europe it became increasingly difficult to have sufficient manning during weekends and for night work. And so, many terminals introduced 4-shift (and later 5-shift) continuous work rosters, covering all 168 hours of the week;

- The described transition was not realized overnight. Human beings and thus port workers as well, are reluctant to change and especially in ports with strong labor unions (Europe, Japan and the US) there was a lot of resistance. The loss of employment and favorable (old-fashioned) benefits from the past triggered labor unions to hold back where possible. Even strikes (from several weeks to a few months) were used to resist changes. For example in 1979 ECT Rotterdam was stopped almost 3 weeks and all shipping lines diverted their vessels to adjacent ports (mainly Antwerp, Felixstowe and Bremerhaven). The labor union TGWU (Transport and General Workers Union) in the UK forced the Southampton Terminal management to continue a rotation of all labor pool workers over all major terminal jobs, causing an inability to build up typical container terminal experience. This resulted in more damage and logistic failures and a poor crane productivity of some 16 moves/hr. Sometimes the requirement for change was enforced with money, later resulting in increased terminal costs (and tariffs). The Japanese labor unions continued in their refusal to work on Sundays causing shipping lines to avoid vessels calling Japan at Sundays with related consequences for connecting ports (US West Coast, Kaohsiung and Hong Kong). In some ports it took 10-20 years before the required changes were accepted. Terminals in new ports (e.g. Kaohsiung and Singapore) and some private terminals (Felixstowe) managed the adjustments in their labor organization rather well;

- Training became an important and professionally supported terminal activity not only in the area of equipment operating but also for familiarization with planning tools (setting of algorithms, handling of non-standard activities) and last but not least the use of steadily expanding information control systems. At the end of the 1980s, the terminals realized that terminal operations were almost completely dependent of well-functioning IT systems. Training was not limited to the use of experienced instructors and detailed operating/maintenance manuals. At the end of this decade the first simulators were introduced. In the beginning they were designed to build up machine-oriented experience (straddle carrier driving and sway control in container cranes), later the operator was trained how to react on breakdowns and/or logistic interruptions. For operations management the first computer-aided management games were developed to show interrelations and complexity of logistic systems and related decision-making. Talking about middle management; they also had to be trained to adapt to new management tools (goals for service and cost, more decentralized decision-making and more responsibility to the work floor). Especially in continuous shift systems it became vital to ensure proper communication between the various management layers;

- Many terminal employees were increasingly working as an individual operator in a rather isolated surrounding, only connected with data-exchange systems to other terminal departments (equipment operators alone in their cabins, checkers in the gate, supervisors in their control tower, etc.). Quite a difference from the old days where teams of dock workers worked for hours together down under in the cargo hold of a general cargo vessel. This encouraged more attention to comfortable and ergonomically designed working places and the associated graphical user interfaces and data communication systems;

- Safety and security became topics with growing importance. In the UK and countries of the commonwealth the health and safety officer was increasingly involved in better working procedures and measures to avoid accidents and damages. Both in equipment design, handling tools and terminal layout safety and security were increasingly integrated. Terminal lay-outs were modified to get transparent traffic flows with one-way driving, ample space for maneuvering or even completely closed areas for stacking with straddle carriers to avoid people and small vehicles entering such areas. The first attempts for remote cargo inspection were encouraged through the intensive inspections of containers required in the Middle East (complete stripping of all cargo, inspection and stuffing again, with all the risks from weather influences, damages, delays, etc.). In 1983, British Aerospace launched the first X-ray imaging systems to inspect containers without opening them. This system was the first development to deter criminal activities such as smuggling drugs, weapons or even people;

- In the 1980s in Western Europe and Japan, terminal management showed more recognition of the influence from the works councils; partly as a result from changing laws and partly as a natural development. Management more and more realized that terminal operations require teamwork with respect for good working conditions and sound labor relations.

In retrospect

At the end of the third decade of containerization in the US (and only the second decade in the other parts of the world) the situation for terminals could be characterized as follows:

- 50 to 100 terminals were serving a globalized container transportation network (rolled out in only 20 years) and they were confronted with five major topics: growth, economies of scale, IT-applications, performance and reliability of handling systems and inland connectivity.

- Labor organizations had changed substantially with considerable reductions in employment and much less use of port labor pools.

- Multi-user terminals became much more in favor of shipping lines (consortia) as many shipping lines stopped their dominating interest in (totally-controlled) dedicated terminals.

Figure 310: First phase ECT Delta Terminal

- Cost control and reliable fast services made shipping lines (consortia) decide to select a limited number of terminals per continent. A shake out took place amongst smaller terminals; many had to accept a moderate growth determined by their local markets, with shipping services from mainline feeders and niche operators. The larger terminals in the US and Europe started a competition in regional importance, based on service level, price and inland connections (see Figure 310).

- In general, every container terminal, handling more than 50,000 TEU annually, used computer systems for administration and tracking & tracing purposes. Terminals in the mainline networks used computer systems and communication systems with some kind of operations control (planning algorithms, appointment systems, etc.).

- The first signals of further breakthroughs were received and some terminals had already started trials with (partly) automated components of handling systems.

12.4. 1986-1996: TERMINAL EXPANSIONS AND FIRST STEPS INTO AUTOMATION

In 1986, the collapse of US Lines was a definite change in the logistic concept and market approach introduced by Malcom McLean in the 1950s and 1960s. US Lines was the last carrier which heavily supported the pure Hub-and-Spoke system with only one or two hubs per trade region. The disappearance of US Lines (with their low-speed jumbo Econships) had a big impact on those terminals serving the US Lines' round-the-world transportation service. But other developments became of importance to the terminals and in this decade both the business environment, the operational demands and the design of terminals changed considerably. In the following, the most interesting aspects will be presented.

General aspects

During this decade the world port handling volumes almost tripled, from approximately 60 million TEU in 1986, towards approximately 170 million TEU in 1996. The changes in global economic growth, (during this decade in Europe 25-30% but in the New Industrial Economies up to 100%!!), deferred terminal developments to the Far East.

The West-East services (Atlantic, Pacific and Europe-Asia) were further intensified and were offered by more shipping lines and consortia and with more ports included in these services. The North-South services (the Americas, Europe-Africa and Intra-Asia) fully matured with many ports converting from general cargo ports into multi-purpose facilities with some pure container terminals when annual volumes justified so (e.g. Santos in Brazil).

Some ports and terminals expanded from feeder terminals towards mainline terminals when their base-volumes supported a calling of mainline vessels and a relay to other (new) regional terminals.

In the 1990s, new relay terminals with a regional function were built in the Mediterranean. After Algeciras (developed as a hub by Sea-Land and later continued by Maersk), Gioia Tauro and Malta were used by the major Europe-Far East carriers and even Piraeus could attract transshipment volumes for the Black Sea, Turkey and the Eastern Mediterranean.

Figure 311: Dubai terminal (Jebel Ali)

At the Arabian peninsula, Dubai developed into a major hub (see Figure 311) and later, when more carriers were looking for hub-terminals with guaranteed services, other terminals in the United Arab Emirates were realized such as Jebel Ali (started with Sea-Land), Fujairah (APL) and Khor Fakkan (Nedlloyd, Maersk, Hapag-Lloyd). These UAE terminals offered sufficient quay length and water depth, which are attractive for transshipment operations of larger carriers.

In Saudi Arabia, in contrast to the UAE-developments, the existing (Damman and Jeddah) and newly built industrial ports (Yanbu and Jubail) were mainly import/export terminals but in general with the same characteristic as in the UAE: sufficient space and no problem to finance expansion; quite a difference with the terminal developments in Africa and South-America.

In those terminals there was still a mixture of general cargo and containers (and even dry bulk) at the existing limited facilities. Carriers (shipping lines) were looking for more space and handling capacity but in many countries the expansion programs could not follow demand (legislation, local area constraints, politics, finance, etc.).

The shipping lines compensated the lack of handling capacity through the use of self-sustained vessels and/or the application of mobile harbor cranes (see Figure 312).

Figure 312: Vessel with on board container handling crane (left) and mobile harbor crane (courtesy Gottwald)

In the Far East, Japan realized impressive expansions in all their major ports but none of these ports developed in a real hub (probably due to the high-labor cost and the service limitations during the weekend). The reclaim activities in Kobe (Port Island and Rokko Island), Tokyo (Aouri Terminal), Nagoya and Yokohama supported the demand from the shipping lines and in Japan many shipping lines and/or consortia could realize their own dedicated facilities within the typical Japanese approach: long-term leases for modular areas with 300-350 m. quay wall and cranes purchased by the port authorities on technical specifications from the tenants.

In this decade South-Korea commenced in a start-up position (mainly in Pusan with a few terminals), but was rapidly expanding. The concentration of container traffic to South-Korea in Pusan pushed this port into the top-5 of 1996. The other top-5 ports (Singapore, Hong-Kong, Rotterdam and Kaohsiung) were major transshipment hubs. Especially Hong Kong and Singapore developed tremendously fast in this decade, together realizing in 1996 about 18% of the whole worlds TEU port handlings.

Hong Kong reached almost 13.5 million TEU and Singapore came close to 13.0 million TEU (both ports doubled their volume within the 5-year period 1991-1996!).

Hong Kong realized some new terminals on expensively obtained reclaimed land and all terminal operators installed dense stacking system. Singapore started its Brani Terminal with a 1 over 8 overhead bridge crane stacking system and the installation of some cranes with built-in second trolley systems (licensed from ECT). Singapore started with a massive further development, the Pasir Panjang Terminals.

Some other terminal developments to be mentioned were shown in Malaysia (Port Klang) and China (Shanghai, Guangzhou and Qingdao), mainly as a result of their important import/export activities supporting the industrial developments in these countries. The rapid growing number of Far Eastern terminals enabled the establishment of an Intra-Asian feeder and domestic shipping network. Also in the Far East the container became increasingly used for shortsea activities.

The massive scale developments for ports and terminals triggered shipping lines and shippers/consignees to increase their drive for cost reductions. Although the cost impact from volume increases at terminals cannot be compared with the benefits from mass-production in the industry still, many terminal customers were negotiating considerable volume rebates. Their threats with a transfer of large volumes to other (adjacent) terminals proved to be successful in areas with fierce competition amongst terminals in the same (regional) cargo catch area e.g. Seattle-Tacoma; Antwerp-Rotterdam; Felixstowe-Southampton. In this context the development of the Tanjung Pelepas Terminal in Malaysia, opposite of Singapore should be mentioned. This terminal development was triggered by the drive of Maersk to have competitive services from terminal operators.

In this competitive field some ports/terminals tried to strengthen their position (in volume!) with the help of price rebates for transshipment cargo (often the second water move was charged at 50% of the first water move).

Both shippers and consignees used their buying power to get better rates and services from shipping lines and often, low-cost carriers grasped the business. For the shippers there was almost no difference, hence their containers were handled at the same terminals with the same (documentation) services. This development encouraged major shipping lines and consortia to establish their own terminals (or at least a controlling share) or to get a dedicated terminal service. That was the established shipping line's answer to show their ability to offer a unique (dedicated) service to shippers for the same or lower price. For these shipping lines, their own or dedicated terminals were often seen as cost centers. However, already in the 1990s shipping line owned terminals were increasingly "invited" by their owners to act as profit centers such as CSX-terminals (Sea-Land) and later Maersk (after the takeover in 2000), Eagle Marine terminals (APL) and Seatainer terminals (OCL).

The large carriers (Sea-Land, APL, Matson, Evergreen and Maersk) were selling a predictable, reliable door-to-door service with an overall cargo care, as they controlled inland transportation, terminal handling as well as vessel operations.

For the land-lord type of port authorities in Japan, Taiwan and the US West Coast the demand for dedicated terminals was no problem, although underutilization of the facilities was a risk (only one or two mainline calls per week per berth). This in contrast to (mostly privately-owned) multi-user terminals such as HHLA and Eurokai in Hamburg, ECT in Rotterdam and PSA in Singapore, which aimed to maintain their independence from shipping lines and who were looking for maximum utilization of their handling facilities, sometimes resulting in minor vessels delays.

In order to combine the better of two worlds (dedicated facility for the shipping line and maximum utilization for the terminal operator) ECT and the Rotterdam Port Authority launched their Delta 2000-8 development plan in 1990. The aim was to have maximum 8 terminals (each with a berth length of 300 m.), by the year 2000 at the Delta-Terminal South side. The project included an extended distribution center and special barge- and rail-facilities. With the Delta 2000-8 concept, ECT could offer a dedicated service concept, with guarantees for a fast vessel turnaround at a dedicated berth and with sufficient (guaranteed) stacking and landside handling capacity.

This concept had a major advantage: a co-use of the most expensive waterside facilities (quay wall and quay cranes) outside of the guaranteed berth hours (see Figure 313).

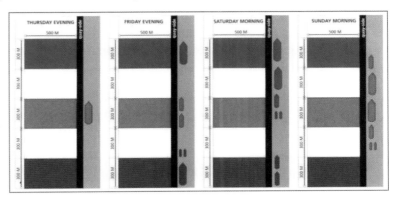

Some alliances accepted this new advanced logistic concept, but other carriers continued to get their own terminal under their own control: within some years this approach resulted in two main terminal types: carrier controlled ded-

Figure 313: Utilization scheme for ECT's Delta 2000-8 concept

icated terminals (service-oriented to their parent shipping line(s)) or multi-user common terminals operated as profit-driven business units, striving for a maximum utilization of their assets.

This decade also showed acceleration in the privatization of ports (e.g. Port Klang and Barcelona). Publicly-controlled port authorities had difficulties in raising funds for the massive investments and were less flexible in their commercial approach.

By the mid-1990s, all major carriers owned or had a controlling interest in 3 to 10 terminals, spread over the world. But shippers were not impressed by this vertical integration and especially the large ones became successful in playing down the dominance of shipping lines in global door-to-door transport. The shippers started to organize their own inland transportation (merchant haulage), forcing the shipping lines to position empty containers at the shippers' cargo loading destination, a prerequisite when they were interested in the shippers business. Examples of such powerful shippers are large chemical companies (BASF and ICI), the automotive industry (Toyota, Mitsubishi, BMW and VW) and breweries (Interbrew, Heineken and Carlsberg). These shippers also affected terminal operations in the areas of dwell time, information flows, onward intermodal connectivity, etc.

Many shippers introduced global supply chain management and stock optimization, resulting in a tendency to leave containerized cargo at the terminals until a delivery to the final production/consumption location at the just-in-time supply date. The shippers saved warehousing cost but the terminals noticed an increase in dwell time, affecting stack demand and productivity (more shuffling/housekeeping).

Another topic of interest for terminals came along at the start of the 1990s: the breaking up of 10-20 year old consortia, like ACT, ScanDutch, TRIO, ANSECS, SAECS.

It was a real blow to many terminals, with an impact on the structure of information flows, the directives for vessel planning, the arrangement of MT-box depots, the tariff-structure, communications with shipping line's representatives, new short-term slot-sharing agreements, etc.

New alliances between carriers resulted in the diversion of large volumes of containers from one to another port, but luckily it didn't cause too much economic disasters for terminals as worldwide volumes in those days were growing with 5-15% per annum (depending on the trades).

In general the consequences of breaking up consortia were limited to new operational procedures, more complexity in terminal logistics and more inland transportation operators, claiming guaranteed services.

The shake-up in shipping lines' alliances also had some positive effects as it allowed terminals to revise their pricing and tariff-structures. Slowly invaded new services could be invoiced (e.g. the handling of side-curtains for containers carrying potatoes, flower bulbs). Also the increasing number of logistic changes (such as overbooking, customs status changes, late minute changes in inland modality and additional reefer checks), with their impact on terminal planning and manning, were defined as additional services with related costs. The registration and invoicing of such services was no problem due to the increasing power of information control systems.

At the end of this decade some large terminal operating companies decided to expand globally, benefitting from sharing technology and operational know-how and being better positioned to negotiate with large shipping lines/consortia. Hutchison Whampoa acquired a majority share (75%) in Felixstowe in 1991 and some years later Hutchison Port Holding made various terminal acquisitions. Similar strategies were developed by Sea-Land (CSX terminals), P&O ports, APM-terminals, Eurokai/Contship and ICTSI (International Container Terminal Services Inc.). In the years after 1995, these Global Terminal Operators would further enlarge their share in the world's overall handling volume.

Terminal operations and handling systems

The tremendous trade volume growth made shipping lines decide to invest in more and larger vessels. Rumors about vessels unable to pass the Panama Canal became stronger and some terminal operators (like ECT in Rotterdam) already during the years 1984 and 1985 installed container cranes capable of handling vessels up to 16-17 containers wide on deck.

During 1986-1987, Gene Pentimonti, the naval architect of American President Lines, ordered 5 Post-Panamax vessels at German shipyards and the first vessel was commissioned in 1988. At that time ECT was the only terminal in Western-Europe, operating cranes with sufficient outreach and so, these vessels could load a lot of containers in Rotterdam when they were transferred from the shipyard to their operating base in the Pacific (APL operated a large coast-to-coast network of double-stack trains, which allowed them to cease Panama Canal transits of large vessels).

Later, many more shipping lines ordered Post-Panamax vessels, causing a boom in the purchase of enlarged cranes. As a result, by the year 1996 almost 2,000 portal type container quay cranes were installed at terminals all over the world (see also Chapter 10). In addition to new cranes, many terminal operators started modification programs to increase the lifting height and outreach of existing cranes, a costly activity (often more than US$ 0.5 million per crane), requiring additional structural components in the portal and an overall check on the crane's stability and structural integrity.

The larger vessel sizes led to larger call sizes and thus a demand for higher terminal productivity to maintain the same time in port. Terminals behind lock systems became less attractive as shipping lines tried to maintain or even improve their ratio port time/sailing time.

The enlarged vessel sizes also included a higher container stacking on deck (4-6 high) a reason for many labor unions and safety authorities to refuse stacking cone handling on these high deck loads. And so, within a few years all major shipping lines introduced the semi-automatic twist lock stackers (SATLs or also mentioned IBCs, Inter Box Connectors) for the lashing of containers higher than the 2nd or 3rd layer on deck.

This development had a major impact on the waterside handling performance, handling cost and safety at the interchange on the apron. Per crane two additional workers at dock level were required and in the beginning the crane operator had to pick up the container from a chassis (or the ground in case of straddle carriers driving under the crane) and then lower the box at 1-1.5 m. above dock level to allow lashers to take out or position the SATLs. Later on, a type of bomb cart with special inserts for the SATLs was applied, allowing SATL handling outside of the quay crane area. On top of the SATL handling in and out of the container the SATLs had to be collected in collecting bins (mostly assembled in 20' open toppers with the help of FLTs) and the surplus of the SATLs had to be brought back on board. For all terminals this additional activity (sometimes for about 50% of all the containers handled during a vessel call) caused a crane cycle time increase of 15-20 seconds, extra manning cost and more safety precautions at the quay crane areas on dock (see also Figure 336).

Automated operations such as the second-trolley crane systems (e.g. ECT in Rotterdam and Seagirt in Baltimore) and the automated unmanned terminal transportation with AGVs at ECT's Delta Sea-Land Terminal were even struck more, as a manual interference was required, asking for extra interchange control in the crane cycle.

Transportation between the quay cranes and the stacking area continued with tractor-trailer systems (RTG and RMG stacking), straddle carriers and reach stacker/top lifters for some smaller terminals. However, the need for cost control and better performance encouraged a scale increase. ECT's multi-trailer transport was introduced in some other European terminals and PSA introduced their so-called "elephant trains", a special 5-axle chassis, designed to handle 4 TEU in two layers. The chassis were provided with a type of cell guides (see Figure 314) to allow 2-high stacking. PSA used these chassis several years, but the increased maintenance to equipment and road infrastructure (the chassis were provided with small wheels). The disappointing savings (tractor remained coupled to the chassis waiting time for the driver) and the more complex logistics did limit a further application.

Figure 314: Double-stacked transportation with PSA's "elephant trains"

During this decade the demands on stacking systems (e.g. stack capacity and handling performance) increased tremendously due to the volume growth, peak loads from clashing of large vessels with call sizes regularly over 3,000 TEU/call, increasing dwell times and pressure from landside operators (trucking and railways) to improve the service.

The straddle carrier concept lost some ground worldwide but remained quite popular in Western Europe and North East Asia, where about 65% of the worldwide straddle carrier population was employed (in 1996, almost 2,400 straddle carriers were operated). The majority could stack 1 over 2 but due to the demand for stack capacity a number of terminal operators purchased the 1 over 3 types.

The rather high operating cost (maintenance, fuel, well-trained operators and damages) and relatively high (US$ 0.6-1.1 million) purchasing cost (limited number of suppliers) encouraged many terminals to shift from straddle carriers to an RTG stacking system.

RTGs could stack 1 over 4 with 5-7 containers wide and one truck lane under the portal. During this decade RTGs were beefed up to even 1 over 7 high stacking, although the majority stayed at 1 over 4 and 1 over 5. The early starter Paceco appointed a number of licensees, but existing and new crane builders entered the market and in the 1990s more than 20 manufacturers were competing to sell RTGs, obviously resulting in attractive purchase prices (US$ 1.0-1.5 million).

The RTG-stacking concept became the preferred concept for many operators due to its favorable ratio purchase price/stack capacity. But some disadvantages showed up, such as traffic problems from the mixing of internal and external truckers; loss of performance from shuffle moves for landside random deliveries and from late-minute changes in export vessel operations. In practice. the stacking height for RTGs was only 50-70% of the maximum feasible stacking height and many terminals suffered from disadvantages such as the need for 6-8 tractor trailers to keep up an acceptable quay crane performance. Insufficient technical reliability and high maintenance and fuel cost were other unfavorable issues. Some terminal operators switched to Rail-Mounted Gantries (RMGs)or Overhead Bridge Cranes (OBCs) asking for a well-thought terminal lay-out and well-designed crane tracks, but offering the possibility of electrical supply (reliable and less pollution) and part or full automation. In Hong Kong (HIT), Israel (Ashdod and Haifa), UAE (Khor Fakkan) and Spain (MacAndrew, Bilbao), terminal operators installed manually-operated RMGs with one or two cantilevers to connect to the transport mode (see Figure 315). Thamesport (Isle of Grain, UK) and ECT Delta Terminal Rotterdam introduced unmanned RMGs without an outreach, but with increased gantry travel speeds necessary for an end-to-end container interchange onto the transportation mode (road trucks and tractor trailers or AGVs).

Figure 315: Wide-span stacking cranes: Israel (left) and Spain

The increased stacking height with related extra unproductive shuffle-moves (RTG and RMG operations) made terminals in Hong Kong and Singapore decide to introduce a kind of truck appointment system; at first sight giving less service to consignees/truckers but definitely an improvement for the truckers' terminal service time.

For small and mid-size terminals the reach-stacker concept was very attractive from a cost and simplicity point of view. The area utilization for full container stacking was less than for the straddle carrier concept, but when stacking MT containers in block stowage, the reach-stackers and MT-handlers (sometimes for up to 8-high block stacking) became very popular. After the first Belotti (late 1960s) many other manufacturers such as Kalmar, Ormig, SISU, SMV, Hyster, PPM and Fantuzzi entered this market and contributed to further price cuts. The concept was basically a spin-off from the heavy top-lifters (FLTs), with a lot of components from the automotive industry, easy to maintain and easy to operate. Another attractive topic was the possibility for leasing, allowing for an off-balance sheet financing and well-suited for the smaller companies (terminals and depots); even rental agreements became available.

MT depots were growing impressively in this decade, but many terminals, who kept empty container stocks for their customers, could no longer provide the stacking space (with regular peak demands from trade imbalances and seasonal peaks). MT depots were pushed to other areas outside the terminals, sometimes at quite a distance. Especially for hub-operations some terminals (e.g. ECT Delta Terminal and Felixstowe) made arrangements with independent depot companies, adjacent to the terminal, to make MT-swaps over an internal road between depot and deepsea-terminal. This allowed late-minute MT-deliveries to fill empty slots at vessels alongside the berth and was a cost saving for the shipping lines (no public road trucking and easy drop-off of leased containers).

The importance of CFS operations decreased in many terminals as a growing number of shippers-consolidators started to run their own facilities outside the terminals. However, in some ports a shortage of space encouraged terminal operators to create CFS services within or connected to their terminal premises. The most extremes were realized in Hong Kong where Modern Terminals, HIT and Sea-Land (Asia Terminals) built multi-storey warehouses offering hectares of storage space. The CFS at the Sea-Land Orient facility (Kwai Chung Berth 3) comprised of 6 storeys (25,000 m² each) on top of a 15 m. high podium, underneath of which there was a 4-high OBC-stacking system with five 40-tons Mitsubishi overhead bridge cranes, sufficient to accommodate about 1,800 40' containers (see Figure 316).

Figure 316: First multi-storey Sea-Land warehouse with ramp (left), Hong Kong

Not surprisingly, such high-density terminals were among the first ones to streamline gate operations with all kinds of (automated) features. For instance in Singapore at the Brani Terminal (opened in 1994) there was an RFID tag-recognition system, to identify trucks passing the gate. These trucks were provided with tags and with the help of radio frequency interference, identification was possible. In this 1990s other terminals introduced equal systems such as Maher Terminals (New Jersey) and some APL-controlled terminals at the US West Coast. APC (the domestic arm of APL) installed tags both on their chassis and trucks to achieve faster gate processing and better equipment control.

Although CFS operations became less important for many terminals, the regional logistic services from shippers and third party logistics were increasingly concentrated around major deepsea terminals. Especially port authorities became keen to develop logistic centers outside of the terminals and no longer under the control of terminal operators or shipping lines.

In some countries the use of self-loading/unloading semi-trailers became rather popular (e.g. Australia, Canada, Malaysia and Sweden) and there the trucks with such a semi-trailer (manufactured by Steadman, Hammar Maskin and others) required special attention at the landside interface. Such self-loading/unloading semi-trailers require a double space when they were side-loading from the ground. For reach stacker and straddle carrier operations, solutions were obtainable although safety was an issue. For RTG and RMG operations, with their parallel interchange, such self-loading semi-trailers caused noticeable delays at the landside handling operations (see Figure 317).

In the 1990s, the outsourcing of all kinds of services became popular, especially in areas with high labor cost or strict working procedures demanded from labor unions. Lashing; quick container repairs; connecting/disconnecting, temperature checks and small repairs to reefers; packing/unpacking at a CFS and equipment maintenance were services that could be fulfilled by specialized small companies often faster and cheaper than the terminals' own labor force. This

Figure 317: Self-loading/unloading semi-trailers requiring special attention

development was beneficial for shipping lines and terminals (better cost/service ratio) but it also increased the complexity of operations control for the terminal's middle management.

To conclude, terminal operations became more complex but were still based on long known handling techniques. The tremendous increases in handling volumes could be accommodated but looking to the handling performance at water and landside, there was not much improvement, despite the introduction of double-trolley systems in quay cranes, faster handling equipment and computer-controlled stacking, etc.

Logistics complexity, conflicts of interest between terminal operators and shipping lines, strict vessel planning rules, more merchant haulage and a lack of forward information resulted in an operational performance almost equal to that of the late 1970s.

Changing attitudes from labor

The on-going growth and the increasing industrial approach changed the attitude and position of labor in ports and their terminals. The application of technology from other industries (automotive, supply chain management and IT), port privatization and globalization reduced the strong (and sometimes even militant) position of labor unions. Three major topics could be recognized:

1. Reduction in workforce and a change in job content.

    Mechanization and controlled operations caused a redundancy in port workers and at the same time the traditional muscle-based jobs disappeared and were replaced by equipment-based handling, logistic planning and service-oriented information exchange; away from teamwork in groups of 10-20 workers (the traditional "gang") towards an individualized job with personal responsibility.

    The ongoing growth helped to absorb the redundancies. On top of that, the support with rather generous redundancy payments and a build-up of special retirement funds made the unions (US and UK) to accept reductions in some jobs and to cooperate in the process of arranging new shift schemes and multi-skill jobs. Labor realized that mechanization and new technologies did result in better working conditions, however it eroded their community thinking and encouraged individual responsibility.

2. The need for terminal-bound workers and limited demand for casual labor.

    The development of specialized container terminals with a rather regular workload stopped the traditional approach of ordering labor from a (portwide) labor pool on a shift-base. Moreover, different terminals in the same port had different equipment (types and makes), different operational procedures and different information control systems with all their consequences on the effectiveness of rotation over various terminal systems. Exemplary was Southampton where the union enforced a rotation of port workers over the various terminals and over the various types of equipment, with all the consequences for productivity (on the job experience) and damages (lack of routine). All over the world terminals learned that a fixed labor force, belonging to the company and well trained, was a must to realize changes in organization, technologies and IT. Productivity increases and improved services (7 days a week, 52 weeks per year) could only be obtained through motivated employees, willing to work in rosters covering 7 days a week, 24 hours per day.

    In Japan productivity was above world average in many terminals, but work on Sundays was a difficult issue for the unions. It took until the late 1980s before the National Council of Dockworkers' Unions of Japan (NCDUJ) accepted work on Sundays with some restrictions. These practices dominated the shipping lines' Transpacific vessel rotations for many years (avoiding Japan during the weekends).

3. Reduced influence from national/regional labor unions.

    During this decade, the influence from unions on job descriptions, rotations in the port and protected work areas diminished considerably. For instance in the US, the longshoremen unions had to accept the entrance of workers from the Teamsters union, after abandoning the so-called 50-mile rule (all port-related work within 50 miles from the port was exclusive for longshoremen union members). US unions remained reluctant to change during this decade, regardless the growing impact from the M&M-agreement, a program allowing a controlled change in manning, towards more company-related (and trained) labor in exchange for early-retirement packages.

In the UK, Mrs. Thatcher terminated the National Dock Labor Scheme (1989), allowing privatization of ports (The British Transport Dock Board was dissolved), which substantially reduced the influence of the Transport and General Workers Union. Similar but less outspoken, reforms were also seen in other European and Asian countries. The increasing privatization resulted in the tendency to move away from branch-related labor agreements towards company-related labor agreements.

In general it can be stated that private terminals better managed their labor relations. They recognized the importance of training, better information and some kind of involvement in decision-making. In Europe and the Far East the introduction of new technologies was less problematic than in the US and Australia.

For example APL did some trials with chassis loaders and multi-trailer systems (some prototype sets were leased from ECT), but the new technology was not accepted partly due to a poor involvement of labor and terminal middle management. Even the support from experienced instructors from ECT could not convince.

So, in this decade, casual labor diminished and service was extended to 7 days a week, 24 hours a day. Good for productivity, safety and service but with a consequence for the cost (modified salary schemes, promotion policies, etc.). The regular underutilization of terminals (berth occupation often below 40%) caused quite some labor idle time, which could only partly be compensated through multi-skill jobs and (some kind of) flexible rosters.

Intermodalism

The pioneers Sea-Land and Matson started with road transportation as the dominant connecting mode between the ocean transport and the customers' door. However, the railway companies slowly took up their share and the double stack developments caused a breakthrough in the US with numerous "land bridges" into the hinterland (e.g. Chicago, Denver and Memphis) and even coast-to coast.

In Europe double-stack was not possible (limited clearance profile and a large number of tunnels), but also regular rail services (with trains up to about 100 TEU length) could not meet demand, due to bureaucracy, insufficient number of slots on the network and priority for passenger trains. On top of that, border-crossing delays (change of locomotives to adapt to electrical supply and safety systems and administrative procedures) and limitations in railcar designs (brake systems and axle loads) caused low average travel speeds. Nevertheless, especially the European Community required a shift towards sustainable mobility (White Paper), encouraging rail and barge transportation by all kinds of studies and investment support (inland rail and barge terminals and new technologies for the road-rail interchange). In the Far East, rail transportation remained limited due to limited networks.

In Australia, Canada and especially the US many large inland terminals were created, often based on simple handling techniques (top lifters, reach stackers and RTGs); only a few large rail facilities introduced rail mounted gantry cranes (RMGs) with one or two outreaches to connect to road haulage and/or storage stacks.

In Europe many existing rail/road terminals were expanded; only a few were built from scratch (a rather complicated process to realize new infrastructure in an existing rail network).

In this decade there came a general understanding that rail shuttles were the only way for railroads to compete with the service-driven and low cost road haulage companies (Figure 318).

In order to compete with road haulage, the shippers and rail operators pressed both the deepsea terminals and inland rail-road terminals into cost reductions. This resulted in many developments for "low-cost" handling techniques for inland terminals (see Figure 319).

Figure 318: Container shuttle train passing RSC, Rotterdam

But, these efforts were not very successful; in general it can be concluded that larger rail-road terminals and deepsea railheads in Europe directed towards rail mounted cranes, supported with reach-stackers or straddle carriers for their storage yards.

The service demands from shipping lines and road haulage companies, forced terminals to improve their turnaround times for truckers,

Figure 319: "Low Cost" handling for inland rail terminal

resulting in some underutilization during the day as most of the inland rail-road terminals had to deal with an early morning and late afternoon peak.

In the US there were many off-dock rail facilities; rail-road terminals operated by railroad companies, originally for domestic transportation but more and more servicing containerized intercontinental trades. This included an additional short road-haulage between deepsea terminal and rail-terminal (varying from 5 to 40 km.) with their related consequences for additional cost, transportation time, logistics complexity and environmental impact.

For that reason, shipping lines with their dedicated deepsea-terminals encouraged port authorities and railroad companies to realize on-dock rail facilities. Some of them were realized with container handling cranes (RMG or RTG), but also the old-fashioned systems with top-lifters (piggy packers), reach stackers and on-wheeled stacking were applied. In the latter case tremendous areas were added to the terminals; some of them dedicated some others more multi-user, controlled by a railroad company (see Figure 320).

Figure 320: Area consuming on-dock rail yards: Los Angeles (left) and Seattle

ICT: becoming a key component for terminals

This decade clearly showed the importance and dependency of information technology: not only control and planning programs, but hardware and data communication systems as well.

Starting with hardware there was a tendency to walk away from mainframes and their expensive brand-related software. Both minicomputers (e.g. Sun Systems) and microcomputers (PC-based) gained more ground due to their rapidly growing computing power and the availability of more universally spread (lower cost) operating systems, such as UNIX and Apple/Microsoft operating systems. It was a step towards PC-based systems.

Early started terminals installed larger mainframes (IBM, Univac, Siemens, etc.) and tailor-made software, but these terminals were more and more confronted with fast growing costs for hard and software. The arrival of more universal application software and database systems (e.g. Oracle relational database), accelerated the introduction of terminal operating control systems from mainframe independent software companies. At the end of this decade, many established large terminals were in the process of converting their in-house developed and maintained operational computer systems into systems available in the IT market and with a multi-vendor approach to hardware. Typical fault-tolerant systems from STRATUS or TANDEM were replaced by universal minicomputers in hot-standby configurations.

Port Community Information systems were further introduced however not always very successfully. Data exchange speeds, limited functionality and relatively high cost made many port users reluctant to support a massive expansion of these systems. The development of standard EDI-messages helped the introduction of bilateral data exchange between the terminals and their users (shipping lines, customs, major shippers and large inland depots and transportation companies).

ICT developed into a key component for efficient terminals and many new applications were introduced, such as:

- Intelligent ship planning systems able to generate a ship planning with smart scheduling for the terminal, to avoid costly shuffle moves as much as possible. The simultaneous access to stack location, container properties and vessel stowage directives together with smart algorithms resulted in more user-friendly ship planning systems;

- Automated container identification systems, mainly based on Optical Character Recognition (OCR) technology. The application of tags (RFID) remained restricted to equipment identification (e.g. APL chassis with tags; Singapore road trucks with tags). This technology helped to speed-up gate processing and to improve quality of information;

- In the field of security (pilferage, illegal retrieval), systems were introduced to identify truckers and to allow pre-allocation at the landside. Vision systems helped to identify and store truckers' information. In Rotterdam a cargo-card was introduced with specific container data and ID-information of truck drivers, whose fingerprint data from readers in the gate could be matched with pre-processed info (biometric recognition);

- Some terminals installed prototype systems for electronic seals, but this development was clearly something more specific for an introduction by shipping lines or shippers. In this decade the electronic seals stayed in the prototype stage. However, they showed their potential for faster handling and clearance in the gate (customs) and for reduced cost of documentation. Especially for ID-systems the software had to assure sufficient preventions for illegal manipulations from outside (or even inside) sources;

- Some terminals installed job control systems for their transportation equipment (straddle carriers, top lifters, reach stacker and terminal tractors). For the required location information, DGPS-systems became popular, although in some terminals laser-based systems (triangulation) were used as back up and control, to assure a proper functioning under various conditions (atmospheric distortions and fading). Location control systems also helped to control and partly automate RTG-operations;

- Remote control systems for fault finding and parameter setting became available for the major handling equipment, allowing maintenance engineers (from the terminal or the manufacturer) to interfere without a physical visit to the equipment.

Obviously, all these rather off-the-shelf applications required quite some interfacing software with all their related reliability threats. The above new (additional) applications and the trend towards decentralized systems with sufficient back-up systems forced terminals to pay much more attention (and money) to their data communication systems and IT-infrastructure (fiber optic network, servers, radio data systems and fire protection). Fortunately the arrival of high-speed LAN-based radio data communication in the GHz-band helped to support the introduction of so many new applications in operations control. By the mid-1990s it became clear that terminal operations were highly dependent on reliable computer control systems. Many terminals learned this the hard way: outages for several hours and a major cost component for hard- and software (systems, employees and outside services).

In retrospect

By the mid-1990s terminals were preparing for even more growth but meanwhile struggling with cost control and performance. Some major topics from this decade can be summarized:

- Port authorities and multi-user terminals were granting dedicated facilities to shipping lines (or alliances). Within a few years shipping lines (Maersk and Sea-Land) used their facilities for business from other shipping lines (often at marginal rates) and that eroded the business for independent multi-user terminal operators. Probably this was the driver for some powerful terminal operators to start a global expansion, later developing into global terminal operators and aimed at securing a major-share in terminal operations with reasonable profits;

- The break-up of consortia and the increasing competition between terminals caused a demise of long-term commitments between terminals and shipping lines. Tariff negotiations became a yearly issue with power play from the large shipping lines;

- China started its tremendous developments in container (terminal) operations making-up much of its backlog;

- A number of major port authorities published their visions for the future (e.g. Long Beach). Los Angeles released its Ports 2020 plan, indicating an upcoming shortage on port area and handling facilities;

- Slowly, all kinds of exotic handling equipment (side-loaders, C-movers, etc.) were phased out. Reach-stackers and RTGs became very popular; the straddle carrier survived and even revived in some areas;

- The community thinking from labor unions further decreased and labor became more loyal to their terminal organization due to the growing number of fixed payroll employees;

- Real terminal automation started with completely unmanned equipment for stacking and transportation (ECT's Delta Sea-Land Terminal in Rotterdam). Only a few terminals in Western Europe (Thamesport, HHLA Hamburg and La Spezia) and the Far East (HIT in Hong Kong and PSA in Singapore) followed and started projects with automation involved (see Chapter 13).

12.5. 1996-2006: INCREASING VESSEL SIZES AND CONTINUING VOLUME GROWTH

The world's economic development during this decade encouraged shipping lines to invest massively in more and larger container vessels. After the introduction of Maersk's Regina Maersk-class (length 318 m, 17 containers wide on deck, officially 6,600 TEU but in reality around 8,500 TEU) the standard mainline vessel became 8,000 TEU, in a few years already grown to 10,000 TEU. At the end of the decade, the *Emma Maersk* set a new maximum: officially 11,000 TEU but capable of carrying ca. 14,500 TEU (later even upgraded to 15,400 TEU). The global economic growth in general but the Chinese trade growth in particular fuelled a tremendous expansion in container handling.

In only 10 years the world port handlings more than doubled from 170 million TEU in 1996 towards 442 million TEU in 2006 and 80% of this volume was handled by approximately 90 ports, handling more than 1 million TEU per year. The container volumes in and out of China showed double digit growth figures for many years and in 2006 an impressive 77 million TEU handlings were realized in Chinese ports only (with Shanghai: 21.7 million TEU and Shenzhen: 18.5 million TEU, ranking in the top 5 ports of the world). The arrival of large vessels required major investments in larger quay cranes, deeper access channels, quay walls with more water depth and especially more handling capacity (in moves per berth-hour) to cope with the demand for a short stay-in-port (preferably < 30 hours) even when call sizes went up to 4,000 container moves or more. The whole containerized supply chain had difficulties to control the year in year out growing volumes, sometimes more than 20% per year. Customs, inland transportation companies and even shippers and consignees could not maintain their regular service levels and this resulted in elongated container dwell times at the terminals; many terminals experienced an increase from 4-5 days towards 6-8 days. This in turn caused performance problems, a demand for more stacking capacity and additional costs (more shuffle and housekeeping moves and larger driving distances).

So, it is no wonder that in the second half of this decade many large terminals were congested and desperately looking for expansion and/or new terminal sites. Amazingly, the boom in shipping volumes did not result in shipping rate improvements (even to the contrary) with all the negative consequences for terminal handling rates, forcing terminals to cost reductions, often leading to staff cutting and extended equipment maintenance intervals.

In a drive to assure sufficient terminal capacity and an increased berth performance at reasonable cost many large shipping lines/alliances acquired long term commitments for dedicated terminal facilities in major ports within their shipping networks. The concentration amongst shipping lines and container terminals triggered a concern about the availability of handling capacity and service, both aspects becoming a key issue during this decade.

General topics for terminals

The tremendous volume growth, the changes in shipping networks (mainline routes, feeder operations) and an accelerating privatization resulted in many topics effecting design and operations of container terminals. The most relevant issues are presented below:

- Privatization and a reduced involvement from port authorities increased the number of tendering processes for concessions, including demands for volume guarantees, revenues, utilization of the facility, etc. Sometimes the concession periods were short, which blocked in-depth investments required for expansion and service improvements. Especially in South-America, South Africa and South East Asia, many new private terminals were built. Examples are in Panama and the Bahamas where new terminals acquired a regional hub function. The HPH terminal at the Bahamas was a good example of private smartness: the expensive civil engineering works could be compensated with the sales of valuable coral sand. Terminal operators were required to pre-qualify with commitments for financing and realization. In many cases the regular profits were insufficient to acquire external financial resources and even regional governments were limited for this type of expansion programs. Not surprising that the Global Terminal Operators and shipping lines became increasingly active in the race for much more terminal capacity. Older facilities (with limited water depth and stacking area) were abandoned or sold to smaller (general) stevedoring companies or restructured in attractive housing (apartments) for the happy few (London, Rotterdam and San Francisco);
- Shipping lines rationalized their networks with various services on the same trade but with different port calls, also allowing for cross-feedering and mainline vessels calling at earlier feeder ports. This was no problem for the big load centers but many terminals saw sudden changes in their yearly volumes (often positive, sometimes negative) as a result of these rapid changes in services;
- Privatization and takeovers caused many disputes with labor unions sometimes resulting in weeks-long strikes, such as in the US East Coast, Australia, France, Brazil, Chile and Greece.

But gradually, labor unions were losing influence, partly due to the diminished number of members and partly through the entrance of new technology and a new type of terminal workers. It became clear that major improvements in working conditions and the approach from management had transferred the old-fashioned, muscle-based port facilities into industrial terminal activities;

- The shipment of high-value chemicals, perishable goods, etc., increased through the availability of refrigerated containers (integrals), tank containers, ventilated containers, bulk containers, etc.; attractive for shipping lines for whom these valuable cargoes did generate a sound profit but with a lot of attention and often restrictions for terminal operations. Separated stacks, stacking height restrictions, electrical supply, regular inspections and a reporting of hazardous cargo are a few of the extra activities to be realized by terminal operators, often without sufficient coverage of the related cost;

- Between 2002 and 2004 quite a number of terminals could not fulfill the shipping lines' service demands. Saturation appeared in many terminals resulting in vessel delays and elongated turnaround times for truckers. Not only the rapidly-growing volumes (sometimes double

Figure 321: Tank containers

digit), but also the increasing dwell times surprised terminal operators. Terminals started to push-out "foreign activities" such as a railhead, the storage and repair of MT-containers and CFS activities. Shipping lines complained about the port/terminal congestions but at the same time immediately collected a congestion surcharge fee from the shippers. Where terminal operators looked for possibilities to externalize area consuming rail operations outside of their terminal, shipping lines expressed their need for on-dock rail facilities for two obvious reasons (from their point of view): a fast transshipment from stack to railcar and at the lowest cost. Nevertheless quite a number of terminals, together with port authorities and rail operators moved intermodal rail activities adjacent to the terminal and settled a cost coverage for the extra transportation activities. The congestion problems strengthened the drive of shipping lines for their own dedicated facilities or at least a guaranteed berthing and service performance (crane availability);

- Intermodal services increased, often with the support of governmental bodies. Shuttle trains (block trains) were the only possibility for railway companies to compete with trucking (see Figure 322). However, only a limited number of terminals experienced substantial numbers of rail

Figure 322: Rail terminals in Antwerp (left) and Felixstowe

handling (say > 20%) at their landside. US West Coast terminals and some Australian and European terminals (Bremerhaven, Antwerp and Felixstowe) had to provide for enlarged railheads;

- Trucking remained the dominant inland mode and to avoid too many delays, clever trucking companies extended their role in the landside logistic chain. Some arranged their own consolidation center decades of kilometers away from the terminal, to combine pickup and delivery trips, to consolidate for shippers/consignees with related VAL-services and to do stock-keeping of special empty containers for shipping lines or merchants. In Europe even rail shuttles and barge shuttles were introduced by large trucking companies, with all the related contractual complexity as terminal operators in general had their service contracts with shipping lines;

- Many terminals became aware of their limitations and started improvement activities. Simulation became a proper tool to analyze measures to reduce saturation and congestion. Dynamic stack planning, pre-notice for truckers, flexible scheduling and pooling of transportation equipment at the waterside were introduced, often as a result of simulation studies. Many larger terminals started the on-line collection of data, necessary for a more in-depth analysis of terminal logistics and evaluation of improvement proposals. It became clear that there was no single linear relation between volume and numbers of equipment. The introduction of stochastic arrival times, operational delays and equipment breakdowns and the use of cycle time distributions for handling processes within their simulation studies, made many terminals aware of the necessity to further study their complicated logistic processes.

Terminal capacity dominated by Global Terminal Operators

The ongoing growth in demand for terminal capacity increased the concern amongst shipping lines about scarcity of terminal capacity along their major shipping networks. At the same time many terminal operators wanted to expand their business, to exploit their expertise in other ports of the world. On top of that, the privatization in ports worldwide made successful terminal operators and investors interested in terminal operations as a profitable business in a steadily growing container shipping world.

In the mid-1990s, there were only a few multi-terminal, international terminal operators such as:

- Hutchison Port Holdings, founded in 1994, with interests in Hong Kong International Terminals (see Figure 323), Felixstowe, Yantian International Container Terminals and a joint venture in Shanghai Container Terminals;

- Sea-Land Terminals (later CSX World Terminals), the terminal operating arm of Sea-Land, but increasingly handling third-party business, although always with preferred service for the Sea-Land vessels (see Figure 324). The increasing number of alliances and joint services encouraged this third-party business;

Figure 323: HIT terminal, Hong Kong

- Stevedoring Services of America, a major stevedoring company in the US with more than 10 terminals (containers, general cargo, breakbulk, etc.) started international activities in Panama (Colon) and in a joint venture with TMM in Mexico (Manzanillo) and the Caribbean (Port of Spain);

- P&O Ports, originally started as an OCL interest in terminals in the UK and Australia to serve the container shipping activities of OCL and some of its consortia (TRIO) partners.

Figure 324: Sea-Land terminal Tacoma

The large majority of international terminal interests was realized by shipping lines (the carriers), not only Sea-Land and OCL, but also Evergreen, Maersk Line, APL, Matson, OOCL and later Hanjin, Hyundai and Cosco, secured their needs for terminal capacity. In most cases these carriers made long-term lease arrangements with a port authority and these terminals could realize sufficient terminal handling volume from their own services and some minor third parties.

Well-established typical private terminal operators like Eurokai (Hamburg), ECT (Rotterdam), Hessenatie (Antwerp) and Maher Terminals (New York) were certainly looking for international expansion (e.g. ECT got a long-term lease in the Italian Trieste Terminal) but it was a slow, difficult process due to the reluctance from shareholders not interested in taking more risk, difficulties in raising sufficient finances, reluctance from employees to move "overseas" and a lack of experience with local conditions not allowing a 1-to-1 duplication of the systems/methods in use with the mother company. The idea of strategic alliances between major worldwide multi-user container terminals was a nice theory but did not emerge.

In the years before 2000, a few events encouraged the take off of some real global operators. Hutchison Whampoa supported Hutchison Port Holdings with ample financial resources and the takeover from Sea-Land by Maersk Line allowed A.P. Møller (the Maersk Line parent) to expand APM Terminals into a global terminal network.

P&O ports joined the global operators with terminal interests in UK, Australia, Italy, Shekou (China), Thailand, India, etc.

After the year 2000, the emergence of global operators accelerated, partly supported through mergers and takeovers in the shipping line world and partly through the entrance of large investors, interested in terminal operations as a long-term investment with guaranteed profits.

It should be noted that the original discrepancy between private terminal conglomerates and carrier-controlled terminal networks evaporated in this decade.

Basically, private terminals marked their business as a profit center whilst the carriers in general defined their terminals as cost centers in their worldwide shipping business. But gradually, the carrier-related global terminal operators (APMT, Evergreen and later Cosco Pacific) were allowed reasonable profit margins for their services to the (parent) shipping lines.

At the end of this decade all major global terminal operators considered their business as profit-driven, exposing a strategy to have worldwide coverage with terminals at the major East-West and North-South shipping routes. It became a major effort (by tendering for concessions and long-term leases) to assure a foothold in all major main ports, regional hubs and port expansion programs in the developing markets (China, India, Indonesia, Brazil, Russia, etc.).

By 2006, there were 7 globally operating terminal conglomerates each handling more than 10 million TEU handlings per year and together realizing more than 55% of the world's port transshipment volume (see Figure 325). Within about 5 years a few global port operators captured market dominance and in this top 5 only 2 of them were shipping line related. Some highlights of these remarkable developments are mentioned below.

	2003	2004	2006
HPH	41.5	47.8	58.0
PSA	28.7	33.1	51.3
APM Terminals	22.3	31.9	43.0
DP World incl. P&O	25.1	33.5	42.0
Cosco Pacific	17.9	23.5	32.5
Eurogate	10.7	11.5	12.6
SSA	5.4	9.9	12.9
Sum 7 GTOs	151.6	191.2	252.3
World Total	317.0	363.7	441.8
Share 7 GTOs	47,8%	52,6%	57.1%

Figure 325: Handling volumes global terminal operators in million TEU (Source Dynamar)

Hutchison Port Holdings

When the British trading house Hutchison Whampoa was sold to Cheung Kong Holdings Limited, the self-made entrepreneur Li Ka-Shing founded Hutchison Port Holdings in 1994 as a subsidiary of the Hong Kong conglomerate. Starting with a majority share in Hong Kong International Terminals, the purchase of a 75% share in Felixstowe was the beginning of an impressive expansion, supported through the clever business approach and financial power of Hong Kong's largest private landlord. The Chinese roots of Li Ka-Shing (a Chinese refugee born in Chaozhou) helped to enter the Chinese terminal market just in time in 1992 with the first investments in Shanghai and Yantian (Shenzhen). At the end of 2006 Hutchison Port Holdings was operating many Chinese terminals (such as Jiuzhou, Ningbo, Shantou, Xiamen and Tianjin). Other Far Eastern facilities were added in Myanmar, South-Korea (Busan and Kwangyang) and Indonesia. Worthwhile to mention was the realization in the 1990s of a regional hub at the Bahamas (Freeport) at the crossing of various trade lanes and this terminal was realized with rather low cost for the facility's civil works as the dredged coral sand could be sold very attractively (see Figure 326).

Figure 326: Hutchison's terminals at Freeport Bahamas and Euromax Rotterdam

The addition of terminals in Cristobal and Balboa assured a strategic position at both ends of the Panama Canal. Another strategic acquisition was a 40% stake in ECT Rotterdam in 1998 later followed by a complete takeover by the end of 2001. The Hong Kong management was rather reserved about

ECT's AGV/ASC-based unmanned operations (in the Far East labor cost were a minority cost in terminal operations) but after thorough financial analysis they finally stood behind these developments and they approved further investments in this direction, including a new fully automated Euromax Terminal. Other terminals added to HPH's European envelope were in Barcelona, Harwich, Thamesport, Gdynia and St. Petersburg.

HPH has always been keen to apply their operational know how developed by HIT and Felixstowe in their newly-acquired or newly-built terminals. Investments were only made on the base of a sound business plan and the selection of terminals was based on their strategy to establish an interlinked chain of hubs at the major trade lanes. HPH's policies and strategy are justified by the healthy profit margins, experienced for many years and often criticized by shipping lines, who failed to make money in the periods of trade volume growth.

PSA

The port of Singapore Authority was transformed in 1997 and became the PSA Corporation for all the Singapore business (various terminals, warehousing, etc.), connected with an international business arm: PSA International. The objective of this restructuring was to become "a world-class corporation with a network of ports, logistics and related business throughout the world". In this decade PSA continued its strong competition with Hong Kong, resulting in a slight advantage over Hong Kong in 2006 (see Figure 327).

	1996	2006
Singapore	12.9	24.8
Hong Kong	13.4	23.5

Figure 327: Port volumes in million TEU

It should be noted that approximately 70% of Singapore's handlings were pure transshipment handlings, this in contrast to Hong Kong's moderate figure of only 25%. Obviously, Hong Kong's port volumes were influenced by the rapid expansion of Chinese ports in South China (Shenzhen terminals, Jiangmen, Jiuzhou, and Guangzhou) close to Hong Kong.

In 1996 PSA started its first overseas terminal activities in Dalian through a joint venture with the Dalian Port Authority. In later years other interests in Chinese ports were obtained such as Fuzhou, Guangzhou, Jiangyin, Qingdao and Tianjin, often in tough competition with HPH.

Remarkable was the entrance in Europe: first in Italy (Venice and Genoa) and later in Portugal (Sines) and Belgium (Antwerp and Zeebrugge). In Antwerp, PSA obtained a considerable market share. Shortly after the merger between Hessenatie and Noordnatie, PSA acquired their interests in 2002 and established the PSA-HNN terminals, operating the Europa-terminal and Noordzee-terminal and a barge terminal in Rotterdam Europoort. After that, the PSA-HNN combination formed a joint-venture with the Hanjin/K Line/Yang Ming alliance, operating the Antwerp International Terminal at the Antwerp Deurganck dock as from 2005.

A year later PSA and MSC started the MSC Home terminal, a major MSC-hub operation at the Delwaide dock. This cooperation with MSC also resulted in a dedicated terminal (MSC-PSA Asia Terminal) at Pasir Panjang Singapore. The appointment of Mr. Kho as managing director of PSA-HNN in Belgium was peculiar as Mr. Kho started with ECT, worked for HIT and HPH and then landed at a PSA subsidiary.

Quite an effort was PSA's agreement to design, build and operate the Aden Container Terminal in Yemen. Being in the catch area of Jeddah, Salalah, Fujairah and Khor Fakkan, this presented some difficulties to attract volume to become a regional hub.

PSA's interests in Busan, Tuticorin and Laem Chebang were in line with the strategy but a real surprise was the acquisition of a 20% share in HPH, a 20% share in HIT Hong Kong and a 31% share in CT3 (the former Sea-Land facility) in Hong Kong for a total amount of US$ 5.65 billion. It showed the strength of PSA International, owned by Temasek, a government supported Singapore investor. This participation in its rival global operator gave PSA an involvement in 63 ports worldwide.

APM Terminals

Although Maersk Line entered somewhat late in container shipping, their strategy with regard to terminals was already developed in the 1990s, looking for terminal operations where possible, with a good service at competitive cost.

In the US Maersk Line had a dedicated terminal in Long Beach, operated by Stevedoring Services of America. In New York, as of end 1970s, they ran a terminal in Port Newark, including a crane sharing agreement with Universal Terminal (see Figure 328).

At Kaohsiung a small straddle carrier based terminal was operated very efficiently (large throughput over only one berth) due to the fact that Maersk effectively controlled the whole hinterland chain between inland Container Freight Stations (Maersk's Mercantile inland organization) and the terminal. Dwell times were very short and the stack planning was completely dedicated towards a productive vessel operation.

Maersk Line's interest in terminals became materialized in Yokohama, Algeciras (Spain) and Yantian (near Hong Kong).

Figure 328: Maersk terminal at Port Newark in the 1990s

In the second half of the 1990s, Maersk clearly stated its demand to get more cost control and better service (berth guarantees and vessel performance) in the major ports of their envisaged global shipping network. Sea-Land (later APM Terminals) realized some important hubs in Salalah (Oman, 1996) and Port Tanjung Pelepas (PTP, see Figure 333), just opposite Singapore, showed the independency Maersk was looking for, an approach applied to many ports and not always appreciated by the existing (public) multi-user terminals. Both terminals (PTP and Salalah) were built from scratch, based upon the simple, cost-effective RTG-stacking system (in low labor cost areas) and the use of Maersk's planning and operations control systems (Navis, BARN and ERP), proven in other terminals of APMT.

It took Maersk more than 2 years to get its own, dedicated facility in Rotterdam, this to the detriment of ECT, who lost quay wall length, terminal area and volume. In those days many Maersk officials negotiated with one firm statement: "We don't take no for an answer". Equal developments took place in other ports such as Bremerhaven. After the takeover of Sea-Land, December 1999/January 2000, more terminal interests came to APMT (although some US terminals remained with CSX) and again there was a big dispute with ECT Rotterdam. There, Sea-Land had a 20-year contract at the automated Delta Sea-Land Terminal and Maersk tried to transfer their combined Maersk Sealand business to its own dedicated facility next to ECT. The resulting legal dispute was settled after a number of years (Maersk reimbursed ECT).

The introduction of the 17-container-wide Regina Maersk-class vessels and the plans for even 22-wide vessels (the later Emma Maersk-class) stimulated APMT to get involved in major new or expansion programs for terminals, allowing them to specify quay cranes with sufficient outreach and lifting height to handle the upcoming leviathan vessels. More than 15 terminals in Europe, more than 20 in Asia including China, over 20 terminals in the Americas and about 10 in Africa marked Maersk's global terminal interests.

At the end of this decade APMT surprised the terminal community with the introduction of an unmanned automated stacking yard at their new facility at Virginia ports. Here, in the US, Maersk retracted its often exposed reluctance for automation as the sky-high labor cost (and may be the setting of an example for the tradition-bound labor unions) made automation very attractive. The competitive shipping world and Maersk's policy for economies of scale supported APMT to further expand in terminal capacity at first class locations but only when possible on a cost-attractive base.

DP World

DP World became a worldwide terminal operator as of the late 1990s. The Dubai Ports Authority (with their large terminals Port Rashid and Jebel Ali and later all concentrated in Jebel Ali, see Figure 329), founded Dubai Ports International (DPI) in 1999 when a major share was taken in the South Container Terminal in the Jeddah Islamic Port. Later, terminal interests were obtained at Djibouti (2000); Visakhapatnam, India (2002) and Constanza, Romania (2003).

In 2005 DPI made a major investment with the acquisition of CSX World Terminals for the sum of US$ 1.14 billion. This caused some discussion in the US about the influence of Arab companies in US terminals (security risk). In September 2005 the Dubai Ports Authority and Dubai Ports International merged into DP World and

Figure 329: DP World terminal at Dubai, Jebel Ali 1

at the year end, DP World finalized negotiations for the takeover of P&O and P&O Ports for the amount of 6.8 billion US$. Within a year, DP world sold its US terminal business (Baltimore, Miami, New Orleans, New York, New Jersey, Philadelphia and general stevedoring activities) to the investment group of a large US insurance company (AIG Global Investment Group) for an amount of just over US$ 1 billion.

With the takeover of P&O Ports, the history of some DP World terminals goes back to the late 1960s when the shipping consortia OCL and ACT became involved in Seatainer Terminals Ltd in Australia (Sydney and Melbourne) to support their Europe-Australia service. Interestingly, in the beginning OCL and ACT could not arrange much interest in the London docks, where a terminal at berth 39 was realized (behind the locks). There, the unions even refused to handle these new containerized services and the two shipping consortia diverted their vessel calls to Antwerp. Probably that experience even more convinced OCL that the assurance of dedicated facilities was crucial for a reliable shipping service. Late 1970s, the OCL/ACT combination transferred to the riverside Northfleet Hope Terminal.

In the 1970s Container Terminals Australia Ltd was set-up, starting terminal operations in Botany Bay (Sydney). In 1976 Tilbury Container Services was added to P&O Ports. In the 1980s and 1990s P&O Ports further expanded internationally with interests in Manila, Shekou, Vostochny, Port Qasim, Mumbai (Nhava Sheva, JNPT), Antwerp, Marseilles, Malta, Le Havre, etc.

The oil and trade-earned buying power transformed DP World in a major player and this process continued. In July 2006 DP World made a long term contract with the Egyptian Government for the port development of Eastern Port Said in addition of the existing public terminal (PSC&CH) and the APMT-operated Suez Canal Container Terminal (SCCT). Other important involvements can be found in Pusan Newport Terminal (Korea), Aden Container Terminal (Yemen) and Callao (Peru). During the last few years of this decade, the large acquisitions and an active tendering for new concessions drove DP World into the top 5 of the world's Global Terminal Operators.

Cosco Pacific

The origin of Cosco Pacific lies in the terminal involvement of Cosco, the first Chinese national carrier. The shipping line's interest in terminals started in the 1990s, with shares in some Hong Kong Terminals, a dedicated facility at Long Beach and a regional hub in Naples (Italy).

In the beginning of this decade, Cosco Pacific had a number of minority shares in Chinese ports (such as Shekou, Yantian, Shanghai and Qingdao) and these interests were expanded, sometimes through joint ventures, such as in the port of Taicang (together with PSA).

At the end of this decade, Cosco Pacific obtained considerable shares in the Euroasia International Terminal at Tianjin (30%) and the phase II terminal at Nansha (58%). Later, a part of its Nansha share was sold to APMT, which in return granted Cosco Pacific a stake in the Beilun Terminal at Ningbo. Other partnerships ensured Cosco Pacific an involvement in the 30-kilometer offshore Yangshan terminals of Shanghai.

To ensure sufficient terminal capacity for Cosco's important Europe-Asia shipping services its subsidiary Cosco Pacific managed to settle terminal interests in Antwerp (Antwerp Gateway), Rotterdam (Euromax) and Genoa.

A bid for a share in HHLA's Tollerort terminal failed, but a time-consuming bidding procedure at Piraeus (Greece) started in 2006 and was finalized successfully a few years later. The tremendous growth of China's port throughputs (in the direction of 100 million TEU per year) supported Cosco Pacific to handle more than 32 million TEU through their terminals in 2006.

Eurogate and SSA

Next to the abovementioned "Big Five" global terminal operators, there were two mid-size, more classical terminal stevedoring companies, however with much smaller volumes than the top 5 GTOs.

In this decade, the Eckelman Eurokai Group acquired a stake in Contship Europe resulting in terminal involvements in La Spezia, Leghorn and Gioia Tauro (Italy) and Lisbon (Portugal). By the end of the decade the Eurokai and Contship groups had founded Eurogate and merged with BLG (Bremer Lagerhaus Gesellschaft), adding terminal interests in Bremerhaven, Wilhelmshaven (Jade Weser Port), Salerno and Ravenna and a terminal in Tangier at the East-West/North-South crossroads. The terminal capacity in North West Europe and Italy provided Eurogate a better market share towards Central Europe, supported with an increasing number of shuttle trains, an interest of DB Cargo and Italian Railways.

In the US, a well-established stevedoring company also made a move into the international terminal business. Founded by Fred R. Smith in 1949, a general stevedoring company in Seattle, later named Seattle Stevedore Co. and as of 1984 Stevedoring Services of America (SSA), slowly but steadily entered into container terminal operations; often as the stevedoring arm of a shipping line, which arranged for terminal leases (5 years or longer) with Port authorities. The SSA Company acquired an interest in the Vancouver container terminal, followed in 1994 with a share in Manzanillo International Terminal (Colon, Panama). In 1996 SSA got a stake (31%) in terminal and warehousing operations in Saigon (Vietnam); later to be followed by joint ventures to develop Cai Mep and terminals in Ho Chi Minh City and Cai Lan Port (2005).

In the year 2000, SSA entered into a partnership with the Mexican shipping line TMM leading to terminal operations at Veracruz, Acapulco, Cozumel and Manzanillo (Mexico). In 2003n Stevedoring Services of America was transferred to SSA Marine and before the end of this decade SSA Marine started a container terminal at Long Beach (via a joint venture with Cosco) and in Oakland: the Howard Terminal and the Oakland International Container Terminal. In some US ports SSA Marine started cooperation with Cooper T. Smith, a general stevedoring company.

Figure 330: SSA terminals in Seattle (left) and Panama (Manzanillo)

Especially at the US West Coast, SSA got a reputation to be very cost conscious and SSA was often mentioned: "The most anti-union maritime operator at the West Coast". In 2003, SSA Marine entered in a very profitable contract for Iraq operations, providing container handling and general stevedoring in the Port of Umm Qasr (Iraq) to support US Army operations.

Of course, besides the independent Global Terminal Operators, the shipping line related terminals continued as well. Interests from APL, Evergreen, OOCL, MSC, CMA/CGM, Hanjin and others were further developed along their liner networks, but the yearly throughput of their global port handlings remained below 10 million TEU by the end of this decade.

The dynamics in the "battle" for terminal capacity, international exposure and guarantees for service will continue. New players emerged in this decade: The Shanghai International Port Group made its first international entrance through a 40% share in the APMT terminal at Zeebrugge. Also China Merchants Holding International (CMHI), a partly state-owned investment company, is active in the fields of port operations, bulk and container transportation and manufacturing (paint and containers). CMHI could build up major interests in Chinese ports (such as Ningbo, Shekou, Shanghai, Qingdao and Tianjin) and related warehousing activities. In a joint venture the first international activities will start in Vietnam; further terminals are planned for Sri Lanka, Taiwan and Nigeria.

Rather new in the world of container terminal operations was the entrance of large civil building contractors, becoming (temporarily) terminal operators through BOT contracts. Companies like Bouyges (France) and Dragados (Spain) in particular became noticeable players, e.g. Dragados not only assured terminal interests in Spain (Bilbao, Cartagena, La Coruña, Malaga, Sagunto and Valencia), but also in Portugal (Las Palmas and Setubal), Asia (Mumbai and Jing Tang) and America (Caucedo and Iquique).

In general, all conglomerates of globally active terminal operators have an approach equal to financial investors: there must be a sound Return On Investment (ROI). In many cases, there is a detailed cost control from headquarters, including the approval of all investment programs. Benefits arise from a multiple application of handling systems and operational planning and control systems, the exchange of qualified personnel, repetitive training programs and economies of scale. The GTOs have an impressive buying power, based upon tough tendering processes for systems and of course standardized equipment, with the focus on a low investment (and in general not on a minimum total life cycle cost); local preferences were very often overruled by headquarters! Most of the GTOs managed to maintain a healthy margin, but unfortunately the focus on profit did result in staff reductions and a degradation of the terminal into an operating unit (influencing the entrepreneurial spirit of the earlier terminal staff).

This strategy could be clearly recognized in the design of many terminals, realized during this decade by the GTOs. Most of them were RTG-based terminals and only a few large ones were based on (partly-automated) RMGs. The emphasis was on the creation of terminal capacity and avoiding risk through the use of proven equipment and operations control software.

Upgrading the terminal handling systems

The vessel size developments (from 16 to 17 wide containers on deck and later even until 18 and in 2006, 22 wide) urged terminal operators to upgrade their fleet of quay cranes in the first place. The outreach (from center waterside rail) increased towards 50 m. and later for some terminals even towards 60 m. to accommodate the Emma Maersk-size (22 wide). The stack height on deck (6-8 high) required an enlarged lifting height above the quay wall, reaching 35-45 m. So, terminals were forced to invest in new larger cranes and to modify existing cranes, some of them not older than 10 years (quite a gap between the technical and economic lifetime!). Productivity improvements could be obtained by increased hoisting/lowering and trolley speeds and the application of twin-lift (2 x 20') and later tandem-lift (2 x 40', parallel).

Another component for productivity improvement was the automated second-trolley but remarkably here a contradictory development came up in this decade. The second trolley pioneer ECT stopped this feature in their cranes due to their vulnerability for breakdowns and the installation of electronic sway control via the main hoist and trolley drives. To ECT's opinion (probably shareholders opinion), the additional investment did not match with the moderate productivity improvement. However, other terminals purposely selected an automated second-trolley system, such as CTA in Hamburg, Euromax in Rotterdam and Port 2000 in Le Havre. Of course a proper design and sufficient maintenance are a prerequisite for a successful second-trolley operation, but if so, some operators saw the productivity benefits (remark: this is a good example of a potential improvement feature which can be unsuccessful when the technical conditions and operating environment are not properly controlled).

Features for load control (anti-sway) became very popular in this decade but in many terminals the crane operators did not like (or even refused to work) these devices as these interfered in their built-up sway control skills. Some terminal managers supported such operators' opinions and they installed crane simulators to train operators in sway control and other operational functions.

In North West Europe some terminals installed special barge/feeder cranes; basically quay cranes on a 30.5 or 35 m. rail gauge but with a much lower lifting height, to reduce the pendulum length and improve sight of the crane operator and thus improving the productivity. Even special shortsea terminals were established, often with wide-span gantries to stack containers in the rail gauge and handle shortsea vessels in their outreach and trains and/or road trucks in the backreach.

In spite of the installed measures to beef up crane productivity, some other issues overruled their potential, such as the additional time for SATL-handling and delays from waiting for transportation and information during a crane cycle. Talking on transportation Noell and Kalmar introduced their Sprinter or Runner, a 4- or 6-wheeled small straddle carrier (1 over 1, see Figure 331) designed for the transportation between the quay cranes and RMG-stacking areas, both in front-end or parallel arrangement. The benefit was the use of buffering under the quay crane, on the ground between the crane rails or in the backreach, and under the RMG. Some terminals supported this development, but many terminals maintained their tractor-trailer transportation, as they appreciated the low operating cost and minimum training efforts for drivers. Some terminals (e.g. Felixstowe and Gioia Tauro) introduced 2- or 3-trailer trains behind a heavy duty terminal tractor.

Figure 331: Small straddle carriers (1 over 1) for transportation (Noell, Kalmar)

An interesting development in horizontal transportation was shown at the Rotterdam Shortsea Terminal (RST) where four so-called Multitainers were installed between the backreach of the wide-span quay cranes and a landside RMG stacking module parallel to the quay wall. These devices allowed the transportation of 18 TEU (a block of 3 x 3 40'/45' containers) by means of a rail-mounted, self-propelled frame (see Figure 332).

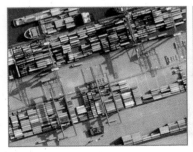 

Figure 332: Multitainer transport frames between quay cranes and stack yard

The tremendous trade growth in the Far East and South America induced a big demand in new terminal handling capacity and an expansion of stacking capacity in existing terminals. Scarcity of land and low investment cost made many terminals select an RTG stacking system. Although started as 1 over 3 and 1 over 4 stacking machines, most of the new RTG-applications were based on RTGs stacking 1 over 5 or 1 over 6 and 6-8 stacking rows with one truck handling lane under the portal. Obviously in many Far Eastern and South-American countries, the somewhat higher labor demand for RTG handling systems (on the RTG but especially the tractor-trailer demand sometimes reached up to 7 TTs per quay crane) was of minor influence as labor cost in countries such as China, Vietnam and Malaysia were rather low. Many newly built terminals in this decade show the simple rectangular lay-out, typical for an RTG stacking system and with an attractive step-by-step expansion possibility (both in quay wall extension direction and in depth). Typical examples are the PTP-terminal in Tanjung Pelepas (Malaysia, see Figure 333), Salalah (Oman), terminals in Gwangyang (Korea) and many Chinese terminals (Shanghai, Shenzhen, Qingdao and Ningbo). Some terminals specified 16-wheel gantry drive configurations allowing for lower wheel loads (savings for the track) and a much easier (90 degrees) turning of the wheels to switch from one stacking block to another (see Figure 334).

Other features such as automated gantry steering and position control systems also became available for RTG systems. Automated steering systems were based on vision sensors, transponder systems, induction wires in the ground, laser based triangulation or DGPS technology. For reliability reasons, sometimes two different systems were installed to ensure a proper functioning under all circumstances. The use of semi-automated positioning also required a certain type of sway control, either by sensors and electronics or through constant tension winches on an additional cable tower for sway control. All these features were meant to assist the operator and to facilitate tracking and tracing of both the RTG and the position where a container was placed or picked up. By the end of the decade, trials were going on with an electric supply to RTGs. The concern about the environment and the maintenance cost of a diesel-electric power set made some operators (e.g. Stockholm) decide to modify the RTG energy source from diesel fuel to electricity, in spite of the reduced flexibility (change-over to other stacking blocks, see Figure 335).

Figure 333: RTG terminal Port Tanjung Pelepas

Figure 334: RTGs with 16-wheels for low wheel loads and easy wheel turning

Terminal safety

During this decade safety issues continued to take a lot of attention both from terminal management, labor representatives, unions and authorities. The increasing scales and denser traffic and equipment movements caused some accidents resulting in all kinds of measures to reduce risks such as personal injuries, damages to equipment and cargo or the environmental impact from leaking hazardous cargo, fire, etc. Traffic types were increasingly separated and in many terminals driving at the terminal with private cars became restricted.

Figure 335: Electrical supply to Rubber Tired Stacking Crane

Another topic was the accessibility to stacked reefer containers. A 3 and 4-high stacking with straddle carriers and even 5 or 6-high with RTGs/RMGs required proper access walkways and stairs. Also in maintenance facilities much more attention was paid to safe and comfortable access to the enlarged equipment types.

A major issue was the lashing of deck-containers, an increasingly dangerous activity as on- deck stacking increased to 5, 6 and even 7-high. Terminal operators were used to lashing cages and special man-carrying cages under the spreader (often an open 20' frame or modified flat rack). In the US these provisions were named shoeboxes (from the name of "shoes" for stacking cones and twist locks) and terminal workers had to wear a safety harness with a spring-loaded line. Nevertheless sometimes severe accidents happened.

In July 1997, the US labor department announced a ban on container top work, to be effective from mid-1999, affecting both shipowners and terminal operators. Within in few years, semi-automated twist locks (SATLs) became the new standard for on-deck lashing as of the second or third tier. This change had a major impact on terminal operations as the placement and/or removal of these SATLs interfered in the quay crane cycle and thus negatively influenced crane productivity. Terminals developed two operational alternatives:

- SATL-handling within the crane cycle e.g. at a platform in the crane at 8-12 m. height and before the WS rail or at quay level before (when discharging) or after (when loading) positioning/hoisting the container onto/from the terminal chassis (or onto/from the ground in case of straddle carrier operations);

- SATL-handling outside the crane cycle when using cornerless bump cars allowing the handling before/after the crane. Another possibility was found for cranes fitted with an (automated) second trolley system where this SATL-handling could be done at the interchange platform between main trolley and second trolley system.

For organizational reasons most of the terminals selected a SATL-handling on dock level, also because of a more simple handling of the SATLs in and out of the collecting bins and placing the bins in a 20' flatrack container with the help of a forklift truck (see Figure 336).Terminals with multi-trailer trains, AGVs and automated second trolley systems had to make costly adjustments, difficult to recover in a competitive market. Some terminals experimented with semi-automatic SATL-positioning/retrieval devices (Tokyo OHI terminal and APMT) but not very successful, due to different SATL-designs and SATLs sticking in the corner castings.

Figure 336: SATL-handling in gauge with storage bins on 20' flats

In general, the introduction of the SATLs was a safety improvement for lashing activities on board of vessels, but the problems were transferred to shore where the terminal operator was faced with more cost, often 2 man more per crane crew (gang) and still a concern about safety when "cone men" could interfere with chassis or (even worse) straddle carrier driving. Some terminals unfortunately registered one or two fatal accidents.

Security

Security was another important issue. Before the year 2001 this in general comprised: the allowance of people on the terminal, the avoidance of pilferage or stealing of complete, loaded containers, the avoidance of stowaways and the preventive measures against smuggling (liquor, cigarettes, drugs, etc.). Gate security systems became more and more sophisticated and in a few countries customs introduced the first applications of X-ray equipment (stationary or mobile) to check the container contents without the need for a complete stripping (and there after stuffing) of the container (by the way this was a regular procedure in many Middle Eastern countries). In the late 1990s some terminal operators introduced a so-called cargo card, basically an ID chip card with personal information about trucker, his company, validity, etc. and biometric data to guarantee a secure permission to pass a gate. At their Brani Terminal, PSA started a system based on RFID-technology identifying the truck provided with a tag in the gate (trucks always stayed in Singapore).

Figure 337: Mobile X-ray equipment for container inspection

Maher Terminals in the US launched the paperless gate system with their Automated Receiving and Delivery (ARD) system with license plate readers, optical character recognition and imaging the drivers face and license for checking and authorization. The ARD-system was integrated with the TOS system. Also in the US (APL), Hong Kong (HIT) and some other Far Eastern terminals trials with RF technology, sensors and recognition systems were initiated, to improve security and accelerate the processing of truckers through the gate.

The terrorist attack at New York's World Trade Center, on 11 September 2001, had a tremendous impact on security procedures, both in ports and its terminals. In the US, legislation was developed within a few years, resulting in a few programs with global impact. The US Bureau of Customs and Border Protection (CBP) launched their Container Security Initiative (CSI) in 2002 with the intent to increase security by screening containers, bound for the US, in their port of origin. Initially the CSI-program focused on the top 20 ports, shipping containers to the US, but later the European Union embraced the program and many ports/terminals got certified to screen containers with an assumed higher risk. The CBP also extended their procedures to the whole supply chain in a voluntary Customs-Trade Partnership Against Terrorism (C-TPAT) allowing reduced CBP inspection activities when companies complied to C-TPAT guidelines in their security procedures. Parallel to CBP's policies, the IMO developed an initiative to enhance maritime security known as the ISPS-code, aimed at safeguarding vessels and to make sure that weapons, explosives, etc. could not come on and off aboard a vessel. In the US this code was the base for legislation: the Maritime Transportation Security Act.

Obviously all these requirements for much better and more in-depth security procedures had a major impact on container terminals; a few examples:

- Terminal access control with positive identification of employees, service providers (e.g. truck drivers), vendors, visitors, etc. This included "smart" ID cards, biometric verification and identity management (passwords, data base management, etc.);

- Proper fencing and monitoring the facility. Many terminals had to upgrade their fences, install automatic barriers, install cameras, encourage awareness and train security guards to maintain procedures and monitor cargo handling and storage areas;

- Designation of a Facility Security Officer responsible for control of procedures and risk management covering security assessment, security plans and security surveys.

On top of the described measures, additional activities could be required depending on different alert levels. Levels 2 and 3 could ask for compulsory registration of visitors (like a prison), more security staff, body checks, etc. Most of the terminals made substantial investments in this area and had to increase their security staff. The resulting costs were passed on to shipping lines (charging their customers) as a security charge to cover costs in the range of 10-15 US$/TEU.

In addition, C-TPAT-terminals had to cooperate with customs (and US customs) to participate in the Automated Manifest System (AMS). An automated risk analysis can select a number of containers to be checked in a customs scan; in some terminals within the terminal in some others outside the terminal. In the beginning the scanning equipment was developed out of available X-ray scanners, not able to image the complete container. After 2004 especially the fixed-site systems became very powerful, providing the image of a complete 40' or 45' container. Some manufacturers developed thermal neutron analysis-based inspection systems capable of detecting vehicular bombs, explosives, etc.

After the Gulf War, the US Department of Defense started to develop a tracking and tracing system, based on RFID tags and readers from Savi Technology. As of 2002, pilot projects started and when Hutchison Port Holdings entered into a joint venture (2005), to set up Navi Networks, a world wide application came into reach. This opened the way to more publicly available applications, especially when the ISO started to standardize such devices in a draft ISO standard PAS 17712. Other electronic seal manufacturers joined this developments and many trials were conducted including customs, shippers (Mitsui and Xerox) to connect either disposable e-seals or active GPS traceable tags and on terminals, (such as ECT and HPH terminals in Hong Kong and Shanghai) to install readers and processing equipment onto their cranes and connected with their terminal data systems.

Although primarily focused on the improvement of security in the whole logistic chain, terminals and logistic service providers could benefit from this time-saving automated reading of tags/e-seals. For sure, the 9/11 incident had tremendous impact on container logistics with large investments and annually-recurring costs for ports and container terminals.

Increasing concern about the Environment

Many Port Authorities took the driver's seat and developed measures for reduced environmental impact. At the marine side, ports installed waste reception facilities and encouraged ballast water management systems (MARPOL), to avoid contaminated water and to avoid the introduction of alien species in the local habitat. Dredging for maintenance and expansion activities became restricted and had to fulfill strict directives for the disposal of polluted sediments and for the renewal of lost or altered habitats. Many terminal expansion projects were delayed by these more stringent rules. For instance: the deepening of some basins in the Port of Oakland took years before the Army Corps of Engineers gave approval and in Western Europe the Habitat Directive forced a number of ports to replace port expansion areas by means of land acquisition to preserve rural sites and typical species (Bremerhaven, Felixstowe, Rotterdam, Antwerp, etc.). In the United Kingdom, the Dibden Bay project for the expansion of Southampton facilities was stopped as a result of too much impact on the environment.

Another topic on the waterside was the water pollution from waterfront run-off (polluted rainwater). Terminals were forced to install sewerage systems without any outlet into the port basin and terminals paid more attention to leakage from hydraulic oils and fuel.

Already in the late 1990s, Rotterdam started a Green Award initiative aimed to reward shipowners when they could fulfill the environmental requirements at the marine side. Later, this initiative was followed by other ports as well.

At the terminals themselves the main focus was on sound and air pollution (NO_x, SO_2, PM and later CO_2), effecting terminal personnel and adjacent areas and proper precautions for the fumigation of containers (often performed with toxic bromide gasses). Equipment manufacturers got more stringent requirements for sound control (better cabins, exhaust systems, insulated power sets, etc.) and ergonomic designs. Limitations in the noise contour (especially during the late evening and night time) interfered in many terminal expansion programs resulting in lay-out adjustments (e.g. to better control noisy MT handling) and sometimes a maximum of operating equipment.

Figure 338: Provisions for Alternative Marine Power

At the waterside interface, California introduced directives towards Alternative Marine Power (AMP), more commonly known as "cold ironing". When berthed the seagoing vessels should stop their auxiliary diesels and use the clean electric supply from the shore (see Figure 338); an important contribution to reduced pollution, especially if one considers the power demand from large container vessels with sometimes over 1,000 reefer connections. Also in Europe some ports (Gothenburg, Stockholm and Zeebrugge) offered this shore power supply on a voluntary base. At the end of the decade it was generally recognized that cold ironing would bring a major contribution to air pollution reduction however, ports could not accelerate the required modification on board the vessels and at terminals. In all countries with a 50 Hz AC frequency, the facilities on shore would be somewhat more complicated as most vessels run a 60 Hz supply network on board. So, at terminals converting stations had to be installed, capable of supplying many megawatts of electric power. Ports realized that the transition to cold ironing would take at least one decade. Ports with regular visits from ferries and barges decided to gradually encourage (reward) the use of cold ironing.

Terminal lighting became a controversial topic. Increased traffic, better working conditions and more security control asked for more lighting, however without impeding vessel entrance and mooring, and preferably invisible for the terminals' neighbors. The conflicting interests could be solved with the installment of proper light pole heights and improved lighting fixtures. Nevertheless light pollution remained a serious issue in the design of new terminals. A similar topic was horizon (skyline) pollution, mainly caused by the growing size of quay container cranes. With their booms up, the 22-wide cranes surpassed the 100 m. height and when

Figure 339: Horizon pollution (Matson, Los Angeles)

painted in a contrasting color scheme, such cranes became poignant landmarks. Some terminals recognized this environmental impact and selected moderated light grey crane colors (see Figure 339).

The increasing diesel fuel prices and the environmental impact triggered some manufacturers of mobile equipment to improve their diesel drivelines. Diesel-electric drives were increasingly introduced and after 2005, diesel-electric drives with variable diesel speeds (to better match demand and to run at a favorable high-torque RPM) were applied in RTGs and AGVs.

In 2006, California announced a levy of US$ 30 for every box handled by its ports, to compensate for the upcoming port improvements in the areas of security, infrastructure and environment. Terminals intended to pass on this charge to shipping lines (and so further to merchants), which made shippers protest against this levy. Although not (yet) introduced in 2006 the levy illustrated the need for cost compensation for all the additional requirements for ports and terminals.

Parallel to the increasing demands on terminals to diminish their environmental impact, environmentalists and governments realized that sea transportation is rather environmentally friendly compared to road and rail transport. Both in Europe and the US, measures were taken to reduce trucking for inland container transport. Rail transport, shortsea shipping (and where possible barging) were promoted, regardless the discussion around the absolute figures for air pollution from long distance trucking and diesel powered rail transport. Modal shift became the buzz word during this decade with all kinds of support to reduce trucking to the terminals.

In the US many intermodal (rail-truck) facilities were located outside port areas and this made some port authorities decide to connect rail transport close (near-dock) or onto (on-dock) the container terminals. One of the most impressive projects in this respect was the Alameda Corridor, a rail-link from intermodal facilities operated by Union Pacific/Southern Pacific and Santa Fe (later merged in BNSF) to the ports of San Pedro Bay (Long Beach and Los Angeles). The massive investments in this rail connection (US$ 2.4 billion), crossing the cities of Long Beach and Los Angeles in an 11 m. deep trench, was justified by the major reduction in delays, congestion and air pollution, caused by trucking containers between the Long Beach and Los Angeles terminals and the major ICTFs (Intermodal Container Transfer Facility) east from LA/LB, with short haul distances from 4 to 25 miles (6.5-40 kms). The construction of the Alameda Corridor started in 1996 and became operational in 2002. In 2006 there were already 60 train movements per day, with a transportation fee of US$ 18 per TEU.

Figure 340: Alameda corridor, partly trenched (Los Angeles)

Another large project to stimulate a modal shift was the "Betuwelijn" in The Netherlands, a dedicated 160 km long double track freight railway between the Port of Rotterdam and the German rail network. Although aimed to reduce the environmental impact from trucking, many environmentalist raised objections as the new rail infrastructure could influence nature and residential areas (the well-known NIMBY syndrome: Not-In-My-Back-Yard). This resulted in years of delay (the works started in 1998 and were finished in 2007) and many costly infrastructural adjustments such as noise insulation panels, tunnels and wildlife passages. No wonder that the first made budget of 1.1 billion euro in 1990 increased to 4.7 billion Euros at the date of finish. This Betuwelijn became part of the Trans-European Transport Networks, a development supported by the European Commission and major railway organizations such as DB Cargo, Fret SNCF, Italian Railways, and Scandinavian Railways. The Port of Rotterdam aimed for an "ideal" inland modal split: 35% trucking, 20% rail and 45% barging. However, during this decade the share of trucking continued to be above 50%. Also in Germany, France and Italy the rail operators were not very successful in transferring containers from truck to rail.

Notwithstanding a lot of governmental support for inland rail terminals, trucking continued to be a low cost, flexible mode for inland transportation. The trucking industry themselves did contribute to a lower environmental impact through smart planning of combined pick-up and delivery trips, the avoidance of empty return trips and the set up of small inland truck terminals to organize an efficient inland transport, in spite of some innovative system developments supported by national governments.

In France a pilot plant for a partly automated rail-rail transfer hub did not materialize (see later Chapter 13). In Germany a full scale rail-feeder system was developed and put into operation. The idea was to collect and distribute smaller numbers of containers by means of short, self-propelled train sets (see Figure 341), to be coupled into large shuttle trains, running between two rail hubs. The planning of such operations proved to be rather complicated and also the operating costs were disappointing. So, this concept of a rail feeder service was discontinued.

Mainly in Europe another environmentally friendly mode was promoted: shortsea shipping. Some shippers tried this type of inland transportation but the more complicated port procedures (security and customs) and a limited flexibility did not help to attract many containers away from trucking.

This decade clearly showed that especially port authorities, supported with regional governments took their responsibility for a bet-

Figure 341: Small feeder trains for Hub-and-Spoke rail transport, Germany

ter environment, with initiatives and directives. In the mid-1990s the European Sea Ports Organization (ESPO) started to raise awareness on environmental issues and in 1999, nine port authorities (Amsterdam, Antwerp, Barcelona, British Ports Association, Gdansk, Genoa, Goteborg, Hamburg and Rotterdam) established "Ecoports "an organization for information exchange and impact assessment for enhanced environmental conscious operations in European ports and terminals". This organization developed a Port Environmental Review System (PERS) in line with more general Environmental Management Systems.

Also the ISO became active in this field but on a voluntary basis. By the end of the 1990s the ISO 14000 series of standards on environmental management was published and one of the first practical standards was the ISO 14001: Certification. This standard can be seen as the environmental addition to ISO 9001, a standard for quality management systems. The ISO 14001 aims to assist in the set up of an environmental management system, starting with an analysis of present and future operations. The result can be a concept of continual improvement in the environmental impact. The Ecoports Foundation expanded to over 100 port members and in 2004 the ESPO published its first Environmental Survey, a review of European performance in port environmental management. In 2006, the ESPO published a reaction on the EC-recommendations on this topics and this showed that all major European ports would actively support environmentally friendly ports and terminals.

This growing environmental awareness was a positive development but it also had a major influence on the realization time for new (or expanded) terminals. Examples in the US, the UK, Germany and The Netherlands showed that some projects required more than 10 years from the first request for approval until the effective start of construction activities. So, in many countries the planning horizon for terminal capacity increased to 10-15 years.

IN RETROSPECT

During this decade, terminal capacity was often lagging behind the growing demand, determined by the shippers and a rapidly-expanding container vessel capacity. The following issues were marked:

- The center of container transshipment in ports shifted from the US and Europe towards the Far East. Chinese ports (existing and newly-built ones) expanded with double digits, realizing more than 17% of the world transshipment volume by 2006;

- Global Terminal Operators gained a majority share in world port handlings, supported through an ongoing port privatization and their own capital;

- In many ports space for expansion became a problem. Increasing environmental concern, habitat directives, slow decision making processes and a limited financing caused delays, resulting in terminal congestion;

- The US' response to 9/11 had major consequences for all ports: better security systems, more customs checks, and a requirement for shipment data in advance, resulting in dwell time increases and additional terminal costs;

- At the end of the decade some port authorities emphasized the importance and competitive edge of Green Ports, stimulating measures to reduce emissions, to apply renewable energy and to encourage a shift from trucking to rail or barge;

- The need for terminal stacking capacity made some terminals decide to install Rail Mounted Stacking Cranes (RMGs), with their increased area utilization and potential for (partly) automation;

- The implementation of full automation was slowly growing. ECT further introduced its AGV-ASC system at their Delta Terminal and CTA Hamburg and P&O Antwerp (later DP World) followed with similar automated concepts;

Figure 342: ECT's automated Delta Sealand Terminal

- At many terminals vessel handling productivity and service to the landside remained below expectations of the shipping lines. However, it should be noted that reduced price levels, dwell-time increases, delays from SATL-handling and a growing share of merchant haulage were negative influences out of the terminal's control.

After the year 2006, terminal operators continued to expand their facilities, most of them maintaining proven handling concepts and equipment (RTGs, RMGs, tractor/trailers and straddle carriers). The economic recession of 2008 slowed down many of these programs for terminal expansion and new facilities were postponed. Only in regions with a growing economy (although at a lower rate), the realization of new terminals continued, often supported with the (financial) interest of a GTO. In general, these terminals adhered to the proven designs and need no further explanation in the context of this book.

However, a few terminals proceeded with the development of new terminal-handling systems applying (partly)-automated stacking and waterside transportation. These developments are presented in Chapter 13.

CHAPTER 13

AUTOMATION

A slow but steady development

After the 1950s, the manufacturing industry (automotive, consumer goods, etc.) showed a tremendous development towards automated manufacturing, based on information control, planning, mechanized handling and standardized processes for handling and machining. This level of automation could be obtained through one simple approach: control the entire process and eliminate non-predictable influences. As from the 1960s the manufacturing industry developed specifications for material characteristics, product-design, tooling, handling equipment and sub-contractor's quality, in order to fulfill the demands from a well-defined manufacturing process.

The introduction of standardized containers, fitting in specially designed container vessels with standardized cells under deck and standardized lashing on deck, resulted in early ideas for automated handling activities, in the second half of the 1950s.

In 1959, the naval architect Doros A. Argyriadis already mentioned the potential of automated ship/shore handling, focusing on the gantry cranes on board a ship. In those days only Matson and Seatrain Line operated shore-based container gantries. Pan-Atlantic (Sea-Land), Grace Line, US Lines, APL and Isbrandtsen Company (still) were in favor of the ship crane system, because of their operational flexibility to call at ports not yet provided with proper container handling cranes (lifting capacity and outreach). Both converted vessels and newly-designed container vessels were provided with these ship cranes (Paceco's "Shiptainer" and LakeShore's "Siporter" (see Figure 343) and some considerations were made about automated control of this ship cranes.

Figure 343: C-frame "Siporter" cranes (Grace)

With the help of a three-dimensional location control, the on-board movements could be realized by pushing a button and then the crane should move gantry and spreader to the selected location. But this idea was never realized in practice, not only because of the estimated high investment (probably an automated operation would have required more than double the investment of a manually operated crane) but as well because of the foreseen difficulties for automated landing of containers onto the shore based chassis (ship's roll, vessel movements alongside berth, heave due to swell, etc.). But anyhow, it was remarkable that already in the late 1950s automated handling was considered.

The standardized dimensions and load ratings triggered many engineers to come up with many conceptual designs for automated container handling, However it would take more than 3 decades before the first fully automated terminal got materialized.

13.1. DEVELOPMENT OF BUILDING BLOCKS FOR TERMINAL AUTOMATION

The introduction of containerization in Europe and the Far East generated sufficient volume to spark thinking on automated container handling. However, the first automation activities started in the field of document handling (administration) and yard inventory control. The large computer companies like IBM, Siemens, DEC and Burroughs installed administrative systems to reduce the amount of paperwork and to assist in sorting data (container shipment properties), to prepare the yard planning and to support vessel stowage planning. Some terminals introduced container ID-cards with barcodes; other terminals applied proven punch-card technology (with Hollerith-machines for sorting). The US-based shipping lines and container terminals showed the way and companies like Sea-Land, APL, and Maher Terminals already operated computer systems in the early 1970s. Of course in those days worldwide data exchange was rather slow, being dependent on telephone connections, inductive loops (Baud rates less than 1,200 bit/sec.) and/or telex.

In Europe early starters like HHLA and Eurokai in Hamburg, ECT and Unitcentre in Rotterdam and OCL and ACT in London-Tilbury and Southampton looked to the European industry (automotive, warehousing and electronics) and installed systems from Siemens, Burroughs and ICL. Almost all the early applicants of administrative computer systems set up their own departments for data control and software development, using software languages such as Assembler, PL-1 and Cobol. At the end of the 1960s the first patent for fully automated container transportation and stacking was filed by Rudiger Franke and Hans Tax. This system (see Figure 344) was based on inductive guided vehicles and automated rail mounted stacking cranes. In the mid-1970s, Mannesmann and Peiner developed an automated system based on high-bay warehouse technology already applied for palletized warehousing of products (automotive, manufacturing of consumers goods, etc.).

In the early 1970s, some fully automated concepts were developed; for instance the Port of Tokyo (MOL Container Terminal) considered a rail based transportation system with movable flat cars running between quay cranes and rail mounted stacking cranes. However these systems were not yet mature and could not convince the risk-avoiding terminal managers, operating in a rather conservative shipping world.

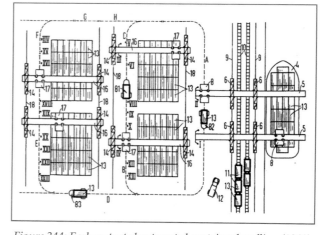

Figure 344: Early patented automated container handling (1968)

The tremendous growth in container throughput and a lack of space on a narrow-shaped terminal site made ECT, Rotterdam decide in 1971 to install wide-span stacking cranes (14 containers wide between the 43 m. rail gauge), suited for 4-high stacking (1 over 4) and provided with automated positioning in trolley and gantry direction (see Figure 345). Cantilevers at both sides (serving three lanes each) were designed for the interchange of containers on tractor/trailers (waterside) or road trucks (landside). At the machinery trolley, an additional constant torque rope system provided sufficient anti-sway for a precise container stacking.

Conrad Stork and Siemens jointly developed this half-automated stacking crane and four units of this type were commissioned in 1972 on a functional specification, demanding 30 moves per hour, in an operational pattern, contractually agreed in advance. The crane operator received stack location instructions by radio communication (VHF), and via pinching a 3-digit position the crane automatically moved to that place and the only thing to do for the operator was hoisting or lowering the box. For those days, gantry travel (120 m./min.) and trolley travel (80 m./min.) were rather high. These characteristics and the structural stiffness de-

Figure 345: Partly-automated RMG at ECT, Rotterdam

mands for reliable positioning resulted in 380 tons heavy duty cranes. A few months later Unitcentre ordered the same cranes however some of them provided with a rotating trolley as one crane stack was serving railroad tracks under the outreach (door direction requirements).

Within a few years more or less similar rail mounted stacking cranes were installed at OHI-terminal 3, 4, 5, Tokyo (Mitsui, 12 wide within the rail span); at Modern Terminals, Hong Kong (Hitachi, 15 wide within the rail span and 6-high stacking) and at Eurokai, Hamburg (Kocks, 11 wide within the rail span, 4-high stacking).

The latter, so-called Constacker system at Eurokai (see Figure 346), was installed in 1976 and in this semi-automated stacking cranes, all three movements (gantry, trolley and main hoist) were electronically controlled by sensors and an on-board minicomputer (Siemens 310). One central computer (Siemens 330) was connected to the three stacking cranes and was continuously monitoring crane movements, stacking positions, yard inventory and stacking profile. The original idea to adjust the hoisting height to the foreseen travel path stack pattern (to minimize hoisting height) was not maintained very long. A further expansion program for even much larger (wider) stacking cranes was not materialized.

In the second half of the 1970s, handling volumes at terminals increased tremendously and thus the yards became larger, stack-density and number of shuffle-moves increased and vessel stowage information often arrived too late to enable pre-planning

Figure 346: Partly-automated RMG (11-wide; 1 over 4) at Eurokai with GUI in cabin

(housekeeping). This all resulted in a lower vessel-handling performance. Some terminals introduced operations research know-how in their management staff (Matson in LA, OCL in Tilbury, ECT in Rotterdam and HHLA in Hamburg) and their research concluded that there were advantages of having process buffers between the various terminal sub-cycles, in particular between the ship-to-shore crane cycle and the transport and stacking cycle.

In 1976, ECT ordered three ship-to-shore cranes with Conrad-Stork (later Nelcon, Kalmar and Cargotec) and one of these cranes should get a prototype fully automated second trolley system, functioning as a process buffer between the ship handling cycle and the transportation to the stacking yard. Research showed some limitations in buffering 2-3 containers in the gantry structure (wheel loads, corner loads) and this, together with a new idea of much cheaper buffering on the dock level, made ECT decide to develop a multi-trailer train (10 TEU) and an automated second-trolley system with a moving platform for only one container. When the train (loaded with 5 to 10 containers or empty) arrived under the crane it should be considered as part of the crane. This was enabled through ECT's patented chassis loaders, a device physically connecting (embracing) the train (trailer by trailer) with a guiding device to the crane. This allowed the crane operator to lower containers onto the trailer through neutralizing the container sway (in the discharging cycle). In the loading cycle the crane operator could use his spreader guides as the 20' boxes were placed on the trailer with some space in between.

The second trolley system was built up from a horizontally moving platform between waterside and landside at about 11 m. high above dock level. The last hoisting/lowering sub-cycle was performed by a fixed hoist in the gantry, picking (or placing) the container from the platform when at the landside and lowering it automatically on the trailer-train (or a normal terminal chassis). The cable reeving system and the zero movement of the second hoist, guaranteed a proper positioning as no sway could be introduced (see Figure 347).

 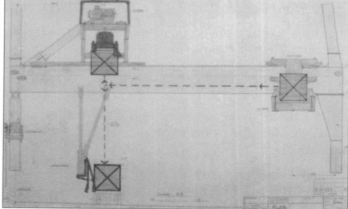

Figure 347: ECT's prototype 2nd trolley system

The entire control of movements, positioning, inter-lockings, etc. was performed by a Siemens PLC (Programmable Logic Controller), which was rather new in those days. Programming this type of automation gave some headaches to Siemens' engineers and finally the OR specialist of ECT, Mr. Ruud van der Ham, programmed the PLC in the typical Siemens Step 3 language. This prototype of a completely automated second trolley system became operational in 1979 (with some teething problems in the system and doubt with the operators) and was further improved in the next two years.

In 1983, four of these systems were ordered for the new Delta Terminal, where the multi-trailer system was selected as the main component for internal terminal transportation. The advantages of a second trolley system were underlined by VIT (Virginia International Terminals). They also ordered a few quay cranes, provided with such a system, however including a height adjustable platform, to create the lowest possible hoisting/lowering distances when working on various vessel sizes (hatch coaming height versus platform height) and various tiers on deck (see Figure 348).

ECT's proprietary second-trolley system was also licensed to EB-ARA (Japan) and through that connection also 3 Sumitomo cranes at the Seagirt Terminal, Baltimore, US were provided with a second trolley system.

During the years 1974-1976, K Line realized a 2-berth terminal in Tokyo (Berth 1 and 2, OHI), provided with a computerized terminal operations system and 8 partly-automated RTGs from Mitsui Engineering and Shipbuilding, a Paceco licensee (see Figure 349).

The computerized terminal operations system comprised subsystems such as yard planning and yard operations, according to the planned scheduling. Transtainer and Portainer (the Paceco brand names for RTGs and quay cranes) handling instructions were supervised by computer as well. For that reason the cabins of Portainers and Transtainers were provided with a work instruction panel (see Figure 350, left) connected with the main computer by means of an inductive radio system, working in polling mode and based on frequency modulation and with a transmission speed of 200 Baud.

Figure 348: 2nd trolley system at VIT

Yard operations were controlled by computer (see Figure 350, right), determining the optimum position of transtainers, based upon vessel stowage, work sequences, priorities, collision avoidance and transtainer utilization. The diesel electric transtainers (RTGs) could stack 1 over 3 and were already provided with automatic steering and position control, with the help of embedded cross twined induction loops. Transportation from stacking yard to quay cranes was a manned tractor-trailer system but the tractor drivers received a computer printed sequence list of their transport moves. Although all equipment was operator controlled, it was already a terminal operation with many computer-controlled processes, already showing the feasibility of further automation.

Figure 349: K Line terminal, Tokyo

Figure 350: Screen in RTG operator's cabin and computerized yard control

Also in the second half of the 1970s, Matson developed a system with some buffer ability between the quayside and the stacking yard. Their innovative approach resulted in the so-called "mouse trap", a container storage for maximum 5 containers either fixed in a quay crane (such as in the prototype system for Richmond California) or as a rubber-tired frame, moving independently from the quay crane, but automatically following the quay crane in the backreach to feed the hook. In the mouse trap, containers could be moved transverse in order to move containers horizontally between the quay crane and wide span rail mounted stacking crane, projected (and built) by Matson (see Figure 351).

The objective from Matson was a completely computer assisted container handling system, between the vessel and the gate and offering a high area utilization (as land area was scarce in Californian ports) and better service performance (vessel handling rate, gate processing).

Figure 351: Prototype automated handling system Richmond

In 1979, a complete pilot terminal was built in the port of Richmond with major contributions from Paceco, Morgan Cranes, TAK Components, IBM, JWD and of course the Matson development engineers.

Paceco provided the quay cranes (50' rail span) with built-in mouse trap (see Figure 352). The mouse trap was a device for horizontally moving the container in the crane between the waterside and a pick-up/delivery position in the backreach, where the automated (gantry + trolley positioning) stacking crane could pick-up or deliver a container. Provisions in the mouse trap (partly hydraulically operated) allowed the handling of 20', 24', 27' and 40' containers. The handling of hatch covers onto dock level was difficult; hatch covers had to remain on-board.

Figure 352: Detail of Quay Crane/RMG interface with buffer

Morgan Cranes was responsible for the wide span, partly automated stacking cranes, an interesting design built-up from one large box girder with an asymmetric overhanging trolley and a C-frame type of portal structure. The stacking yard covered by this stacking crane could be handled by two rubber-tired transtainers as well, allowing separate simultaneous vessel operations and landside receivals and/or deliveries. The rubber-tired transtainers could pass under the Morgan cranes' main

Figure 353: Wide-span RMG with RTGs underneath passing

girder, a useful characteristic for flexibility and redundancy (see Figure 353). The rather narrow terminal design allowed lighting from the landside terminal edge with two large lighting structures, designed by JWD. Probably JWD was also involved in some more layout and system design topics.

TAK Components was responsible for the machine automation (mouse trap and cranes) and the interface to the Terminal Operating System, running on two series 1 IBM computers. TAK Components designed the machine automation on partly self-developed powerful PLCs (for those days) and 1,200 Baud rate data links between machines and host computers. Due to the large variety in box length the yard was based on 0.1-ft grid increments, allowing maximum yard utilization in container length direction. The overall terminal control functionality encompassed terminal planning, container stack position assignment, yard inventory control, gate handling (equipment interchange and digital scales), job sequencing and of course data interchange.

Operators in the quay crane and in the yard cranes were supported with displays (called CRTs in those days), to give them pre-determined assignments and to allow positive identification of container ID numbers.

In Richmond it took quite some time to get the overall system up and running at an acceptable rate of service and reliability. For some reason the Richmond pilot plant did not mature, probably due to the overall system design complexity, the limitation in technology those days and the reluctance from the labor unions. The Matson facility in Los Angeles (see Figure 354) was also provided with the wide span stacking cranes and there a transfer car was installed at the end of the stacking yard, to transfer stacking cranes from one stack (parallel to the quay wall) to the other. Here, rubber-mounted mouse traps were installed, to transport (and buffer) 4-8 containers between the quay cranes and the wide span stacking cranes. But also in LA the original overall system concept was not successful. After some years of trials the mouse trap operation was stopped and replaced by the well-known tractor-trailer system.

The wide span stacking cranes were continued, but their automatic positioning was not always precise enough and the operator remained necessary to adjust gantry and trolley movements.

It was the author's (Joan Rijsenbrij) opinion that budgetary limits, an underestimation of some component's detailed engineering quality and impatience from the Matson board eventually triggered the decision to stay with more conventional technology. However, this

Figure 354: Matson facility with rubber tired travelling interchanges

Matson concept definitely showed the feasibility of a partly-automated terminal handling but may be a little bit too early and with too many partners in the project, struggling with their interface engineering topics.

In Italy, the port of La Spezia was also limited in space and developed a system based on the direct transfer of containers from the quay crane (fitted with some buffer positions) to the rail mounted stacking cranes (see Figure 355). The Italian crane manufacturer MGM (Magrini Galileo Meccanica) made a partnership with Nelcon and this combined experience resulted in a terminal system realized in the mid-1980s. However, the planned direct transfer of containers from quay crane to stacking crane was sometimes difficult. The quay crane had to wait for the availability of the stacking crane and there was the continuous attention for aligning the stacking crane with the quay crane (always the leading cycle). So, in the end the transfer of containers was either realized via temporarily buffering on the ground (quay crane backreach) or via transportation with tractor/trailers. But this La Spezia concept showed already a rather dense operation with connection to the road and the rail, all serviced with rail mounted stacking cranes.

In the early 1980s, Sea-Land was running out of space at their Hong Kong facility (Terminal 3), equipped with only 3 quay cranes, but running at berth utilization above 60%. The typical Hong Kong container and warehousing operations made Sea-Land decide to build a multi-floor warehouse facility on their berth 3 premises with a 4 high stacking system on ground level,

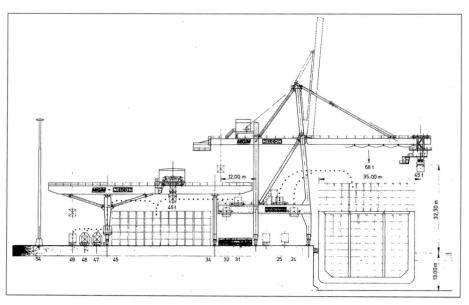

Figure 355: La Spezia automated-handling quay crane

based on semi-automated overhead bridge cranes from Mitsui (a Paceco licensee). This system has 4 stack bays and just as in Matson's LA stacking concept, a transfer facility at the end, to replace a crane in case of a major breakdown or for normal planned maintenance. Here as well the crane movements were controlled from a central host computer. In Hong Kong, the low labor costs did not encourage Sea-Land to go for a completely unmanned operation and thus this facility was basically computer supported with automated positioning (gantry and trolley) and a hoisting height indication, to facilitate yard inventory control. In the same period also HIT (Hong Kong International Terminals) started computer-assisted operations for their rubber tired transtainers and later rail-mounted stacking cranes.

The fast growing (hub) terminals realized that the scale of internal transportation was rapidly increasing, resulting in developments towards more containers behind one driver. ECT installed the 10-TEU Multi-Trailer-System (MTS) and the port of Singapore introduced the 5-axle trailer for 2-high transport (max 4 TEU). Also the Swedish LUF system and later a Buiscar development for 2-high stacking at the MTS aimed to increase transport capacity per unit. Theoretically, these systems could

be automated however nobody gave it a try due to complexity, location control, etc. Noell, Germany developed an automated transport system based on carts driven by linear motors (see Figure 356) and with the ability to move in rectangular patterns. Some small prototype installations were realized at Eurokai, Germany (for waterside transportation) and at a Noell facility (to demonstrate the potential for Noell's Megahub concept for large rail terminals).

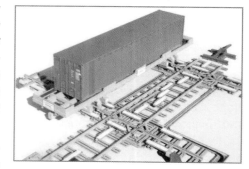

Figure 356: Noell linear motor concept

All the above-mentioned developments concerned smaller or larger components/sub-systems for a terminal. A fully automated terminal seemed feasible, but a satisfactorily working concept could not (yet) be realized.

13.2. AUTOMATED TERMINAL HANDLING CONCEPT

Only a few passed the feasibility check

Already in the 1970s a number of handling equipment manufacturers and engineering consultants got triggered by the prosperous developments of containerization, the rising labor cost and the first signs of limitations of space in ports: it made them design innovative automated container handling systems. This resulted in a variety of new handling concepts; many of them with automated container storage systems, some of them with connecting automated horizontal transportation.

Figure 357: Meeusen concept

In the early seventies Meeusen Consultants (The Netherlands) presented a concept for a fast vessel discharge/loading directly into a stacking system with portal cranes. The concept involved a new vessel design as well (see Figure 357) and the whole concept required such a combined support from shipping lines (the vessels), port authorities (the special berth arrangement) and terminal operators (the terminal handling system with related planning and control features) that an application was not considered as realistic.

Another early, more terminal-related, concept came from Kaiser Engineers (Kaiser-SpeedTainer System), designed around a high-bay warehouse, connected through rail mounted cars feeding containers to the 1-3 quay cranes. At the landside, containers were swapped between these rail mounted cars and road trucks.

Figure 358: Kaiser Engineers' high-bay warehouse

Mannesmann Demag presented a somewhat similar concept in 1978 (see Figure 359) however here each of the 4 container quay cranes was connected with the 11-high, high-bay warehouse with their own conveyor belt. At the landside, various interchange areas should transfer container to trucks and rail.

Harry Lässig's design for an automated rail facility (see Figure 359) shows how this landside interface could be configured, in combination with automated pallet loading.

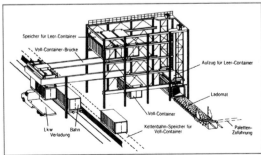

Figure 359: Mannesmann Demag automated high-bay warehouse and Harry Lässig system for connection to rail transport

Some engineering companies proposed cylindrical designs which even could be connected into honey comb-like constructions (see Figure 360 for such GEC and Babcock silo concepts). The leading demands were high area utilization and random accessibility to every container. The ratio stack capacity/handling capacity was not very attractive and neither were the projected overall cost.

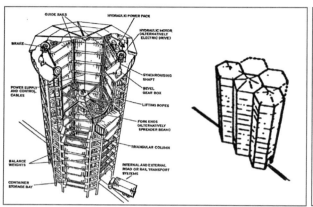 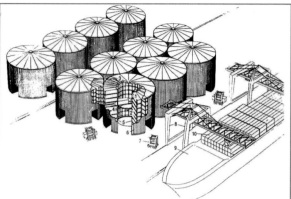

Figure 360: Cylindrical automated high-bay warehouses from GEC (left) and Babcock

The entrance of Conrad-Stork (later Nelcon/Kalmar, now Cargotec) in the market for container cranes (stacking cranes in 1971 and quay cranes in 1976) encouraged Conrad-Stork to develop an integrated terminal concept, hopefully attractive for terminals with limited space (e.g. ECT and Eurokai). The concept (see Figure 361) encompassed a sophisticated quay crane, fitted with a second trolley system and a waterside buffer in the crane (somewhat similar to the Matson system at Richmond). The transportation to and from the yard was projected with a number of conveyors interconnected with travelling lift vehicles (small straddle carriers). Reverse movements of conveying components were de-

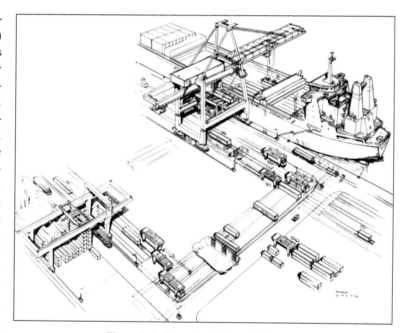

Figure 361: Conrad-Stork terminal system

signed underground and this combination of horizontal transportation equipment should allow sufficient flexibility to connect every quay crane with the stacking yard and with an increased number of containers per hour. The artist impression from Rudolf Das (see Figure 361) learns that rather massive civil works were involved, only possible in green field situations and probably rather costly. Nevertheless it was an example from crane manufacturers showing their ability in systems engineering, attractive for customers.

Besides Matson, who designed a new concept (see section 13.1) and even brought it into the application stage in Richmond and Los Angeles, also Sea-Land showed interest in automated operations. After the completion of the SL-7 program, Sea-Land's engineering department (managed by VP Ron Katims) started looking at automation for a few of their major terminals. Their house consultants Bob Gottlieb, Mike Jordan (JWD) and McKay Engineers cooperated with Sea-Land engineers such as Jules Nagy, who presented various concepts with automated OBCs. In Hong Kong an OBC based stacking system got realized under the multi-floor warehouse and was already prepared to be fully automated in a later stage. Rising labor cost and a drive to maintain their innovative leadership made Sea-Land decide to further investigate an automated handling system.

In 1985, Translift (known from cable conveyors e.g. for the transport of concrete for the Itaipu dam) got involved in a feasibility study, initiated by ECT and conducted by students and assistant professors from the Technical Universities in Delft and Karlsruhe. Although not ECT's choice, Translift developed a number of automated container conveyor systems with elevated carriageways and trolleys provided with winches and a simple spreader and supplied with energy and control data through contact lines in the conveyor rails (see Figure 362). This system with overhead monorails was further developed by Translift and IFK Karlsruhe (a university institute) and was presented to Sea-Land by means of a large scaled model, showing the monorails, the various interfaces and some buffer provisions at land and waterside (as earlier shown by Matson and Paceco); see Figure 363.

Some Sea-Land executives got enthusiastic, but a few in-depth cost/performance studies showed insufficient feasibility. Moreover, the large number of new, unproven components was a too big risk.

After the pioneering automation efforts from ECT in the early 1990s,

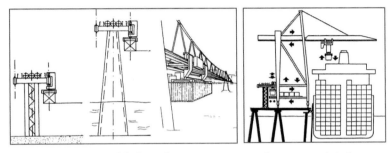

Figure 362: Translift elevated transport system and quay crane interface

Figure 363: Scale model of Translift overhead monorail system for Sea-Land

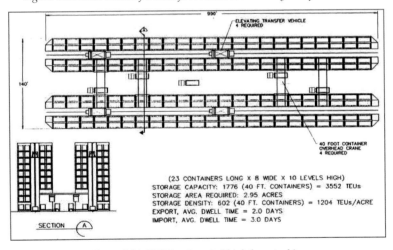

(23 CONTAINERS LONG X 8 WIDE X 10 LEVELS HIGH)
STORAGE CAPACITY: 1776 (40 FT. CONTAINERS) = 3552 TEUs
STORAGE AREA REQUIRED: 2.95 ACRES
STORAGE DENSITY: 602 (40 FT. CONTAINERS) = 1204 TEUs/ACRE
EXPORT, AVG. DWELL TIME = 2.0 DAYS
IMPORT, AVG. DWELL TIME = 3.0 DAYS

Figure 364: SCSS automated high-bay stacking

a revival of conceptual designs for automated high-bay container handling systems came up. The SCSS company from the US presented a high-rise stacking system for the port of Kaohsiung in 1993.

Later to be followed by a similar design, but with only two rows per bay, to allow random access (see Figure 364).

In 1996, Fata Automation, Italy patented an integrated automated container terminal as shown in Figure 365. The system shows various container rotation devices to ease the logistic demands in a high-bay warehouse and to allow the positioning onto an internal transportation system connecting the rail and long-term stacking. The drawings show a variety of components: a real challenge for a control system!

Also Earl's Industries, Vancouver ("Computainer Concept", 1990), Mitsui, Japan (1997) and Robotic Container Handling, US

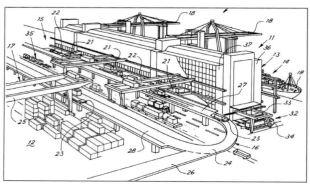

Figure 365: Fata Automation fully-automated container handling

(1998) developed such high-bay warehouse concepts, including equipment for transport, stacking and the landside connection. The Mitsui system showed overhead bridge cranes (OBCs) with a complicated spreader system, allowing the positioning of containers sideways into the racks (see Figure 366).

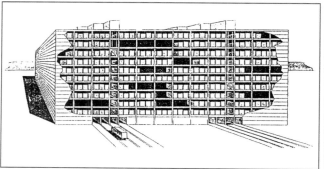
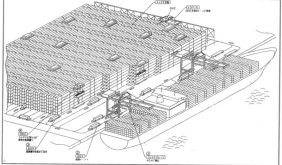

Figure 366: Automated high-bay warehouses connected through AGVs (Earl's Industries, left, Mitsui, right)

Robotic presented horizontal conveyors connected to a rather small high-bay warehouse and from there conveyor connections to a long-term stacking area, a rail-head or the CFS by means of overhead carriageways (see Figure 367).

Figure 367: Robotic's automated high-bay warehouse

Around the turn of the century some more concepts for high-bay container storage systems connected with AGV transportation were presented by Gottwald/Dematic. In the year 2000 ASSA Industries from Israel presented their CHESSCONT automated storage system, probably applying some car parking sorter technology in the warehouse. The published artist impression (see Figure 368) could not convince and raised doubts about the realizable yearly throughput.

Figure 368: CHESSCONT automated storage with shuffle sorters

To conclude this summary of drawing board concepts, Figure 369 shows the SPEEDPORT concept, a massive design from the ACTA Maritime Development Corporation with two indented docks and an amount of large overhead bridge cranes (OBCs) to handle containers directly from vessels into a stacking system with the help of traversing "spiders" also applicable for transfers alongside the docks. Obviously terminal operators were rather doubtful about the limitations for vessel sizes and the complete dependency on high-mounted OBCs with all the related issues such as sway-control, positioning tolerances, flexibility for last minute changes, maintenance, etc.

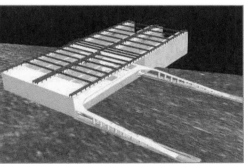

Figure 369: SPEEDPORT with indented docks and large overhead bridge cranes

All the above mentioned concepts had one major characteristic in common: they were never realized as they could not prove their attractiveness for terminal operators and/or shipping lines. Most of them were not suited for integration in existing terminal systems and quite a number of these concepts were presented by engineering companies, not very experienced in the handling of loads up to 40 tons in volumes of several thousands per day (fatigue) and in an environment with rather complex information control. The business risk for this kind of unproven large scale concepts (investments of hundreds of million dollars) was too large.

In the area of intermodal terminals (mainly rail/road) a few concepts matured into a prototype stage. Both the German and French governments supported the modal shift from the road to the rail and in the 1990s some concepts were selected as promising for the automation of intermodal terminals.

Krupp Fördertechnik presented their "Schnellumschlaganlage" as an automated concept for the discharging and loading of trains and connected to a high-bay warehouse. During the train handling, the train kept slowly moving (requiring long rail tracks at both sides of the system) and the crane was synchronized with this train speed when picking/placing containers at the railcars. A prototype was built and tested (see Figure 370), but up till now there is no terminal operating this concept.

Figure 370: Krupp's "schnellumschlaganlage"; model (left) and prototype plant

Another German manufacturer Noell presented automated concepts as well. A high-bay handling concept was designed but not tested. However, the idea of a mega-hub concept got attention. This concept, especially developed for a fast and flexible transfer of containers in the major nodes of a rail shuttle network was based on wide span cranes and shuttle cars driven with linear motors, for the horizontal movements in the transfer stack area (Noell Mega Hub).

Prototypes for the innovative linear motor driven carts were installed at Noell's premises and at the Eurokai Terminal in Hamburg. Complex technology and costs were major disadvantages resulting in no further developments so far.

In France, the Commuter concept was developed for large rail hub terminals and prototypes, including handling cranes, automated vehicles and of course a logistic control system was built. But just like in Germany, so far this Commuter concept got stuck in the prototype stage.

In Switzerland, Tuchschmid developed the compact terminal as an automated terminal for rail-road interchange. After the first conceptual designs in 1993 it took more than 15 years before a first application was realized (see Figure 371). The first terminal is operational indeed, but the degree of automation is still limited as operators are manning the Overhead Bridge Cranes.

Figure 371: Tuchschmid's automated rail-road terminal; design (left) and realization

In spite of all the efforts to get installed automated (high-bay) container handling systems in container terminals, only a few terminals entered into automation. Almost all the here presented automated concepts were not feasible and especially the high-bay warehouse types require such massive (expensive) civil works, making it questionable whether these will ever become reality. Some concepts entered the prototype stage, however with mixed feelings about their success.

13.3. THE FIRST AUTOMATED TERMINAL, INSTALLED BY ECT

During the autumn of 1983 the R&D department of ECT started research into the possibilities for an automated container terminal. The president Mr. Wormmeester was convinced that shipping lines such as Sea-Land, US Lines and Evergreen would continue to look for cost leadership and so, the rapidly growing labor cost in Western Europe, together with the fast growing handling volumes supported the possible benefits from automation. Unfortunately, but good for ECT's expansion, the ECT staff was fully occupied with procurement and building of their first Delta Terminal at the Maasvlakte; nevertheless, the R&D team together with some master students from TU Delft started the development of some promising automated concepts.

The announcement of US Lines by the late 1970s to invest in 12 Econships (to be built by Daewoo, Korea) for a new world spanning network indicated volume increases for the main ports. Such "Hub-and-spoke" operations would result in a large percentage of feedering in the main ports (hubs) and so ECT developed the expression "Majority-Sea-to-Sea" (or MSS) for their new automated concepts. The focus was on much relay cargo and rather short dwell times (2-4 days) and possibly random access in the stacking yard for reasons of flexibility.

In those days the only proven, reliable automated horizontal transport systems were rail based, such as shuttle systems for satellite airport terminals and the automated handling of heavy loads in the steel and manufacturing industry.

The first concept for an automated MSS terminal was based on an OBC stacking area with a crossing loop, to allow for a positioning of containers on the small trains with a correct door direction; an artist impression is shown in Figure 372.

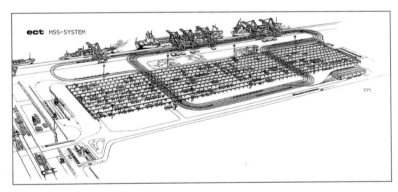

In the years 1984-1987 various alternatives were studied and the most promising ones were simulated, using the toolkit MUST, an improvement on earlier simulation tools, from ECT's operations research specialist Ruud van der Ham. These studies showed the inflexibility of a rail based transport system and the chance on too high peak loads on the limited number of interfaces at the stacking yard.

Figure 372: ECT's MSS system (artist impression Rudolf Das)

After finalizing the first stage of ECT's Delta Terminal the R&D department started looking for other horizontal transport systems, including an Automated Guided Vehicle (AGV) already suggested by the late 1960s, but so far only applied indoor and for loads up to 10 tons, traveling about 1 m./sec.

In a combined study between the Technical University of Delft (Department of Transportation Engineering from prof. ir. G. Prins), the Technical University of Karlsruhe (Abteilung fur Logistik from prof. dr. ing. E.H. Bahke) and ECT's R&D staff, three alternatives were analyzed: small trains, trolleys running under overhead monorails and automated guided vehicles. The study concluded a preference for AGVs: more flexible, less cost for infrastructure, better resistance against equipment breakdowns and the design could benefit from components from the automotive and manufacturing industry. For the stacking yard, the most flexible solution proved to be rail mounted stacking cranes with a few issues still to be solved: which crane dimensions and speeds and how to control the load, to guarantee precise positioning?

After the commissioning of the first stage of ECT's Delta Terminal (with 7 quay cranes, multi-trailer systems and straddle carrier and RMG stacking), the R&D team organized an evaluation of the whole terminal design and commissioning process to record and save the lessons learned, may be useful for the next stage after 5-10 years. The team had no idea that these experiences would be useable much earlier.

After the demise of US Lines in 1986, Sea-Land acquired some of US Lines' volume and would secure its market share and concluded a need for new terminal capacity in Western Europe, as the capacity at ECT's Willem Alexander Harbor was at his limits. Sea-Land presented a Request For Proposal (RFP) specifying a terminal facility with expansion potential and above all at competitive cost. On top of that Sea-Land was looking for a terminal, to be "an example for the industry". Sea-Land had already shown interest in second-trolley cranes with a built-in buffer and also the fast positioning of containers onto chassis or alike was studied (see Figure 373, courtesy McKay Engineers).

At ECT, president Wormmeester saw the opportunities for an automated terminal, stating: "Why building a terminal with the technology of the 1970s when you want something state-of-the-art that should last for the next 30 years". Converting an existing facility into an automated one was definitely too complex and too expensive. So, ECT decided to offer a few alternatives; one of them an automated terminal at a green field site on the Maasvlakte, with a guar-

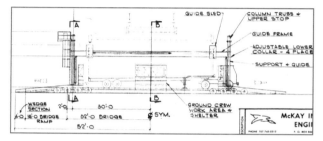

Figure 373: Concept for fast container positioning onto chassis

antee for the Sea-Land required crane productivity of 600 moves per day (and after a few years 630 moves/crane/day). Not surprisingly, the automated alternative in ECT's RFP (Rotterdam Facility Plan) was the most attractive for the projected 20-year contract, hence labor cost could be reduced and equipment could be amortized over a long period. After long negotiations and major efforts in convincing Sea-Land with all kinds of information (simulation results, artist impressions from Rudolf Das, see Figure 374) and of course guarantees with fall-back scenarios, Sea-Land agreed with an automated terminal in the beginning of 1988.

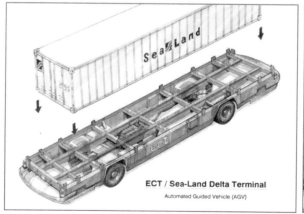

Figure 374: ECT's artist impressions of AGV transportation (Rudolf Das)

However with one pertinent statement: the development should be 5 years instead of ECT's projection of 7 years. The system offered consisted of 8 quay cranes of which 4 were provided with a second trolley system and all of them equipped with ECT's patented container guide system (see Figure 375).

The stacking yard was designed of 25 stack modules with only one rail-mounted high-speed Automated Stacking Crane (ASC) per module; at the waterside connected through AGVs running between the quay cranes and interfaces with four container exchange places at each ASC module. At the landside 1 over 1 diesel-electric straddle carriers were shuttling containers between the stacking yard and road trucks or rail and barge containers onto the MTS system for longer distance movements to the railhead and the barge terminal.

Figure 375: Adjustable guide system between AGV and crane

For the realization of this completely automated terminal with all its newly to be developed equipment and software, ECT arranged a comprehensive project organization managed by one executive, ECT's technical director Joan Rijsenbrij. One of the lessons learned in the past was, that for such a project you need one responsible manager, overlooking all technical, organizational and financial issues. The project management decided to divide the work in 3 stages:

- First, the development of the most critical equipment: the ASC and the AGV including their equipment management software and shake-hand controls (see Figure 376);

Figure 376: Prototypes ASC and AGV at the interchange

- Second, a pilot plant, a small "terminal" system with 4 ASCs, 8 AGVs and a dummy quay crane (a converted 16 wheel Nelcon RTG, called "Rubberen Robbie", which was earlier tested for automated yard operations but not found as sufficiently positioning). In this small terminal configuration all equipment, control software and data communication could be tested on the first stage of all civil works (4 stack modules, with rail tracks, foundation, power supply, fiber optics, etc.).

- Third, the gradual commissioning of the whole system, including the testing of all (58) EDI standard messages defined by ECT and Sea-Land for the logistics order control, documentation, tracking and tracing and data exchange. In this phase all testing and acceptance was carried out by the new terminal organization. Only they could assess whether the commissioned components were up to the specifications and standards they required to enable them to deliver the guaranteed services to Sea-Land, the dedicated customer of the automated terminal.

The first goal was to get reliable manufacturers for the key components. The ASCs were specified with a gantry travel speed of 240 m./min., all AC drives, fully automatic spreader, fiber optics for data exchange, fault monitoring systems and a required reliability factor (MTBF) by far in excess of current techniques (one ASC per module!!). Nelcon got the order, applying a HOLEC electrical installation and Stinis telescopic spreaders. The cable-reeving concept was based on ECT's research with the TU Delft, enabling sway control in trolley travel direction. In gantry travel direction (high acceleration/deceleration) an additional constant torque anti-sway winch was installed. A systems approach for the crane/rail track combination resulted in a sleeper-based PRI 85 rail and a lightweight but rather stiff monobox girder ASC, travelling on 8 driven wheels with horizontal guiding wheels (see Figure 377).

Figure 377: Monobox girder ASC with sway-controlled reeving and guided gantry travel trucks

For the cranes, there were sufficient suppliers but where to get outdoor running AGVs, designed for 40 tons load and a lifetime of 50,000 running hours? Some suppliers out of the heavy truck business (DAF, Mercedes and GHH) came up with quotations, however too expensive and not enough commitment. ECT was familiar with Gottwald for their mobile harbor cranes and when their chief engineer Joachim Kröll noticed ECT's demand for AGVs, he showed all kinds of automated handling concepts he had been working on during the last couple of years.

This remarkably innovative and driven engineer settled a contract with Joan Rijsenbrij for the first AGV prototype at a fixed price and to be delivered in about 10 months. The prototype's drive line consisted of a DAF diesel engine and a 2-stage VOITH variable transmission and Gottwald themselves engineered the PLC-based vehicle automation including all kinds of control functions. The navigation system was specified by ECT and one of the potential suppliers was the Dutch company FROG Systems a name derived from Free Ranging On Grid. That could be an advantage (no induction cables in the apron) but, it was never applied in outdoor situations. FROG was invited to show their system's capabilities and for that reason ECT provided a terminal tractor that FROG used for testing and demonstrations at one of ECT's sites; it also helped to familiarize the maintenance engineers and the labor unions which were rather reluctant about the automation developments.

It was ECT's specific requirement to fully separate vehicle automation and navigation system to ensure that FROG and Gottwald would not point at each other in case of malfunctioning. The interface was clearly described and the first prototype did quite well, however the required positioning tolerances in length direction could not be met by the VOITH transmission, too much influence from temperatures and transmission fluid viscosity; a pity as it was a simple straightforward design. Kröll and Rijsenbrij decided to develop a second prototype with a completely redesigned drive line based on the secondary hydrostatic drives from Rexroth (a Mannesmann company). This improvement was encouraging and ECT ordered a next series of 8 AGVs with Gottwald, to demonstrate fleet management, route planning, sequencing, etc., in the pilot plant (8 AGVs, 4 ASCs, 1 dummy quay crane; see Figure 378).

One major obstacle occurred when Gottwald was taken over by Mannesmann. The management of that industrial conglomerate had a different philosophy about profit and risk. But, ECT had a deadline and after some weeks of radio silence in the communication between Mannesmann/Gottwald and ECT the driven Joachim Kröll started renegotiations finally concluding a contract for another 40 AGVs. The entrance of Gottwald in this field has never been regretted. Up till 2011, Gottwald delivered almost 500 AGVs to the terminal industry.

Figure 378: ECT's pilot plant for the Delta Sea-Land terminal

The pilot plant started in 1991 and was already located at the first 4 stacking modules of the definite terminal layout. The pilot plant proved to be very helpful in testing the equipment, control software and data communication systems. In the meantime the civil engineering activities continued and the overall terminal infrastructure (stack modules, pavement, power supply, buildings, lighting, etc.) was ready before the end of 1992.

Already by mid-1992, the first vessel operations got started, demonstrating the potential of the concept, however with still a lot of teething problems to be solved. Both Sea-Land and ECT knew that the whole world was looking at this project and that stimulated the project teams to do the impossible in order to get the terminal up and running. For the new operational organization, it was sometimes very difficult to realize that they could do nothing when the Process Control System (PCS) was not available. This was a major difference with manual operations because in a manual controlled and operated system, operations management and operators start to improvize when a breakdown in a sub-system occurs. Not in an automated terminal: at the moment you start improvising outside the control of stack management/sequencing/interchange management, than you blow the whole synchronization, resulting in massive works for new settings and updates of order control and data bases.

The commissioning and start-up phase took some more months than planned, but the terminal throughput rapidly raised above the 200,000 lifts (about 350,000 TEU) per year and in June 1993 there was a festive opening ceremony by the Dutch Queen Beatrix.

Specific topics from the first automation project

During the more than 5 years of development, design and commissioning of this first automation project, a number of topics are worthwhile mentioning:

- Probably equally important as the technical innovations were the innovations in the operational organization and the participation of labor in the day-to-day operational decisions. For the automated terminal a new flat management structure was created in basically three layers: the operators (quay cranes, straddle carriers and MT handlers), the planners and the operations managers (shift related). The operations managers were weekly rotating in line and staff functions, assuring a balance between the daily on-the-job (hectic) activities and the more long-term issues such as process improvement, training of operational personnel, HR activities, etc. The overall terminal manager was already appointed 3 years before the terminal start date and was made fully responsible for the setup of his new operational team and the commissioning of all systems, equipment and facilities for the new terminal. He managed training programs, the selection of operators, education of the ins-and-outs of automated logistics and of course a proper understanding with the labor unions. From the beginning it was made clear that all disciplines (operations, IT, maintenance, HR, etc.) had to report to this new terminal manager, ensuring that everybody had the same goal: make the terminal into a success, being a good service to Sea-Land, rewarding working conditions for the operators and some profit for ECT.

- Already a year after the contract date (1988), the first changes in terminal design specifications were announced by Sea-Land: yes, the terminal should handle 45' containers; yes, we will bring partner business (other shipping lines cooperating with Sea-Land with their own and leased containers and thus more difficulties for ship planning and stacking); yes, the terminal has to deal with SATLs for lashing on deck; yes, the terminal must accept an average dwell time increase (specified to be maximum 3 days, but increasing due to market influences). This of course required some in-depth modifications for equipment and control systems.

- The facility design could benefit from the civil engineering know-how built up during the construction of the Delta Terminal (1982-1985), including the service road before the WS rail, electric supply and data communication network. However for the design of buildings, a more user oriented approach was followed, especially for the operations/maintenance building at the waterside and the container inspection facility at the landside. For instance, the rooms for IT monitoring and equipment maintenance were located very close to the central operations control

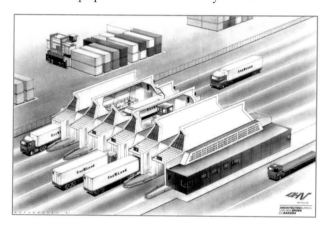

Figure 379: Special design of the inspection building

room (close connections) and the maintenance facility was dedicated to the automated equipment. All over the world, inspection facilities were suffering from wind blowing under the canapee, bad lighting levels for inspection cameras and uncomfortable working conditions for the inspection operators. An improved design was made and a model was tested in a wind tunnel to see the impact from wind. This resulted in wind pressure relief holes in some side walls, a special column design, a roof with optimized camera positions and provisions for safe, comfortable working conditions (see Figure 379). This design supported a short inspection cycle time, a requirement, to ensure a short truck turnaround time at the landside (gate-in/gate-out time: less than 30 min.).

In the buildings' design stage one issue took remarkably much attention: Sea-Land's Marine Dining Room in the Admin Building. This fancy facility on the top floor gave a magnificent view over the terminal and from that room Sea-Land would like to entertain their customers (the shippers), under while showing them their ability for a fast, reliable and cost-effective container transport. It became one of the most frequently discussed topics.

- It was quite an effort to keep the project teams (ECT, Vendors, Port Authority, etc.) focused on the final objective. During the 5-year project period many gatherings were arranged to communicate the status, the critical issues, the expectations, etc. For this communication and progress control a few experienced women did a very good job, with extraordinary approaches, underlining the uniqueness of the project.

- Sea-Land operated a large M&R facility at the terminal, including repair shops for chassis and containers. They even installed an automated cleaning station for reefer containers. All these depot functions did attract quite some MT container flows. For that reason a direct interchange between the waterside AGV system and a side lift truck operated MT depot, was installed with all the related complexity when going from an automatic (AGV) to a manual (MT handler)operation. Here again, technology provided safe operations.

- In the beginning transponders were damaged! What was the reason: seagulls were looking for food and thus picking the transponders assuming they were eatable. Later, completely glass-shielded transponders were applied, very well mounted some centimeters below dock level. But seagulls caused more trouble. When they were flying a few meters before an AGV, the (ECT-developed) collision safety system triggered the AGV emergency brakes, stopping the operation. Of course, it took some time before this completely unexpected breakdown was recognized. Thereafter the solution was simple, short (some hundreds of milliseconds) sensor signals were ignored.

- Also weather conditions resulted in some special provisions. For instance the wet and salty ASC rail tracks gave sometimes problems with precise positioning. This was cured by making ASC travels over the whole track length at least once per day. Another surprise was the damage from lightning, when the lightning entered the inductive cables for AGV navigation mounted in the apron pavement. This was improved through special provisions in the supply transformers.

- The labor unions focused on safety and working conditions. One of their issues was the safety for the straddle carrier operators shuttling containers between automatic stacking yard and the road truck interchange. According to the design team, the travel area was spacious enough and moreover only 3-4 straddles were operating at an area of about 700 x 40 m. But the unions/operators were not convinced and ECT decided to show the "real world" by applying techniques used for the assessment of tunnel designs in road traffic. A precise mock-up was made and with special (small) cameras on the scaled straddle

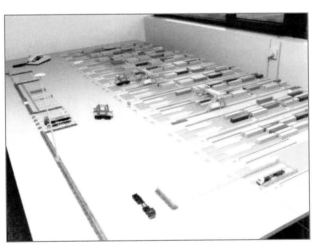

Figure 380: Land-side scale model to show safety and operability

carriers, the operators could get an idea of their work space and travel conditions (see Figure 380). This made the future operators convince of the safe working conditions which were much better than for instance the dense traffic of straddle carriers in a manual operation between quay cranes and stacking yard (like at the Europa Terminal in Antwerp and HHLA's Burchard Kai in Hamburg).

- The selection of hardware and software was one of the toughest issues for ECT. In many automation projects in the automotive and manufacturing industry, control systems were running on DEC machines and that made project management decide to go for the DEC-VAX line instead of the Univac machines, common to ECT. In spite of the interest from many (often smaller) software companies ECT continued its policy to develop (and maintain) its own software. Basically three areas were covered: PCS, the real process control software with many algorithms developed with the help of advanced simulations, PAS the software for message control, tracking and tracing and the important data (message) exchange with Sea-Land and last but not least the data communication hardware and software for the glass fiber networks and radio communication (in the GHz band) with mobile equipment.

- For reefer inspections, the reefer checkers had to cross the straddle carriers (only 2-4), shuttling containers between the automated stack and the truck interchanges at the landside. Being unfamiliar with this operations and always afraid of unsafe operations the labor representatives insisted on building a special vehicle, designed to survive a possible collision with a straddle carrier, with a small curve radius and provisions to carry material for reefer connecting. A committee designed a very expensive vehicle (see Figure 381),

Figure 381: Custom-built vehicle for reefer inspection activities

completely to the theoretically defined specifications, but when it became operational it showed a very unpractical, uncomfortable driving, however……. very safe. So be aware of designs by committees.

The funny (tank-like) vehicle was named "Oma Duck" and later replaced by a much cheaper industrial vehicle and an off-the-shelf small SUV with a roll bar inside! It was one of the examples where non-acquaintance resulted in overdone provisions (characteristic for the introduction of new innovative systems).

- The decision to go for a 6-wide ASC and only one machine per module was based on the requirement for maximum random access (Sea-Land) and optimized investments (ECT). Hence the utmost attention for a reliable ASC design and what to do in case of a major ASC breakdown. For that reason ECT and Nelcon developed a Rescue ASC, essentially a standard ASC with the same drives and automation but additionally equipped with a gen-set, rubber tires and a hydraulically powered steering systems to allow this Rescue ASC to travel from a parked posi-

Figure 382: Back-up ASC on Scheuerle heavy-lift vehicle

tion to any of the 25 stacking module tracks. This Rescue ASC was provided with a cabin, to maneuver the ASC into position. Later this rather complex Rescue ASC was followed up by a special Scheuerle heavy-lift vehicle, suited to transport an ASC from its track, by means of simple lifting provisions at each ASC (see Figure 382).

Teamwork and a tremendous effort from the vendors and ECT's staff made this first automated terminal into a success. It took almost 10 years before the next fully automated terminal was up and running. With improvements and some modifications, but the basic concept is still "an example for the industry".

13.4. AUTOMATION CONTINUES; SLOWER THAN EXPECTED

In the 1990s much more terminals analyzed the feasibility of an automated terminal and the general opinion was that automation would be attractive for new terminals in areas with high labor cost, growing volumes and skilled staff to support new technologies. Nevertheless many terminals were reluctant due to financial constraints, risk-avoiding management and expected resistance from labor unions. But the potential rewards of automation were obvious and thus some brave terminals started automation projects. Unfortunately the growing dominance of global operators caused some slowdowns as these organizations supported standard solutions to be duplicated for many of their terminals. An outline of the realized terminal automation projects will be given below.

Thamesport, Isle of Grain, UK

Two key executives from the Port of Felixstowe: Geoffrey Parker and Robin MacLeod started a new terminal in 1988 at the Isle of Grain, on a vacated industrial area, opposite Sheerness, close to London. Their drive to be a cost leader and this new greenfield site triggered them to install automation, where economically appropriate. However, they had to fulfill two major goals: start up the terminal as soon as possible (get revenues!) and minimize investments in the start-up phase.

The available area resulted in a layout with stack modules parallel to the quay wall, which was connected to the shore with a few traffic bridges (see Figure 383).

Robin MacLeod formed a small team of keen experts that realized an automated stacking yard with the objective to automate transportation to the quay cranes in a later stage. With his enthusiastic and driven team, Robin MacLeod (who used to call his team a "bunch of Lunatics", as they had to do the almost impossible) got the first phase up and running by the end of 1990; four stack modules with 8 rail mounted

Figure 383: Thamesport terminal with automated stacking yard

cranes from Magrini Galileo Meccanica (MGM), stacking 8 wide and 1 over 4 with a gantry travel speed of 150 m./min. and prepared for unmanned operations. Within half a year the first crane was already running automatically and at the beginning of 1992 all cranes were unmanned. The long stack modules (approximately 550 m. long) were divided in two parts: the basic stack yard (60 TEU long) and a so-called magazine (± 15 TEU long) a kind of buffer area, to stack pre-planned containers shortly before vessel loading or to dump containers during a discharge operation. This allowed short cycle distances (efficient!) for tractor/trailers to the quay (see Figure 384), but also included a crossing of terminal tractors with the stacking cranes (feeding the magazine). At first the uncompromising Health and Safety Officer would not allow this type of operation but after some time he got convinced by the rather innovative safety controls (with GPS sensors at the tractors, the crane positioning algorithms and overall collision avoidance software), rapidly developed by MacLeod's team of smart guys. Another topic helping the terminal to get automated within a rather short time (about 18 months!) was the fact that MacLeod only engaged operators having no former experience in sea ports. Such people were open-minded, not infected by the typical dockworkers attitude, to be skeptical of any change suggested by management.

Innovative was the handling of containers in and out of the magazine, operated by the terminal tractor drivers themselves. When positioned at a magazine slot, within the stacking crane rail gauge, the driver connected (through Radio Data Transmission) himself to the stacking crane and with a simple control device in his terminal tractor cabin, he could lower (or hoist) a container from his chassis and thereafter, the crane automatically handled the follow-up of that cycle. Of course the terminal tractors were connected to the process control system through the VDU in the cabin.

Figure 384: Stacking yard with "magazine" area (circled)

Being always in a shortage of (investment) money, the terminal managed to realize a low cost process control system at standard PCs (first only 2 model 386 and later 4 x 386) programmed by their own in-house experts. Later, when the terminal expanded the 386 models were replaced by the 486 models. Road truckers got a (magnetic) smartcard, and when traffic allowed, they were diverted through the inspection gate to a pre-determined exchange place at one of the stacking crane interchange zones at one end of the terminal.

The stacking crane automatically delivered a container and only the final hand shake (container on road-truck chassis) was done with the help of remote control from an operator walking in the interchange area. In the end stage (9 modules) only 3 remotely controlling operators could manage 9 stacking cranes (of course in quiet periods only 1 or 2 operators could do the job).

Already in 1991, 3 more stack modules were ordered, as the terminal handled already 100,000 TEU in 1991. The 6 new stacking cranes were delivered by Morris Cranes and commissioned in 1992/1993.

A few years later, the terminal was completed to 9 stacking modules and the last 4 stacking cranes came from Morris Cranes as well, although now with twin-lift capability (50 tons lift capacity), and much faster gantry travel speeds (design speed 300 m./min.).

The automation of the waterside transportation was considered as well. Demonstrations at a Robotics Laboratory of the Oxford University supported the terminal's belief in further automation. The Dutch tractor manufacturer Terberg developed a 2-axle AGV, provided with navigation and control software from Firefly (David Avery); obviously this development

Figure 385: Prototype Terberg AGV developed for Thamesport

required a lot of attention to solve teething problems and to improve the first prototype design (see Figure 385). However, the terminal and the companies developing the AGV were running out of money and also the UK government would not support this applied research. So, the Thamesport automation remained limited to an automated stacking system with semi-automated interchanges to the waterside and landside. Still, it was remarkable that Thamesport was developed in a rather short time, with limited amounts of money. Enthusiasm and smart thinking were major characteristics behind this success.

In later years this medium-sized terminal (7 quay cranes, 650 m. quay wall) handled up to approximately 1 million TEU. In the 2000s, the terminal was taken over by HPH, neutralizing Thamesport's cost-attractive competition with Felixstowe (another nearby HPH terminal).

Container Terminal Altenwerder (CTA), Hamburg

On a green field site in Hamburg (close to HHLA's Burchardkai terminal), HHLA and Hapag-Lloyd developed a completely new automated terminal as of the late 1990s.

CTA started their design work a decade later than ECT and in those 10 years container transport showed many changes such as: much larger container vessels (call size!) changing consortia arrangements (planning and documentation) much more on-deck containers, predominantly lashed with SATLs and more influence from shippers (more merchant haulage) resulting in a requirement for landside flexibility.

CTA's own analysis and the experiences at the Delta Sea-Land terminal and Thamesport made CTA select an automated RMG stacking system, however with two stacking cranes per stack module (10 containers wide and 37 TEU long) that could pass each other, resulting in a double rail track per module (higher investment and increased corner loads) and one crane per module larger, higher and heavier, to enable passing of the other crane. The lessons from Thamesport (reliability of the RMG) and ECT (AGVs driving within the quay crane gauge, and critical sequencing) caused some reluctance from HHLA and Hapag-Lloyd against the application of AGVs. Besides, some others (Hessenatie, Kalmar) showed the attraction of straddle carriers or shuttle carriers working in the quay crane's backreach. However, HHLA had their experiences with straddle carrier operations including the impact on the environment and the costs for manning, fuel and maintenance (damages!).

It was again Joachim Kröll from Gottwald who convinced the CTA board of the cost effectiveness of Gottwald's AGVs. He offered a fixed price for a first series of AGVs (35) including fleet management system, an interface to CTA's process control system. The diesel-hydraulic AGVs were equipped with Gottwald's in-house developed Navimatic system (instead of the earlier FROG system). Compared to the first ECT automated terminal, the CTA automated terminal (see Figure 386) showed the following developments/improvements:

Figure 386: Automation in Hamburg: Container Terminal Altenwerder

- All quay cranes were provided with a second trolley system in automated mode; connecting to the AGVs via a 2 container capacity elevated platform accommodating SATL handling and container ID check (see Figure 387).

Figure 387: Interchange platform in quay crane, with 2 container positions

- The AGVs were handled in the quay cranes' backreach with 4 AGV lanes available. The AGVs were running at higher speeds and had twin lift capability (60 tons payload).

- Between the quay cranes and the automated stacking crane interchanges, the AGVs could be positioned in a buffer area to better allow cycle time pulling from the quay cranes and better support sequencing and late minute changes.

- The crossing stacking cranes (cross twin ASC) gave an improved redundancy and (slightly) better handling productivity per module (but, at a much higher investment).

- At the landside, road truckers were directly handled in the ASC interchange areas. A formal hand-shake was achieved through remote control operators (far away in a comfortable control room) monitoring the manual final hoisting/lowering with cameras. This required only 1-4 operators (depending on the workload) for the whole landside area. In a later stage, the handling of landside containers onto (from) terminal chassis for transportation to the railhead could be done completely automated without interference from the remote control operators.

The first phase of CTA, for about 1.1 million TEU annual throughput, started with a 950 m. berth, 9 quay cranes, 22 stacking cranes at 11 stack modules and 35 AGVs; the whole process supported with an in-house built process control system running at fault tolerant hardware. Later the system was expanded to 26-stack modules supporting 16 quay cranes, with a throughput of around 3 million TEU/year. The fleet of AGVs was extended with diesel-electric

Figure 388: Battery-supplied AGV in operation at CTA

268

Gottwald AGVs (a fuel saving design with improved operating cost) and in 2011 the first 2 full electric, battery driven AGVs were put into operation together with a fully automated battery exchange and charging station. This zero emission AGVs inaugurated a new era in sustainable, environmentally friendly transportation at container terminals (see Figure 388).

Deurganck Dock Antwerp: Hessenatie sows; DP world reaps

Already from the mid-1990s, Hessenatie considered automation, knowing the costs of a labor and maintenance intensive straddle carrier operation. By the end of the century, the Antwerp Port Authority finalized the planning of a new left bank harbor and Hessenatie, together with its major customer MSC (Mediterranean Shipping Company, Geneva) acquired a concession for a part of that new harbor, which is attractive because of the absence of locks and sufficient draft. Automation was heavily considered and the decision was made to apply Gottwald overhead stacking cranes, with a guiding beam for precise positioning. Again it was the drive of Joachim Kröll from Gottwald who arranged a prototype installation at a Hessenatie terminal at the Churchill Dock. Here the stacking of the OBC and the handshake with a Gottwald AGV was tested (see Figure 389). But, unfortunately for the course of automation, the Antwerp terminal business environment got dramatically shaken. In June 2000, Hessenatie (a CMB subsidiary company since 1988) and Noordnatie announced merger discussions that should be finalized by mid-2001. Meanwhile the design of a new automated terminal, to be operated by Hessenatie and MSC at the Deurganck Dock, continued (see Figure 390, courtesy of Gottwald).

Figure 389: Prototype automated overhead stacking crane

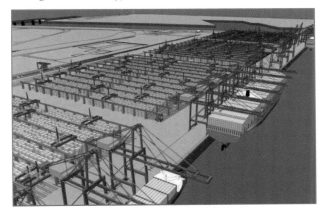

Figure 390: Automated terminal concept at Deurganck Dock

The imminent shortage of handling capacity triggered P&O Ports and P&O/NedLloyd to apply for a Deurganck Dock concession (opposite of Hessenatie/MSC) as well. Only a few months earlier (May 2000), P&O Ports acquired Seaport Terminals and thereafter ACT. These P&O container terminal activities were managed by Roger Roels, a former Sea-Land executive.

Unfortunately, after the start (September 1999) of building the Deurganck Dock, the Belgium Council of State stopped the activities due to procedural mistakes in the building permit (June 2000). This was corrected some months later but then the European Commission noticed problems with the habitat and again the project was stopped. By the end of 2002, the building activities were continued again.

In the meantime, terminal ownerships had changed considerably. The merger process between Hessenatie en Noordnatie took much longer and after the final agreement, March 2002, the new combination HesseNoordNatie was sold to PSA, still interested in a Deurganck Dock concession. The fast growing MSC decided to concentrate its hub operations around the Delwaide Dock and then P&O Ports, together with P&O NedLloyd and Duisburg Port applied for a concession on the Deurganck Dock as well. In February 2003 the concession partition was settled: P&O Ports got the east side and PSA/HNN the west side. The rather conservative PSA board decided for a manual operation first and P&O Ports started with a manual straddle carrier terminal in July 2005. But, for the second phase an automated stacking system from Gottwald was selected. Some former Hessenatie staff members (by then working for P&O), continued what Hessenatie started in the 1990s, however with some changes, for a part encouraged after DP World acquired P&O Ports in 2006.

Today, the Antwerp Gateway Terminal phase II shows 7 stack modules (40 TEU long, see Figure 391), each with two Gottwald ASCs (stacking 9 wide, 1 over 5) and Gottwald software for stack control, ASC assignment, collision control and the fully automated interchange at the landside. Here, special

Figure 391: Antwerp Gateway Terminal with automated stacking cranes from Gottwald

vision technology allows an automated positioning of containers onto road chassis (even when they are not very well aligned). It is still in the air whether an automation of the waterside transportation will take place somewhere in the future. In 2011, DP World expressed its interest in transportation with lift AGVs for another terminal development (London Gateway). It is a matter of regret that an unfortunate permission process and business takeovers stopped an almost definite decision to go for a fully automated terminal in Antwerp.

Patrick's AutoStrad Terminal in Brisbane, Australia

The Australian dockworkers have been known, not only for their high hourly labor cost but also for their reluctance against innovations. All the more remarkable were the developments Patrick Stevedores and Kalmar initiated at the Fisherman's Island Terminal in Brisbane. After some experiments at the Sydney University the two companies cooperated in the development of a driverless straddle carrier, provided with a free-ranging navigation system and technology for tracking and tracing, order processing and collision avoidance (it is likely that Kalmar used its Valmet experience, obtained from a carrier automation project with the Dutch Hoogovens, IJmuiden, during the 1980s).

In 2001, Patrick decided to go for a pilot plant and retrofitted 5 Kalmar straddle carriers. As of mid-2002 these already called AutoStrads were tested in real life operations for Cosco's Sino Service. The promising results culminated in an order for 14 E-drive AutoStrads (diesel-electric drives with AC-technology), October 2004. In 2006, Patrick's 3-berth facility in Brisbane started operations and nowadays is running with 27 AutoStrads (see Figure 392). The AutoStrads function with the help of DGPS, millimeter wave radar and laser technology. The WS interchange is in the quay crane's backreach and the LS interchange is still semi-automated, with the interference of a tele operator (remote control) mainly for import operations. Of course, the whole container yard was fenced off. Parallel to the AutoStrad development itself, Patrick developed terminal control and yard management systems as well and this technology is marketed through a joint company (Patrick Technology and Systems) with Kalmar (15%) and Asciano Ltd (a Toll Holdings subsidiary) wherein Patrick has the IP-rights.

Figure 392: Fisherman Island AutoStrad Terminal (Brisbane)

In 2010, the new Fisherman Islands AutoStrad Terminal opened at berth 10, a new 40 ha facility, with a throughput capacity of 1-1.2 million TEU/year and all the latest planning (NAVIS yard planning) and process control software developed by PTS, including smart yard management (dual cycling) and pooling of AutoStrads. The building's design was impressive and got an architecture award.

During the almost 10 years from the first tests to a mature fully-operational terminal, the Patrick executives maintained their drive, which resulted in an automated system that might be interesting for other straddle carrier operated terminals (the Aarhus stevedoring company Cargo Service has already shown its interest).It is for sure that Patrick's automation efforts will influence Australia's labor attitude. Their next application could well be the Asciano terminal in Botany Bay, Sydney.

APM Terminals Portsmouth, Virginia, US

During the years 2002 and 2003, APMT studied the potential of automation for their terminals and in April 2004 APMT surprisingly announced the plan for an automated terminal on a new site at Portsmouth, Virginia. Of all places, APMT selected the US East Coast for their first automation project. Probably, the availability of a greenfield site, the prospect of considerable cost savings in a high labor cost environment and the support of a local driven management team turned the scale. Already in an early stage RMGs were selected for an auto-

Figure 393: Aerial view APMT terminal Portsmouth, Virginia

mated yard but the choice for a horizontal transportation system was more difficult. Cassette systems (manual and automated), AGVs and shuttle carriers (manual) were analyzed with the help of simulation studies and cost analyses. Aiming for proven technology and afraid to go too advanced and to be too dependent on reliable control software, APMT went for manual shuttle carriers at the waterside and manual translifters (TTS) with cassettes for the drayage to the close by 6-track railhead. The choice for manual shuttle carriers was spurred by the goal for high crane productivity on vessels, using twin-lift, dual cycling and even tandem lift (2 x 40') when appropriate (Figure 393 and Figure 394).

The 15 stack modules (60 TEU long) were provided with 2 RMGs (Konecranes with GE-electrics), stacking 8 wide, 1 over 5. At the waterside the manual 6-wheel shuttle carriers could pick-up the containers within the crane gauge and connect to 4 TEU-deep interchanges at the WS stack-end.

On the landside, the truckers position their chassis at the LS stack-end (5 positions per module) and get (or deliver) their box with remote control for the final hand-shake. In the 12-lane gate-in and 12-lane gate-out facilities, state-of-the-art ID and data processing techniques have been applied.

After 3 years of construction this (partly) automated terminal was officially opened September the 17th, 2007, but got in full swing during 2008. Unexpected, in July 2010, APMT made a

Figure 394: Automated stacking yard and interchange areas

long-term arrangement with Virginian International Terminals to operate this new facility for them. It is unknown whether APMT was satisfied or not by the cost savings and productivity gains or the handling volumes, they had in mind, when introducing this concept in 2005.

Euromax, Rotterdam

In the second half of the 1990s an increasing number of shipping lines were looking for dedicated capacity in their main hub ports. In Rotterdam, ECT's 2000-8 approach could not convince some shipping lines. The Rotterdam Port Authority projected a new terminal Northwest from ECT (west from the Maasvlakte Oil Terminal) and here P&O Nedlloyd, together with ECT started the planning of a new automated terminal, after the settlement of a 50/50 joint venture for the building of this Euromax Terminal (November 2000). The first concepts were published in 2000-2001, but the planning process was slow, partly because of some economic drawbacks in 2002-2003 and a hold-up of the EU-commission who finally (in December 2004) cleared the joint venture.

Mid-2005, the building of the first 1,900 m. quay wall started and thereafter Euromax finalized the conceptual design with AGV transportation at the waterside and automated rail mounted gantries for the stacking yard. However, again in 2005 some delay came up when Maersk acquired P&O Nedlloyd (for 2.3 billion Euros). Maersk had already a commitment for a new terminal at the Second Maasvlakte and the involvement in a third terminal in Rotterdam was firmly criticized. But in November 2006 ECT got 100% ownership of the Euromax terminal, in an operational partnership with the CKYH Alliance (Cosco, K Line, Yang Ming and

Figure 395: Euromax automated terminal, Maasvlakte Rotterdam

Hanjin Shipping). From that time the project got accelerated again and the Euromax terminal opening celebration was in September 2008. The start-up took more than half a year, but in June 2009 the terminal was fully up and running and the first million handling moves were realized until autumn 2010.

The first phase (1,500 m. operational quay wall) showed 12 ZPMC quay cranes, all fitted with second trolley systems, connecting to the AGVs in the backreach (see Figure 396). In order to optimize the main trolley handling cycle, the interchange platform (about 16 m. above dock level) was located at the landside of the crane rail gauge. In addition 4 smaller ZPMC barge-feeder cranes were installed, lower than the large STS cranes (improved visibility and sway control on small vessels) and without 2nd trolley systems. The 96 Gottwald AGVs had a diesel-electric drive and were provided with Gottwald's Navimatic system for routing and positioning. Just like at CTA, the AGVs could be staged at a waterside buffer area, between quay cranes and the stacking yard. The refueling of AGVs was realized at a fully automated fuel station.

Each of the 29 stack modules was provided with 2 ARMGs, stacking 10 wide, 1 over 5 and with 300 m./min. gantry travel. The stack modules have an insert at the waterside to allow AGVs entering into the stack in order to get the possibility of both ARMGs working at the waterside (for increased vessel handling performance). At the landside stack interchange, the road truck drivers were allowed (after a short training) to position the container onto their road chassis by themselves, however, the unions turned back this concept.

Figure 396: Interchange AGV

In early design concepts the connection between stacking yard and railhead (6 rail tracks) was designed with AGVs but later this was reversed to a simple tractor-trailer system with chassis parking perpendicular to the rail tracks (equal to CTA). At the end of the 6 rail tracks a transfer car for locomotives helped to minimize track length and still allowing incoming trains with pulling locomotives and loc's returning via a bypass track (see Figure 397).

Also the gate processing was highly automated: after pre-notification and using his cargo card, the trucker can do the complete gate-in/gate-out process without leaving his cabin and meanwhile passing identification (hand scan for the driver), a photo gate and a check on radioactive radiation.

Figure 397: Loc transfer car

The overall terminal operations control system was developed by Navis/Gottwald-Teams and included some new features, triggered by ECT's experience with earlier automation projects.

Although the Euromax terminal design could benefit from developments of ECT, CTA and DP World still the commissioning took quite some time, partly because of the entrance of new vendors (ZPMC and ABB), which had to go through their own teething period as well.

Tobishima Container Berth Co, Nagoya, Japan

The Japanese Government established a so-called Super Hub Port project in the early 2000s. This effort was meant to considerably reduce the port entry fees (minus 30%) in order to keep in line with rival ports in Busan and Kaohsiung. For that reason, the Japanese Government appointed some ports and these ports were challenged (with research and financial support) to install state-of-the-art terminal facilities at competitive cost. In the Nagoya area at Ise Bay a new medium-size innovative terminal was established with a berth length of 750 m. (400 m. in the first phase), a terminal depth of 500 m. and the "introduction of cutting-edge IT systems and fully-automated container terminal handling equipment". The graph of this governmental program (including financial support) is shown in Figure 398.

The concept was based on automated RTGs, all terminal transportation with AGVs and at the landside interchange, transfer cranes should swap containers between road trucks and AGVs. This helped to avoid road trucks entering the RTG yard (always giving traffic problems, waiting and damages) and allow double handling for AGVs. For that reason, the RTG modules were designed with two driving lanes in the crane gauge. It was planned to achieve a full automated terminal in a step-by-step approach and the first focus was on automated RTGs. Already in the mid-1970s Japan installed a semi-automated RTG terminal at the K Line

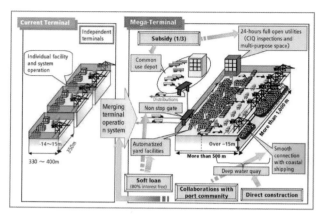

Figure 398: Scheme for transition to automated terminals (Japan)

terminal at OHI, Tokyo with Paceco/Mitsui RTGs. For this Tobishima South Side Container Terminal project, Mitsubishi Heavy Industries (MHI) was selected and they developed a fully automated RTG, including automated drives (hoist, trolley and gantry), gantry travel auto steering, anti-collision sensors, stack profile detection, a "Magic Eye" system for precise container positioning using CCD cameras, vision techniques and anti-sway control. Internal transport was projected with AGVs but in the first phase (2005-2006) 12 RTGs were installed and no AGVs but terminal tractors.

For the second phase (operational in 2010) the Toyota Material Handling division supplied 20 AGVs (Toyota also was financially interested in the terminal) with design speeds up to 7 m./sec. and 40 tons pay load (see Figure 399). The operations control system was provided with dynamic assignment features for RTG and AGV and algorithms to realize as much as possible dual cycles (combining import and export moves, both at the water and landside). So far it is not known to the authors whether this show-case facility has met the target: 40 moves/hr per crane! (6 quay cranes at 750 m. berth).

Figure 399: Automated Tobishima Terminal with automated RTGs and AGVs

Busan New Port Container Terminals, Korea

At the phase 2-2 New Port Development in Busan (at Gaduk Island) two terminals were realized with automated stacking yards. The first one, Hyundai Pusan New Port Terminal (HPNT) with an 1,150 m. quay wall, installed 36 double cantilever RMGs manufactured by ZPMC/Scoho, stacking 10 wide 1 over 5 in 350 m. stacking blocks parallel to the quay wall. The transportation was realized with tractor/trailers however, pooled and with multi-cycling, controlled via a smart terminal operating system, developed by a Hyundai subsidiary: Hyundai Ubiquitous & Information Technology. Although not yet completely unmanned, the operations for 36 stacking cranes could be managed by maximum 9 operators, with the help of remote control consoles in a central operations room.

The second New Port Terminal was realized at phase 2-3 with 19 stack modules perpendicular to the quay wall, each about 330 m. long and each provided with 2 ARMGs (ZPMC). The waterside transportation is realized with TEREX Sprinters (shuttle carriers).

TTI, Algeciras, Spain

In 2010, Total Terminals International (TTI) at the latest expansion in Algeciras installed automated stacking cranes (ZPMC) in modules perpendicular to the quay wall and Cargotec Sprinters for the waterside transportation (see Figure 400).

Figure 400: Automated stacking with automated ASCs and manual sprinters

13.5. INTRODUCTION OF NEW CONCEPTUAL DESIGNS, BUT .....NO APPLICATIONS

Just like in the 1980s, crane manufacturers, engineering companies and consultants continued to develop automated handling systems during the 1990s and the 21st century; some of the most promising ones will be presented below.

Octopus

In 1995, Reggiane, Italy, launched its "revolutionary" system called Octopus aiming to get more quay cranes efficiently working on a Post-Panamax vessel (see Chapter 10). The system was based on very narrow quay cranes, operating at an elevated crane track, close to each other. The concept showed a split in loading and unloading operations, by means of vehicle positioning under the loading cranes and a type of conveyor at the waterside for fast unloading. The automation part was projected in the yard system and the waterside transport. An octopus control system was foreseen to coordinate the crane assignment on the vessel and to coordinate activities between the yard and the waterside transportation system(s). The promised but unproven reduction of more than 50% in vessel berth time could not convince potential users.

FAMAS

During the second half of the 1990s the Dutch Centre of Transport Technology (CTT) managed a variety of studies on terminal handling systems and equipment under the umbrella FAMAS (First All Modes All Sizes). Research was done by a consortium of companies from the container handling and port industry together with the universities of Delft and Rotterdam. The outlook was 2020 with at that time foreseen jumbo vessels of 8,000 TEU, possibly growing towards 12,500 TEU (the outlook on the future in those days!). Service requirements, defined in 1996-1997, included the need for a vessel performance, for such jumbo vessels, of 300 moves/hour, to be realized with a maximum of 6 quay cranes.

Major research topics were the jumbo crane itself (see Chapter 10), smart AGVs with decentralized control (SMAGIC), improved performances, smart terminal control features and a better integration with landside modalities. The research focused on the Rotterdam Maasvlakte II, where until 2030 massive growth was predicted.

Interesting to mention here are two concepts: the CRAFE concept and a centralized Barge Service Center (BSC).

The CRAFE concept (CRAne FEeding system) was developed to realize an average crane productivity of 50 containers/hour, with peaks up to 100 containers/hour. Due to the increased vessel beam height, an elevated dock level was proposed (12-15 m. above sea level) to realize the shortest crane cycle times varying from 35-95 secs/cycle (max 20 wide containers on deck, foreseen in those days). The required design changes for quay wall and quay crane (see Figure 401) showed cost advantages. The CRAFE concept (various alternatives were developed) offered a large buffer capacity for the vessel operation with provisions to take the time-consuming SATL handling (coning/deconing) away from the quay crane towards centralized coning/deconing stations, to allow better efficiency and a potential for automated SATL handling (see Figure 402).

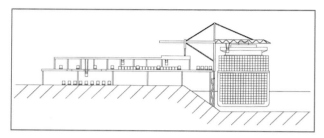

Figure 401: The CRAFE concept (FAMAS)

Figure 402: Artist impression of FAMAS' CRAFE concept

Simulations showed the high vessel performance potential, but of course with a related investment and a demand for a combined approach in civil and crane engineering.

The Barge Service Center (BSC) was a development to concentrate all barge handling at one dedicated handling site, to allow (semi)-automated barge operations and to support larger call sizes for barges, as they often collect containers for a multitude of customers (shipping lines, merchants) and destinations.

The concept shows Overhead Bridge Cranes, both for stacking and barge-handling (see Figure 403), allowing fast barge handling at the predicted high yearly barge volumes (several millions/year).

Figure 403: Barge Service Centre with overhead bridge cranes

The BSC concept showed to be attractive for a multi-user operation with high equipment utilization, attractive high area utilization and of course a very good service to barge operators which were offered a quick turnaround and high barge utilization. However the reverse side could be the related additional (costly) internal transport and an investment and operation from an "independent" BSC operator.

Container conveyor Promo-Teus

A number of automated handling systems considered continuously moving conveyors as a promising concept, especially for unloading operations and internal yard transportation. In the late 1990s Halmij, a Dutch company involved with Noell, presented a conveyor, based on coupled, synchronized modules, each provided with electrically-driven rubber-covered belts, sliding over steel bars and with a hydraulically automated lift mechanism at crossing points (see Figure 404). In 2001, a demonstration prototype was realized, conveying at 1 m./sec. and showing a rectangular crossroad. This concept development stayed in the prototype stage, probably due to the limited transportation capacity, limited flexibility in larger terminals and the impact of a breakdown (equal to rail track systems).

Figure 404: Prototype container conveyor

TTS automated cassette AGV

At the end of the 1990s, TTS was involved in a European development project IPSI, for the fast loading and unloading of Ro-Ro vessels in coastal operations. This system comprised of cassettes, for 2 x 40' or 4 x 20' containers which could be transported by low-bed AGVs (see Figure 405). This concept was further developed into an automated system for container terminals. Cassettes were (un)loaded under the quay crane and the stacking crane and the AGVs transported the cassettes over the waterside apron. Decoupling at the yard was an advantage, decoupling at the quay crane could give problems when the quay crane had to reposition over the vessel.

Later this concept was modified, with new cassette designs provided with long corner guides for easy positioning (see Figure 405). Also a new 8-wheel, all-electric AGV was presented, with a 90-degree turning capability for the wheel sets, allowing rectangular routings and "crab driving". The concept design mentioned contactless energy transfer technology (e.g. at the quay cranes and at the stacking crane interchange) using induction and capacitors onboard of the AGV.

Figure 405: TTS cassette system: double-stack concepts (top) and prototype (below)

ZPMC rail-mounted shuttle-car concept

In 2006-2007, ZPMC launched an automated handling system, based on rail-mounted shuttle cars with rectangular container transport lanes at multi-levels for the transfer of boxes between the quay cranes and the stacking yard (see Figure 406). The system can handle tandem 40' containers to be moved with flat trolleys and lifting trolleys, running on elevated tracks, parallel to the quay wall. At certain spots, the boxes (still in tandem) are lifted and 90 degrees rotated and again placed on flat trolleys moving to a position under a rail-mounted stacking crane.

The ZPMC management was convinced of the advantages of this system and to demonstrate the capabilities of the concept built a prototype at its Changxing Island manufacturing plant. In 2009, SSA Marine showed their interest in the concept for one of their US West Coast terminals, but so far no firm commitments for an operational system have been made.

Figure 406: ZPMC automated terminal concept (left) and demonstration prototype (right)

ZMPC promoted the system with two major advantages: a major saving in labor cost (according to ZPMC up to 90%) and zero environmental impact due to the rail-mounted and fully electric-driven transfer trolleys. However, some terminal experts showed their doubts mentioning topics like layout flexibility, cost of track foundations, maintenance of the steel structures for the elevated tracks and the recovery (or working around) in case of breakdowns.

Paceco SegCart and CP&A conveyor system

At the end of 2010, two US engineering companies published concepts for the automated transport of containers between the apron (or landside truck interchange) and RMG stacks to the quay wall. Both concepts aim to reduce RMG long travel considerably, allowing a simplified RMG design and RMG rail tracks.

Paceco's SegCart system proposes battery driven carts operating at separate rail tracks (probably a normal railway gauge) within and along the RMG stack modules (see Figure 407). The carts are independently controlled, operating in a loop between an apron interchange and the RMG, and with controls for proper positioning and spacing. At dedicated queuing areas, the recharging of batteries can be done with induction technology. The small (lightweight) carts only support the containers at their ends (somewhat similar to the RoadRailer bogies) and can even be configured as small trains. For the exchange of containers at the landside (trucking) and the waterside (AGVs or shuttle carriers) Paceco suggested overhead bridge cranes for container swapping.

Figure 407: Automated rail-based transport parallel to stack (Paceco SegCart)

Caspar, Phillips & Associates proposed a stationary conveyor in between the stack modules and elevated about 1.5 m. above dock level (see Figure 408) The conveyors are supposed to be built up from powered transport modules of about 15 m. length (to accommodate containers up to 45' length), combined with side shift modules, turntable modules and non-driven idler modules. The proposed conveyor concept will use chains for the support and movement of containers (this as contrasted with the Promo-Teus conveyor system which used a belt). According to CP&A, conveyor transport capacity should be sufficient to provide 50 containers per hour to a number of quay cranes. Similar to Paceco, the exchange with AGVs or shuttle carriers is foreseen with OBCs, also providing some buffer capacity.

Remarkably, the two concepts show some similarities with earlier terminal automation concepts, published between 1975 and 1990. Both concepts are aimed to improve RMG productivity with reduced RMG investments however, at the expense of additional components with additional control systems and special, rather rigid, tracks for carts or conveyors. Moreover this extra transport system will decrease the area utilization and when peak RMG productivity is required the Euromax concept already offers the possibility of driving into

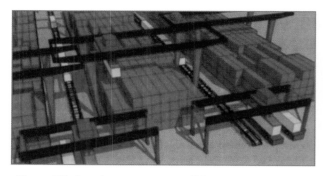

Figure 408: Container conveyors parallel to automated stacking

stack modules with the help of AGVs. At the time of writing there were no plans for a prototype or first application known to the authors.

Kalmar's AutoShuttle

After the maturing of the automated straddle carrier at the Patrick Terminal in Brisbane (see Section 13.4), Kalmar proposed an automated 6-wheel shuttle carrier as a further cost-saving component for the waterside transportation between quay cranes and stacking yard. This concept was presented in early 2008 and could be one step further than shown in the APMT terminal with manual shuttle carriers in Virginia. Coincidentally, the know-how of FROG Navigation, used for the first AGVs at ECT, was further developed by FROG's follow-up: Advanced Cargo Transshipment (ACT) a Dutch company acquired by Kalmar. This company earlier developed a free ranging navigation system using embedded magnets, for a passenger bus system in The Netherlands. This technology is also proposed for the AutoShuttle in combination with an advanced equipment management system, which should be capable of avoiding/solving deadlock situations and updating job orders including a proper sequencing. Up till now there are no applications registered, probably because of the doubts, whether such an automated shuttle carrier system will be capable of realizing productivities equal to those from manually operated shuttle carriers. On top of that the impact on the environment (AutoShuttles are heavier than AGVs and diesel-electric driven, with more maintenance cost for driveline and telescopic spreader) may cause reluctance due to the risk of more cost and vulnerability for breakdowns.

Nevertheless, the abovementioned new concepts for automated terminals showed the drive for further developments in automation. However, from a cost and reliability point of view the terminals could have considered to concentrate on a limited number of concepts to be matured and improved on topics like maintainability, elongated MTBF, lifetime, environmental impact and sustainability. The success of concepts with automated stacking cranes, directly connected with the landside and a low cost automated transport between quay cranes and stacking system may encourage terminals and manufacturers to further improve this simple reliable concept.

13.6. ICT: A CRITICAL SUCCESS FACTOR

The automation of container handling systems could only take-off after the availability of powerful hard and software for the control of movements of equipment, the process control of handling systems and related issues such as equipment management, assignment, sequencing and the tracking and tracing of containers at the terminal. Moreover the exchange of data for large terminals, often realizing more than 1,000 container movements per hour, required high-speed, reliable data communication systems both fixed in the facility (mainly fiber optics) and by radio to mobile equipment.

During the last three decades, wherein automation was introduced, a number of issues are worthwhile to mention here:

- In spite of a maturing period of about 3 decades, ICT is still considered a risk element in the design/operation of container terminals and automated concepts in particular. Both the internal information flows and the information exchange with the terminal's stakeholders require properly designed data base management systems, capable of following the continuously growing demand for faster and more info. The standardization of message transfers (EDIFACT) has helped to control this all but still, all kinds of information/documentation are stakeholder specific (e.g. customs manifests, security checks, trade statistics, status queries from shipping lines/shippers), which require special interfaces to fulfill requests on formatting and update frequencies. Moreover, many of these info exchanges tend to migrate to web based applications, universally available, but not always reliably built. In this environment with constant changes (update from systems software, expanding functionality, failing support from software/hardware suppliers), the terminals must maintain the software for their EDI engine, an effort with a high risk on bugs.

- Technology in the ICT world developed with an amazing speed. In the field of data transmission the availability of fiber optics and spread spectrum technology in the 2 GHz and 5 GHz bands allow high density data exchange far more than 10 Mbps for remote vision systems, on-line seal checking, RFID, transponder based ID checks, OCR systems, etc. For the position control of equipment, manufacturers have a choice out of many technologies: transponder navigation, laser based triangulation, differential global positioning systems (DGPS), electronic gyroscopes and recently local positioning radar in the license-free 5.8 GHz ISM band. The power of software and hardware is immense, allowing a high processing speed in information control systems, often in combination with relational data base management systems and smart SQL's. Hardware can be configured in fault-tolerant systems for essential information systems and also recovery algorithms for start-up after a breakdown are increasingly implemented.

- Planning systems, in use for vessel stowage, quay crane assignment, container stacking, equipment scheduling, etc. are nowadays developed to support improved terminal equipment productivity and better service to trucking and shipping. More and more, automated optimization algorithms are built in, allowing operations management to monitor the logistic processes and to intervene only in case of irregularities or last minute changes. Some suppliers of terminal operating systems have integrated some of these planning functions but often tailor-made solutions are required due to local conditions. Also the integration with one or more equipment management systems (pooling of tractor-trailers, AGV transportation, stacking crane systems) is an important issue.

- ICT developments have supported the automation of gate processes, important to realize a fast trucker's turn around in and out the terminal. It also helped to reduce the costs for inspection, equipment interchange, damage control and ID checks. OCR techniques became faster and much more reliable, but RFID tags are promising. Already some shipping lines (e.g. APL) provide their own equipment with tags (chassis, reefers) and RFID readers in their dedicated gate lanes. Unfortunately these developments are not yet worldwide spread and are awaiting standardization. The ongoing work on the ISO 18186 standard may in the coming years result in a much wider support for these new RFID technologies.

- When newly installing or replacing/modifying an ICT system (e.g. a terminal operating system, an EDI engine or a berth planning system), there is always a fair risk of encountering major problems ("bugs") in performance and functionality. For that reason training and testing are of utmost importance, especially in the case of a running terminal which should continue services 24 hours per day, 7 days a week. Advanced simulation models (with control algorithms almost equal to the real life process control software) have resulted in emulation software, allowing vendors and users to test control software on functionality, robustness and performance. During the last five years this new technology has been embraced both by major software suppliers and large terminals and has resulted in a better quality at the moment of going live. However, the complexity of today's control software and the integration of subsystems from various vendors make the implementation of automated terminal operations a risk-full activity. The many vendors and the tailor-made solutions required by terminals have prevented the evolution of one de facto standard. The industry is still far away from plug-and-play. "Plug-and-pray" does not help either and thus sufficient time and money for proper training and testing is required; an experience learned in the last decades.

- The involvement of operators and operations management is essential when implementing ICT systems not the least because of the fear for job reductions. In general, the introduction of planning and control systems, combined with (partly) automated operations (stacking, gate and info exchange), will erode manpower demands. Fully automated terminals show a considerable reduction in operators for equipment, but also in partly automated terminals, the control over equipment is done remotely, allowing only a few operators (in a central control building) to control 3-6 machines. For process managers as well (planners, yard dispatchers, etc.), the availability of advanced control systems resulted in a change from continuous activities (presenting job orders and proper sequencing) towards a continuous monitoring and only interfering in case of hiccups and/or last-minute changes. Also in the area of administrative functions and info exchange with shipping lines, customs, inland transportation companies, etc., the manpower demand is substantially reduced. Fortunately, during the last decade much more attention has been paid to the interaction between operators/controllers and their software tools and nowadays the design of Graphical User Interfaces (GUI) includes involvement of the users. But still, ICT system developers tend to present too much or irrelevant information for on-the-job decisions to be made by controllers/operators.

In the early days large terminals had their own in-house ICT development teams both for new building, modifications and daily monitoring. But for cost reasons, ICT services are increasingly outsourced, with all the consequences for service and fast response in case of breakdowns. Moreover outsourcing may result in an erosion of in-house know-how, so much required for the control over complex logistic processes wherein information management is of utmost importance.

Looking to the ongoing automation in the fields of stacking and internal transport, the physical characteristics of the various applied handling systems have many similarities but the control software tends to differentiate due to a growing number of software suppliers entering this ICT applications area. Up till now, the interchangeability of software systems is far away, causing a dependency of software suppliers.

13.7. PROJECTS IN PROGRESS

Up until summer 2012, a number of terminal automation projects were decided and in progress and again the differences came from the concept of transportation between the quay cranes and the automated stacking yard. The following projects are already in the realization stage:

HHLA Container Terminal Burchardkai, Hamburg

Volume developments made HHLA decide to upgrade their Burchardkai facility. A new, longer quay wall was realized in front of the older quay wall (designed at the end of the 1960s), allowing the installation of quay cranes at 35 m. gauge provided with second trolley systems (interchange at the backreach), almost equal to the CTA quay cranes. The required service to trucking and rail and the increased demand for stack capacity resulted in an automated stacking crane system with 3 stacking cranes per stack module: two stacking cranes on one track (stacking 1 over 5) and the third, somewhat higher crane (stacking 1 over 6) on an additional track allowing this third crane to pass the other two at any place of the 50-TEU long stack module (see Figure 409). Obviously the operational flexibility of these 3 cranes will give a good performance both to the waterside and landside however at a price (double tracks per module and expensive cranes). For the first stage of the plan to gradually convert CTB from straddle carriers to ASCs, 8 stack modules with 24 ASCs are under construction and by the end of 2011, the manufacturer Cargotec had fifteen stacking cranes commissioned.

The transportation of containers between the quay cranes and the waterside interchange at the stacking modules will remain with straddle carriers.

 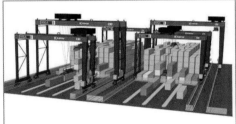 

Figure 409: Automated stacking with 3 ASCs (2 crossing) at BCT, Hamburg

HPH TerCat, Barcelona

After acquiring TerCat in 2010, Hutchison Port Holdings planned to realize a second, semi-automated terminal at the Muelle Prat, Barcelona. For this development HPH had to invest approximately 515 million Euros. In the first stage, the 60 ha terminal is to have 1,000 m. of quay wall and 18 stacking modules with 36 stacking cranes from Konecranes, each stacking 1 over 5. Transportation is realized with the help of shuttle carriers. For

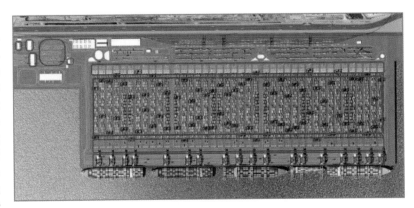

Figure 410: Layout Muelle Prat Terminal, Barcelona

the operations control the TerCat terminal is to use the newly (HPH in-house) developed nGen operating system. The first operations are planned for the second half of 2012. In later stages the quay wall can be extended to 1,500 m. and the total terminal area may expand up to 100 ha (see Figure 410).

Khalifa Terminal, Abu Dhabi

The required terminal expansion and shortage of labor made Abu Dhabi Ports decide to build a semi-automated container terminal at the first phase of their new port. The new 2 million TEU capacity terminal with 1,000 m, quay wall will have 26 stack modules in the end stage. The first stage will start with 15 stack modules (each with 2 ASCs from Konecranes) which will be connected to the quay cranes through a shuttle carrier system (TEREX "Sprinters"). The terminal operating system will be SPARCS-N4 delivered by Navis (a Cargotec subsidiary); furthermore a fully-automated gate will be installed including active RFID and OCR technology. The first batches of stacking cranes were delivered in the autumn of 2011 and the terminal started operations in September 2012.

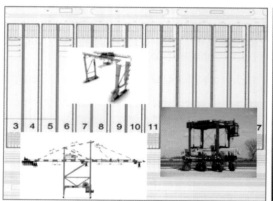

Figure 411: Khalifa automated terminal with ASCs and Sprinters

DP World Terminals Brisbane, London, Rotterdam

The experience with automated stacking cranes encouraged DP world to continue this concept for other terminals. The new Brisbane terminal is built with an automated stacking crane system (8 stack modules, each with 2 ASCs) and shuttle carriers for transportation at the waterside. But DP Worlds' London Gateway Terminal might be further automated. In the first phase there will be an automated stacking system with 19 stack modules, each 10 TEU wide and 30-39 TEU long, and each provided with 2 ASCs from Cargotec. Waterside transportation will start with Cargotec's shuttle carriers, but it could well be that these shuttle carriers will be automated in a later stage. Hence, Cargotec (Kalmar) has experience in that field with Patrick Stevedoring and moreover Cargotec has acquired FROG Systems, many years involved with navigation systems for AGVs.

For its Rotterdam World Gateway terminal (at Maasvlakte II), DP World has decided to go for an automated stacking yard and an AGV transportation system. Remarkably the stacking yard will have approximately 17 stack modules with two 10-wide ASCs per module but on top of that 9 stack modules with fully automated single cantilever ASCs, stacking 12 wide within the crane gauge (1 over 5). This allows the AGVs to further penetrate in the stacking yard, resulting in shorter ASC-cycle times and higher stacking-crane productivity. The AGVs will be battery powered for zero emission and batteries will be charged in a fully-automated high-bay battery exchange and charging station.

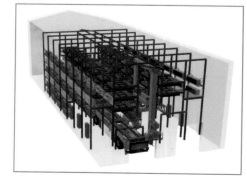

Figure 412: Automated battery exchange station

APMT Rotterdam

At Maasvlakte II, APMT is building a second terminal, with 1,000 m. deepsea quay wall and 500 m. barge/feeder quay wall in the first stage. That terminal will get an automated stacking yard with 27 stacking modules, 42 TEU long and each provided with 2 stacking cranes (ARMGs), stacking 9-wide, 1 over 5. Battery-powered lift-AGVs (Gottwald) will provide transportation at the waterside (deepsea vessels, feeders and barges) and to the rail head at the landside of the terminal Also, the handling of trucks at the landside stack end will be automatic. Only in case of irregularities a remote stacking crane control will be used. It is envisaged to install a partly automated gate and a fast truck turna-round time will be supported through a truck appointment system and electronic pre-announcement of truck arrivals. The start-up of the first stage is planned in 2014.

In the end stage this automated terminal may comprise of 2.5 km. deepsea quay wall; 0.8 km. barge/feeder quay wall; 75 stack modules, almost 100 AGVs, and an 8-track rail head. This should be sufficient to handle approximately 11 million TEU per year at the waterside (deepsea, feeder and barge).

In addition to the above automation projects coming on stream between 2012 and 2014, some more projects are in the preparation stage, but not yet decided. The following projects are known.

APMT Port of Savona (Vado Ligura)

The limited space at this port made APMT to select an automated stacking system parallel to the quay wall (see Figure 413). The projected layout shows 14 stack modules with portal cranes (stacking 7-wide within the gauge), con-nected to the quay cranes with either tractor/ trailers or shuttle carriers.

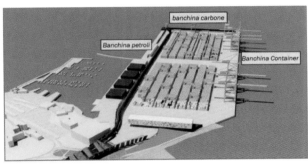

Figure 413: Terminal automation with parallel RMG stacking

Projects in the US

On the West Coast three projects around Los Angeles/Long Beach indicate that automation of more terminals (after APMT Virginia) is seriously considered in the US. The Long Beach Container Termi-nal seems to be designed with an automated stacking system (about 27 modules perpendicular on the quay wall), with two ARMGs per module and AGVs for the waterside transportation.

Also APL (LA) is planning an automated stacking system with AGVs for transportation. However there might be an intermediate handling with fast cranes, swapping containers between public truck-ing and the terminals' AGVs. Another terminal upgrade in Los Angeles, the Trapac Terminal (parent company Mitsui OSK Lines) has committed itself to redesign the berth 136-147 facility into a state-of-the-art terminal, complying with the clean air program and focused on a low environmental impact. Some conceptual designs indicate in the direction of a partly automated terminal with rail mounted stacking cranes, but in the first stage both transportation and stacking will be realized with AutoStrads.

For their Oakland terminal, Ports of America has issued tenders for a cassette based transportation system connecting the quay operations with an automated stacking system with rail mounted gan-tries.

For the redesign of the Global Terminal in New York an automated stacking system with stack modules perpendicular on the quay wall is projected. The transportation system seems to remain a manually operated shuttle carrier system.

The terminal automation projects nowadays in progress clearly show that only a few terminals have decided to go for full automation (yard, transportation and gate). But the developments outside of Europe indicate an increasing interest in terminal automation worldwide.

IN RETROSPECT

The introduction of automation was driven by the vision of a few people believing in the advantages of automated operations and was enabled through standardized cargo and procedures and technology. During two decades, many concepts for automated handling were developed and presented, but only a few entered the prototype stage. The management of the handful fully-automated terminals (stacking and transportation) learned that the realization of this type (and size) of projects is not only a matter of design and purchasing the systems but also includes risk management, problem solving (teething problems), changes in operations control, training and attention for performance improvements.

Terminal automation requires a sound logistic concept with dedicated equipment (modified from standard equipment) and control software. That explains why all larger automation projects were established at greenfield sites. Step by step automation in existing terminals was up till now limited to automation of the stacking yard with remote control for handling and interchange activities.

Unfortunately, all of the automation projects suffered from long start-up learning curves and (almost equal) teething problems. In spite of rather similar functionalities for automated stacking, (partly-)automated transport and logistics control, the projects were realized with many different vendors and equipment types with everybody inventing the automation wheel again.

Most of the presented innovative handling concepts were technically realizable but not suited for the logistic demands, such as the ability for high peak loads, flexibility and a high average performance simultaneously at the waterside and landside. Moreover, the installation of a completely new concept (investment probably > 500 million US Dollar) including new one-of-a-kind equipment is a too large risk both for operators, shipping lines and bankers.

Built-in buffer techniques (2nd trolley platform, WS interchange and vehicle buffers at the apron) proved to be helpful in smoothing the process and increasing equipment utilization when pooling.

The individual logistic nature of a container still hampered the feasibility of continuous transport concepts (like the container conveyor); it is doubtful whether the conversion from unit load handling to continuous flows (as suggested in the past by some vendors) is feasible for automated container transportation. It was learned, that the implementation of automation in container terminal handling required more effort than a conventional manual system. However, once installed and properly running, it takes less energy to train people in equipment driving, damages are greatly reduced and it is easier to maintain or even improve a steady service performance.

Terminal automation is under way for already two decades however, the speed of transition to automation may accelerate, as indicated by the many projects, in progress and announced. The success of such automated concepts will highly depend on the proper selection of reliable systems and equipment but above all on the dedication of a knowledgeable project team, with a drive to balance all disciplines (civil, equipment, IT, operations), required for a good performing automated terminal.

CHAPTER 14

TIME FOR A BREAK
2006 - Present

The previous period showed mergers, massive takeovers and a reshuffling of alliances. From 2002 on, the extra demand for container shipping exceeded 10% annually. Shipping lines reacted by ordering large volumes of additional TEU capacity. Ship sizes increased rapidly, with Maersk Line in the driver's seat. However, MSC, CMA CGM and the Chinese shipping lines followed suit and Korean shipyards operated near full capacity. Container liner shipping seemed to sail towards a bright future.

Yet, economic developments were less predictable than expected. The demand in container shipping depended on economic growth with a cyclical character. Since newbuildings were often ordered during an upswing and delivered during a downturn, new containerships often put downward pressure on freight rates. To remain profitable, shipping lines lowered their operational costs by slow steaming and rerouting, whereas scrapping, laying idle and postponing newbuildings also reduced capacity. But was it enough?

14.1. SHIP DEVELOPMENT

Ship size

From 2003 on, the demand of shipping lines for TEU capacity had soared and even when the economic downturn started in 2005 the ordering of newbuildings stabilized at an all-time high. Therefore, a large number of new containerships were delivered at the start of this period. At that time, the 9,178-TEU MSC Pamela-class vessels were officially the biggest containerships and the only ones with a beam of 45.6 m. In February 2006, a longer (350.6 m.) but less wide (42.8 m.) containership, the 9,469-

Figure 414: COSCO Guangzhou meeting COSCO Yantian

TEU *COSCO Guangzhou*, became the new record holder. Also, in another respect a record was broken. At the Hyundai shipyard the first diesel engine to exceed the 100,000-bhp, a 74,760-kw MAN B&W 12K98MC, was installed. A few months later, China Shipping Container Lines' 9,580-TEU *Xin Los Angeles* surpassed the *COSCO Guangzhou*, with a beam of 45.6 m. and a length over all of 336.7 m.

Once again, Maersk Line made a quantum leap in ship size with a series of eight containerships: 397.7 m. long, 56.6 m. beam and a maximum draft of 15.5 m. These vessels were designed with double hull and double bottom technology and had an improved hull form, which increased the cargo capacity and decreased the water resistance during operations. Officially the 170.794-grt/156,907-dwt *Emma*

Maersk could carry 11,000 EU (if all containers are full). According to the standard method of defining capacity, they could carry 14,770 TEU. In May 2010, the *Ebba Maersk* set a class record of 15,011 TEU in Tangiers. On the Maersk Line website their capacity is now listed as 15,550 TEU.

The *Emma Maersk* was launched at the company's Odense Steel Shipyard on 18 May 2006. Welding work during construction caused a fire within her superstructure that spread rapidly through the accommodation section and bridge. In order to reduce the delay the accommodation block was removed and the nearly completed superstructure of the *Estelle Maersk* was lifted onto the *Emma Maersk* instead. The *Emma Maersk* was named after the late wife of Maersk's chairman Arnold Mærsk Mc-Kinney Møller who died in April 2012 at the age of 98. The vessel was christened by their daughter on 12 August 2006 and set sail to the Far East on 8 September.

Figure 415: The Christening of Emma Maersk

The eight Emma Maersk-class (also referred to as PS-class vessels) were equipped with the new 80,000-kw 14 cylinder Wärtsilä-Sulzer common-rail diesel engines. This engine stands at 13.5 m. high, is 27.3 long, weighs over 2300 tons and is currently the world's largest single diesel unit. These engines enable a service speed of 25.5 knots. For maximum performance the engine needs 14,000 liters of heavy fuel per hour. In order to save costs the service speed was lowered, so-called slow steaming. This raised some concern about sufficient cooling of the engine, however, to no avail.

Exhaust heat recovery is used to improve economy and lower emissions; internal funnels capture the waste heat and use it to drive two turbines which exert extra power onto the 130-ton propeller. Maersk stated that this technique cuts fuel consumption by about 10%.

Other environmental friendly features included an extra slippery silicon paint on the giant hull and the use of water for cooling reefers (container ID prefix: MWCU=Maersk Water Cooled Unit). In the year 2007 the *Emma Maersk* was the recipient of the prestigious Lloyd's List Ship of the Year-award for being carried out in an environmentally and ecologically sound manner.

However, the *Emma Maersk* as well as other ships has been criticized for burning cheap bunker fuel with a sulfur content of 2.5 to 4.5 percent except for designated Sulphur Emission Control Areas (SECAs) where a maximum sulfur content of only 1% is allowed since July 2010.

The Emma Maersk-class containerships will not be able to use the new locks in the Panama Canal. The Panama Canal expansion project will create a new lane of traffic along the canal by constructing two new lock complexes with three chambers, one each on the Atlantic and Pacific sides. New access channels will be exca-

Figure 416: Estelle Maersk on her maiden voyage

vated and existing channels will be widened and deepened. Finally, the water level of Gatun Lake will be raised by 0.46 m. The new lock chambers are 427 m. long, 55 m. wide and 18.3 m. deep. Contrary to the existing procedure with small locomotives, tugs will be used to position the ships in the locks. This explains the large difference between the locks and maximum dimensions of vessels; the so-called New-Panamax containerships are subject to the following maximum dimensions: 366 m. LOA x 49 m. beam x 15.2 m. draft in tropical fresh water (TFW). The new canal is scheduled for completion in 2014, exactly 100 years after opening, and will be fully operational in 2015.

It took some time before the first vessels built according to the New-Panamax dimensions, were launched. CMA CGM and MSC had containerships built that matched the New-Panamax dimensions in length but the beam was one row of containers smaller. The first vessels that fully complied with the new limits were Maersk's 13,092 TEU containerships. On 2 July 2010, four of these vessels were christened at the Hyundai Heavy Industries' Ulsan shipyard. Containers are carried 17-wide below deck and 19-wide on the hatch covers. In the eight vessels owned by the Rickmers Group, 68,640-kw Hyundai-Wärtsilä 12RT-flex 96C engines were installed that enabled a service speed of 24.3 knots. The five containerships chartered from Zodiac Maritime had equally powerful MAN-B&W 12K98ME engines but their service speed was significantly higher: 25.8 knots.

Shipping lines MSC and CMA CGM soon followed with their 12,562-TEU New-Panamax vessels, built by Samsung. Meanwhile the three Korean shipbuilding companies have delivered quite a few of these vessels to various shipping lines.

An interesting design feature of the New-Panamax containerships is the separation between the engine room and the deckhouse. The latter's position in the forward part of the ship permits an increase in container capacity due to a better visibility from the bridge, and a reduction in ballast water. The *MSC Daniela* was probably the first containership with this characteristic. This vessel was ordered in July 2006 and delivered by Samsung's Geoje Shipyard at the end of 2008. With an overall length of 366.1 m., a beam of 51.2 m. and a draft of 15.0 m., the 156,301-dwt *MSC Daniela* could carry 13,798

Figure 417: New-Panamax containership Al Riffa of the UASC

TEU and was one of the largest containerships in the world. Nowadays the superstructure of containerships with a capacity over 12,500 TEU, is mostly located forward of amidships.

Quite remarkably, the ultimate 5,300 TEU Panamax containership also has a deckhouse that is not fitted on top of the ship's engine room but in a more forward position (see Figure 418).

The restrictions for New-Panamax vessels are not applicable for containerships deployed in the Far East-Europe trade. Shipping lines heavily involved in this trade took delivery of approximately 366 m. long containerships with a beam of around 51 m. The *MSC Danit* built by

Figure 418: Panamax containership CSAV Recife

Daewoo and commissioned in 2009 was 365.5 m. long and had a beam of 51.2 m. and draft of 16.0 m. The service speed amounts to 24.1 knots. The seventeen(!) 165,517-dwt vessels of this series can carry up to 14,000 TEU. The five CMA CGM's Christophe Colomb-class containerships bear a close resemblance to the MSC vessels but have a stronger 14 cylinder engine. China Shipping Container Lines ordered eight containerships at Samsung's, the *CSCL Star* and sister ships could carry over 14,000 TEU (see Figure 423). Other Asian shipping lines currently stick to the New-Panamax dimensions, thus emphasizing the importance of the US market.

The next increase in size will be the *CMA CGM Marco Polo* which maiden voyage starts in Shanghai on 3 November 2012. With an overall length of 395 m., beam of 54 m. and a draft of 16 m., this containership can carry approximately 16,000 TEU. This series of three vessels is actually an enlarged version of an existing design. With their 21 rows of containers on deck they can call at all major ports between Asia and Northern Europe without modifying the existing port infrastructure.

In February 2011, Maersk announced orders for a new class of containerships: Triple-E (Economy of scale, Energy efficient and Environmentally improved). The vessels will be 400 m. long and 59 m. wide. The draft of (only) 14.5 m. is less than the Suezmax requirement of 16.0 m. The Triple-E-class is only 3 m. longer and 3 m. wider than the Emma Maersk-class. This allows an additional row of containers, but can carry approximately 18,300 TEU, an increase of 16%. This is enhanced by the U-shaped hull and a deckhouse that is located further forward.

Speed plays an important role in energy efficiency. This class has a so-called 'twin skeg' propulsion system. Two 32,000-kw ultra-long two-stroke diesel engines are installed, each driving (at 80 rpm) a separate propeller at a design speed of 19 knots. The top speed would still be 23 knots but steaming at 20 knots reduces fuel consumption by 37%, and at 17.5 knots fuel consumption would be halved. However, slower speeds would add several days to journey times on the Far East-Europe route, and 19 knots is considered the optimum speed.

Ultra-long two-stroke diesel engines were mostly used for tankers and bulk carriers. These engines have lower specific fuel consumption than the short-stroke engine types, which will reduce fuel consumption and greenhouse gasses. State-of-the-art environmental features including a waste heat recovery system are estimated to cost US$ 30 million per ship. The Triple-E containership is supposed to emit 20% less carbon dioxide per container than the Emma Maersk-class vessels.

Moreover, all the materials used to construct the Triple-E-class ships are recorded in the vessel's "cradle-to-cradle passport". At the time the vessels are retired from service, materials can be put to good use through recycling or, if required, correctly be disposed. These actions will be carried out under safe and controllable conditions, and in the most effective manner.

The Triple-E-class containerships are being built at the Daewoo shipyard. The initial order for ten ships was valued at US$ 1.9 billion. Maersk had options to buy a further twenty ships. In June 2011, Maersk announced that ten more ships had been ordered but an option for a third series of ten ships was not lifted. The first ten vessels will be delivered in 2013 and 2014; the second series of vessels is scheduled for completion in 2014 and 2015. The impact to ports and rates was heavily discussed, but during the year 2011 already a substantial number

Figure 419: Artist impression of theTriple-E-class (source: Maersk)

of ports assured sufficient cranes with large enough outreach to accommodate this type of vessels (the 23-wide containers on deck require an outreach of at least 60 m. from fender side). Nevertheless a service demand from Maersk for 5,000 lifts in 24 hours will be a challenge for many terminals.

Other developments

In the year 2006/2007, Maersk Line launched seven B-class containerships specifically designed for high-speed transportation between China and the US West Coast and East Coast. They were built by the German Volkswerft Stralsund GmbH. The 4,100-TEU *Maersk Boston*, the first vessel to be launched, was 294 m. long, had a beam of 32 m. and a draft of 13 m. A twelve-cylinder, 50,485-kW engine enabled a service speed of 29.2 knots. During trials the *Maersk Beaumont* reached a top speed of 32 knots. To achieve this speed the hull form is very fine and the only space where a large engine fits is in the mid-body of the vessel. Their fuel consumption of 300 tons per day makes them vulnerable for high fuel prices and shippers are apparently not willing to pay more for a fast container service. Although, reducing the operating speed to 12 knots was an option (with a fuel consumption of 50 tons per day), other vessels were more economical to operate. Five B-class containerships were laid up in Loch Striven on the Clyde in Scotland (some months together with one former US Lines Econship) and the remaining vessels at Laem Chabang in Thailand. After ten months, Maersk Boston left Loch Striven on 11 June 2010. The vessels are not deployed in their initial service anymore.

Other shipping lines also ordered fast containerships. Mid-2006, Hanjin took delivery of eight 6,655 TEU Bremerhaven-class vessels that had a service speed 26.5 knots. In January 2008 the first of eight 8,562-TEU Hyundai vessels was commissioned. These containerships were equipped with a 14-cylinder engine that provided a service speed of 27 knots.

The economic recession in the late 2000s caused a growing concern about the cost to operate vessels at average speeds of 22 knots or more.

Figure 420: Maersk B-class vessels laid up in Loch Striven

Especially when bunker prices exceeded US$ 500 per ton the trade-off with the slightly reduced sailing time was debatable.

14.2. CONTAINER LINER SHIPPING BUSINESS

2005 had been a year with a growth of 10.6% in demand for TEU capacity, perfectly matched by the actual increase of the container fleet. From 2002 on, the extra demand for container shipping had exceeded 10% annually and between 2005 and 2009 the orders for additional TEU vessel capacity were also over 10% of the existing fleet. To put this in perspective, as of January 2007 all containerships on order amounted to 4.36 million TEU, which was nearly half of the existing fleet at that time.

In due course the increase in TEU capacity began to outpace the growth in demand. In 2006, the Transpacific trade was still the biggest by volume, but was surpassed by the Asia-Europe trade in 2007 when the growth rate between Asia and the US was around 3% compared to 15.5% in the Asia-Europe trade. The next year, the absolute decrease in demand was in the Transpacific significantly higher than in the also deteriorating Asia-Europe trade. Freight rates showed a different pattern. The Transpacific trade had low rates in 2006, picking up in 2007 and staying high until the last quarter of 2008. In the Asia-Europe trade freight rates started to rise earlier (second part of 2006) but declined sooner (start of 2008). Increased competition due to the deployment of new 10,000+ TEU containerships of MSC, CMA CGM (see Figure 421), Maersk and Cosco could be an explanation. In order to cut fuel costs many shipping lines adopted a policy of slow steaming. As a consequence extra vessels were needed which reduced overcapacity.

Sometimes containerships were rerouted via Cape of Good Hoop in order to avoid the tolls for the Suez Canal; around US$ 600,000 for large vessels. Moreover, the pirate hotspot near Somalia was left aside.

Whereas 2007 had been a good year for shipping lines, the year 2008 showed reduced profits. In September the financial shake-up slowed down the economic growth, especially in the US and Europe. At the same time shipping lines were confronted with fast rising fuel cost: bunker prices touched US$ 700 per ton in July 2008 and surprisingly came down to US$ 200 at

Figure 421: CMA CGM Thalassa in Zeebrugge

the year end. During the last quarter, freight rates dropped substantially and service frequencies and rotations were reduced to adjust capacity to the decreased trade volumes. Consequently, profits were much lower although in general still in the black. The change in economic climate caused NOL to withdraw their bid for Hapag-Lloyd, which allowed the Hamburg-based Albert Ballin consortium to acquire the majority stake put up for sale by parent company TUI. In Rotterdam the port expansion program was under discussion for a short while, but the works for the Maasvlakte 2 port expansion officially started in September 2008. At the end of the year, around 500,000-TEU vessel capacity (>200 vessels) were laid up. The published operating fleet capacity was 12.4 million TEU and the order book comprised 6.3 million TEU.

Decreasing container volumes and falling freight rates continued at an even higher pace in 2009. The TEU volume from Asia to Europe contracted by 14.8%, whereas in the past an annual growth rate of about 20% was common. Trade on the transpacific route (eastbound) declined by 14.2%. Even the less important Transatlantic trades slumped; eastbound by 20.1% and westbound by 25.1%. Total trade volumes in 2009 reached an estimated 124 million TEU, down from 137 million TEU in 2008. These developments put pressure on the already decreasing freight rates (sometimes more than 30%). Many carriers restructured their services; two carriers (China Shipping and Hanjin) withdrew services completely and lost their status as global carrier. Several shipping lines started to downsize their fleet by returning chartered vessels to their owners and laying up others. By November 2009, the total number of idle vessels was 551, representing a combined capacity of 1.18 million TEU. Moreover, there were over a hundred cancellations of earlier-ordered vessels; quite a number of these orders were converted into bulk carriers and old tonnage was sold to ship breakers. For example, Evergreen got rid of its 31 G/GL/GX-class containerships, built between 1983 and 1988, and so reduced its TEU capacity in 2009 by 5.9%. Subsequently, the losses per TEU were moderate compared to other shipping lines. Albeit 3% of the existing container capacity was scrapped in 2009, total TEU capacity was 4.9% higher partly due to the arrival of a large number of approximately 14,000 TEU newbuildings such as Samsung-built *CMA CGM Christophe Colomb* and *MSC Daniela*, and the slightly larger *MSC Danit* from Daewoo. Certainly, the reduced increase of new tonnage and capacity reduction measures helped to turn around the negative trend in freight rates at the end of the year but still, the collective financial loss for the top 30 shipping lines was estimated to be US$ 19.4 billion, from a reported US$ 5 billion profit the year before. Orders for newbuildings obviously decreased, but those who ordered new vessels could benefit from attractive prices, lower than US$ 13,000 per TEU ship capacity.

In 2010, global container trade volumes bounced back at 12.9% over the figure of 2009. In the Transatlantic and Asia-Europe trade the container flows returned, more or less, to their 2009 levels whereas the TEU volumes on the transpacific route were significantly higher. Robust growth also occurred on the North-South trades e.g. Europe to South/Central America and non-main lane East-West trades. In these trades reefer containers were increasingly penetrating in the conventional reefer vessel services. A number of container shipping lines introduced vessels with a high reefer capacity (often more than 1,000 reefer plugs on board). The frontrunners Maersk and Hamburg Süd were getting more competition from Evergreen, Hanjin, UASC and others.

The container sector was caught by surprise and, among others, not enough (empty) containers were available. This triggered the US Federal Maritime Commission to investigate the (non-)availability of supply capacity on the transpacific trade. Although no signs of foul play were found, the Alliances, the Transpacific Stabilization Agreement and the Westbound Transpacific Stabilization Agreement now have to report changes in overall capacity on a monthly basis. The shortage of containers resulted in a return to a healthy container building program for the next year.

The year 2010 saw 260 newly built vessels delivered including the first 13,100-TEU New-Panamax containerships. In TEU capacity, the container fleet increased by 8.7%. For the first time since 2005, growth in supply was below the growth of demand in container shipping. Freight rates soared and reached an all-time high in early 2010. On average they were 78% over the 2009 level. Due to the brighter outlook, the ordering of new vessels took up again and the order book at the end of 2010 stood at 3.8 million TEU. Besides the increasing demand and restricted supply in the global container trade, shipping lines also benefitted from a fall (up to 30%) in fuel prices. In 2010, the top 30 companies made a total profit of US$ 17 billion.

The rollercoaster ride of trade growth, freight rates, profits and losses continued in 2011. At the start of the year expectations rode high but by the third quarter most shipping lines reported losses. A disappointing, nearly 8% increase of demand and a destructive fight for market share due to overcapacity put pressure on freight rates. Actually, rates on the Asia-Europe route had already started to drop in the third quarter of 2010. Redeployment of large containerships spread the problem of overcapacity to other trade lanes. Throughout 2011, 188 containerships encompassing 47 10,000+ TEU vessels, with a total capacity of 1,230,000 TEU, were launched. This resulted in a worldwide vessel fleet of 270 vessels with a 10,000+ TEU capacity, totaling over 3.5 million TEU. To fill all these vessels shipping lines lowered their freight rates. Due to high fuel prices (bunker prices reached again US$ 650-700 per ton at the end of the year), containers were even transported below cost levels. Although most shipping lines carried more containers in 2011, the financial results for 16 of the top 20 shipping lines indicated an average loss of US$ 102 per TEU (against a profit of US$ 149/TEU in 2010). For the first 9 months the Chinese Cosco group and Chilean CSAV were the unfortunate top scorers with losses of US$ 752 million and US$ 859 million respectively. And again by early December 2011, almost 3% of the existing TEU fleet capacity was laid up or was idle otherwise. While shipping lines saw their revenues per TEU fall in 2011, forwarders such as Kühne & Nagel and Panalpina, increased their TEU revenues up to 8.5%.

Amazingly, 2011 saw the ordering of 240 containerships (equal to 1,770,000 TEU), including twenty of Maersk's 18,300-TEU Triple-E-class vessels. Only the Malaysia International Shipping Corporation (MISC Berhad) announced its withdrawal from the container liner business, by June 2012, after already having left the Asia-Europe trade to focus on an Intra-Asian model. The company had considerable doubts about earning back its investments in "a depressed freight rate environment, which was not expected to improve any time soon" (press release 24 November 2011).

At the end of 2011, Alexander & Baldwin (the owners of Matson and more) was split into two separate companies: one for the real estate and agricultural business; the other one Matson with two operating arms: Matson Navigation Company Inc. and Matson Logistics Inc. The Matson assets comprised of 17 container vessels; 47,000 containers and a 35% interest in the terminals of SSA (Stevedoring Services of America). In the present perspectives quite a moderate number of assets, considering the pioneering and innovative role, Matson played in the first two decades of containerization.

Figure 422: MISC's Bunga Mas 9 near Singapore

Some shipping lines attracted new financial resources. The Turkish Yildirim Group, for example, bought at a cost of US$ 500 million 20% of CMA CGM and acquired three out of ten seats on the board. Soon, the influence of Turkish businessman Robert Yildirim became apparent when he vetoed a proposed order for up to twenty 10,000 TEU containerships. Instead CMA CGM takes delivery of three 16,000-TEU containerships in 2012.

The ever-falling freight rates on the Asia-Europe route made Maersk look for new opportunities. "Daily Maersk" was introduced on the Asia-North Europe trade lane with ships departing at the same time seven (later six) days a week, and arriving daily at the same time at the four Asian ports of Ningbo, Shanghai, Shenzhen-Yantian and Tanjung Pelepas, and at the three European ports of Felixstowe, Rotterdam and Bremerhaven. The new service, operated by seventy 8,500-15,000-TEU vessels totaling 57,000 TEU weekly, started 24 October 2011.

The "Daily Maersk" scheme came with a money back guarantee: US$ 100 per container if consignments were delayed three days and US$ 300 per box if delayed four days or more. But when containers to be shipped on the Asia-North Europe trade are late, and in fact 44% is, a no-show fee from shippers who book space and fail to deliver was considered. The reliable "conveyor belt" service boosted Maersk's Asia-Europe market share to an all-time high of 19.4% by the end of 2011.

Figure 423: China Shipping's 14,300-TEU CSCL Star (courtesy Frans Waals)

Other shipping lines joined forces to compete with "Daily Maersk". The Grand Alliance (Hapag-Lloyd, NYK and OOCL) and the New World Alliance (APL, Hyundai and MOL) set up the G6 Alliance to operate six joint services from the Far East to North Europe and two to the Mediterranean. CKYH-the Green Alliance (Cosco, K Line, Yang Ming and Hanjin) and Evergreen exchange slots in eight North European and five Mediterranean loops. China Shipping Container Line and Cosco share space in three North European services as well as three Mediterranean services. Finally, CMA CGM and MSC (short: CCMSC) share ships and slots not only to/from the North European and Mediterranean regions but also to South Africa and Latin America. This new partnership (sometimes called DRA, the Diego (Aponte) and Rodolpho (Saadé) Alliance), brought together almost 90 vessels in the 10,000-17,000 TEU range. On the three main routes the CCMSC consortium could potentially match Maersk Line, which further distanced the top three shipping lines from their competitors. At the end of 2011 Maersk Line had a 16% share in the world container fleet, MSC 13% and CMA CGM 8%. And again, the recovered shipping market forced shipping lines to provide containers to their customers. However most of them were unable to raise funds for new containers. So, the container lease companies did good business: daily rates returned to US$ 1.10 per day per 20-ft box. Newbuilding prices for 20-ft dry containers reached to 2,800 US$ and even more. For years, they were around US$ 2,000.

Effective as of 1 March 2012, shipping lines raised their rates with US$ 600 to US$ 900 per TEU. Mid-February the Asia-North Europe spot rates were US$ 711/TEU according to the Shanghai Containerized Freight Index (SCFI). The new rates were close to the average Shanghai-North Europe spot rate of US$ 1,340 in January 2011 but lower than US$ 1,900 in mid-2010. At the end of June 2012, another rate increase of US$ 339 per TEU was imposed. However, within two weeks rates came down by US$ 141 per TEU. Yet, US$ 1,747 per TEU is quite an achievement in a very competitive market.

As from October 2008, following the repeal of Regulation 4056/86, shipping conferences are strictly prohibited in the EU but the 2010 version of Block Exemption Regulation 823/2000 allows groupings that not exceed 30% of the overall annualized capacity. After establishing the new consortia, only Green Alliance member Cosco that has a slot swap with China Shipping Container Lines 'controlled' 31% of the trade. Also the large number of 10,000+ TEU containerships ultimately available for the CCMSC consortium may enhance a (too) dominant position. Should the European Commission find evidence of infringement of competition laws, fines will be substantial.

In the US, liner shipping groupings are exempted from antitrust due to the Ocean Shipping Reform Act. The Federal Maritime Commission (FMC), the relevant regulatory body, actively watches the rules.

The Global Shippers' Forum and, in particular, national member organizations will also safeguard the interests of shippers engaged in international trade. In the 1990s, they were successful against the Trans-Atlantic Conference Agreement (TACA).

IN RETROSPECT

This period explicitly showed the cyclical nature of the container liner shipping industry. Business cycles are characterized by economic upturns followed by economic downturns; in 2008 a severe and prolonged recession. The sudden and huge increase in demand for container shipping in 2010 is still difficult to explain.

Since shipping lines are focused on (predicted) economic developments, ordering of additional TEU capacity often occurs in periods with economic growth and increased demand for container shipping but newbuildings are frequently delivered when the economic tide is low. From 2006 to 2009 the increase of supply in container shipping exceeded the growth of demand although shipyard deliveries in 2009 were adjusted downwards. The year 2010 sent a wrong signal to the shipping lines, many of them ordering large numbers of 10,000+ TEU vessels, which put pressure on freight rates and profits. In order to cope with these developments, especially in the Asia-Europe trade, new consortia were formed. However, the cooperation between CMA CGM and MSC (CCMSC) had a more global nature.

The first aim of these consortia, raising freight rates, was obtained; the increased rate level allowed for a (small) profit. However, cooperation is put under strain when new TEU tonnage enters the market and demand for container shipping is hardly growing. Lowering freight rates to fill the large containerships seems obvious from the perspective of a single shipping line, but will prove disastrous for the entire sector. Shipping lines such as Evergreen and OOCL showed in 2009 that reducing TEU capacity could be the best strategy. Therefore, the negative spiral of overcapacity and low rates needs to be breached. It is time for a break.

CHAPTER 15

OUTLOOK ON THE FUTURE
Continuous improvements or new breakthroughs??

The previous chapters described the history of containerization and the subsequent massive developments realized in shipping, ports, terminals and inland transportation. However, those were the past and the present. Obviously, stakeholders in containerized transport would like to know what developments may be expected in the coming decades. Such a forecast is risky, because when you are wrong nobody will forget, but when you are right nobody will remember (Josh Billings, US journalist 1818-1885). Nevertheless, as we learned so much from the past here we present our outlook on the future, which probably will show much more than we can imagine now.

15.1. VOLUME DEVELOPMENT

Globalization is still going on and especially the development of China into the world's workshop has led to a doubling of worldwide container handlings within only one decade, from 300 million TEU in 2003 to approximately 600 million TEU in 2012! This growth will not end in the coming decades. In general, trade volume increases twice as fast as economic growth and as long as wealth improves, trade will continue to grow. Especially when transport costs remain relatively low, the shipment of low revenue commodities (waste paper, hay, recycled plastics, etc.) will be maintained. This always happens at the thin leg of imbalanced trade routes. The existence of (very) low labor cost areas will encourage manufacturers (traders) to ship large volumes of components, semi-finished products and consumer goods all over the world, as long as the transportation cost do not offset the cost savings.

However, it is questionable what will happen when the standard of living (and thus labor cost) in China, India and some other Far Eastern countries has increased and the transportation costs are rising due to increasing costs for energy, labor, scarce materials, etc.

Also the increasing unemployment in countries from the "old world" (Europe and US) may change the strategy of outsourcing labor intensive manufacturing to low labor cost areas. These long term developments (50-100 years) may balance worldwide transport volumes.

On the other hand a number of (scarce) raw materials will remain to be unequally spread over the world. The drive for development in the countries where such raw materials are mined will encourage such countries to install industrial activities directly connected to the availability of these raw materials (bauxite, limestone, oil and gas, metal ores, etc.). Nowadays such trends can already be recognized in the Middle East, Brazil, South Africa, Chili, etc. This will result in a shift from the transportation of raw materials in large bulk vessels towards the shipment of semi-finished products and base commodities either in specially designed vessels (see Stora-Enso) or as containerized cargo.

Thus the future volume developments seem rather unpredictable, however, in general, they can be estimated with the following relation of parameters:

Future volume of port handlings = Present volume x Population index x World purchasing power parity index x Ratio transportation growth/economic growth.

The population index for the next 50 years is approximately 1.5. The world population at present is approximately 7 billion people and may reach 10.5 billion people around 2050 (based on a medium-fertility scenario). See Figure 424, showing UN population projections for the world and major regions, such as Africa and the Far East.

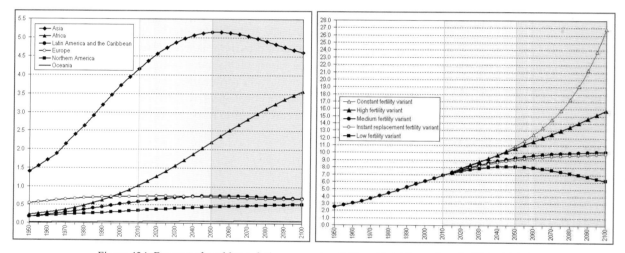

Figure 424: Forecast of world population; per region (left) and total for various fertilities (right)

The world's purchasing power parity growth (equals wealth growth) has been impressive over the last 50 years (between 200 and 500%). Considering a stabilizing wealth in the rich countries, it is plausible to assume a world purchasing power parity growth of 75%. When looking to the tremendous growth in China over the last 25 years and looking to the potential of India with a population growing to more than 1.5 billion people, this figure could easily stay around 200% but we took a moderate approach with 75% growth and thus a 1.75 index.

Over the last 25 years the growth rate in containerized trade has been twice the average economic growth rate. But, the impact of increasing energy cost on transportation cost and a slowdown in production diverging to low labor cost countries may decrease this ratio to about 1.5.

The above parameter development assumptions will result in:

Container handlings in 2050 = 600 million TEU (present) x 1.5 (population growth) x 1.75 (wealth growth) x 1.5 (transportation/economic growth ratio) = 2500 million TEU in 2050.

It should be noted that this volume reflects handlings in ports worldwide. The full container trade (in shipments) may be 600 million TEU. During the last decade the number of port handlings is consistently 4 times larger than the number of full container shipments, explained by the seagoing voyage (2 handlings per trip) and additional handlings for connecting feeder transport and the repositioning of empty containers. A worldwide 4-fold growth in containerized volume by the year 2050 is imaginable however, not equal for every region. Europe and the US will grow much more moderate or even stabilize, as the world's growth is expected to be in the BRIC countries, Vietnam, Indonesia and of course the African continent that may show a 3-fold population growth (see Figure 424). Preparing for this tremendous growth is a challenge both for the realization of sufficient infrastructure and for organizations responsible for the inland drayage of such massive volumes of containers.

15.2. SHIPPING AND VESSEL DEVELOPMENTS

The forecasted tremendous volume growth will only partly be realized at the major existing trade routes. A large contribution will come from new services connecting new (enlarged) production and consumption regions. Major port expansion programs in the Americas, Africa and the Far East will allow the application of larger vessels (even larger than 10,000 TEU) in services so far operated with vessels of Panamax size (< 5,000 TEU). Gradually, draft limitations will be reduced through port expansion programs and the realization of new (hub) ports at better accessible locations.

Recent port developments in China, India and Vietnam and especially port expansion programs along the African coast learn that shipping patterns increasingly tend towards multi-port vessel rotations (schedules) with 15-20 ports of call. Concentration of traffic flows by means of a Hub-and-Spoke system is less attractive for regions where the population is living in coastal areas. In such regions it will be attractive to serve a number of ports, each with their own hinterland of 5-25 million people. A limitation to only one or two main ports would result in large, expensive inland traffic flows and/or feeder operations.

In 2011, Maersk surprised the shipping world with their announcement to order ten 18,300-TEU vessels, later extended to a total of twenty vessels. The published vessel design for the Triple-E-class vessels (Triple-E=Environmental effective, Energy efficient, Economies of scale) showed a full body with 23 containers across on deck, an aft engine room with two diesels, each connecting a 9.4 m. diameter propeller (see Figure 425). The indicated capacity of 18,300 TEU and the proposed cruising speed of 19 knots (maximum 23 knots) explained the order size of 2x10 vessels (10 in one Far East-Europe loop) and showed Maersk Line's policy to aspire to cost leadership (not so easy with "lean and mean" competitors like MSC and CMA CGM).

Figure 425: Maersk Triple-E-class: The end of the range?

Comparing this Maersk Triple-E vessel design with the much earlier published Malacca Max (Wijnolst, Scholtens and Waals, 1999), makes clear that a further vessel enlargement might be feasible in the future.

From an energy and environment point of view, it will make sense to maintain a moderate speed (18-20 knots). It is plausible that shippers will accept a somewhat longer sea voyage time, as long as the overall door-to-door time remains the same (through controlled port dwell times and short intermodal connecting times) and transportation costs remain attractive. Besides, more frequent sailings (e.g. "Daily Maersk") also reduce connection times.

From a technology point of view vessel sizes up to 30,000 TEU can be developed, however restrictions in vessel length (turning basin) and limited deployment areas may cause reluctance for investments in these vessels, especially as the world's trade flows may change in the next 20-50 years. The dimensions of the New Panama Canal locks have set a New-Panamax vessel size (366 m. length, 49 m. beam width and 15.2 m. draft) which may support the 10,000-13,000 TEU vessel size to become the universal workhorse all over the world. This assumption coincides with a recent Maersk decision to enlarge their fleet of S-class vessels. Smaller shipping lines will be encouraged to form alliances in combined services, allowing such 10,000-13,000 TEU vessels. It could well be that 20,000+ TEU-class vessels will only be deployed by four to eight large shipping lines, mainly operating in alliances.

Reduction of operating cost per TEU will remain a key issue encouraging shipowners and ship designers to find a balance between cruising speed, vessel size and type of propulsion. Energy consumption and environmental impact will become increasingly important. Worldwide demands for reduced sulfur and CO_2 emissions will stimulate the application of more environmentally friendly fuels. The application of dual fuel engines (LNG/HFO) will increase although the limited number of LNG bunker facilities may raise restrictions.

The development of vessel propulsion based on renewable energy has started and the first designs have already been presented (see Figure 426).

Figure 426: Future vessel propulsion: LNG (left) and renewable energy sources (right)

Fuel cost developments and worldwide environmental directives will determine whether these new (and more expensive) technologies will be applied in the next two decades. Vessel life time, cost and a traditionally conservative shipping world will maintain diesel engines as the dominant propulsion for container vessels in the next decades.

15.3. PORTS AND TERMINAL FACILITIES

Doubtlessly, ports and terminals will be enlarged to accommodate the larger vessels and the 2-5 fold increased yearly volumes. Hundreds of ports will handle more than 2 million TEU per year but some ports, or better said port conglomerates, will grow beyond 25 million TEU/year (e.g. Shanghai, Pusan, Los Angeles/Long Beach, Rotterdam, Singapore, Hong Kong and Shenzhen), but these volumes will be spread over a number of terminals, each handling 5-10 million TEU/year. Such terminals will have 1.5-5 km of quay wall length and 100-300 hectares for the storage of containers and related services (MT depot, M&R, etc.). Scarcity of land will put stronger demands on better area utilization and such requirements will be reflected in lease and concession contracts. Objectives for yearly utilization rates will be 4,000 TEU/meter quay wall and 40,000 TEU/ha terminal area or even beyond. A key issue in this respect will be the dwell time of containers at the terminal. When shipping lines (carrier haulage) and shippers (merchant haulage) do not succeed to limit this dwell time to an average of 3-4 days then, terminal congestion and/or excessive cost will be the consequence. Maximum supply chain efficiency (speed, cost) can only be realized when one party is responsible for the whole chain (door-to-door!). Obviously this will require a good coordination between all parties involved, but that should be no problem with all the available IT tools.

In the future, an increasing number of ports will be connected with so-called satellite terminals (inland or coastal), with frequent shuttle services between the deepsea (coastline) terminals and inland satellite(s). For efficiency reasons the deepsea terminals should control the shuttle operations, however, this will require support from shipping lines and shippers to provide sufficient and above all reliable information. Especially barging will be suited for this type of high volume transportation in particular as barging can support peak demands (much better than rail). However in countries without navigable waterways, rail transportation is suitable as well but it will require on-dock (near-dock) rail facilities for proper cost control.

Ongoing in the future, ports and terminals will be confronted with their longstanding dilemma; is our strategy cost or service driven? Non shipping line related GTOs (like HPH, PSA, Eurogate and SSA) will be eager to make a fair profit, whereas terminals owned by shipping lines will tend to go for service.

This dilemma (cost or service driven) will remain when it comes to agreements about berth performance. Increased call sizes (handlings per vessel call) and stronger demands for limited times in port (24-36 hrs.) will result in performance requirements of 250-350 moves per vessel berth hour. Such demands will be even more essential for vessels with a reduced speed (and installed horsepower) as they will have limited surplus power to be able to catch up port delays. Cost-conscious terminal operators will try to realize this with 6 to 8 quay cranes, which requires a crane productivity (sustained during the entire vessel call) of 40-60 containers per hour. This will be quite a challenge, especially when considering the increased quay crane dimensions (50-55 m. lifting height above quay; 75-80 m. outreach) and the logistic complexity at the apron when handling three to five 15,000+ vessels simultaneously at one terminal. With the arrival of much more ULCVs, more than 50% of all vessel handlings will be deck loads (with all related problems from twist lock stackers) and the large handling volumes per vessel hatch (hatch capacity will be about 900 TEU) will thwart a crane operation planning. So far, the indented dock (the CERES terminal, Amsterdam never became fully operational) has not convinced the industry about its productivity potential.

Dual cycling, twin lift, tandem lift and even block lift (2 containers high and 2 containers wide under one spreader) will be further encouraged however the bottleneck will be the transportation (and proper sequencing when loading) between the quay cranes and the storage yard. On top of that terminals (and shipping lines) will be increasingly confronted with special stowage demands, off-standard containers (pallet-wide, overheight/overwide) and even swap bodies. Tank containers and 2.5 m. wide swap body tanks are becoming increasingly attractive for the globalized trade in chemical products, however requiring more space for hazardous cargo.

Automation will be applied on a much larger scale however in a controlled way. Reliability will remain a major concern just like the increasing complexity of terminal operating systems with integrated planning functions, transport and sequence optimization, etc. The future may bring control systems with interaction between equipment, systems and containers (provided with an active tag). Within one or two decades containers may communicate with their environment about destination, type of cargo, travel priorities, etc. However, will it be possible to close the gap between available technology and organizational control?

Nevertheless, automated (driverless) operations will be further applied not only for cost saving reasons but also to guarantee the control over large volume operations with increasing logistic complexity and much more customer requirements and security and safety procedures. Some equipment and system manufacturers will develop and offer all-in service contracts but terminals should consider whether such a strategy will support a long-term control over priorities and costs of their own operations.

Port authorities and terminal operators are already increasingly confronted with demands for more sustainability, both in their terminal design and in their daily operations. Environmentalists advocate an approach towards minimum life cycle cost including the cost of environmental impact. In this way ports and terminal operators will increasingly include the materialized impact of the rate of sustainability both from equipment, facilities, operations and even outsourced services. This trend is already observable in eco-conscious regions like California and North West Europe. Slowly but steady, more port authorities will enforce sustainable operations however, this process will take several decades (certainly in the developing countries).

The following areas for sustainability in ports and terminals will get increased attention in the future:

- Eco-efficient operations and facility designs.

  This will include the application of eco-friendly terminal equipment (reduced sound emission, reduced toxicity) and provisions for cold-ironing. In terminal designs, area utilization will be improved and waiting times for intermodal activities (the container swap from mode to mode) will be reduced. System designs and buildings will increasingly show socio-technical approaches to allow participative management and operations control. Obviously this will ask for changes in labor skills and attitude.

- Reduction of energy use.

  Substantial savings will be realized with more efficient equipment drive lines. Gradually, diesel-powered equipment will be replaced by electric supplied equipment (direct from the grid or through batteries). Automated handling will allow much lower lighting levels and where lighting is required (buildings, access roads), energy-efficient armatures will be applied. Covered areas for reefer containers (avoidance of sun radiation) and the application of heat pumps for heating and air conditioning will be seen in the future. The use of renewable energy sources will get much more attention.

- Durable facilities and handling systems.

  The growing awareness about sustainability (and the society's assessment of companies in this respect), will encourage the building of terminal facilities with a long life time and low maintenance demand, designed with renewable/reusable materials (e.g. high quality concrete, wooden structures, glass panels, etc.). Handling equipment can easily be designed for 20-30 years of operational life and terminals can be modular designed, allowing for future expansion without major modifications.

Fortunately automated terminal operations with high-density stacking systems definitely support the drive for more sustainable port facilities. The benefits are for the neighboring environment and the society as a whole. Probably, the reluctance from many terminal operators to invest in sustainable terminal operating systems will slowly evaporate. Nevertheless port authorities will increasingly take the lead to realize more sustainable port facilities. For example, the tender for a new container terminal in the port of Rotterdam contained a claim in relation to maximum emissions of trucks visiting the premises.

15.4. INLAND TRANSPORTATION

At present the cost of inland transportation represents a majority part in the overall cost for intercontinental door-to-door container transport. The tremendous cost savings from economies of scale and fierce competition in sea transportation could not be matched by inland transportation offered by trucking, barging, railways or shortsea services. To the contrary: road pricing, rising fuel cost (from increasing crude oil prices and taxes), rail track pricing, environmental requirements, limitations in infrastructure and last but not least, increasing labor cost tend to further enlarge the relative share of inland transportation in door-to-door transport costs.

The next decades will show a further urbanization, in some regions up to 90% (see Figure 427) and this will result in more concentrated cargo flows towards urban conglomerates, not only the large distribution centers and consumer shopping centers, but as well the industrial and service activities at suburban locations. This will offer challenges and threats. Large container flows into such areas can benefit from high-volume transportation offered by barging, railways and shortsea. However, only when such densely populated regions can be connected (shortsea for coastal areas, barging needs navigable waterways and railways need a track network with sufficient penetration). Often, the final leg is trucking and that will become a major threat for inland transportation to urban regions.

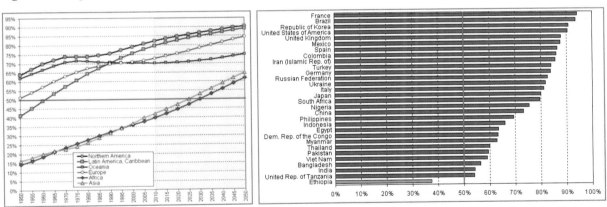

Figure 427: Increasing urbanization (left); Some countries even exceeding 80% by 2050 (right)

Shortsea will become more attractive for distribution to coastal (or near-coastal) producer and consumer centers. However legislation, customs regulations, security, administrative procedures and port dues do not support fast, low cost shortsea operations.

Ferry-type operations with reliable (fixed time schedules) services will be attractive for short-distance distribution along the coast in archipelagos.

Barging is a high potential for inland transportation over more than 100 km, when navigable waters are available. Depending on water depth and lock dimensions, motor barges of up to 800 TEU will be used for shuttle services, although many inland destinations along waterways will be short of volume to justify a daily service with such large motor barges (see Figure 428).

For long rivers (Mississippi, Yangtze, Rhine, Amazon and Ganges) with 15-30 inland terminals, push-barge systems operating in a stop-and-drop system will become attractive. Push-barge convoys with 6-12 barges/lighters (each carrying up to 200 TEU) will stop at an inland terminal to drop (or exchange) one or more barges, which can be collected in the return trip from the same or another convoy.

Figure 428: High-capacity barging for inland shuttles

Such large systems have a tremendous capacity potential as the infrastructure does hardly put any constraints and when connecting road transport is not required, this really low cost inland transportation with a small environmental impact can cope with the increasing inland container flows. Recently, the first dual fuel (LNG/MDO) diesel engines are applied for barging and this in combination with a diesel-electric drive line (also helpful to accommodate reefers connected on board), will further reduce the carbon footprint per TEU. For many commodities the moderate travel speed will be acceptable, as the service is reliable and the products on board can be considered rolling stock in the supply chain.

The limited operating range (along the river, often close to urban areas) is attractive for green drive lines (such as LNG or even fuel cells), which require only a few special fuel bunker stations (LNG, Hydrogen) along the waterway as the bunker capacity of such barges will be large enough for their operating area.

Obviously the required investments and related business risk for such high-capacity barge systems will require a commitment from shipping lines and/or shippers/consignees.

Until the 1950s, rail transportation used to be the dominant mode for the inland transportation of general cargo. But later, in containerized transport, rail operators were not very successful in maintaining a reasonable market share, with exception of the US. Limited rail networks, difficulties in keeping up average speeds and schedules, lack of standardization (electric supply and safety systems, car types, axle loads), track pricing and limited operational flexibility caused a drop in the share of rail-bound inland container movements, in most of the countries. But, the growing resistance against trucking (traffic congestion, environmental impact), the high transport potential and relatively moderate environmental impact made many governments decide to upgrade existing rail networks and invest in new infrastructure and equipment.

In Europe the many country-related regulations and a priority for passenger trains will result in moderate growth. The objective to get a 20-40% share in inland container transport is very ambitious and requires longer trains (proposed length 1,000 m.), increased average speeds (at present often below 50 km./hr) and well organized shuttle services. Also high-speed cargo trains (160-200 km./hr) may be introduced on some trunk routes. Bundling of short trains into one large long-distance shuttle, which is broken up afterwards for final delivery to a number of destinations has been promoted for years but will not be broadly applied. Coupling of train sets is time consuming, it requires large, "shunting" yards and the repositioning of train sets is a complex exercise. In the future, the mega-hub concept (swapping containers by means of portal-type cranes between train shuttles, serving various destinations) will be further applied. The US shows already some (partly automated) inland rail hubs capable of handling thousands of containers per day. Increasingly there will be a mixing of domestic trade with maritime (intermodal) containers which will cause some logistic complexity as many land-based containers (pallet-wide, swap-bodies, 53'-long, etc.) show off-standard characteristics.

Especially on longer distances (>500 km) rail transportation for containers will increase in the coming decades. Countries with a long-term vision and investment power have decided to encourage rail transportation (new networks, double stack railcars, new locomotives, etc.). China, India and Middle Eastern countries already made commitments for billions of dollars to expand their inland rail networks. Double track connections and the set up of shuttle services will result in a growing share for rail transport especially in these larger countries.

Russia, China and India will expand their rail systems, supported through the fact that they cover long distances (up to 5,000 km) under the same regulations. When the Trans-Siberian rail link is upgraded to a completely double track link between (Eastern) Europe and the Pacific, a real Trans-Siberian Express Service could be realized. Ruskaya Troyka is promoting this 11,000 km rail link, often taking about 25 days travel time (partly single track and many other users). However a double rail track might reduce this to approximately 16 days and then this will be an attractive alternative for deepsea shipping, especially for the connection with Mid and Western China. Some trials for a weekly service between Antwerp (Belgium) and Chongqing (1,500 km west of Shanghai), via Poland and Belarus, already learned that such a service is interesting for automotive parts, chemicals, machinery, etc. A more southern route from Istanbul to China (via Azerbaijan and Kazakhstan, partly parallel to the early Silk Road) could be feasible as well. Two or three rail connections between Europe and Asia could be successful and absorb some maritime containers, but this will remain a small share in the overall Europe-Asia trade.

In Africa the realization of a reliable rail network will be much more complicated as a result of the many countries involved, the political instability, the rough terrain conditions and issues like safety and security. Besides the required capacity in rail networks and equipment, successful rail transportation requires state-of-the-art logistic control systems, a market-oriented organization and flexibility for last minute changes and peak demands.

The conversion to eco-friendly locomotives is no problem from a technology point of view. Dual fuel (LNG/MDO) and fuel cell technology is very suited for locomotives (see Figure 429) and fuelling is no problem: either at a few locations along the track or carried by the trains themselves (like in the old days, the tender behind the locomotive). Such new technologies will only be applied on a large scale when companies like Siemens and General Electric take the lead in the design and marketing of

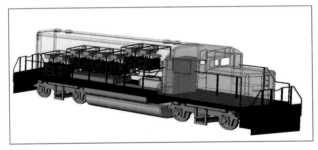

Figure 429: Locomotive with fuel cell drive line

this eco-friendly equipment. A first contribution from such eco-friendly locomotives could be the application for last-mile solutions when connecting the rail terminal with an electrified main track.

Regardless the major efforts to accomplish a modal shift to railways, barging and shortsea, it is likely that trucking will continue to be the dominant inland mode worldwide. Threats such as road pricing, shortages of drivers (in some areas), environmental demands and fuel taxes will be offset by the service flexibility, transparent cost structure, fast delivery, excellent infrastructure and simplicity of logistics.

Technology can even further support the preference for low cost inland road transportation. The road infrastructure is always there and cost savings can be realized through the application of road trains carrying up to 8 TEU behind one driver. In Europe, these road trains will probably be limited to a maximum of 4 TEU (length < 32 m.), but in the US, Australia, South America, Africa, China and India, longer road trains will definitely support the demand for inland transportation, especially when rail and barge transportation cannot deliver or are too expensive.

The growing resistance against trucking in densely populated and traffic congested areas could be conquered with road trains in (shuttle) networks driving outside the rush hours e.g. later in the evenings and during the night (see Figure 430).

Figure 430: Road train on public infrastructure

Even automated road trains could be applied and this was already shown in a demonstration project in 1999 in the Netherlands. Track-keeping technology (available from AGVs) and track-keeping road trains such as developed by TU Delft and ECT (multi-trailer system) were combined and applied on an existing road infrastructure (see Figure 431). This would be a much less expensive concept compared to automated road haulage, running on a separate infrastructure (e.g. as proposed by Combi-Road). In spite of the availability of technology and the promising cost advantages, it is doubtful whether the society will accept such developments on their public road systems. During the coming decades, safety, damage risk, red tape and slow-changing legislation will make automated container transport over public roads difficult to implement. Howewer, first trials have started in Nevada (US), which state gave a licence for tests with driverless cars.

Figure 431: Prototype AGV-pulled road train

More probable will be the set up of inland satellite terminals where large quantities of containers are shuttled between major deepsea container terminals and their inland satellites by means of rail, barges or road trains. From these distant inland terminals (at tens to hundreds of km distance from the deepsea terminal) collection and delivery with traditional trucking could be realized and when required even with a green drive technology. The present developments for electro mobility may become available for 40-50 tons road haulage in the 0-100 km range (battery powered electric drive lines). For longer distances improved fuel-efficient diesel engines will remain the preferred power source. But in case fuel prices would rise dramatically, fuel cells and induction technologies could become of interest.

The society will increasingly require reduced environmental impact and better utilization of infrastructure and transport equipment. In that respect carriers (shipping lines) and merchants should much more focus on an efficient door-to-door transport. Short connecting times at terminals (deepsea and inland) should be a primary goal.

A pre-planning of connecting inland transport will help to balance capacity and to shift container movements towards rail, shortsea and barging; modes with a potential for economies of scale and reduced environmental impact. Partnerships and trust amongst each other will support shipping lines, shippers and inland transport companies to arrange the fast growing future inland container flows in an efficient way.

15.5. INFORMATION AND COMMUNICATION TECHNOLOGY

The area of information and communication technology will probably be the one with the highest rate of development in the coming decades, compared to equipment and facility developments.

Planning and control tools will develop in the direction of self-decisive systems based on pre-processed information and decision rules, pre-determined by logistic planners from shippers, terminals and shipping lines.

Planning tasks such as vessel, yard and equipment planning will be further automated. Today, shipping lines and terminals require a lot of manning (24/7), to operate extensive manual planning processes, although with the help of computer systems. The future will bring tools for automated planning tasks, where the operator sets objectives, conditions and boundaries and monitors the integrity of data (built-in checks). Then the computer will execute the standard tasks whereafter the operator may intervene in case of signaled irregularities. From there, automated equipment will be assigned according required sequencing and priorities. For manually operated equipment, the assignments will be generated automatically, but equipment operators will get smart user interfaces, allowing them to overrule when they want to optimize or safeguard their operating process. For sure, a large number of manual activities will diminish, however control and checking functions will remain with operators, who will have to monitor more complex decisions. The user interfaces should get more attention with much better logical instructions. Voice recognition is a promising tool, but still suffering from a lot of shortcomings. New techniques for user friendly interfaces will be developed in the future.

The monitoring and control of actual operations against the planned activities will further develop. In this area, tracking and tracing is of utmost importance and the future will show a complete tracing of all equipment (manual and automated) and containers. For safety reasons also personnel in risk full areas (apron, reefer monitoring, salvage of broken down equipment, etc.) will be traced (active DGPS, transponders, RFID technology, heat sensors, vision techniques, etc.) and will be controlled by computer systems.

Tracking and tracing demands a 100% reliability of the identification of equipment and containers when passing essential interchange areas (gate, ship-shore interchange, rail terminal, customs X-ray checking station, etc.). Optical character reading and passive transponders will be further applied, although all kinds of RFID applications are showing their future potential. Reliability (preferably 100%) and cost will be the key characteristics, determining the future choices. The past learnt that standardization will support a widely accepted application and performance improvement, however it is questionable whether the continuous flow of innovations in this field can be canalized through standardized interfaces and message structuring.

Future sensor technology, logging systems and equipment status control will support a complete equipment monitoring. Not only for FMEA purposes (Failure Mode and Effect Analysis) but also to increase productivity, to improve maintenance activities (stagger line info, preventive maintenance) and to indicate required training and education of operators (drivers' ID connected to equipment).

Research is increasingly focusing on agent-based technology where equipment is self-decisive in routing, order picking, etc. This approach may work for a container as well, when provided with an active tag, containing origin, destination, intermodal voyage numbers and all relevant shipper and transshipment data. All kinds of checking, control and planning functions, nowadays executed by operators from shipping lines, terminals and intermodal operators will then be performed by the container itself when crossing essential interchanges. The active tag at the container could signal days in advance that the next connecting phase should be prepared (and approved), including all kinds of key administrative procedures (bill of lading, customs clearance, payments), which so often hinder a smooth flow through the logistic chain (think of terminal dwell times or no shows).

Instead of active tags on board of the container, web-based apps could fulfill part of such functionality as well; however this will entirely depend on an online, reliable tracking and tracing over the whole voyage. In this area much can be learned from the parcel industry however with one complication: in the parcel industry all logistic decisions are made by one operator (e.g. UPS and DHL); in containerized transport 2-6 parties may be involved in all logistic decision making (shipper, shipping line, terminal, inland operator, consignee, etc.).

Container operations control systems (terminals, inland transport) will be further developed, comprising much more functionality. It will be possible to run simulations 1-3 days ahead, with various decision and parameter settings and based on the actual operational situation. After an evaluation of the outcome, the best combination of decisions/settings can be made for the next 24 hours of operation.

It is still unclear whether the trend to install off-the-shelve operations control software will continue. Especially larger shipping lines and Global Terminal Operators (GTOs) can afford to design their own overall systems, which can be used in multiple ways for all their worldwide subsidiaries. And of course some consolidation in this technology field will help to get properly trained and experienced staff to run the increasingly more complex control systems.

The drive for cost control will focus on the avoidance of peak loads (at terminals) and a better utilization of equipment and transport means (feeders, trains, trucks and barges). Vehicle booking systems will increasingly be applied to avoid peaks at terminals (gate and landside interchange). Not only trucking, but also barging and even rail operations could benefit from a time slot allocation with a guaranteed short service time.

An increase of utilization for seagoing vessels, trains, trucks and barges could be obtained with a kind of advance allocating and auction, which can be realized when shippers specify their demands in time and place and then, select their preferred transportation channel (just like already in place for passenger airline ticketing and parcel transport), based on time schedule and cost. Especially the underutilized capacity in barging, railways and return trucking could benefit from such early booking/low price policies, known from the airlines. However this could result in market instability. A better solution will be to present all worldwide transport legs including available slots, costs and time schedules. Then the shipper/shipping line could make reservations at agreed costs. Of course no shows should be penalized.

The development and control of software and middleware for this type of improvements in vertically integrated activities in the logistic chain will be a complicated issue. Hence, which party will take the lead and responsibility for such intelligent algorithms, their quality and service guarantees? The past has learned that shipping communities are reluctant to support (and pay for) general services

(Dacosy, Seagha and Intis). Nevertheless the future will bring much more web-based services for supply chain optimization.

The growing demands on advance information will further develop EDI procedures/messages and databases, accessible for multiple partners in the supply chain. Only when partners allow access to their shipping data (data sharing) then new applications can be developed for a more intelligent utilization of supply chain systems. It is questionable whether all such new applications will be made available in the public domain; the impact of cybercrime will increase, asking for better protected data networks.

15.6. CONCLUDING REMARKS

In about half a century, containerized transport developed into a worldwide utility indispensable for the global economy. The coming decades will undoubtedly bring many improvements to support a further growth in containerized transport. New technologies will be implemented and the containerized supply chains will be improved and further expanded into new markets (liquid and dry bulk specialties, minerals, etc.). Looking back, it can be learned which impressive achievements could be obtained through entrepreneurship and technology, in a period of only five decades. This may continue, however our society is increasingly aware of the world's limitations. Examples from the past show that economies of scale are not infinite (Ultra Large Crude Carriers larger than 400,000 dwt disappeared) and especially for door-to-door transport, there must be a balance in scales. Nevertheless, the future will bring new developments, although, with more attention for stabilization and the human scale.

Breakthroughs should not be precluded because feasible innovative concepts may come up as a result of major changes in the global economy and a growing awareness of our scarce global resources. New methods for transport will be launched but, it should be realized that at present thousands of billions US$ have been invested in vessels, containers, port facilities, inland transportation, information systems and capable organizations for the control of containerized cargo movements. A possible breakthrough will only stand a fair chance if the present container transport systems can be beaten on cost, transport times and environmental impact; quite a challenge! And if so, it will take a long time before all parties in the chain will be convinced that an (too) early amortization of their assets is required to stay in transport business, certainly when realizing that new methods only will become successful after a worldwide acceptance.

The world benefits from a matured container transport, initiated and developed through entrepreneurship and technology. Standardization and economy of scale have supported the worldwide spread of containerization. Its simplicity, low cost and reliable service may further consolidate the position of containerization as the world's transport utility.

REFERENCES

Alix, Y., Slack, B., and Comtois, C., (1999), *"Alliance or Acquisition? Strategies for Growth in the Container Industry: The Case of CP Ships"*, Journal of Transport Geography 7, pp. 203-208

Angeloudis, P., and Bell, M.G.H., (2011), *"A Review of Container Terminal Simulation Models"*, Maritime Policy & Management, Vol. 38, no. 5, pp. 523-540

Argyriadis, D.A., (1959), *"Cargo Container Ships"*, presented to the Institution of Naval Architects, March 25, 1959

Ashar, A., (2000), *"The Fourth Revolution and Transshipment Potentials for Panama Ports"*, In: Proceedings TOC 2000

Assel, K.H., (1995), *"Ship-to-Shore Crane Design: A Comparison"*, Port Technology International 2nd edition, ICG Publishing Ltd, London

Atkins, W.H., (1983), *"Modern Marine Terminal: Operations and Management"*, Port of Oakland, The Compage Company, San Francisco, California

Baird, A.J., (1999), *"Analysis of Private Seaport Development: The Port of Felixstowe"*, Transport Policy, Vol. 6, Issue 2, pp. 109-122

Baird, A.J., (1999, May), *"Container Vessels of the Next generation: Are Seaports Ready to Face the Challenge"*, In: Proceedings 21st World Ports Conference of the IAPH, 12-21 May, 1999.

Baird, A.J., (2001), *"Container Vessels in the New Millennium: Implications for Seaports"*, Singapore Maritime & Port Journal, pp. 141-174

Beddow, M., (2007), *"Floored"*, Cover story on Maersk, Containerisation International, January 2007, 34-35

Bendall, H.B., and Stent, A.F., (1996), *"Hatchcoverless container ships: Productivity gains from a new technology"*, Maritime Policy & Management Vol.23 (2), pp. 187-199

Bendall, H.B., and Stent, A.F., (1999), *"Longhaul Feeder Services in an Era of Changing Technology: An Asia-Pacific Perspective"*, Maritime Policy & Management Vol. 26 (2), pp. 145-159

Bhimani, A.K. & Hoite, S., (1998), *"Machinery Trolley Crane"*, In: Proceedings Ports '98, Long Beach, California

Bhimani, A.K. & Hsieh, J.K., (2001, May), *"Cranes to Serve Ship in the Slip Ceres Paragon terminal, Amsterdam"*, In: Proceedings ASCE Conference, Norfolk

Bhimani, A.K., Jordan, M.A. (2001), *"Crane Purchase Specifications: Tailor Made or Off-the-Shelf?"*, In: Proceedings TOC 2001, Lisbon

Bhimani, A.K., Jordan, M.A. (2003, December), *"A Few Facts about Jumbo Cranes"*, In: Proceedings TOC Americas 2003, Panama

Bird, J.H. (1971), *"Seaports and Seaport Terminals"*, London: Hutchinson

Blagden, A., (1998), *"Developments in Container Handling Technology"*, Cargo Systems Report, IIR Publications, London

Blauwens, G., De Baere, P. and Voorde, E. van de (2002) *," Transport Economics"*, Antwerp: De Boeck

Boer, C.A., and Saanen, Y., (2008), *„Controls: Emulation to Improve the Performance of Container Terminals"*, In: Proceedings of the 40th Conference on Winter Simulation, December 7-10, Miami, FL

Boer, P.J., (1992), *"Piggyback and Containers"*, Golden West Books, San Marino, California, ISBN 0-87095-108-4

Boevé, W., (2011), *"The Future of Freight Transport"*, Publication of Europe Container Terminals BV

Bohlman, M.R., Chun, H., Lacey, H., (1983), *"Remote Reefer Monitoring"*, In: Proceedings 3rd Terminal Operations Conference, Amsterdam, 13th-16th June 1983.

Bos, W. van den, and Rijsenbrij, J.C., (2002), *"Design Optimization of Space Frame Structures"*, World Class Crane Management Seminar Europe, Marriot Hotel Amsterdam, may 27-29

Böse, J.W., (2011), *"Handbook of Terminal Planning"*, Springer, New-York, ISBN 978-1-4419-8408-1

Bouwman, T. (1993), *Containers, Logistiek en Arbeid"*, Stichting FNV Pers, Amsterdam

British Rail, (s.n.), *"Freightliner"*, brochure, Publicity Arts Ltd, London

Broeze, F., (2002), *"The Globalisation of the Oceans: Containerisation from the 1950s to the Present"*, St. Johns, NF, Canada: International Maritime Economic History Association

Brooks, M.R., (2000), *"Restructuring in the Liner Shipping Industry"*, discussion paper, Centre for International Trade and Transportation, Dalhousie University, Halifax

Bruun, P., (1989), *"Port Engineering"*, Vol. 1, Gulf Publishing Comp., Houston, ISBN 0-87201-843-1

Burg, G. van den, (1969), *"Containerisation: A Modern Transport System"*, Hutchinson & Co Ltd, London

Casper, W.L., (1983), *"Modernization and Upgrading of Shoreside Container Cranes"*, Proceedings of Ports '83, Specialty Conference on Port Modernization, Upgrading and Repairs, ASCE, New Orleans, Louisiana, March 21-23

Cheung, R.K., Tong J.H. and Slack, B., (2003), *"The Transition from Freight Consolidation to Logistics: The case of Hong Kong"*, Journal of Transport Geography 11, pp. 245-253

Clemmetsen, O.M., (1972), *"Cellular Container Ships"*, Lloyd's Register of Shipping, London

Comtois, C., (1994), *"The Evolution of Containerization in East Asia"*, Maritime Policy & Management Vol.21 (3), pp. 195-205

Containerisation Study Group, (1967), *"Report on Containerisation"*, National Joint Council on Materials Handling, UK

Cudahy, B.J., (2006), *"Box Boats"*, Fordham University Press, New York, ISBN 0-8232-2578-2

Cullinane, K. and Khanna M. (1997), *"The Economics of Deploying Large Containerships"*, International Conference of Maritime Economists, London: International Association of Maritime Economists (IAME)

Damas, P., (1997), *"Who's Making Money"*, American Shipper, Editorial Supplement: Revenues and Markets, July 1997

Detlefsen, G.U., (2006), *"Schiffahrt im Bild, Containerschiffe III"*, Verlag H.M. Hauschild, Bremen, Germany, ISBN 3-89757-345-8

Dobner, M., (2001),*"The Design, Application and Economics of AGVs"*, AAPA Facilities Engineering Seminar, November 2001, Oakland, California

Dobner, M., and Rijsenbrij, J.C., (1999), *"Equipment Selection and Utilisation – Key Factors for Smaller Terminals"*, AAPA Facilities Engineering Seminar, February 3-5, Corpus Christi, Texas

Dokkum, K. van, (2003), *"Scheepskennis: Een Moderne Encyclopedie"*, DOKMAR, Enkhuizen (NL), ISBN 90-806330-2-X

Donovan, A., and Gibson, A., (1997), *"Testimony of Les Harlander at the Matson Building"*, interview, 19 June, San Francisco

Donovan, A., (1999), *"Longshoremen and Mechanization. A Tale of Two Cities"*, in Journal for Maritime Research, Vol. 1, December 1999.

Donovan, A., and Bonney, J., (2006), *"The Box That Changed the World"*, The Journal of Commerce, Commonwealth Business Media, N.J., USA, ISBN 978-1-891131-95-0

Driel, H. van, and Schot, J.W., (2002), *"Techniek in Nederland in de 20ste eeuw: Indirecte overslag en de komst van de container"*, part V, pp. 97-113, ISBN 90-5730-068-0

Eckelmann, T. and Schiffer, E., (2006), *"Eurogate bringt Wilhelmshaven ins Containergeschäft"*, HANSA International Maritime Journal-143, 2006, nr 4

ECT and GHR, (1990), *"Delta 2000-8: Naar een Grootschalig Containeroverslag- en Goederendistributiecentrum op de Maasvlakte"*, Joint publication of Europe Combined Terminals and Rotterdam Port Authority, November 1990

ECT, (1992), *"Met het Oog op Morgen: Vijfentwintig Jaar ECT, 1967-1992"*, Published by ECT Corporate Communications, Rotterdam

Egyedi, T.M., (2000), *"The Standardised Container: Gateway Technologies in Cargo Transport"*, In: Manfred Holler & Esko Niskanen (Eds.), EURAS Yearbook of Standardization, Vol. 3 / Homo Oeconomicus XVII(3) pp. 231-262. Munich: Accedo

Ehira, H., (1998), *"Next Generation Supertainer Crane"*, Seminar on Port Design and Operation Technology, Singapore, 4-5 November

Elshof, H.L.J., and Boer, J. de, (1998, May), *"Ship Dimensions in 2020: A Study on the Trends in the Dimensions of Representative Ships that Could Call at Rotterdam in the Year 2020"*, Lloyd's Register of Shipping

Fischer, G.L., (2002), *"Crane Life Cycle management II: Getting the Control Specifications right"*, In: Proceedings TOC Asia, Kuala Lumpur

Fossey, J., (2007), *"Shifting Sands"*, Containerisation International, 40th Anniversary, pp. 35-39

Foxcroft, A., (1997), *"Straddling, a Tough Market"*, Cargo Today, Vol. 3, issue 5, October

Frémont, A. (2009), *"Shipping Lines and Logistics"*, Transport Reviews, 29:4, pp. 537-554

Gardner, B., (1985), *"The Container Revolution and its Effect on the Structure of Traditional UK Liner Shipping Companies"*, Maritime Policy & Management Vol. 12 (3), pp. 195-208

Gianquinto, P.A., (1980), *"Trends in Containerization; Their Effects on Terminal Design"*, ICHCA-USA Conference: "Intermodal Containerization and Marine Terminal Development", New York

Gisnås, H., Holte, E., Rialland, A. and Wergeland, T., (2008), *"Industry Analysis of the Container Market in the Baltic Sea Region"*, EU Work Package D-A1-E, Activity A32-Develop Scenarios, Part 1 Industry Analysis, Brussels

Guy, E. and Alix, Y., (2007), *"A Successful River Port? Container Shipping in Montreal"*, Journal of Transport Geography 15, pp. 46-55

Ham, J.C. van, (1991), *"ROTTERDAM: Still Going Strong"* In: Portus Vol. 6, nr. 3 pp. 10-15 / *"ROTTERDAM: Image de la Hollande Entreprenante"*, In: Portus Vol. 6, nr. 3 pp. 22-26

Ham, J.C. van, and Koppenjan, J.F.M., (2002). *"Port Expansion and Public-Private Partnership: The Case of Rotterdam"*, in: Maritime Engineering & Ports III, CA Brebbia & G Sciutto (eds.), WIT Press, Southampton

Ham, J.C. van, (2004), *"Den Gutertransport im Blut: Starke Position der Niederlandischen Transporteure"*, Neue Zürcher Zeitung (05-24-2004), Zürich

Ham, J.C. van, (2005), *"The Feasibility of Mega Container Vessels"*, European Transport / Trasporti Europei n. 25-26, pp. 89-98

Ham, J.C. van, Autekie, P., (2005), *"Container Terminals in the Mediterranean Region"*, In: Maritime heritage and modern ports, R Marcet i Barbe & CA Brebbia (eds.), WIT Press, Southampton, UK

Ham, J.C. van and Duin, J.H.R. van, (2001), *"The Second Container Revolution: Assessing and Managing Risks in Port Development"* in: First International Congress on Maritime Transport, J. Olivella, R. Rodriguez-Martos & R .Gonzalez Blanco (eds.), Grup Artyplan-Artympres, S.A Barcelona.

Ham, J.C. van, and Kuipers, B., (2004). *"E-Commerce and the Container Shipping Industry"* in: Transport developments and innovations in an evolving world, M. Beuthe & V. Himanen (eds.), Springer, Berlin

Ham, J.C. van, and Rijsenbrij, J.C., (2006), *"The Disordered Start of Containerization"*, in: Maritime Transport III, J.O. Puig, R.M.I Barbé and V.G. Carcellé (eds.), Barcelona: Technical University of Catalonia/Museu Maritim.

Ham, R.Th. van der, (1988), *"De Rol van Simulaties bij het Ontwerp van de ECT/Sea-Land Delta Terminal"*, Symposium University of Technology Delft, department Transport Technology and KIVI, December 15th

Harlander, L.A., (1959), *"Engineering Development of a Container System for the West Coast-Hawaiian Trade"*, paper presented at Meeting of North. Cal. Section of the Society of Naval Architects and Marine Engineers, June 1959, San Francisco, California

Harlander, L.A., (1961, April), *"Further Developments of a Container System for the West Coast-Hawaiian Trade"*, Spring Meeting of the Society of Naval Architects and Marine Engineers, San Francisco, California, April 10-11

Harlander, L.A., (1982, October), *"Container System Design Developments Over Two Decades"*, Marine Technology, Vol. 19, nr. 4, pp. 364-376

Haussmann, G., (1968), *"Transcontainer Umschlag"*, Book Serie Fördern und Heben, Krauskopf-Verlag, Mainz

Hayuth, Y. (1978),*"Containerization and the Load Center Concept"*, PhD thesis, Seattle: University of Washington

Hearth, J.M.A., (1964), *"Progress in Cargo Handling Volume IV"*, Proceedings of the Sixth Biennial Technical Conference ICHCA, Fairplay Publications, London

Hebeler, H., (1978), *"Container Terminal Operating Experience: The Rail-Mounted Gantry Crane System"*, Terminal Operations Conference 1978, Amsterdam

Hengst, S., (2001), *"5000 Years of Shipping"*, Farewell address Delft University of Technology, ISBN 90-806734-1-2

Hensel, F., (2012), *"The Containership: Its Chances and Challenges"*, HANSA Int. Mar. Journal, Vol. 149, nr. 3, pp. 71-74

Hodd, M., (1979), *"Matsonisation: 'Phenomenal' Technology the Key"*, Cargo Systems, Vol. 6, nr. 11, November

Hodd, M., (1979), *"Automation Implications Challenge Terminal Operators"*, Cargo Systems, Vol. 6, nr. 11, November

Hollmann, M., (2005), *"Container Ship Development, Pamela the Great"*, In: Nonstop Issue No. 3/2005, Germanischer Lloyd, Hamburg

Hornby, O., (1988), *"With Constant Care..:A.P. Møller: Shipowner 1876-1965"*, J.H. Schultz Information, Copenhagen, Denmark, ISBN 87-569-2358-9

Horssen, W.van, (1982), *"The Story of the Port's Growth in a Period of only Half a Century"*, In: Rotterdam Europoort Delta 82/2, Rotterdam

Houston Port Authority (1956), *"Trailer Ships Now Serve Houston"*, Houston Port Book, Spring, 1956, Houston

Howarth, D. and S., (1986), *"The Story of P&O"*, Weidenfeld and Nicholson Ltd, London, ISBN 0297789651

Ignarski, S., TT Club, (1995), *"The Box: An Anthology Celebrating 25 Years of Containerisation and the TT Club"*, EMAP Business Communications, London, ISBN 1854383051

Jansen, E.B.P., (2006, April), *"A Short History on Container Transport: Period 1960-2006"*, Literature survey, Delft University of Technology, Department Transportation Engineering

Jeffery, K., (1999), *"Recent Developments in Information Technology for Container Terminals"*, Cargo Systems, January 1999, IIR Publications, London

Jordan, M.A., (1986), *"Streamlining Structure Design"*, PDI Container Crane Supplement, pp. 2-7

Jordan, M.A., (1986), *"Advances in Container Crane Design"*, Cargo Systems Publications Ltd

Jordan, M.A., (1997), *"Super Productive Cranes"*, In: Proceedings TOC 1997, Barcelona

Jordan, M.A. (1998), *"Purchasing Cranes in a Changing World"*, In: Proceedings Ports '98, ASCE, Long Beach, California, pp. 591-602

Jordan, M.A., (2001, October), *"Future-Proof Your Crane"*, In: Proceedings TOC Americas 2001, Miami, Florida

Jordan, M.A., Morris, C.A., and Dix, A., (2007, March), *"The Floaterm Concept: Reducing Terminal Congestion with Waterside Cranes"*, In: Proceedings ASCE Ports Conference 2007, San Diego, California

Journal of Commerce, (2006), *"50 Years of Containerization"*, A Special Commemorative Supplement, April 2006

Jung, A., (2005), *"The Box that Makes the World Go Round"*, Spiegel Special – Globalization: The New World, nr. 7

Kataoka, K., (1978), *"Container Terminal Operating Experience: The Rubber-Tired Gantry Crane System"*, In: Proceedings TOC 1978, Amsterdam

Klaassens, J.B., Honderd, G., El Azzouzi, A., Cheok, K.C., and Smid, G.E., (1999), *"3D Modeling Visualization for Studying Controls of the Jumbo Container Crane"*, FAMAS Program, Faculty ITS, Delft University of Technology

Klein Breteler, A.J., (1999), *"Design Aspects of a Mechanism for Automated Container Handling"*, 10th World Congress on the Theory of Machines, Oulu, Finland, June 20-24

Klein Breteler, A.J., (2003), *"On the Design of a Twist-Lock Manipulator"*, 11th World Congress on Mechanism and Machine Science, August 18-21, Tianjin, China

Kleiss, R., and Derks, K., (2004, June), *"From Strength to Strength"*, Cargo Systems, June 2004, pp. 52-55

Kondoh, R., (2005), *"An Inland of Hidden Treasure"*, Container Management, November 2005, pp. 46-49

Krüger-Kopiske, K.K. (2003), *"Die Schiffe von Hapag-Lloyd"*, Koehlers Verlag, Hamburg ISBN 3-7822-0861-7.

Lacey, H.M., (1980), *"The Interrelationship of Terminal Design and Equipment Selection"*, ICHCA-USA Conference, New-York

Larkin, J.E., (1983, June), *"An Integrated Short Sea container Service"*, Container Handling and Transport, pp. 183-186

Lauring, K., (2008), *"ContainerTrafik Gennem 50 år/Container Traffic for 50 years"*, Søhistoriske Skrifter nr. 24, Handels- og Søfartsmuseet, Helsingør (DK), ISBN 978-87-7015-001-9

Lee, K., Vazifdar, F.R., and Wong, S.L.H., (2001, May), *"Useful Structural Life Assessment of Dockside Container Cranes"*, In: Proceedings ASCE Conference, Norfolk

Lee, T.W., *"Restructuring of the Economy and its Impact on the Korean Maritime Industry"*, Maritime Policy & Management Vol. 26 (4), pp. 311-325

Levinson, M., (2006), *"The box: How the Shipping Container Made the World Smaller and the World Economy Bigger"*, Princeton UP, Princeton

Lim, S. M., (1996), *"Round-the-World Service: The Rise of Evergreen and the Fall of US Lines"*, Maritime Policy & Management Vol.23 (2), pp. 119-144

Lind, D., Jordan, M.A. & Hsieh, J., (2007), *"Tandem 40 Dockside Cranes and Their Impact on Terminals"*, In: Proceedings ASCE Ports 2007 Conference, San Diego, California

Lindner, E., (2008), *"Die Herren der Container"*, Hoffmann und Campe Verlag, Hamburg, ISBN 978-3-455-50090-5

Lloyd's Register and Ocean Shipping Consultants Ltd (2003) , *"Container Ships: Design Aspects of Larger Vessels"*, London

Losey, M.D., (1963), *"Conex: A Decade of Service"*, In: Military Review 43 (September 1963), pp. 32-37

Lowe, A. and Bonney, J., (2006), *"Intermodal Freight Transport"*, Elsevier Butterworth-Heinermann, Burlington, MA, USA

Lundquist, E.M., Harmon, B., and Hinson, K., (2000), *"Gunderson, A history of an Oregon Company"*, The Greenbeer Companies, Portland

Luttekes, E. and Rijsenbrij, J.C., (2003), *"The Carrier Crane, a Wide Body Crane Concept for Ship to Shore Container Handling"*, The Container Port Terminal Equipment and Technology Conference, Rotterdam WTC, Rotterdam

Lygo, A.J.D., (1978), *"Container Terminal Operating Experience: Rail-mounted Cranes in Combination with Straddle Carriers"*, In: Proceedings TOC 1978, Amsterdam

Macleod, R., (2001), *"The Human Cost"*, Cargo Systems, September 2001, pp. 58-59

Macleod, R., (2001), *"Doing the Maths"*, Cargo Systems, October 2001, pp. 54-55

Macleod, R., (2002), *"Welcome to the Machine"*, Cargo Systems, January 2002, pp. 44-45

Macleod, R., (2002), *"Automated to the Core"*, Cargo Systems, March 2002, pp. 52-53

Maher, M.E., (1980), *"Sole-User vs. Multi-User Container Terminals"*, ICHCA-USA Conference, New-York

Marcus, H.S., (1974), *"Planning Ship Replacement in the Containerization Era"*, Lexington Books, D.C. Heath and Company, Lexington, Massachusetts

McCalla, R.J., (1999), *"Global Change, Local Pain: Intermodal Seaport Terminals and Their Service Areas"*, Journal of Transport Geography 7, pp. 247-254

McCarthy, J., (1987), *"Ship to Shore Gantry Cranes and Ancillary Equipment"*, Special Report, Containerisation International, September, pp. 3-34

McKinsey & Company, Inc., (1967), *Containerization: The Key to Low-cost Transport"*, report for the British Transport Docks Board

McLellan, R.G., (1997), *"Bigger Vessels: How big is too Big?"*, Maritime Policy & Management Vol. 24 no.2, pp. 193-211

Meek, M., Adams, R., Chapman, J.C., Reibel, H., and Wieske, P., (1971), *"The Structural Design of the OCL Container Ships"*, In: Proceedings Royal Institution of Naval Architects, April 28, 1971, London

Miyahara, K., (2005), *"Making History"*, NYK 120th Anniversary, Containerisation International November 2005, pp. 106-112.

Miyata, N., Nishiokam M., Ukita, T., Monzen, T., and Toyohara, T., (2001, June), *"Development of Feedforward Anti-Sway Control for Highly Efficient and Safety Crane Operation"*, Mitsubishi Heavy Industries Ltd, Technical Review, Vol. 38, nr. 2

Morgan, R., and Gatto, F., (1998), *"Risk Management of Rail Mounted Machines"*, In: Proceedings Ports '98, Long Beach, California

Morris, C.A., and McCarthy, P.W., (2001, May), *"The Impact of Jumbo Cranes on Wharves"*, In: Proceedings of Ports '01, ASCE Conference, Norfolk, Virginia

Muller, G., (1999), *Intermodal Freight Transportation"*, 4th Edition, Eno Transportation Foundation and Intermodal Association of North America, Washington DC/Greenbelt MD, USA

Nagel, A.N., (1986), *"Tractor Trailer Systems, Now and in the Future"*, 4th Terminal Operations Conference, Amsterdam, October

Nagel, A.N., (2006), *"Krane-Einsatzgemäß Ausgelegt"*, HANSA Intern. Mar. Journal 143 no. 6 pp. 68-72

Nagel, A.N., (2010), *"A Qualitative Evaluation of Automated Stack Design Principles: 1-track vs. 2-track Configurations"*, In: Port Technology International 34, 6 pages

Niven, J., (1987), *"The American President Lines and its Forebears' 1848-1984"*, University of Delaware Press, London and Toronto; Ass. Univ. Presses, ISBN 0-87413-299-1

Norris, F., (1992), *"Cargoes North: Containerization and Alaska's Postwar Shipping Crisis"*, In: James H. Ducker (Ed.), Alaska History, Vol.7, pp. 16-30, Anchorage: Alaska Historical Society

Novacek, A.C., (2006), *"One Step Ahead"*, Main Street Rag Publishing Company, Charlotte, NC, USA, ISBN 1-59948-026-3

O'Mahoney, H., (1998), *"Opportunities for Container Ports"*, Cargo Systems Report, IIR Publications, London.

Paparis, B., Quadagno, M., Buzzoni, G., McQueen, J., and Lizzo, J. (2004). *"Modernizing a Three Decade Old Wharf Structure for the generation of Containerships"*, paper, New York.

Pearson, R., (1988), *"Container Ships and Shipping"*, Fairplay Publications Ltd., London, ISBN 0-905045-90-4

Pedraja, R. De La, (1992), *"The Rise and Decline of U.S. Merchant Shipping in the Twentieth Century"*, Twayne Publishers, New York, ISBN 0-8057-9826-9

Permanent Technical Committee on Ports (1962, February), *"Status of Shipping Containers, United States of America and Europa"*, Washington D.C.

Peschiera, R., (2006), *"Straddling the Future"*, Container Management, January/February 2006

Port of Rotterdam, (1996), *"Container Yearbook 1996"*, WYT Uitgeefgroep, Rotterdam, ISBN 90-600-7-761-x

Pottinger, J.A. (2010), *"Seatrain Gas Turbine Ships"*, in: Sea Breezes Magazine, April 2010 issue

Ragucci, C., (1980), *"Optimal Loading and Unloading of Containerships; Effect of Chassis Scheduling'*, ICHCA-USA Conference: "Intermodal Containerization and Marine Terminal Development", New York

Rimmer, P.J., (1998), *"Ocean Liner Shipping Services: Corporate Restructuring and Port Selection/Competition"*, Asia Pacific Viewpoint, Vol. 39, No. 2, pp. 193-208

Roberts, A.H., (1983), *"Computer Supported Terminal Communications"*, In: Proceedings 3rd Terminal Operations Conference, Amsterdam, 13th-16th June, 1983.

Robinson, R. (1998), *"Asian Hub/Feeder Nets: the Dynamics of Restructuring"* In: Maritime Policy & Management, vol. 25(1), pp. 21-40

Robinson, B., (2007), *"Ship-to-Shore cranes survey: Orders Swing Westwards"*, Cargo Systems, March 2007, pp. 33-37

Rosenstein, R. (2000), *"The Rise of Maritime Containerization in the Port of Oakland 1950 - 1970"*, MA-thesis, New York University, New York

Rudolf III, C.D., (1999), *"The Dual Hoist Crane's Influence on Productivity"*, Port Technology International, 10th edition, ICG Publishing

Rudolf III, C.D., (2007, June), *"Ship-to-Shore Productivity: Can it keep Up With Mega-Ship Size Increases? Part 1"*, Port Technology International, 34th edition, ICG Publishing

Rijsenbrij, J.C., (1978), *"Future Trends in the Development of Container Handling Equipment"*, 1st Terminal Operations Conference, Amsterdam

Rijsenbrij, J.C., (1983), *"ECT Delta Terminal; Strategy Through to 2000 and Beyond"*, 3rd Terminal Operations Conference, Amsterdam

Rijsenbrij, J.C., & Prins, G., (1985), *"Trends in High-throughput Container Handling"*, ICHCA 17th Biennial Conference Rotterdam, May 1985, Rotterdam

Rijsenbrij, J.C., (1986), *"Service Demand, Productivity and Profit; Where's the Balance"*, 4th Terminal Operations Conference, Amsterdam

Rijsenbrij, J.C., (1986), *"Terminal Productivity at ECT: A Variety of Factors"*, Improving Productivity in U.S. Marine Container Terminals, National Academy Press, Washington DC, ISBN 0-309-03694-1.

Rijsenbrij, J.C., (1996, April), *"Terminal Automation: Challenges and Threats"*, In: Proceedings ICHCA Biennial Conference, Jerusalem

Rijsenbrij, J.C., (2000, April), *"Standardization: A Must for Global Spreading"*, Dynamar Workshop: "Liner Shipping 2020", Rotterdam

Rijsenbrij, J.C., (2000, April), *"The Infrastructure for Tomorrow's Ships"*, Dynamar Workshop: "Liner Shipping 2020", Rotterdam

Rijsenbrij, J.C., (2000, October 24-25), *"Landside Operations: A delicate Balance Between Performance and Cost"*, In: Proceedings Medtrade 2000

Rijsenbrij, J.C., (2001, June),*"The Impact of Tomorrow's Ships on Landside Infrastructure"*, In: Proceedings TOC 2001, Lisbon

Rijsenbrij, J.C., (2001), *"Flexi-Trains: Cost Effective Equipment for Medium-Sized Terminals"*, Port Technology International, pp. 101-106

Rijsenbrij, J.C. & Luttekes, E., (2002, May), *"Double or Quit? New Concepts in Crane Cesign"*, TOC Conference, Bouwcentrum Antwerp, Belgium

Rijsenbrij, J.C. & Luttekes, E., (2002, May), *"Ship Shore Handling of Ultra Large Containerships"*, In: Proceedings World Class Crane Management Seminar, Amsterdam

Rijsenbrij, J.C., & Visser, W.F.J., (2004), *"Application of New Technology"*, Lloyds Maritime Academy, London, September 29th – 30th, London

Rijsenbrij, J.C., Nagel, A.N., & Diekman, W.A., (2005), *"Verkenning Ontwikkeltraject Shortsea Terminals Rotterdam"*, Internal Report for the Rotterdam Port Authority, Rotterdam

Rijsenbrij, J.C., Ottjes, J.A., Veeke, H.P.M., Duinkerken, M.B., Lodewijks, G., (2006, May), *"Simulation of a Multiterminal System for Container Handling"*, OR Spectrum, vol. 28, pp. 447-468

Rijsenbrij, J.C., Bos, W. van den, & Luttekes, E., (2005), *"The Increasing Importance of Wind Loads on Port Operations"*, In: Proceedings International Conference on Port-Maritime Development and Innovation

Rijsenbrij, J.C., Ham, J.C.van, Ham, R.P.W., (2006, May), *"50 years of Containerization in Retrospect"*, In: Proceedings TOC 2006, Hamburg

Rijsenbrij J.C., & Wieschemann A., (2006), *"Robotized Stacking Cranes"*, TOC Conference Asia 2006, March 14-16th., Busan, South Korea

Rijsenbrij, J.C., & Saanen, Y., (2007, June), *"Which System Fits Your Hub?"*, In: Flüsse - Kanäle - Häfen: Kernelemente der Wirtschaftinfrastruktur und Cargo Systems June/07

Rijsenbrij J.C., and Pielage B.A., (2007), *"Future Short Sea Container Terminals: Concept development and evaluation methods"*, 2nd International Maritime-Port Technology and Development Conference (MTEC 2007) 26-28 September 2007, Singapore

Rijsenbrij, J.C., (2008), *"Container Handling in Mainports: a Dilemma about Future Scales"*, In: The Future of Intermodal Freight Transport, Edward Elgar Publishing Ltd, Cheltenham, ISBN 978-1-84542-238-7

Rijsenbrij J.C., & Wieschemann A., (2011), *"Sustainable Container Terminals: A Design Approach"*, In: ISBN Handbook of Terminal Planning, Springer, New-York, 978-1-4419-8408-1

Saanen, Y.A., (2004), *"An approach for designing robotized marine container terminals"*, PhD Thesis, Delft

Saanen, Y.A., (2004), *"Container Yard Performance and Optimisation"*, Port Management Seminar, Lloyd's Maritime Academy, September 29th-30th, London

Sauerbier, C.L., (1956), *"Marine Cargo Operations"*, John Wiley & Sons, New York

Sawyer, L.A., & Mitchell, W.H., (1974), *"Victory Ships and Tankers"*, David & Charles Ltd, Newton Abbot, Devon, UK, ISBN 0715360361

Schuylenburg, M. van, and Veldhuyzen, W., (2001), *"Twenty-Two Containers Across"*, Schip en Werf de Zee, July/August 2001

Sea-Land Industries, (1983, June), *"Integrated Deep Sea Service Based on the Sea-Land philosophy"*, Container Handling and Transport, pp. 177-182

Seidelmann, Ch., (2010), *"40 years of Road-Rail Combined Transport in Europe"*, International Union of Combined Road-Rail transport companies (UIRR), Brussels

Shaw, J., (2000), *"New Ideas in Container Terminal Design and Construction"*, Asian Shipping, June, pp. 14-18

Shinji Hara, (1995), *"Advanced Technology for Fully Automated Yard Operations"*, Port Technology International 2nd Edition, ICG Publications Ltd, London

Slack, B., Comtois, C. and Sletmo, G., (1996), *"Shipping Lines as Agents of Change in the Port Industry"*, Maritime Policy & Management Vol. 23 (3), pp. 289-300

Slack, B., Comtois, C. and McCalla, R., (2002), *"Strategic Alliances in the Container Shipping Industry: A Global Perspective"*, Maritime Policy & Management Vol. 29 (1), pp. 65-76

Smithsonian Institution (s.n.), *"America on the Move, Transforming the Waterfront"*, permanent exhibition, National Museum of American History, Washington.

Starner, D.E., (1998), *"The Straddle Carrier: From Beginning to Present"*, Vidagraph Publications, Lowel, Oregon

Tally, W.K., (1988), *"The Role of US Ocean Ports in Promoting an Efficient Ocean Transportation System"*, in: Maritime Policy & Management, vol. 15(2), pp. 147-155

Tantlinger, K.W., (1982), *"U.S. Containerization: From the Beginning through Standardization"*, Lecture held at the Republic Technical Center, USA, and in 5th Terminal Operators Conference, april 1982, Rotterdam

Tax, H., (1989), *"Specifying Quayside Cranes for Operations in the Year 2009"*, In: Proceedings TOC 1989

Tax, H., (1995), *"The 'Driverless Dream' Quay Crane towards the Unmanned Terminals"*. In: Proceedings TOC 1995, Singapore

Thanopoulou, H.A., Ryoo, D.K., and Lee, T.W., (1999), *"Korean Liner Shipping in the Era of Global Alliances"* in: Maritime Policy & Management, vol. 26(3), pp. 209-229

Thoresen, C.A., (2003), *"Container Terminals"*, In: Port Designer's Handbook, ISBN 0727732285

Thorsøe, S., (1991), *"DFDS 1866-1991, Ship Development Through 125 years from Paddle Steamer to Ro/Ro Ship / Skibsudvikling Gennem 125 år fra Hjuldamper til Rulleskib"*, World Ship Society, London

Thuong, L.T., (1989), *"From Piggyback to Double-stack Intermodalism"*, in: Maritime Policy & Management, vol. 16(1), pp. 69-81

Truck Trailer Manufacturers Association (1960, July), *"The Outlook for Containerization"*, panel discussion 12th Annual Summer Meeting, July, 13, Hot Springs, Virginia

UNCTAD, (s.n.), *"Review of Maritime Transport"* (various years), United Nations, New York and Geneva

U.S. Department of Transportation, (1998), *"The Impact of Changes in Ship Design on Transportation, Infrastructure and Operations"*, Publication from the Office of Intermodalism

Veenstra, A.W., (1999), *"Quantitative Analysis of Shipping Markets"*, PhD Thesis, Erasmus University, Rotterdam, Delft University Press, Delft, ISBN 90-407-1876-8

Verschoof, J., (2002), *"Cranes: Design, Practice and Maintenance"*, Professional Engineering Publishing Ltd., London, ISBN 1-86058-130-7

Vetter, H. et al, (1978), *"Handbuch Container-Transportsystem"*, Transpress VEB, Verlag für Verkehrswesen, Berlin

VIA Port of NY-NJ, (1986), *"Happy 30th Anniversary"*, Special issue, April 1986

Vickerman, J., Zachary, J.M., Miller, B., (1987), *"Future Terminal Facility Requirements"*, Study for San Pedro Bay Ports: Plan 2020

Vietsch Engineering, (1957), *"Containership Cranes"*, Summary Report Prepared for Matson Navigation Co., San Leandro, California, November 4, 1957

Vossnack, E., Buys, C.T., Vriend, S.G., Bosschaart, B., (1982), *"Liner Fleet Retonnaging-Vessel Development"*, Nedlloyd Internal Paper

Vossnack, E., (1985), *"33 Jaar Scheepsontwerp"*, Farewell address, Nedlloyd Publication

Vossnack, E., (1996), *"Fatal Influence of Gross Tonnage on Safety-Pollution-Sound Ship Design"*, Publication Delft University of Technology and Kennis Centrum

Ward, T.A., & Woodman, R.A., (1997), *"Terminal of the Future"*, Proceedings TOC Asia '97, Singapore, September 16-18, 9 pages

Wasacz, M.S., (1980), *"Advances in Marine Container Terminals"*, ICHCA-USA Conference: "Intermodal Containerization and Marine Terminal Development", New York

Watanabe, I., (1996), *"Containerisation enters the Fourth Generation"*, Ports and Harbors, June 1985, pp. 14-21

Watanabe, I., (2006), *"The Wake of Containerships"*, Seizando, ISBN4-425-71371-0

Witthöft, H.J., (1977), *"Container; Transportrevolution Unseres Jahrhundert"*, Koehlers Verlag, Hamburg, ISBN 3-7822-0129-9

Witthöft, H.J., (2000), *"Container: Eine Kiste Macht Revolution"*, Koehlers Verlag, Hamburg ISBN 3-7822-0777-7.

Witthöft, H.J., (2002), *"125 Jahre Blohm und Voss"*, Hamburg, ISBN 978-3782208475.

Witthöft, H.J., (2004), *"Container, die Mega-Carrier Kommen"*, Koehlers Verlag, Hamburg ISBN 378220882-X.

Witthöft, H.J., (2010), *"Giganten der Meere; Containerschiffe-Motoren der Globaliserung"*, Koehlers Verlag, Hamburg ISBN 978-3-7822-0992-2

Woodman, R., (1997), *"The History of the Ship"*, Conway Maritime Press, London, ISBN 1-55821-681-2

Worden, W.L., (1981), *"CARGOES, Matson's First Century in the Pacific"*, University Press of Hawaii, Honolulu, ISBN 0-8248-0708-1

World Bank, (1999), *"The Evolution of Ports in a Competitive World"*, The Port Reform Toolkit Module 2, World Bank Transport Division

Wormmeester, G.J., (1972), *"Enige Opmerkingen over het Automatiseren van Containerhandling in de Havens"*, Internal publication ECT

Wormmeester, G.J., and Rijsenbrij, J.C., (1975), *"High Throughput Terminals"*, Cargo Systems/ICHCA-Conference, November 1975, London

Wormmeester, G.J., (1978), *"The Future For the Container Terminal"*, Terminal Operations Conference, Amsterdam

Wijnolst, N., Scholtens, M., & Waals, F., (1999), *"Malacca-Max: The Ultimate Container Carrier"*, Delft University Press, Delft, ISBN 90-407-1947-0

Zijderveld, E.J.A. van, (1995), *"A structured Terminal Design Method with a Focus on Rail container terminals"*, PhD dissertation, Delft, ISBN 90-370-0120-3

In addition to the above references, the authors have used information published in a variety of journals, magazines and websites, i.e.:

- Cargo Systems
- Container Management
- Containerisation International
- DynaLiners Trades Review
- Dredging and Port Construction
- HANSA International Maritime Journal
- Jane's Freight Containers, Yearbooks
- Lloyd's Ship Manager
- Maritime Policy & Management
- Port Strategy
- Sea Breezes
- Schip en werf / Schip en werf de zee/ SWZ Maritime
- The Motorship
- World Cargo News
- World Port Development

- http://myweb.tiscali.co.uk/gansg/index.htm#unit
- http://www.containershipregister.nl/
- http://www.containership-info.com/
- http://www.marinetraffic.com/
- http://www.shipsnostalgia.com/
- http://www.shipspotting.com/
- http://www.vesseltracker.com/

CURRICULA VITAE

Johannes Cornelis (Hans) van Ham

Hans van Ham was born on July 1956 in Meppel (The Netherlands). He attended local secondary school (Atheneum-b) and studied economics at Groningen State University, where he specialized in regional and transport economics. In his master research he studied the principles of tariff-making in public transport from a company's as well as society's point of view. He graduated with honors. In 1985 he started teaching at the Traffic Academy in Tilburg. He specialized in freight transport and his expertise comprised freight flows research, quantitative as well as qualitative.

During the academic year 1990/1991 he spent a 'sabbatical year' at Canada Ports Corporation in Ottawa, Ontario. This organization acted as an intermediary between the local ports and the federal government. As a research fellow he focused on the development of double stack trains. At that time the introduction of double stack container services in Canada was a hot issue because the competitive position of the port of Vancouver was deteriorating.

Voortgangsnota Zeehavenbeleid

After his return in the Netherlands he applied for a position at the Ministry of Transport and became a senior policy advisor in the field of sea ports. He was secretary of a project group that prepared the policy document 'Voortgangsnota Zeehavenbeleid'. One of his main achievements was to set up a directive for financial contributions. Between 1996 and 2004 nearly 100 million euros were spent on 'small' port projects. Yet, implementing policies lost its fascination.

His next step was to study policy processes from a theoretical point of view at Delft University of Technology. At the end of 1995 he joined the staff of the department of Transport Policy and Logistics at the faculty of Technology, Policy and Management.

He lectures and investigates the economic, technical as well as policy aspects of freight transport systems, in particular, intermodal transport chains (incl. sea ports).Together with a colleague he published a book on Public Private Partnership in Transport Infrastructure. A PhD thesis on public decision-making in relation to port investments was completed in 2010. He is a member of the scientific organization NECTAR (Network on European Communications and Transport Activities Research) and the Belgian\Dutch Association of Transport Economists (BIVEC).

Joannes Cornelis (Joan) Rijsenbrij

Joan Rijsenbrij, born September 1944 in Amsterdam, attended high school at the 5-year HBS-B, Keizersgracht Amsterdam. After a bachelor's degree in mechanical engineering (1965, Institute of Technology Amsterdam), he worked as assistant plant manager for a building contractor and after which he served in the army for over 2 years as technical officer, responsible for procurement specifications. In 1968, he started studying at the Delft University of Technology, where he graduated cum laude (MSc, 1972) in mechanical engineering, specialization cargo transportation systems and equipment. After working with Holland Handling Engineering and Hewitt Robins in the field of bulk materials handling and port facilities, he joined ECT in January 1974.

During a 23-year ECT employment he started as manager R&D and later director equipment engineering, responsible for many new features such as the multi trailer system, the first automated second trolley system and diesel-electric straddle carriers. In 1987, he was appointed as Vice-President engineering and R&D, in charge of ECT's development, design and procurement of all equipment and terminal facilities. During 1988-1993 he was the project manager for the automated Delta/Sea-Land terminal responsible for design, purchasing and commissioning of equipment (such as automated guided vehicles and automated stacking cranes), facilities, information systems and the set-up of a new labor organization. As Managing Director of ECT's Delta Container Division (all Maasvlakte terminals), he encouraged ECT's ongoing expansion and further automation (1991-1997).

In 1997, he started his own consultancy activities covering strategic planning, development of automated handling systems, city logistics and port facilities. From 1998 onwards, he is a professor at the Delft University of Technology with the chair of Large Scale Transport Systems, lecturing for and coaching master students.

During his more than 40 years of engineering activities, he built up a broad experience in the design of (automated) handling systems and equipment. This is illustrated by patents, the Medal of Honor from the Dutch Royal Institute of Engineers (1986) and his appointment in Paris (1987), as Euro-Engineer, one of the first three Dutch nominees.